"Kwasi Ampene's *Asante Court Music and Verbal Arts in Ghana* is an exemplary study of patient interdisciplinarity. Though much has been written on the subject, no one has attempted to understand Asante court music as a cultural management discourse that entails central dramatis personae as well as reiterative mnemonic system enshrined in instruments, the way they are played, and the manner in which they are spoken about by knowledgeable cultural brokers. This book is a significant contribution not just to the field of African musicology but also to African cultural studies in general."

—*Ato Quayson, FGA, FRSC, FBA, Professor of English,*
Department of English, Stanford University, USA

"Kwasi Ampene's *Asante Court Music and Verbal Arts in Ghana* is a work of singal importance. Based on ten years of painstaking research at Manhyia Palace, Kumase, the book charts the history of Asante court music and explicates the poetry of various instrumental and vocal performances. Notable is the deep valuation of language as manifest in speech, song and drummed language. Ampene makes good on the unrestricted access he was granted to centuries-old materials preserved at the court, and produces a book rich with information, including an account of a recent (2016) *Akwasidae* public assembly. Africanists, ethnomusicologists, anthropologists and linguists will find much of value here. With this book, Ampene consolidates his position as the pre-eminent scholar of Asante musical culture."

—*Kofi Agawu, Distinguished Professor, The Graduate Center,*
City University of New York, USA

Asante Court Music and Verbal Arts in Ghana

Asante Court Music and Verbal Arts in Ghana is a comprehensive portrait of Asante court musical arts. Weaving together historical narratives with analyses of texts performed on drums, ivory trumpets, and a cane flute, the book includes a critical assembly of ancient song texts, the poetry of bards (kwadwom), and referential poetry performed by members of the constabulary (apae). The focus is on the intersections between lived experience, music, and values, and refers to musical examples drawn from court ceremonies, rituals, festivals, as well as casual performances elicited in the course of fieldwork. For the Asante, the performing arts are complex sites for recording and storing personal experiences, and they have done so for centuries with remarkable consistency and self-consciousness.

This book draws on archaeological, archival, historical, ethnographical and analytical sources to craft a view of the Asante experience as manifested in its musical and allied arts. Its goal is to privilege the voices of the Asante and how they express their history, religious philosophy, social values, economic, and political experiences through the musical and allied arts. The author's theoretical formulation includes the concept of value, referring to ideas, worldview concepts, beliefs, and social relationships that inform musical practices and choices in Asante.

Kwasi Ampene is Associate Professor of Ethnomusicology at the University of Michigan (USA). He specializes in the rich musical traditions of the Akan people of Ghana, West Africa. He is the author of *Female Song Tradition and the Akan Ghana* (Ashgate); *Engaging Modernity: Asante in the Twenty-First Century* (Michigan Publishing); and the producer of the documentary film, *Gone to the Village*.

SOAS Studies in Music Series

Series Editors:
Rachel Harris, *SOAS, University of London, UK*
Rowan Pease, *SOAS, University of London, UK*

Board Members:
Angela Impey, *SOAS, University of London, UK*
Noriko Manabe, *Temple University, USA*
Suzel Reily, *Universidade Estadual de Campinas, Brazil*
Martin Stokes, *Kings College London, UK*
Richard Widdess, *SOAS, University of London, UK*

SOAS Studies in Music Series is today one of the world's leading series in the discipline of ethnomusicology. Our core mission is to produce high-quality, ethnographically rich studies of music-making in the world's diverse musical cultures. We publish monographs and edited volumes that explore musical repertories and performance practice, critical issues in ethnomusicology, sound studies, historical and analytical approaches to music across the globe. We recognize the value of applied, interdisciplinary and collaborative research, and our authors draw on current approaches in musicology and anthropology, psychology, media and gender studies. We welcome monographs that investigate global contemporary, classical and popular musics, the effects of digital mediation and transnational flows.

Theory and Practice in the Music of the Islamic World
Essays in Honour of Owen Wright
Edited by Rachel Harris and Martin Stokes

Singing the Gospel along Scotland's North-East Coast, 1859–2009
Frances Wilkins

Turkic Soundscapes
From Shamanic Voices to Hip-Hop
Edited by Razia Sultanova and Megan Rancier

The Indian Drum of the King-God and the Pakhāwaj of Nathdwara
Paolo Pacciolla

Asante Court Music and Verbal Arts in Ghana
The Porcupine and the Gold Stool
Kwasi Ampene

For more information about this series, please visit: www.routledge.com/music/series/SOASMS

Asante Court Music and Verbal Arts in Ghana

The Porcupine and the Gold Stool

Kwasi Ampene

Routledge
Taylor & Francis Group

LONDON AND NEW YORK

First published 2020
by Routledge
2 Park Square, Milton Park, Abingdon, Oxon OX14 4RN

and by Routledge
52 Vanderbilt Avenue, New York, NY 10017

Routledge is an imprint of the Taylor & Francis Group, an informa business

British Library Cataloguing-in-Publication Data
A catalogue record for this book is available from the British Library

Library of Congress Cataloging-in-Publication Data
A catalog record for this book has been requested

ISBN: 978-0-367-35610-1 (hbk)
ISBN: 978-0-429-34062-8 (ebk)

Typeset in Times New Roman
by Apex CoVantage, LLC

The audio examples can be accessed via the online Routledge Music
Research Portal: www.routledgemusicresearch.co.uk. Please enter the
activation word **RRMusic** and your email address when prompted. You
will immediately be sent an automated email containing an access token
and instructions, which will allow you to log in to the site.

Contents

Figures

Music examples

Acknowledgments

Asante Court Music and Verbal Arts in Ghana is the fourth outcome of ten years
of field research at the Manhyia Palace in Kumase, Ghana, that began in the summer of 2009. I am profoundly grateful to His Royal Majesty, Otumfoɔ Ɔseɛ Tutu II,
for ensuring my unrestricted access to the more than five centuries of Asante court
music and verbal arts at Manhyia Palace. As the sixteenth occupant of the Gold
Stool, his unparalleled vision and foresight for formal education underlie his commitment to facilitating my scholarly engagement with the aural and oral practices
associated with the musical arts at Manhyia Palace. Notwithstanding his busy
schedule, Otumfoɔ always finds time to meet with me to assess my progress and
to offer advice and encouragement. I would like to register my indebtedness to
the Asantehene's Sanaahene, Nana Kwadwo Nyantakyi III (the chief of treasury).
As the presiding chief of my field research, he is responsible for inviting and
setting up my meetings and interview sessions with all the custodians, chiefs of
ensembles, court musicians, and poets mentioned in this monograph. Nana Nyantakyi's encyclopedic knowledge of Akan and Asante culture is breathtaking. He
made critical contributions of oral history and cultural memory to enhance my
interviews with courtiers and during my one-on-one playback sessions with him.
My sincere gratitude to Ɔheneba Akwasi Abayie (Otumfoɔ Akɔmfɛrehene), for
generously sharing his extensive knowledge of the genealogy of Asante kings and
ahemaa (roughly translated as queens) with me. I am grateful to Nana Otimpie
Aben II (Asantehene Sasaamohene) for his willingness to serve Asanteman in
diverse ways, and in my case, at critical stages of my projects. My communications with Manhyia Palace are facilitated by the exceptional support of officers
and the staff at the Asantehene's Office. They are Kofi Badu (the chief of staff),
Nana Effah-Apenteng (Bompatahene), Mr. Kofi Owusu Boateng (secretary to the
Asantehene), Mr. Ernest Saahene (chief of protocol), Ms. Monica Amoako (secretary to the chief of staff), and Kwame Mensah (personal assistant to the chief
of staff). Without reservation, I would like to register my utmost appreciation to
the courtiers, custodians, chiefs of ensembles, and poets who appear throughout the book for being so diligent and kind with their time and knowledge, and
for patiently answering my never-ending questions. As custodians of Akan and
Asante lore, they are all my teachers and as a result, I take full responsibility for
any omissions and errors in this monograph.

Writing a book manuscript can be a solitary and lonely endeavor. I have benefited enormously from interactions with those who blazed the trail in the expressive cultures of the Akan. Posthumously, I would like to recognize J.H. Kwabena Nketia for his pioneering research and publications on the musical expressions of the Akan and for making time for my annual meetings with him to discuss several aspects of my project. My knowledge of Akan religion, ethics, and culture owe a great deal to my discussions with His Grace Akwasi Sarpong (Catholic Archbishop Emeritus of Kumase) and Kofi Asare Opoku, and I am grateful to them. My discussion of the spiritual essence of the numbers three, four, and seven in Akan owe a great deal to my conversations with Kofi Asare Opoku. I have had the opportunity on numerous occasions to discuss aspects of this project with Kofi Agawu and I am grateful for his critical comments. My interactions and collaborations with the following colleagues have been inspirational and critical to the success of this project: Lester Monts, Kelly Askew, Kwesi Yankah, Franc Nunoo-Quarcoo, Kofi Agyekum, Ruth Stone, Portia Owusu, and Ray Silverman. Kofi Agyekum particularly introduced me to two experts of the Twi language, Appenteng-Sackey and Baning Peprah, who assisted me with the Twi orthography and English translations of instrumental and song texts as well as poetry of the bards (kwadwom) and members of the constabulary (apae). I am thankful to archivist Judith Opoku-Boateng and her terrific staff at the Nketia Audio-Visual Archives at the University of Ghana for making available to me Nketia's audio recordings of kwadwom in the 1960s and his unpublished manuscript of the same. A study that seeks to unravel the interconnections between music and historical experience is inherently interdisciplinary, and I am forever grateful to the late James Anquandah for sharing archaeological insights and objects with me. Similarly, my discussion of culture management systems is the result of my conversations with Ato Quayson, while my rationale for beginning and ending this monograph with an event—the Akwasidae Public Assembly—is informed by my conversations with Jocelyne Guilbault. I am grateful to Vanessa Compton and Maria Phillips for years of friendship and for their commitment to cultural heritage and preservation. Dr. Sam Jonah deserves special mention for his interest, support, and encouragement. I thank Peter Agbeko, Baba Abdulai (Paa Kwesi), and all our social networks for their unwavering support and advice.

Field research is capital intensive, and I would like to register my appreciation to the following units for providing much-needed financial support: the Leadership Education for Advancement and Promotion (LEAP), Council on Research and Creative Work (CRCW) Faculty Fellowship, and the Graduate Council on the Arts and Humanities (GCAH) at the University of Colorado Boulder. From 2011, a generous research fund from the University of Michigan exponentially transformed my field research and made it possible for me to purchase high-end audio-visual recording devices for documentation. Additional support came from the University of Michigan Office of Research (UMOR), College of Literature, Science and the Arts Scholarship/Research Fund (LSA), the African Studies Center (ASC), the Department of Afroamerican and African Studies (DAAS), the Michigan Musical Heritage Project (MMHP), the Office of Diversity, Equity and

Inclusion (ODEI), and the African Humanities and Heritage Initiative (AHHI) at the ASC.

For their valuable service in the trenches, my research assistants in Ghana deserve special mention. They are Enoch Osei Nyantakyi (Nana Kwame), Kwaku Ofori Mensah (Kɔkroanya), Kwaku Nketia, John Dadieh, Kwabena Tawiah, Kwame Owusu, and Atta Poku. At the University of Michigan, I had the pleasure and honor of working with Kristina Johnson, Khairah Green, Simeneh Gebre-mariam, Dairatou Kaba, and Emmanuela Arhin as student research assistants. Many thanks to Constance Ditzel, the acquisition editor and my editorial assistant at Routledge Publishing, for her thorough work on my manuscript. Finally, my heartfelt gratitude to my dear wife, Awura Akua, and our children, Akosua Darkwaa Ampene, Nana Kwadwo Ekye Ampene, Adwoa Ampenebea Ampene, and Akosua Dadie Ampene for their love and support. Awura Akua provided an environment that enabled me to embark on fieldwork far away from home, tran-scribe my research materials, write the book manuscript and journal articles, and complete the documentary film, *Gone to the Village: Royal Funerary Rites for Asantehemaa Nana Afia Kobi Serwaa Ampem II* (2019).

Prologue

Akwasidae public assembly at Manhyia Palace-Kumase

It is Sunday morning, July 17, 2016, and the spacious courtyard (*Efikɛseɛm*) inside Manhyia Palace—the official residence of the Asante king (or Asantehene) and the Asantehemaa in Kumase—is filled with the sounds of multiple ensembles performing vigorously. It is a few minutes before eleven o'clock, and the occasion is the periodic Akwasidae Public Assembly that occurs every forty-two days on the Akan calendar. This plural performance environment, to borrow Kofi Agawu's useful interpretation, is a response to the procession of the Asante King, Otumfoɔ Osei Tutu II, and the custodians of the palace (the *Gyaase*) from the inner chamber (*Asankroase*) to the courtyard.[1] The celebratory element in Akwasidae is made evident by the splendid collection of brightly colored clothing and jewelry. The chiefs, courtiers, and the general public are wearing some of the most sumptuous kente and adinkra cloths, along with fine gold jewelry. The Akan calendar consists of forty-two-day cycles, with two fixed holy days: *Akwasidae*, which falls on a Sunday, and *Awukudae*, which falls on a Wednesday. *Adae* literally means a sleeping place, or more broadly a resting moment. It is a religious feast day when Akan chiefs and elders worship and perform rituals in communion with the spirits of their deceased forebears. Early in the morning and before taking part in the General Assembly, all occupants of stools in the kingdom perform a special worship in the chapel or in the "sleeping" places of black stools located in their respective communities. For his part, the Asantehene leads the worship in special chapels located both in and outside of Manhyia. The first worship is in the Temple of Stools (*Nkonwafieso*) in the palace, followed by a trip to the mausoleum (*Banmu*) at *Akyeremade* and *Bampenase*, after which they return to the palace and head straight to the chapel in the Asantehemaa's residence for the final ritual. The primary goal of worship in the various locations is to honor and celebrate the life of illustrious forebears, and to keep alive memories of the good deeds performed by those who held leadership positions and, in some cases, paid the ultimate price for defending the kingdom against outside forces. This worship inside and outside of the palace affirms the Akan belief in the supremacy and omnipotence of God or the Supreme Being (*Nyankopɔn*), who has absolute authority over two worlds—the natural world of the living and the supernatural world of ancestors and lesser gods. Far from the notion of "ancestral worship," this worship in communion with the departed is informed by the Akan religious belief that the good never dies. The exemplary accomplishments of male and female leaders and the citizenry, along with the sacrifices they made for posterity, are never to be forgotten. In light of the previous, and as a Holy Day, Akwasidae creates a treasured space for the Akan to focus on the celebratory facets of life, while Awukudae is a time for reflection on the ethos of death. The Adae Public Assembly on this Holy Sunday morning is a social gathering that brings together all levels of society to perform aspects of Asante history and lived experience and to strengthen Asante identity and values.[2]

Various ensembles have mapped out their space in the courtyard. Strategically positioned under a shed, and directly facing the area where the ruler will eventually sit, are members of the *fɔntɔmfrɔm* ensemble. I am standing close to the open doorway that connects the umbrella room (*Nkyiniyɛdanmu*) to the courtyard, facing the *fɔntɔmfrɔm* drum ensemble from about seventy feet away. In this seemingly tight space, the booming sounds of the *fɔntɔmfrɔm* ensemble provides a sonic umbrella, a spiritually charged shield that leaves participants without doubt of the heroic expressions that outline its repertoire and dance suites. Stationed to my right and under another shed are two popular vocal ensembles, Manhyia Tete Nnwonkorɔ and Kaakyire Badu's Nyame Akwan Nnwonkorɔ and Adowa.[3] To my far left, performing under another canopy, is another vocal ensemble: Sika Adowa Nnwonkorɔ, led by Nana Adowaa.[4] Out of the three vocal ensembles, Kaakyire Badu's group specializes in two genres, *nnwonkorɔ* and *adowa*.[5] Unlike court musicians, the participation of popular bands in court ceremonies is voluntary, and in addition to enriching the ceremony, performing at such events raises the profile of such groups in the community.[6] Meanwhile the chief of drummers, Nana Akofena Bediako II, is keenly watching the proceedings, as fourteen of the relatively smaller *mmedie* drums are tactically lined up near the open doorway. The fourteen drummers hold two straight sticks as they stand behind each drum, ready to play a piece as soon as the ruler enters the courtyard. It is unlikely the ruler will miss the *mmedie* drums in this position.

The procession is already underway and unfolding in sequences of three distinct but seamless groups: the Advance Group, the Gold Stool Group, and finally the Asantehene's Group. The priests and physicians (*nsumankwaafoɔ*) are the first of the Advance Group to emerge from the inner chambers. The Advance Group begins with a priest who is by now spiritually possessed and carrying the medicinal brass basin (*samanka*) on his head, supported by two assistants holding large horse tails on both sides, while one of the divisions of the Constabulary (*asekanfo*) guards them with swords. Next in line are members of the Treasury (*afotosanfoɔ*), consisting of two fairly young men each holding a bunch of black keys (*nsafoabre*) in their raised palms. The first group of ivory trumpeters (*nkɔtwema*), are next, and by the mechanics of instrumental speech surrogacy, they intermittently play instrumental verses to announce the imminent arrival of the king. Members of another ivory trumpet group (*ntahera*) use similar tactics, but play different texts to herald the approach of his royal majesty. Wearing rectangular-shaped gold-plated hats (*ɛsɛn*) are seven Couriers and Court Criers (*nsɛneɛfoɔ*) whose duty, among others, is to maintain order at the Public Assembly. The lively music of the *sekye* drum and dance ensemble is next in line and performing one of their drum pieces, though surprisingly without the usual female dancers. The third ivory trumpet group, Kɔkroanya, like the two ivory trumpeters before them, are on hand to herald the upcoming arrival of the ruler with instrumental verses. The Gold Stool Group made up of chairs (*nkonwa*) are next in line. As it turns out, the Gold Stool (*Sikadwa Kofi*) is conspicuously absent from today's assembly, but some of the associated items, including the Lion Skin Carpet (*Gyata Nnwoma*), a Cushion (*Atɛ*), a Footrest (*Akrokroa*), and the ornamented chair (*Hwedɔm*), are held high by the Stool Carriers (*Nkonwasoafoɔ*), who are canopied under a huge colorful umbrella (*bɛnkyinyɛ*) and are all part of the procession. The Stool Group are preceded by the *Nkofe* ivory trumpeters and followed by four men—two on each side—bearing gold-plated swords (*mfenatene*). Typical of the ivory trumpeters, members of the *Nkofe* sporadically sound out poetic verses by way of instrumental surrogacy to herald the arrival of the Asantehene.

It is now the turn of the Asantehene's Group, which reveals three sequential groups including the Forward Group (*Animfoɔ*), the Inner Circle (the *Asantehene Mpɛsua*), and the Rear Group (*Akyirefoɔ*). The pair of *mpebi ne nkrawiri* drums, another apparatus of instrumental surrogacy, are on hand to lead the Forward Group by sounding relatively short, repeated signals. Having been activated, the Shield Bearers (*Ɛkyɛmfoɔ*) are vigorously spinning and throwing the shields into the air, catching them with superb mastery. Forming a buffer zone that protects the space between the Forward Group and the king's Inner Circle are the males from the royal household (*Adehyemranteɛ*), children of past kings (*Ahenemma*), and grandchildren and great-grandchildren of past kings (*Ahenenananom*). The Asantehene finally enters the courtyard with a large retinue of sword bearers (*afenasoafoɔ*), wearing gold-decorated hats and gold-plated pectoral discs (*akrafokɔnmu*) and carrying gold-leafed swords with gold-cast ornaments (*abɔsodeɛ*) on their sheaths, and canopied under three large appliqued umbrellas (*bɛnkyinyɛ*). Split into two sections and forming two lines to the right and left of the Asantehene are fourteen Sword Bearers. On the Asantehene's right-hand side are the Swords of the Soul (*Akrafena*), while Deity Swords (*Abosomfena*) are lined up on his left-hand side. Momentarily, the *Ananta* and *Dadiesoba* Chiefs, whose duty is to protect the Inner Circle, fire rounds of gunpowder from nineteenth-century Danish guns that often disturb unsuspecting guests not familiar with such ear-shattering sounds at close range. In the space between the Sword Bearers is *Animosum* (a member of the constabulary), slowly walking backwards and guiding the ruler, while members of the Constabulary (*Abrafoɔ*) busily weave in and out of the royals and Sword Bearers to ensure that the procession is moving along smoothly. As expected, the Asantehene pauses to listen to the drum texts issuing forth from the *mmedie* drums as soon as he enters the courtyard, nodding his head in appreciation for the message and thanking the drummers by waving his right hand before moving on. To his immediate right is the chief of the ubiquitous Silver Casket (*Dwetɛ Kuduo*) carrying the regalia object on his head.

The moment the king steps into the courtyard divisional chiefs and *ahemaa* of the Kumase Traditional Council, a handful of territorial chiefs and *ahemaa* in the

Asante Kingdom, courtiers, visitors from far and near, government officials, and the general public all rise in deference. The procession is moving at a snail's pace as the Asantehene walks majestically in synchrony with the rhythms of gourd drums (*mpintin*) behind him. Immediately behind the ruler are the short ivory trumpeters (*mmɛntiafoɔ*) sounding short formulaic verses, while the cane flutist (*durugyakani*) follows quietly with his flute in hand. Also walking closely behind the ruler are the bards (*kwadwomfoɔ*), who intermittently recite short poetic verses in unison while members of the constabulary are busily making sure that there is order and the procession is progressing smoothly and without incident. As the procession moves along slowly, the Asantehene occasionally nods his head or waves his right hand to acknowledge greetings, or briefly pauses to listen to the poetic verse of the ivory trumpets. When he is not greeting during the procession, the ruler holds the hilt of one of the swords (*mpɔnpɔnsɔn* sword). The rear group is made up of a dozen or so men who constitute the king's bodyguards (*Atuotumfoɔ*). They carry gold-decorated long-barreled guns with gold-cast ornaments attached to the stocks. They wear skullcaps (*krɔbɔnkyɛ*) and a collection of haversacks, straps, and bandoliers (*ntoa*), along with containers for gunpowder or bullets (*danka*). At the very end of the procession are the chief of the Home Guard (*Ankɔbeahene*) and some of the elders of his division.

As soon as the ruler turns the corner towards his seat, the ivory trumpet groups made up of *nkontwema*, *ntahera*, *kɔkroanya*, and *nkofe* begin taking turns sounding proverbial language and poetic verses to *speak*—by way of instrumental surrogacy—to him. Predictably, each time they begin to sound their formulaic code of expression, the Asantehene pauses for a moment, listens thoughtfully, and acknowledges the message by nodding his head before moving on. The drummers of the *mpebi ne nkrawiri* drums momentarily take over from the ivory trumpeters to sound short phrases meant to guide His Majesty to his seat. Just before he gets to his seat, the *Samanka* Priest stretches the medicinal basin with both arms towards the ruler. For his part, the ruler places his right palm in the basin three times, and at the end of the third time, a member of the constabulary who is standing by the side of the *Samanka* Priest acknowledges the gesture by pulling his sword in and out of its sheath, making clicking metallic sounds. Holding on to the sheaths of the swords, the Sword Bearers bow as the ruler makes his way to his ornamented chair. A handful of courtiers with pieces of cloth immediately surround him, while the huge umbrella is lowered to cover the top to prevent the general public from seeing them place him on the chair. His clothing and jewelry are re-adjusted by the attendants to ensure that all of the jewelry and the headband (*abotire*) are in their proper place. While that is going on, the *mpintin* ensemble that includes six *donno*, five *mpintintoa*, and one *gyamadudu* are performing, as members of the ensemble line up from where the last Sword Bearer is seated at the far end of the rows of seats.

The cloths and umbrella are finally removed, and the Asantehene is formally seated while the stage is set for him to share the blessings and graces flowing from the morning worship (*Adae Tɔkye*) with his subjects. Still drumming, the *mpintin* drummers leave to make room for the next stage in the assembly. The seating format for this Akwasidae is understood as Asanteman when the ruler faces the Asawase suburb.[7] Standing behind the Asantehene are the flutist (*durugyakani*), two bards (*kwadwomfoɔ*), and the players of short ivory trumpets (*mmɛntiafoɔ*), who take turns sounding poetic verses that remind the ruler of the exalted position he occupies and the responsibilities that come with it. The bards proclaim in cryptic poetry the glorious deeds of his forebears and entreat the Asantehene to rival or surpass their selflessness and accomplishments. Similar to the bards who use the human voice to recite poetic verses, there are about eight men from the constabulary (*Abrafoɔ*) who take turns reciting verses of referential poetry known in Akan as *apae*. Unlike the bards, the *Abrafoɔ* perform in front of the Asantehene with a sword in their right hand and dramatic shades that are tailored to the occasion. Against the backdrop of verbal poetry by the bards and members of the constabulary, the plural performance of all the groups intensify as members of the Asantehemaa's household, chiefs and *ahemaa*, and the general public take turns to greet, congratulate, and wish the ruler well. After an hour of greetings, all the musical activities eventually stop, and the *kwadwomfoɔ* seize the moment to intone a long verse that lasts for about eight minutes. At the end of this verse, all of the sound-producing instruments respond with brief statements to congratulate the bards. The *Abrafoɔ* take turns again, with intermittent input from the *durugya* flutist, the short ivory trumpeters, and the long ivory trumpet ensembles.

All musical performances and poetic verses momentarily cease to pave the way for the Chief Protocol Officer Ernest Sarhene to introduce the guests. The guest list includes His Royal Majesty, Kgosi Leruo Molotlegi, the King of Royal Bafokeng Nation in South Africa; His Excellency, Former President John Agyekum Kuffour, the Asante Regional Minister; members of the Regional Security Council; the people of Kankyire, led by Ɔheneba Akwasi Abayie (Otumfoɔ Akɔmferehene); and others. Observing the norms of Akan communication protocols in formal events, as Kwesi Yankah frames it, Mr. Sarhene does not address the Asantehene directly; rather, he turns and faces the royal spokespersons (*Akyeame*) seated to his left, directing his message to them "so it might reach the king" (Yankah, 1995: x). The Protocol Officer presents high-ranking visitors to the Royal Spokespersons, who in turn present them to the king. Most of the guests come bearing gifts. After that, the Asantehene distributes offertory drinks (*Adae Nsa*) to the assembled chiefs, courtiers, and visitors. Compared to the General Assembly of chiefs that attend Asanteman Adaekɛseɛ, celebrated every five years, today's public ceremony is relatively small and intimate. However, the intensity and density of multisensory performance of history and lived experience, to reference Ray Silverman's useful description, makes the focus of the Asante Akwasidae Public Assembly undeniable (Silverman, 2016: 10).[8]

Notes

1 For a concise view of simultaneous performances at festivals and other social gatherings, see Kofi Agawu, 2016: 301–303. The *Gyaase*, with several divisions, are one of the largest groups of court officials who are responsible for the affairs and management of the palace.

2 See Osafo K. Osei (1997) for an in-depth discussion of the significance of the Akan calendar.
3 Although the legendary Nnwonkorɔhemaa Nana Afia Abasa passed away in 2000, the signboard in front of Manhyia Tete group still retains her name as the leader of the group.
4 Sika Adowa Nnwonkorɔ is a splinter group from Manhyia Tete.
5 The previously-named vocal ensembles are not, technically speaking, court ensembles, but rather fall under established traditional Popular Bands that primarily perform for funerary rites and other festivities. In his classic *Drumming in Akan Communities of Ghana,* Nketia devotes a chapter to popular bands (1963: 67–74). Another monograph on Akan popular bands, Nnwonkorɔ, is Ampene (2005).
6 A classic example is Nketia's chapter "Popular Bands" in *Drumming in Akan Communities of Ghana* (1963: 67–74).
7 Another seating arrangement is Kumase Traditional Council, where he faces Asante New Town.
8 See Ray Silverman's Preface in *Engaging Modernity*, 2nd edition, p. 10. For a full description of the 2014 Adaekɛseɛ General Assembly, see Kwasi Ampene and Nyantakyi III (2016) *Engaging Modernity,* pages 24–121.

References

Agawu, Kofi. 2016. *The African Imagination in Music:* New York: Oxford University Press.

Ampene, Kwasi. 2005. *Female Song Tradition and the Akan of Ghana: The Creative Process in Nnwonkorɔ.* Aldershot, UK: Ashgate Publishing Ltd.

Nketia, J.H. Kwabena. 1963. *Drumming in Akan Communities of Ghana.* London: Thomas Nelson and Sons Ltd.

Osei, Osafo K. 1997. *A Discourse on Akan Perpertual Calendar: For Religious Ceremonies and Festivals (1700–2200 A.D.).* Accra, Ghana: Domak Press Ltd.

Silverman, Raymond. 2016. "Preface." In *Engaging Modernity: Asante in the Twenty-First Century,* edited by Kwasi Ampene and Nana Kwadwo Nyantakyi III. Ann Arbor, MI: Michigan Publishing.

Yankah, Kwesi. 1995. *Speaking for the Chief: Okyeame and the Politics of Akan Royal Oratory.* Bloomington & Indianapolis: Indiana University Press.

1 Introduction

Ananse Ntentan (The Spider's Web: Symbol of wisdom, creativity, and the complexities of life). Akan Adinkra pictographic writing.

While by no means exhaustive, my description of a present-day Akwasidae Public Assembly at Manhyia Palace is meant to highlight the centrality of court music and verbal arts as fundamental pillars of socio-political and religious life in Asante. With religious undertones, the periodic assembly is a performance of history, experience, and values. Knowledge of history is power, and the assembly provides a space for the performance of Asante history, as well as lived and current experience. The past and historical experience are encoded in the variety of musical arts in terms of instrumentation as mediating material culture, instrumental texts, drumming and dancing, songs, and referential and chronicle poetry. Artistic expressions are not restricted to the past; ongoing and current challenges are also artistically expressed. My rationale for choosing performing arts in the royal court is founded on the premise that since antiquity, Akan royal courts have been the focal point of the highest artistic expressions for the orderly function of state.[1] In addition to aesthetic and artistic value, the performing arts lend credibility, prestige, and power to chieftaincy and political structures. Court musicians are quick to point out how in the days of warfare and territorial conquests, several wars were won or lost just by capturing the musical instruments belonging to an adversary. This is succinctly expressed in instrumental verse by the *nkɔntwema* ivory trumpet group as: *Nipa ɔne wo sɛ, kyerɛ wo mmɛn, kyerɛ wo dɔm* ("those who claim your status, they should show their trumpets, they should show their people" (See Example 3.6). Power and prestige, meant to elevate the status of the occupant of the Gold Stool, is not limited to ivory trumpets, but also includes the variety of drums and court musicians. The previous situation is not unique to the Asante or the Akan. During the restoration of the Buganda monarchy in 1993, Peter Cooke describes a performance involving over 220 *mujaguzo* drums, an unnamed number of trumpeters, and seventy-four "praise drummers" (Cooke, 1996: 439). For the masses, artistic expressions at the courts "stimulate and maintain collective consciousness of state" (Nketia, 1987: 201). We may add issues of identity, as the word of caution in the Akan proverb seems to affirm: if you forget the motto of your chief's ivory trumpets, you will be lost in a festival (*sɛ wo werɛ firi wo kurom hene abɛn a, wo yera wɔ dwaboɔ ase*). That is, in Public Assemblies with several varieties of ivory trumpets sounding verses specific to their respective chiefs in a plural performance space, participants are able to identify where they belong by picking out the motto or philosophical statement of their chief's ivory trumpets. Without that, they would be lost in a festival and the resulting plural soundscape.

Although the constant presence of court music and poetry in rituals and ceremonies is often observed, scholars have often been restricted from access to the vast resources of the Asantehene's court, including the musical arts and their mediating material culture. However, my ethnographic description of the Akwasidae Public Assembly raises a number of fascinating questions that guide my study. For instance, using the July 17, 2016 Akwasidae as our frame of reference, how do we access the text-laden performances involving *fontomfrɔm*, *mpintin*, and *kete* drum ensembles? What were the ivory trumpeters, both short and long, expressing in the instrumental texts? How do we unpack ancient song texts, the verbal poetry of the bards, and the referential poetry of the constabulary? In order to address these questions, I weave together historical narratives with detailed analyses of texts performed on drums, ivory trumpets, and short trumpets. Additionally, I include a critical assembly of song texts, chronicle poetry of the bards (*kwadwom*), and referential poetry by members of the constabulary (*apae*). The focus throughout is on the intersections between lived experience, music, and values, and I refer to a variety of musical examples drawn from court ceremonies, rituals, and festivals, as well as from intimate performances elicited in the course of fieldwork. Since the performing arts are complex sites for recording and storing lived experience, and they have done so for centuries with remarkable consistency and self-consciousness, I will include the contemporary experience of the Asante in post-colonial Ghana. My description of the Adae Public Assembly brings into sharp focus a well-known practice in African cultures, where all modes of artistic expressions are tightly knit together in a holistic performance. Writing on the same subject, Ruth Stone refers to this conceptual framework as a "constellation of arts" and demonstrates how the Kpelle of Liberia, for instance, use the single word *sang* to describe three different types of artistic forms: an exceptional dance movement, a beautifully sung phrase, and outstanding drumming (Stone, 2000: 7–12). Due to disciplinary focus and space limitations, I shall limit my inquiry to court music and verbal arts, and occasionally make reference to visual arts and dance gestures when necessary for a fuller appreciation and understanding. As the official residence of the Asante king and the Asantehemaa, Manhyia Palace in Kumase has the largest collection of Asante visual and performing arts, and thus provides rich resources in a single space for scholarly engagement.

Unlike the court music of Renaissance Europe, which was generally based on love songs and social class, Asante court music is not based on courtly love or the entertainment of the ruler. As we shall see in the following chapters, Asante court music and verbal arts are ritualistic, and depending on the type of ritual, all citizens can and do participate in court music.[2] Asante court music refers to all forms of music associated with Akan chieftaincy. Known as *ahengorɔ* in the Twi language, court music is different from popular bands including *adowa, nnwonkorɔ, adenkum, akatape, asɔnkɔ, ntwiise, sanga*, and others. It is also different from music for occupational groups such as hunters' associations, fishermen, and farmers, or music performed as part of divination by traditional priests (*akɔm*). Furthermore, it is quite distinct from music for nubility rites for girls, children's games, or song interludes for storytelling (*anansesɛm*).[3] But there are noticeable overlaps, as in the use of *atumpan* drums in *adowa* ensembles and the court. In such cases, the *atumpan* at the courts tend to be bigger than those used in *adowa* groups.[4] Similarly, the lead drummer in *adowa* ensembles may be referred to as *Ɔkyerɛma*, and he may play the speech mode type of drumming during performances, but he is not considered to be the Creator's Drummer (*Ɔdomankoma Kyerɛma*). Such titles are reserved for the court drummer, who, among his duties, is to play drum poetry (*ayan*), send messages, play eulogies, offer condolences, and other activities. The leader of an *adowa* group (*adowahemaa*) is also one of the elders at the court of the *ɔhemaa*. Apart from the *atumpan* drums, the shapes and sizes of drums such as the *apentema* and *petia* drums in the public domain are the same as those used at the courts. Another area of overlap is the participation of popular bands at festivals, funerals, and other events, when rulers lead the communities or when performances are at a ruler's palace as described in the Prologue. My observations imply that, although court music may be different on several levels from music in the community, it is seen as being on a continuum of different domains of musical expression. The notion of a continuum of music in the communities and the courts results in both domains being featured performances during festivals or funerals. All citizens, rich or poor, do participate in court dances as long as they know how to dance to, say, *fɔntɔmfrɔm* or *kete*. Asante or Akan court music is not based on class, since court musicians and their families are from the same communities as other citizens, and Asante court music is not conceived as entertainment for rulers. Unlike the practice in other kingdoms in Africa, including the *Jali* among the Mande or the *Lunsi* among the Dagbon, Asante court musicians are not professional musicians who are able to perform for compensation outside of their roles at the court.

Despite the ubiquity of court music and poetry, and the variety of musical instruments and ensembles at Manhyia Palace, it was not until the early twentieth century that aspects of Asante arts appeared in R.S. Rattary's trilogy (1923, 1927, 1929). Based on anthropological research, Rattary's monographs essentially fulfilled his mandate as the head of the newly created Anthropological Office in the colonial Gold Coast, and the resulting colonial bias is to be expected. From the mid-twentieth century, especially in the days leading up to and just after independence, Ghanaian scholars became engaged with traditions that had been neglected during the colonial era and began producing their own publications based on field research. Pioneering research by Kwabena Nketia (1963) and A.A.Y. Kyerematen (1966) introduced a few drums, ivory trumpets, and some ensembles to the general public and academics. Yet, while more recent specialized studies by William Carter (1971, 1984), Joseph Kaminski (2012), and Kwasi Ampene (2016) have contributed to our understanding, the astonishing variety of royal instruments, ensembles, and repertoires remain relatively unknown. Starting in 2009, I became the first ethnomusicologist, since the 1980s, to be granted unrestricted access to the centuries-old court music and verbal arts practiced at Manhyia Palace. In order to ensure the success of my research, the Asantehene elected the Chief of Treasury, Nana Kwadwo Nyantakyi III, to preside over and coordinate my meetings with courtiers and court musicians. Known in Akan as the *Sanaahene*, the Chief of Treasury is responsible for the practical day-to-day running of Manhyia Palace, making his responsibility all-encompassing. He provides funds for the royal household, including the *Asantehemaa*'s court, for the making of new regalia and the repair of existing ones including sound-producing and musical instruments. Further, he provides funds for royal funerary rites, funerary rites for courtiers (*nhenkwaa*), palace chiefs and officials, and for those inside and outside the kingdom. Similarly, he provides items for rituals at various locations within the kingdom.[5] Having served three kings—Otumfoɔ Agyeman Prempeh II (1935–1970), Otumfoɔ Opoku Ware II (1970–1999), and Otumfoɔ Osei Tutu II (since 1999)—Nana Nyantakyi III has accumulated an extraordinary wealth of knowledge on Akan and Asante culture spanning over five decades. Fortunately for me, I worked with him previously, although unofficially, from 1995 to 1998 during my field research on the Akan vocal genre *Nnwonkorɔ* for my doctoral dissertation and first monograph (see Ampene, 2005). In those early days of my academic career, I was impressed by his encyclopedic knowledge of Asante and Akan traditional political systems and the associated material culture.

Since 2009, I have consistently spent two or three months of the summer in Kumase recording the oral histories of sound-producing instruments and ensembles, as well as collecting drums and songs, the texts of a variety of ivory trumpet groups, and the poetic texts of court musicians, chiefs, and courtiers. As the presiding chief of the project, Nana Nyantakyi III was responsible for setting up our meetings and conversations with all of the custodians of regalia and court musicians, and working with him brought to my attention some of the challenges facing oral traditions in contemporary times. He pointed to gaps and generational disparities among courtiers and court musicians and the relative loss of historical practices that has resulted from the older generation passing on without adequately transmitting the oral history of regalia objects, musical instruments, and repertoire to the younger generation. He also pointed out the inaccuracies in the 1963 publication, *Ashanti Stool Histories*, where most courtiers credit the founder of the Asante Kingdom, Ɔpemsoɔ Osei Tutu (c. 1680–1717), with the creation of their respective objects or musical ensembles.[6]

It seems that by associating King Osei Tutu with the creation of particular objects, they validate their existence as well as elevate the status of custodians. The result is a significant number of errors in both the oral and written histories of the material culture associated with Asante kinship that have been replicated in several publications over the years. This is one of the challenges that scholars working in primarily oral cultures face, and my project is no different. However, with the institutional knowledge of Nana Nyantakyi III, we were able to identify inconsistencies in the oral history and make sure we effectively corrected errors with the approval of custodians. A case in point is that while recording the oral history of the elephant tail and ostrich feathers, known by their court name as *Ɛmena ne Kɔkɔsɛsɛ*, the chief of this group gave credit to Ɔpemsoɔ Osei Tutu for their creation. It was after a series of questions from Nana Nyantakyi III that he finally revealed and admitted that they were created by the third king, Asantehene Kusi Oboadum (1750–1764). How did we validate the latter date as historically accurate? We arrived at our conclusion by reckoning that custodians of this group were selected exclusively from grandchildren of past and present kings. According to Nana Nyantakyi III, Asanthene Obuodum's original idea for creating this group was for his grandchildren to stand around him to whisk away flies and other bugs by using the elephant tail and ostrich feathers during court ceremonies. In keeping with tradition over the centuries, not only do we now have the grandchildren of succeeding kings, but we also have great-grandchildren who are members of this group. The crucial point here is that, as the founder of the kingdom, Ɔpemsoɔ Osei Tutu did not have grandchildren at the time and could not have created these regalia items.

I was also concerned with the challenges facing oral histories, as courtiers and custodians are exposed to western formal education and all of the entrapments of the information age. The capacity to memorize over 500 years of history becomes daunting in such circumstances. There are also gaps where acute generational disparities exist, with the older generation passing on without adequately transmitting the oral history and repertoire to the younger generation. Based on these concerns, Nana Nyantakyi III encouraged me not to limit the scope of my inquiry to only court music and verbal arts, but to expand my coverage to include all regalia objects. As an ethnomusicologist, this decision altered my research agenda while at the same time presenting a welcome development I could not resist. Although disciplinary praxis requires me to focus entirely on music, I stand to benefit from such a holistic approach for the following reasons. As an Akan, I am keenly aware that the diverse artistic expressions at the court are not micro-entities in airtight compartments, but rather are connected to a variety of artistic domains that reinforce and maintain the socio-political order. An example of the notion of music in a tightly bound constellation of the arts is when the recitation of referential poetry (*apae*) by members of the constabulary is punctuated by the pair of tribunal drums, *mpebi ne nkrawiri*. Similarly, the set of five or seven huge umbrellas (*bɛnkyinyɛ*) that provide shade for the chiefs and *ahemaa* are moved up and down in synchrony with the rhythms of the gourd drums (*mpintin*), *fɔntɔmfrɔm*, or *kete* ensembles, or when chiefs dance to vocal ensembles such as *adowa* or *nnwonkorɔ*.

There is interconnection between ivory trumpets and the huge umbrellas when a visual representation of an ivory trumpet is placed on top of one of the huge umbrellas to signify the war trumpet (*akobɛn*). Considered on their own, shields (*ɛkyɛm*) might be visual expressions of defense or protection in the days of warfare and conquest, but one of the dance suites performed by the *fɔntɔmfrɔm* ensemble (*ɛkyɛm*) is reserved for only the shield bearers to demonstrate valor and dexterity through dance gestures.[7] There are times when regalia items interact with musical performances, such as when the Asantehene dances *fɔntɔmfrɔma atopretia* with a sword known as *mpɔnpɔnson* and a gun. The five examples offered previously are enough to support a holistic field research approach to the sounded and unsounded domains for my project.

Three years into the project, Nana Nyantakyi III asked me if I could publish a commemorative book as part of the 2014 Grand Adae Festival (Asanteman Adaekɛseɛ). Once again, I was excited at the potential of publishing a community-engaged book for Asanteman for the simple reason that such a request affirms the recognition of my work and the collaborative nature of my field research. Essentially, they created the regalia items including the music and poetry and, given the nature of the request, were looking for publications to ensure continuity for posterity. It became critical for us to first document the oral histories and publish the urtext, a definitive history, of all regalia items including musical and sound-producing instruments. In March 2014, I published *Engaging Modernity: Asante in the Twenty-First Century*, which was launched in Kumase by the Asantehene a few days before the Grand Adae Festival that is celebrated every five years. Despite the challenges with institutional praxis in the United States, which requires single authorship with an academic publisher, I published the book with a private press and added the name of my main consultant at Manhyia Palace as a co-author. On May 9, 2014, the Asantehene launched the book, *Engaging Modernity: Asante in the Twenty-First Century*, as part of the Asanteman Adaekɛseɛ (Grand Adae Festival). Since I was in Kumase at the time, I documented the Adaekɛseɛ on Sunday, May 11, 2014 and the convocation of chiefs at the Baba Yara Sports Stadium. In 2016, I published an expanded second edition of *Engaging Modernity* with ethnographic descriptions of the 2014 Grand Adae Festival (Michigan Publishing, 2016). The second edition also features Nana Nyantakyi III as co-author, with similar implications as before. Cast within two broad sections, I examine the religious and social purpose, and the history of the festival, as well as an ethnographic account of the Asantehene's procession with extensive lists of regalia items in context.[8] Also referred to as Convocation of Chiefs, the contextual account illuminates the temporal and historical narratives of the regalia objects, including musical performances of the various ensembles rendered as they move through space and time, as well as the metalanguage embodied in the regalia objects and the symbolic language they convey. In contrast to the first section, the second part consists of over 200 photographs of objects and custodians with detailed descriptions and definitive histories.[9] The third tangible outcome of my research in Manhyia Palace is my recent documentary film, *Gone To The Village*, that essentially captures the collective mourning, the burial, and the final funerary rites of the Asantehemaa Nana Afia Kobi Serwaa Ampem II in January and December 2017.[10] Although a video documentary, the single thread that connects it to the current monograph is its emphasis on a multifaceted and multidirectional documentary that registers the blending of oral traditions, political authority, and national unity with the musical, visual, and performative arts of Asante. As a result, the documentary film enriches previously published and forthcoming books on Asante court music and verbal arts.

With my focus on the interconnections between music, lived experience, and social values, *Asante Court Music and Verbal* Arts expands and bridges the groundbreaking works of J.H. Kwabena Nketia in ethnomusicology and A.A.Y. Kyerematen in social anthropology, while addressing current scholarship in post-colonial kingdoms in Africa. Recognized as the preeminent scholar of African musicology, Nketia published several articles and monographs on the royal music of the Akan in general and the Asante in particular. Nketia's *Drumming in Akan Communities of Ghana* (1963) and *Funeral Dirges of the Akan People* (1969) are two classic monographs but are currently out of print. On a much higher plane in the analysis of instrumental texts in Africa are Nketia's two chapters in the multi-authored volume *Current Trends in Linguistics* (1971a: 699–732), "The Surrogate Languages of Africa" and "The Linguistic Aspect of Style in African Languages" (Nketia, 1971b: 733–757). A social anthropologist, Kyerematen focused on Asante kingship and regalia in his 1966 doctoral dissertation presented to the University of Oxford. Although he includes musical instruments in his publications, including *Panoply of Ghana* (1964) and the small pamphlet *Kingship & Ceremony in Ashanti* (1969), his critical contribution is in the area of Asante kingship and regalia, or what he refers to as ornamental arts. Unfortunately, he did not publish his dissertation, and as a result, his critical and pioneering work is not readily available to academic institutions, scholars, or the general public. I will like to comment on my choice of the crested porcupine and the Gold Stool as the sub-title of this monograph.

The porcupine

The crested porcupine (*kɔtɔkɔ* in Twi) and the Gold Stool (*Sikadwa Kofi*) are potent symbols of Asante history, religious views, and identity. The evocative subtitle, "the Porcupine," is informed by a predominating ethos and ideology that continue to guide the Asante in all of their undertakings. The Asante aversion to injustice, according to Kwame Donkoh Fordwor, has been misrepresented by the uninformed as pride or arrogance. While the Asante have a high tolerance for unkind friendship, continues Fordwor, they cannot withstand deceit or prejudice, for they are prepared to fight against injustice in all circumstances (Fordwor, 2009: 6). It is considerations such as this that led the founders to adopt the characteristics of the crested porcupine as the sacred totem of the Asante. The use of animals or plants as clan totems is widespread across Africa; for example, in his monograph on the Buganda Kingdom, Damascus Kafumbe examines a complex system of primary and secondary totems associated with over fifty patrilineal clans (Kafumbe, 2018: 1–5).[11]

Known in Twi as *kɔtɔkɔ*, the crested porcupine is a rodent and classified as an herbivorous animal that occasionally eats insects and carrion. In that sense, it is not a carnivorous animal, nor is it a predator or an aggressive animal. The foot-long quills of the crested porcupine are only used as a deterrent for potential foes, especially predators. As a defensive mechanism, porcupines raise and vibrate the normally flat-lying quills and turn their back towards the predator. In case they lose quills in an encounter with a predator, porcupines grow new ones to replace them. The Asante heroic cry "Asante the porcupines, if you kill a thousand, they will be replaced by a thousand (*Asante Kɔtɔkɔ, wokum apem a, apem bɛba*)" is informed by the biological attributes of the porcupine that ensures quills will not be depleted. Since the porcupine is not seen as an aggressor or a predator, it is misleading to refer to the Asante as the "porcupine warriors," for they are never belligerent or pugnacious. The porcupine is never known to harass, threaten, or chase animals. The Asante perception of the porcupine, then, signifies that they are invincible, insuperable, and unconquerable. The Asante non-aggressive ethos is expressed in a variety of ways in the musical arts (as well as the visual arts) where the Asantehene, for instance, is referred to as *Kɔtɔkɔhene* (king of porcupines) while the Asante as a people are collectively represented by the metaphoric allusion *kɔtɔkɔ* (Asante, the porcupines). The metaphoric allusions of the porcupine (*kɔtɔkɔ*) is one of several stock expressions in compositions for instrumental, song texts, and verbal arts in this book as seen in Examples 1.1, 3.1, 3.11, and others in Chapters 4 to 6.

The Gold Stool

In the formative years of the Asante Kingdom, the need for an all-encompassing ideology that could bring independent states together to fight and free themselves from their powerful overlord Dɛnkyera was the underlying motive that inspired the creation of one of the most enduring and potent ideological symbols, *Sikadwa Kofi* (the Gold Stool born on Friday). Unfortunately, the widespread use of the label Golden Stool, as the English translation of the Twi word *Sikadwa*, is a misnomer. An accurate translation of *sika* is gold, and the question is, how, when, and by who was this designated as "golden" in the English translation? Second, Kyerematen describes *Sikadwa* as made of a mass of solid gold; in all circumstances, a solid mass of gold cannot be "golden." Consequently, I will use Gold Stool throughout this book. In his version of oral history, Kyerematen informs us that in a gathering of chiefs in Kumase, the great priest Ɔkɔmfo Anɔkye appealed to the Supreme Being and brought the Gold Stool from the heavens.[12] The heavenly origins of the Gold Stool ascribes a divine origin, a special gift from God (*Onyankopɔn*)—the Creator of all things and Sovereign Lord of all (Kwame Donkoh Fordwor, 2009: 5). Sometimes referred to as *Abɛnwa*, this singular object embodies the soul, identity, strength, and power of the Asante kingdom, and it has undoubtedly been the single most unifying force in Asante. Ultimately, the Gold Stool is a spiritual as well as an ideological object. In 1896, when the Asantehene Agyemang Prempeh realized that defeat by the British was imminent, he gave himself up in order to prevent the British forces from capturing the Gold Stool. The same stool was at the center of the last Anglo-Asante conflict from April 1900 to March 1901, when a remarkably brave woman in her mid-sixties, Nana Yaa Asantewaa (*Ɛdwesohemaa*), led the Asante army to defend and prevent the British governor Frederick Hodgson and his soldiers from taking away the stool. The war is aptly referred to as the War of the Gold Stool or the Yaa Asantewaa War, among other labels.[13] The relevance of the Gold Stool to my overall thesis is that, although it features prominently in all historical accounts of the Asante, sound-producing and musical instruments attached to it are rarely mentioned in the literature. The only exceptions are Kyerematen (1966) and Nketia (1982). According to oral narratives recorded by Kyerematen, the stool descended from the heavens with a "bell made of an alloy of brass and copper" strapped to it.[14] Known as the Great Bell (*Dɔnkɛseɛ*), it is said that it "compels the people to gather" when the custodians ring the bell, and the bell represents the Gold Stool in the Chapel of Stools and receives sacrifices intended for the Gold Stool. The only time it is strapped to the Gold Stool is when the latter is being taken to the battlefield. Additional sound-producing instruments strapped to the Gold Stool are the Gold Bell (*Sikadɔn*) and two brass bells called *Adomiredɔn* that are rung to alert the general public when the stool is carried as part of the procession. It should be noted that brass bells (*adomire*) are not unique to the Gold Stool, and they are also strapped to the black stools representing past kings. Further, Opoku Ware (1720–1750), who succeeded Ɔpemsoɔ Ɔseɛ Tutu, attached three gold bells in the forms of effigies of defeated adversaries and a regular bell. The three effigies are that of the King of Dɛnkyera Ntim Gyakari, who, as we shall see in Chapter 2, was defeated by Ɔpemsoɔ Ɔseɛ Tutu. The remaining two are King Ofosu Apenten of Akyem Kotoku and King Abo Kwabena of Gyaaman, both defeated by Opoku Ware, for a total of seven bells. Osei Asibe Bonsu (1804–1824) added the eighth bell representing the effigy of Nana Adinkra Kwame, another vanquished king of Gyaaman. In 1824, the gold-cast effigy of the defeated and decapitated British General Sir Charles MacCartey was attached to the Gold Stool. Kyerematen goes on to identify musical instruments attached to the Gold Stool and regarded as regalia objects of the stool. They are the *Apirede* drum ensemble, *Sikakua* (gold-plated drum; relatively small *akukua* type), *Sika Sankuo* (six-string gold-plated harp-lute known in Akan as *Seperewa*), *Asikabɛn* (gold-plated short ivory trumpet known in Akan as *abɛntia*), and *Nkofe* (a set of seven large ivory trumpets) (Kyerematen, 1966: 227–241, 374–377). For his part, Nketia identifies only two musical instruments, a gold model of *akukua*, a small high-pitched drum, and two gold models of *sankuo* or *seperawa* as artistic objects that are paraded with the Gold Stool (Nketia, 1982: 51). The relevance of the foregoing to my overall discussion of *Asante Court Music and Verbal Arts* is that all of the preceding items are material and symbolic objects of history, for they represent specific historical epochs in the Asante kingdom. They embody lived experience and value systems and, for that matter, the previous objects are socially maintained to the present day not by being kept in a room, but by being used by custodians who participate consistently in court ceremonies and rituals. The events and rituals continue to define the Asante in Ghana.

With references to the porcupine (*kɔtɔkɔ*) in music and verbal arts, historical bells attached to the Gold Stool, and musical ensembles and instruments as regalia objects, this study of *Asante Court Music and Verbal Arts* is inherently a case study of the porcupine and the Gold Stool.

Along similar lines, I would like to briefly remark on the acceptability of the English words "queen" or "queenmother" as translations for the Akan word *ɔhemaa*. The Akan have a complex system of socio-political organization embedded in a matrilineal kinship system. In order to ensure equilibrium, harmony, and social balance, they practice dual male-female leadership roles. Beginning at the family level, a male head (*Abusuapanin*) is assisted by his female counterpart (*Ɔbaapanin*). The male chief or king is referred to as *ɔhene*, while his female counterpart is *ɔhemaa*. The gendered word, *ɔ-he-ne*, is the masculine, while the diminutive *maa*, as in *ɔ-he-maa*, denotes the feminine label. Since they are from the same matriclan, the *ɔhemaa* cannot be the wife of a chief or a king, but she can be the mother, sister, or aunt. Crucially, it is the *ɔhemaa* who nominates a chief or king when the stool becomes vacant, or if he is destooled for any reason. She provides critical counseling to the chief or king in matters of state, as well as being entirely responsible for the affairs of women. Similarly, it is the chief or king who appoints a female member from the matriclan to the position of *ɔhemaa*. The dual leadership role has its functional equivalence in the organization of musical ensembles such as the male and female *atumpan* drums. It bears noting that in Asante (and all Akan for that matter), the quintessential "talking drums" are the pair of *atumpan* drums used by the Creator's Drummer (*Ɔdomankoma Kyerɛma*) to send messages as well as to play long verses of drum poetry (*ayan*). Although there are single drums that are played on limited bases to send signals or play short and repetitive motives, it is the pair of *atumpan* drums, with their noted male and female designations, that are used effectively in drum communications. Similarly, the sheer size and powerful sound of the *bɔmmaa* drums represent heroism, and when two are used, the huge pair of *bɔmaa* drums in *fɔntɔmfrɔm* ensembles are similarly labeled as male and female drums. The English words "queen" or "queen mother" are inadequate to fully capture these cultural nuances and implications of the Akan word *ɔhemaa*. As a result, I will retain the Akan titles *ɔhemaa* or *Asantehemaa*, since there is no one-to-one translation in English.

As an Asante, my interest in the musical arts at the court is due to my lived experience growing up in several Akan states. I was fortunate in a sense; my father, Kwame Ampene, was a teacher in the Ghana Education Service, and he was regularly transferred and stationed in several Akan towns. I grew up in four out of the sixteen regions of Ghana: Asante, Brong East, Central, and Eastern (see Figure 2.2). In all of these places, I was exposed to performances of traditional popular bands and court music traditions at diverse events. Like kids everywhere, understanding sometimes came from playmates, and at other times comprehension came from our elders, who are always prepared to answer my numerous questions. My representation of Akan performance arts in this study is therefore based on how I accessed Akan culture growing up, even before I studied "music" in the School of Performing Arts at the University of Ghana. My participation in several musical situations was not predicated on melody, harmony, and rhythm;

rather, I internalized the underlying text, along with its symbolism and significa-
tion and the total feel of performances—instrumental, singing, and dancing. We
learned how to sing, dance, or handclap to accompany singing by watching and
imitating adults. We used mnemonics for bell patterns, sometimes with translat-
able texts or words without linguistic meanings, but were able to represent the
sounds.

I began contemplating a systematic study of court music in 1996 when I began
my field research in *nnwonkɔrɔ* for my doctoral dissertation in ethnomusicology.
At the time, I accompanied Manhyia Tete Nnwonkɔrɔ, led by the late Nana Afua
Abasa (*Nnwonkɔrɔhemaa*), on numerous occasions to Manhyia Palace. Since a
reigning Asantehene is a life patron of Manhyia Tete Nnwonkɔrɔ, they perform
regularly every forty-two days during the Akwasidae Public Assembly, or for
royal funerary rites or in other locations in Kumase and the surrounding areas.
During the court events, it dawned on me that although a few ensembles like the
fɔntɔmfrom, kete, and *ntahera* ivory trumpets are well-known to the outside world,
academics have repeatedly written studies on the same ensembles, while the vast
majority of ensembles and verbal art forms remain unknown. When I searched
databases at the two major universities in Accra and Kumase, I found a few theses
on aspects of court music, but research was not as comprehensive as one might
imagine. My current study is a personal journey that began in my childhood with
my utmost interest in musical events. The opportunity to study with custodians
and knowledgeable experts of Akan and Asante court music and verbal arts, and
the extraordinary opportunity to share that knowledge with the Akan and non-
Akan all over the world, is priceless.

Filling the void in Akan and Asante musicological studies

There are essentially two types of literature on Akan and Asante court music.
The first contains scattered non-specialist accounts in the pre-colonial and colonial periods of various Akan groups and their musical arts. The second involves
systematic accounts by specialists in the post-colonial era and includes Asante
royal music. Non-specialist documentary evidence of a highly developed system of court music and verbal arts appears in the writings of fifteenth-century
European explorers, traders, administrators, and missionaries who went to the
then-Guinea Coast and encountered an Akan civilization in full bloom. Some of
them are Diego d'Azambuya (1482), Pieter de Marees (1602), William Bosman
(1705), John Barbot (1732), Thomas E. Bowdich (1819), John Beecham (1841),
Alfred Burdon Ellis (1887), and Richard Austin Freeman (1898). As expected,
the descriptions of music, musical instruments, and musical events were grossly
inadequate in detail and quite subjective. They describe a variety of idiophones
including clapperless bells and castanets made of iron, flat sticks possibly made of
bamboo stems, and gourd rattles of various shapes and sizes. There are accounts
of melodic idiophones such as the *penpensua*; aerophones in the descriptions
include *atɛntɛ* or *atɛntɛben, durugya*, shorter ivory trumpets (*mmɛntia*), and the
fairly large ivory trumpets (*ntahera*) that are played in groups of seven. There

is also a description of a single type of chordophone, *seperewa*, and a mouth bow (*bɛnta*) that resists classification as a string instrument. Not surprisingly, the early non-specialist Europeans were struck by the variety of drums and provided graphic descriptions of drums, along with the wood, leather, playing techniques that included the use of hands and curved sticks (*nkonta*), and how some of them were carried or hung on the shoulder during processions.

One of the most substantial accounts of elaborate court music from the early nineteenth century is *Mission from Cape Coast to Ashantee* by the British merchant Thomas E. Bowdich (1819). A representative of the Royal African Company, Bowdich traveled to Kumase in 1817 to establish trade with the Asante Kingdom, and ended up writing and publishing in vivid detail his travel and reception in Kumase by the Asante King Ɔsɛe Asibe Bonsu. He described what he refers to as the "Yam Festival," and, with assistance from his cartographer, provided for the first time a colorful drawing of the General Assembly of Chiefs. A little over a century later, and with colonialism in full force, the head of the newly created Anthropological Department of Ashanti, Robert Sutherland Rattray, published a series of books that were vastly different from earlier publications. More than previous authors, though not without colonial bias, he described musical activities and instruments in a systematic way. Rattary's books, including *Religion and Art in Ashanti* (1927), were based on anthropological methods and were published for the benefit of the colonial government.[15]

In a bid to restore the positive aspects of Ghanaian culture that had been tainted with Eurocentrism during the colonial period, Ghanaian scholars in post-colonial Ghana took on a larger role in writing about their own culture. The title of Kofi Antubam's *Ghana's Heritage of Culture* (1963) captures the sentiments at the time by covering every aspect of life in Ghana as a whole. Although very general and with scanty information, court music and material culture do appear throughout the book. The pioneering works of J.H. Kwabena Nketia, such as *Akanfoɔ Nnwom Bi* (1949), were published before independence. Written in the Akan Twi language and based on transcriptions of songs and instrumental texts of seven vocal and instrumental genres—*adowa, adenkum, sobom, nnwonkorɔ, mmobomme, asafo nnwom*, and *mmɛn*—*Akanfoɔ Nnwom Bi* is based on the kind of systematic study that precedes the discipline of ethnomusicology in the West by almost a decade. Another groundbreaking study written in English by Nketia is *Drumming in Akan Communities of Ghana* (1963), which contains a chapter titled "State Drumming" that references all forms of drumming associated with Akan chieftaincy. Another classic, *The Funeral Dirges of the Akan People* (1969), covers the linguistic, literary, and musical style of the Akan dirge. In 1974, Nketia published an extensive anthology of *Ayan* (drum poetry) performed by the Creator's Drummers (Akyerɛma) from Manhyia Palace in Kumase, Kokofu, and Kwawu Abetifi on the pair of Atumpan drums. Following *Akanfoɔ Nnwom Bi*, *Ayan* is written entirely in Twi with four sections grouped under greetings and announcements—those performed at dawn on Akwasidae to wake the king and chiefs, praise poetry of past and present kings and chiefs, and proverbs in *fɔntɔmfrɔm* Akantam (oath swearing dance). Outside court drums, Nketia published two groundbreaking studies of ivory trumpets: "The Hocket Technique in African Music" (1962) and "The Surrogate Languages of Africa" (1971a). One of the most detailed studies of ivory trumpets was produced by Nketia's student at UCLA, Carter G. Woodson, whose master's thesis *The Ntahera Horn Ensemble of the Dwaben Court: An Ashanti Surrogating Medium* (1971) and doctoral dissertation, titled *Asante Music in Old and New Juaben* (1984), present both linguistic analysis and the mechanisms of trumpet speech. One of the most comprehensive works from the mid-twentieth century is A.A.Y. Kyerematen's doctoral thesis *Ashanti Royal Regalia: Their History and Functions* (1966). Presented to the Faculties of Anthropology and Geography at the University of Oxford, Kyerematen's pivotal study is farsighted and critical to my current work. Not only did Kyerematen present a catalogue and description of Asante royal regalia, he also described the regalia "as reflecting the history, beliefs, values and social institutions of the people" (Kyerematen, 1966: 32). Additionally, he includes court instruments, music, and verbal art forms as parts of stool regalia.[16]

In 1990, Peter Akwasi Sarpong, a social anthropologist and expert in Akan and Asante culture, published *The Ceremonial Horns of the Ashanti* (Sarpong, 1990). Although a fairly small booklet, Sarpong provides a general description of the trumpets and concludes the book with a sample of what he refers to as "horn language with English translations."[17] A recent monograph on *ntahera*, one of the ivory trumpet groups with a fairly wide distribution in Akan, is Joseph Kaminski's *Asante Ntahera Trumpets in Ghana: Culture, Tradition, and Sound Barrage* (2012). Although the notion of a "sound barrage" is problematic, Kaminski's monograph is based on field research in Kumase with the Asantehene's *ntahera* ivory trumpet group. Kaminski draws heavily on Nketia and Carter's works referenced previously, but as a trumpeter he expands existing works with technical insights of sound production and the insights he gained as a participant observer. In addition to his doctoral dissertation, Kaminski has published five articles on ivory trumpets in scholarly journals. My analysis of instrumental and song texts, as well as poetry, benefit from publications by Akan literary scholars, including Kwesi Yankah's "To Praise or Not to Praise the King: The Akan 'Apae' in the Context of Referential Poetry" (1983), along with Akosua L. Anyidoho's "Linguistic Parallels in Traditional Akan Appellation Poetry" (1991) and *Gender and Language Use: The Case of Two Akan Verbal Art Forms* (1993). Published in *Research in African Literatures*, Yankah's article is based on his 1975 field research in three different Akan states: Dɛnkyera, Akwamu, and Asante. He combines the poetic verses he documented with those collected and transcribed by J.H. Kwabena Nketia. Akosua Anyidoho's first article is based on a collection of published poems by Ɔkyeame Boafo Akuffo, while the second work is an unpublished dissertation. William Anku's *Procedures in African Drumming: A Study of Akan/Ewe Traditions and African Drumming in Pittsburgh* (1988) is also an unpublished dissertation based on an ethnomusicological analysis of *Kete*, which emphasizes drum patterns in order to establish a theory of African rhythm. Other valuable sources for Akan court music are the unpublished master's theses and doctoral dissertations in the School of Performing Arts at the University of Ghana. They include M.H.N. Agyeman's *Fontomfrom Music in the Adonten Traditional Area of Akwapem Royal Instrumental Ensemble* (1983), Osafo E. Onwona's *The Music of Fontomfrom* and *Mpintin and Osoode in Ohum Festival of Mampong-Akuapim* (1988), Samuel O. Bampo's *Mpintin Music in Akropong-Akuapim* (1990), and Kenneth K. Bonsu's *Music and Identity: The Standpoint of Fontomfrom Music in Peki* (2011). This indicates that although a few ensembles—particularly the *fontomfrom*, *kete*, *ntahera* ivory trumpets, and *mmɛntia*—are well known, the vast resources of the Asantehene and the Asantehemaa's courts, which include the musical arts and their mediating material culture, have largely been sequestered from academic scrutiny. *Asante Court Music and Verbal Arts in Ghana* is my attempt to fill this ethnomusicological void by presenting the wide variety of instruments, ensembles, songs, and sounded texts together in a single volume.

Comparable literature in Africa and Asia

Outside Akan and Asante sources, the range of literature generated about African kingdoms is too long to list here. One of the most recent monographs on the court music of the Buganda Kingdom is Damascus Kafumbi's *Tuning the Kingdom: Kawuugulu Musical Performance, Politics, and Storytelling in Buganda* (2018). Based on field research, along with oral and written accounts and archival research, *Tuning the Kingdom* is a welcome addition to a growing scholarly interest in the musical heritage of pre-colonial, colonial, and post-colonial kingdoms in Africa. Kafumbe's critical assessment of the Kawuugulu Royal Musical Ensemble and performances highlights three domains—kinship, clanship, and kingship—as the foundations of Kiganda politics. Court music of Uganda's southern kingdoms feature prominently in the early publications of Gerhard Kubik. Published in 1964, "Xylophone Playing in Southern Uganda" introduced the *amadinda* and *akadinda* xylophones and court musicians from the Buganda Kingdom to a wider readership (Kubik, 1964: 138–159). Peter Cooke's article "Music in a Uganda Court" (1996) describes performance practices associated with the seven groups of solo and ensemble musicians who perform at various times of the day. Cooke also examines stylistic and structural aspects of the music with a particular emphasis on "rhythmic density" (Cooke, 1996: 439–452).

Although the titles of the following publications do not explicitly reflect royal or court music traditions, they nevertheless deal with court music expressions and musical instruments in Africa. Bode Omojola's *Yorùbá Music in the Twentieth Century*, for example, allocates two chapters to songs of the king's wives and the song tradition of Yorùbá female chiefs (Omojola, 2012: 70–90, 91–112). West African *jali* performance traditions (*jeliya*; griots in French) are among the topics covered in a major comprehensive book, *Mande Music: Traditional and Modern Music of the Maninka and Madinka of Western Africa*, by Eric Charry (2000). In the centralized medieval kingdoms of Ghana, Mali, and Songhey established by the Mande, the *jali*'s multiple identities include verbal artists, genealogists, historians, diplomats, and entertainers. Although they served wealthy merchants in the ancient kingdoms, they were primarily court musicians who are described

by Charry as state-sanctioned guardians of certain Mande musical and oral traditions (Charry, 2000: 3). Jacqueline Djedje's *Fiddling in West Africa: Touching the Spirit in Fulbe, Hausa, and Dagbamba Cultures* (2008) devotes its last
chapter to the one-string fiddle (*gondze*), a highly placed court instrument and
music in the kingdom of Dagbon in Northern Ghana (Djedje, 2008: 169–241).
Although David Locke's *Drum Damba: Talking Drum Lessons* (1990) focuses
on "the purely music meaning" of *Damba* drumming and dance, his interlocutors
are the hereditary drummers known as *lunsi* from the same kingdom as Djedje's
gondze players. While their main instruments are the armpit squeeze drum (*luna*)
and the cylindrical *gungon* drums, like the *jali* they are verbal artists, genealogists, historians, diplomats, and entertainers who perform for wealthy patrons as
well as general households in the communities; however, they are primarily court
musicians. Unlike the *jali*, who have lost their status as royal musicians with the
collapse of the Mande kingdoms, the *lunsi* still perform for royalty, since the
Dagbon kingdom, like the Asante, is still thriving under the new political setup
in post-colonial Ghana. A distinctive feature between the *lunsi* drummers and
the court drummers (*akyerɛma*, singular *ɔkyerɛma*) in Asante is that, whereas the
lunsi combine verbal texts (or storytelling) with instrumental texts played on the
luna drum, court drummers in Asante do not verbalize their poetry. As a rule, all
poetry and instrumental texts are played on drums. For the ivory trumpets covered
in this book, there are comparable studies of Banda Linda horn music in Simha
Arom's *African Polyphony and Polyrhythm* (1991).

   Beyond Africa, contemporary performance and scholarship on court music
and dance traditions across Asia offer a rich analogous repository of materials
for analysis. José Maceda's "The Structure of Principal Court Musics of East and
Southeast Asia" (2001) is an excellent overview of instrumental court ensembles from China, Japan, Korea, Java, Bali, Thailand, and Kampuchea. Guided
by Confucian philosophy, court music in China exerted profound influence in
Asia, from ancient dynasties to the end of the Imperial period in 1911, providing
a window into this wide geographic expanse. The following articles by Joseph
S.C. Lam constitute some of the representative literature on court music in China:
"Huizong's Dashengyue, a Musical performance of Emperorship and Officialdom" (2006) and "The Yin and Yang of Chinese Music Historiography: The Case
of Confucian Ceremonial Music" (1995). In 1991, the Beijing Song and Dance
Ensemble staged a grand music and dance performance of the imperial courts of
eight Chinese dynasties under the broad theme "The Spell of Antiquity" (Lanxing,
1991). One of the oldest examples of imperial court music in Japan is Gagaku.
Since the 1950s, an increase in scholarship across Japan, the US, and Europe—
in addition to the work of performing ensembles—has contributed to renewed
interest in Gagaku. Of particular interest to my thesis is the understanding that
contemporary staged performances involving Gagaku imply performances of history—not only Japan's history but also Gagaku's "unique position in Pan-Asian
history" (Malm, 1971: 8). According to Malm, Gagaku is a special court music,
and "its ability to evoke Japan's most brilliant courtly period" (1971: 4–8) is a
conduit to the glorious past for the current generation. Two articles among several

others are LeRon James Harrison's "Gagaku in Place and Practice: A Philosophical Inquiry into the Place of Japanese Imperial Court Music in Contemporary Culture" (2017) and Andrea Giolai's "Passion Attendance: Becoming a Sensitized Practitioner in Japanese Court Music" (2016). Other examples from South Korea, Java, and Vietnam include Hee-sun Kim (2012), Bambang Sunarto (2006), and Phan Thuan Thao (2015).

Theoretical considerations

My theoretical framework—the intersections between music, lived experience, and values—resonates with research paradigms that continue to animate a large body of texts in ethnomusicology and allied disciplines in the humanities for the past forty years. However, my use of experience differs substantially from the subjective and reflexive overlays in ethnographic texts, where indigenous knowledge is often treated as mere data instead of theory. Essentially, existing scholarship can be filtered through two lines of thought. The first is where the authors are subjectively central in the texts (e.g. Cottrell, 2004), while the second emphasizes the experience of music by individuals expressing shared cultural values (e.g. Wade, 2009). Unwavering interest among ethnomusicologists led to the *Global Music Series* edited by Bonnie C. Wade. Similar to the first edition, the third edition of the framing volume for the series, *Thinking Musically: Experiencing Music, Expressing Culture* (2013), is informed by dialectical pairings of experience and expressions, producing twenty-two regional case studies and potentially generating more. Unlike the Global Music Series, whose authors are all card-carrying ethnomusicologists, Martin Clayton, Byron Dueck, and Laura Leante spearheaded an interdisciplinary collaboration involving ethnomusicologists, social psychologists, and sociologists to produce the seminal volume *Experience and Meaning in Music Performance* (2013). In this volume, ethnographies of Hindustani music are combined with computer-generated algorithms, but like previous literature, they are framed with theories drawn from phenomenology and dialectical relationships, and their analysis extends to entrainment and the theory of embodied cognition and a host of scientific methods.[18]

Fundamentally, my use of experience aligns with Wade et al. and is predicated on the understanding that the construction of sound-producing and musical instruments—along with the creation of songs, instrumental accompaniments, dances, and verbal art forms—all stem from the lived experiences of social groups. Further, lived experience involves centuries of reflection, as a social group goes through life and reflects upon the meaning of life and the world around them (see, e.g., Opoku, 1982: 61). It is undeniable that centuries of reflections morphed into the practical and embodied knowledge encoded in the thousands of proverbs, visual symbols, verbal arts, music and dance, and musical instruments passed down from generation to generation.[19] A case in point is how events led to the creation of the royal drum ensemble *Kwantenpɔnmuta*. According to oral history narrated to me by the presiding elder of the group,

Nana Konadu Brayie II, in 1818, the Asantehene Osei Asibe Bonsu created the previously-named drum after the Asante-Gyaaman War and the defeat of Gyaaman King, Nana Adinkra Kofi. The Asantehene and his men were reported to have been lost in the forest for several days and could not find the path that would lead them back to Kumase. When the ruler accidentally landed on a foot-path that he and his soldiers could follow, he asked those with him to carve a drum and use it to send a message to the infantry that *ma bɛsi kwan mu ta nti obiara mra* (lit. "I have landed on a good trail so they should all come"). It is said that the king placed the drums in the custody of one Kwame Asiedu and honored him with the title *Kofoɔ* (lit. "the fighter"), so he became known as Kwame Asiedu Kofoɔ. The original drum resembles the hourglass drum, but it is slightly bigger. Currently, the ensemble includes one *adawura* (a boat-shaped metal idiophone), one *donno*, and one *petia*. *Kwantenpɔnmuta* is now part of the Asantehene's procession, and heroism in the dance recalls the history, while the repeated drum text—*kwantenpɔnmuta, kwantenpɔnmuta, kwantenpɔnmuta*—is interpreted as "the Asantehene walks in broadways and not bypaths" (Ampene and Nyantakyi, 2016: 228–229). In that sense, it is clear that when the Asante perform *kwantenpɔnmuta* as part of court ceremonies and rituals, the perfor-mance is mediated by history; that is, the Asante-Gyaaman War of 1818, along with the memory and experience of the king and his soldiers losing their trail in the forest and accidentally finding a path leading them back to Kumase. Conse-quently, each new performance of *Kwantenpɔnmuta* recalls nearly two centuries of the Asante-Gyaaman War, including memories of places and events. Although the incident previously involved the king and a group of soldiers, making it a uniquely personal experience, they later shared it with the larger Asante King-dom, just as we all share stories. The oral knowledge about kwantenpɔnmuta has been socially maintained over time by placing it in the custody of Kwame Asiedu Kofoɔ and successive generations of his family, as well as by making it a vital part of royal processions and rituals. The performance of the previously-named drum ensemble in processions connects performers and participants to past lived experience—and the present generation of Asante, who are negotiat-ing challenges in their post-colonial environment—in a grand continuum of his-tory. This singular example is one of several that I will examine here. Figure 1.1 is a picture of the *kwantenpɔnmuta* drum ensemble in a procession.

Guided by the previous example, my notion of music and historical experience privileges the voices of the Asante and how they express their history, religious philosophy, social values, and political experiences through musical performances and the allied arts. When appropriate, I will include personal narratives, but I will not engage in reflexive discourse as the main actor. My approach corresponds to findings from heuristic ethnography in anthropology as exemplified by the works of John C. McCall (2000), Andrew Apter (1992), Michael Jackson (1982, 1989), Paul Stoller (1987, 1997), Edith Turner, Blodgett, Kahona, and Benwa (1992), and Steven Feld (1982). In his ethnography with the Ohafia Igbo in Nigeria, McCall proactively treats knowledge from his interlocutors as theory, thus relinquish-ing long-held assumptions in Euro-American discourse that "'Their' knowledge

Figure 1.1 Kwantenpɔnmuta drum ensemble in a procession during the Akwasidae Public
Assembly, July 30, 2017.

Source: Picture by author.

produces data and 'Our' knowledge produces theory" (McCall, 2000: 14). It bears
stating, however, that recognizing indigenous knowledge does not negate a rigorous and critical assessment of historical memory; rather, it provides a basis for
inductive analysis and an awareness that all forms of knowledge are "socially situated constructs and not 'objective' models of social reality" (*ibid*, 2000: 18). In
that sense, the oral history of the *kwantenpɔnmuta* drum ensemble is socially situated within an Asante construction of a historical incident, the Asante-Gyaaman
War of 1818, but missing from Nana Konadu Brayie's account is the Gyaman
version of the same war. Listing a host of scenarios and the global presence of
contemporary Yoruba in the "postmodern world" in Nigeria, the United States, the
Caribbean, and South America (especially Brazil), Andrew Apter explains why it
is no longer feasible or, in his own words, "conscionable for non-Yoruba scholars
to write 'about' or 'for' the Yoruba, but rather with the Yoruba, within a complex
discursive field" (Apter, 1992: 2–10). Apter aligns his monograph, *Black Critics & Kings: The Hermeneutics of Power in Yoruba Society*, with Robert Farris
Thompson's work on Yoruba art by prioritizing indigenous or vernacular forms of
knowledge and understanding. For Apter, working with the Yoruba on their social
constructs made it possible for Yoruba politics and religious experience to become
accessible to not only scholars from Euro-American institutions, but the Yoruba
themselves (*ibid*, 1992: 4–5). Similarly, in *Sensuous Scholarship* (1997), Paul

Stoller stresses the need for scholars to "tune in to local wavelengths of theory" in order to comprehend the nature of epistemologies of Songhay sorcerers and griots in Mali and Niger.[20]

In order to extend the notion of experience in Asante to other domains, I expand my theoretical formulation to include the concept of *value*. By value, I refer to ideas, worldviews, concepts, beliefs, and social relationships that inform musical practices and choices. In reference to the *kwantenpɔnmuta* drum ensemble, we can conclude that there is value in persistence because the returning soldiers did not give up when they were lost in a dense impenetrable forest, but instead they kept searching until they found a trail that led them to Kumase. For the Asante, there is value in exemplary leadership, along with strength, courage, sacrifice, heroism, honor, responsibility, deference to authority, and other traits that will no doubt come up in the following chapters.[21] An example is in order: the Asantehene Otumfoɔ Ɔsɛe Tutu II is formally seated and presiding over a ceremony, and the territorial chiefs and *ahemaa* are taking turns to greet him. A courtier is sounding the following epigram on the short trumpet (*abɛntia*) in their usual position behind the king.

Example 1.1 Mo Bɛ Kae Me (You Will Remember Me), *abɛntia.*

Lead Abɛntia	Lead Abɛntia
1. Kɔtɔkɔ mo bɛ kae me	Porcupines, you will remember me
2. Kɔtɔkɔ mo bɛ kae me	Porcupines, you will remember me
3. Asante Kɔtɔkɔ mo bɛ kae me	Asante the Porcupines, you will remember me
4. Asante Kɔtɔkɔ mo bɛ kae me	Asante the Porcupines, you will remember me

According to the chief of the short trumpet group, Nana Owusu Mran (*Mmɛntiahene*), the previous verse was composed for Ɔpemsoɔ Ɔsɛe Tutu (c. 1680–1717) and is recognized as an enduring philosophical statement from the founder of the kingdom to his subjects. Although there may be more than a dozen short trumpeters, the verse is invariably performed by one trumpeter, for there was only one short trumpet in the days of Ɔsɛe Tutu. The relatively less aggressive phrase *mo bɛ kae me* ("you will remember me"), in all four lines, negates the forcefulness of a statement like "you should remember me." Aggression is muted in order to soften the message due to the presence of territorial chiefs and *ahemaa*. *Kɔtɔkɔ* (porcupines) as the opening phrase in Lines 1 and 2, and *Asante Kɔtɔkɔ* (Asante the Porcupines) in Lines 3 and 4, illustrates my earlier discussion of the adaptation of known characteristics of the porcupine (*kɔtɔkɔ*) as the totem and emblem of the Asante Kingdom. The opening phrase *kɔtɔkɔ* in lines 1 and 2 refers to all Asante, followed by the emphatic single syllable *mo* (literally, you all). In line 3, *Kɔtɔkɔ* is preceded by Asante in order to remove ambiguity or doubt that he is in fact referring to his subjects. While the accomplishments of Ɔpemsoɔ Ɔsɛe Tutu as the founder of one of the most powerful West African states is well documented, his personal sacrifices are not equally lauded. Here is a short list for the benefit of those who may not be familiar with his record of accomplishments and sacrifices:

- He brought together formerly independent states to defeat their overlord, the powerful Dɛnkyera Kingdom, in 1701.
- He formed a union of states and built an enduring kingdom.
- Together with his spiritual advisor and counselor, Kɔmfo Anɔkye, he created an ideology—the Gold Stool—as the soul, unity, identity, and strength of the kingdom.
- He embarked on wars of conquest to expand the kingdom. Although a symbolic reference, he is said to have fought seventy-seven wars.
- He was a military strategist and created army units and divisions.
- He was an astute constitutionalist, and in another symbolic statement in collaboration with Kɔmfo Anɔkye, he is said to have passed seventy-seven injunctions including religious, political, judicial, economic, and moral laws.
- He created several of the stool regalia and captured some of them from defeated chiefs.

This partial list of Ɔsee Tutu's accomplishments is meant to highlight the personal sacrifices he had to make on the way to his ultimate sacrifice on the battlefield. It is upon years of reflection that he concluded that his subjects in the kingdom owed him endless gratitude and that they would forever be grateful for his lifetime of work long after his death. There is no question about that statement, for after more than three centuries, the achievements of Ɔpemsoɔ Ɔsee Tutu, as well as his personal sacrifices, are talked about as if he were still alive. In the final analysis, there is value in sacrifice, there is value in courage, and there is value in gratitude. It is considerations such as the previous that underlie Reginald Byron's observation that "the value of a piece of music as music is inseparable from its value as an expression of human experience" (Byron, 1995: 31). The sounding of Ɔsee Tutu's epigram on a short trumpet (*abɛntia*) composed over three centuries ago, as part of a present-day Akwasidae Public Assembly, bears ample testimony to historical markers in material objects: a short trumpet (*abɛntia*) and a sounded statement that are socially maintained over time through use in rituals and ceremonies. The previous example is a historical construct that lives in the present. There are value judgements associated with the performative arts in terms of what constitutes an outstanding performance, including verbal agility, voice quality, drum knowledge, and preferred instrumental timbres.

Methodological determinants

The work in this volume is based on ten years of intensive field research at Manhyia Palace in Kumase. Starting in 2009, I became the first ethnomusicologist to be granted unrestricted access, since the 1980s, to the centuries-old court music and verbal arts practiced at Manhyia Palace, the official residence of the Asante king and Asantehemaa in Ghana. In a prototypical participant-observer approach to gathering primary data, I usually spent two or three months in the summer taking part in and recording court ceremonies, rituals, festivals, and funerary rites, as well as engaging in formal and informal interviews with court musicians and culture experts. Outside of the summer months, I collected data during the historical burial and final funerary rites of the Asantehemaa Nana Afia Kobi Serwaa Ampem II in January and December 2017.[22] Data gathering is based on three primary situations: documentation of live events, formal meetings and interviews with ensemble members and leaders, and feedback interviews. My field equipment includes a video camera, a still camera, and a digital audio recording device and accessories. During formal meetings and interviews with members of ensembles, I recorded both the oral history of instruments and ensembles as well as the repertoire. Upon my return from the field, I transcribed all of the conversations and repertoires and edited my audio-visual recordings and still photographs to provide a basis for my analysis. On my return trip the following year, I took my transcriptions back to the court musicians for another round of corrections and further clarification. During the writing stage, I worked with language experts in the Linguistics Department at the University of Ghana to refine the Twi orthography and English translations of texts. My secondary data include library and archival materials from the University of Ghana for extant literature on Akan court music, the Archaeology Department in the same institution, archives and museums at Manhyia Palace in Kumase, the British Museum and British Library in London, and the World Museum of Ethnology in Leiden (the Netherlands).

A critical method of interpreting recorded events while at my field site involved playing back video recordings of prior events for participants to reveal crucial information not readily available through regular conversations or interviews. The playback method is a distinctly qualitative method that was highly favored over four decades ago by ethnomusicologists Ruth Stone, who referred to it as feedback interview (see Stone and Stone, 1981), and Simha Arom, who used the term playback (1976).[23] In particular, the spiritual undertones of court events invariably take participants into the spiritual realm, and in such a spiritual space, court musicians are able to switch to ritual memory, whereby actions and behaviors in an ongoing event are guided by embodied knowledge. While some participants were able to recall aspects of the ceremony to the minutest level of detail after the event, others were unable to articulate or answer my questions very well, leaving the impression they were not conscious of their role in the event. With the video feedback interview, I was able to obtain a rich and textured analysis, using Stone-McDonald and Ruth Stone's useful phrase, that yielded a bountiful collection of data.[24] Since my field research at Manhyia Palace involved recording multi-hour events, I found the video feedback interview to be extremely useful in stimulating a rich polyphony of the combined voices of the researcher and the researched. For instance, when I played back the Remembrance Rites at Breman for the royal drummers of the *fɔntɔmfrɔm* ensemble, they were able to describe drum texts and cues, in addition to the dance gestures and props of the Asantehene, to the *Atopretia* dance suite (see Figure 1.2). In another setting, I played the procession of the Remembrance Rites for the Royal *Kete* drummers at Mpasaatia, and that

Figure 1.2 Feedback analysis with three members of Fɔntɔmfrɔm ensemble: Kwabena
     Atta Panin, Kwabena Adjei Tawiah, and Kwabena Atta Kakra.
Source: Picture by Nana Kwame.

yielded all kinds of comments from the drummers, not the least of which was the
procession drumming they performed on the day. My analyses of *kete* songs in
Chapter 5 stem from my video-feedback interviews with members of the chorus
and the insights they provided. Similarly, there were times when I engaged my
main consultant, Nana Nyantakyi III, in watching a clip of an Akwasidae Public
Assembly or funerary rites that led to the generation of rich data on a wide range
of topics. My video feedback sessions with Nana Nyantakyi III were especially
valuable because they were interactive and allowed for deeper conversations and
observations on varied events; he was able to provide insights into a ceremony or
a ritual that I might otherwise have missed. Similarly, my video playback sessions
made it possible for Opanin Fofie to clarify the utterly dense verses of chronicle
poetry by the bards (*kwadwom*) in Chapter 6. Although the umbrellas are not
musical instruments *per se*, my video feedback interview with the chief of umbrella,
Nana Bogyabiyɛdɔm II, revealed not only the formation of umbrellas in processions, but crucially, also the technique of moving the umbrellas in synchrony with
processional music and rhythms including *fɔntɔmfrɔm, kete, mpintin,* and vocal
ensembles such as *adowa* and *nnwonkorɔ* (see Figure 1.3).

Through the feedback technique, several court musicians contributed more
nuanced insights of the complex layers of symbolism, and historical processes
imbedded in Asante court rituals, to my understanding. During video feedback
interviews, I inserted a Secure Digital (SD) card or an external Hard Drive (HD)
into my MacBook Pro laptop and played a previously recorded event for my consultants. As we watched, a cameraman recorded our conversations with a Sony

Figure 1.3 Feedback analysis with Opanin Kofi Fofie (*kwadwom*) and Nana Bogyabiyɛdɔm II (Kyinyɛkyimfoɔhene).

Source: Picture by Nana Kwame.

hand-cam while I recorded with my Zoom H4 digital audio recorder. Despite the time and resources needed for video feedback interviews, the upside far outweighed the known drawbacks, particularly in non-scribal cultures such as the Asante where an overwhelming amount of research data is based on live events.

The culture management system and the insider-outsider conundrum

Despite official recognition and access to court musicians and courtiers at Manhyia Palace, my research was not without some of the usual drawbacks and politics of field research, for cultural knowledge such as the Asante's is subject to a highly sophisticated system of cultural management.[25] The modes by which I was given access to different knowledgeable persons and custodians represent forms of circuit validation that impose time constraints on the researcher. For instance, traditional formalities involving introductions, negotiations, and acceptance takes time. A formal meeting with an elder or a custodian chief is channeled through proverbs and sophisticated modes of speech that constantly gauged my patience, while at the same time I was being tutored in different forms of rhetorical competence. All of these were designed to manage the temporality of my access to what I thought was my research subject, but which they, in their wisdom, moderated as they deemed fit. There were times when conversations led unexpectedly to topics not in the public domain and I was asked to turn off my audio-visual equipment. At other times, I was told not to publish particular information when they realized

I had already recorded it. Because of my positionality as both a culture "insider" and "outsider," when it comes to the subjects of court music and verbal arts, I was aware of some of these dynamics. I have been particularly guided by what Bode Omojola refers to as the dilemma of not being "fully inside nor outside" (Omojola, 2012: 11–12). The culture management system and circuit validation is not only limited to the Asante court or the Yorùbá, in the case of Omojola, but is widespread across Africa in various ways. For example, although a native of the Buganda Kingdom in Uganda, spirit mediums and custodians of cultural knowledge managed the temporality of Damascus Kafumbe's access to critical materials. According to Kafumbe, some spirit mediums did not permit him to record interviews with audio-visual gadgets, including still photography, while others were not forthcoming or did not want to be interviewed at all. The spirit mediums wondered, and rightly so: why did he want to audio or video tape information that had historically been transmitted orally? Others thought Kafumbe was too young and lived too far away in the United States to be trusted as a faithful gatekeeper of such information (Kafumbe, 2018: 18–22). In spite of my "insider" status, I strongly believe that I would have faced similar challenges if I had approached court musicians and custodians alone, without the Asantehene's approval and interest in my work. It is considerations such as the previous that led Nana Nyantakyi III to suggest at the beginning that I should not go alone to the villages to meet with court musicians, since some of them would still harbor doubts as to whether the Asantehene had actually given his blessings to my research. Nana Nyantakyi III made sure that all of our meetings and interviews with court musicians took place in one of the inner spaces of the palace. In his view, bringing and working with groups inside the walls of Manhyia Palace was all the validation they needed to demonstrate that the Asantehene was really behind my work. The exceptions were when the chief of an ensemble or a lead performer in a group was advanced in age, or if some of the members were sick, in which case we went to the villages and towns of the court musicians.

Linked to the culture management system is an incident that happened when we interviewed one of the Constabulary groups known as *Tɔprɛfoɔ*. In the course of recording the oral history of this group, Nana Nyantakyi III asked the chief why they did not bring the main drum (known as *tɔprɛ*). The chief, Nana Twumasi Panin, explained that since they stopped executing criminals over 100 years ago, they also ceased to bring out the *tɔprɛ* drum. He continued to explain that the only way they can bring the drum out is for the Asantehene to perform a series of rituals. Nana Nyantakyi III then asked him to take me to his house the following morning so that I could take pictures of the *tɔprɛ* drum. The next day, we left the palace around eleven a.m., and upon reaching his house, Nana Panin showed me into a dimly lit room where, placed on a short chair (*asipimtia*) and covered with a camel blanket (*nsaa*), was the *tɔprɛ* drum. On the right was a bed covered with about five or six camel blankets, and in the far left corner of the room were ritual objects.[26] I stepped out of the room to set up my camera, and when I returned to take pictures of the drum, to my utter surprise my EOS 60D Canon Camera would not work! The shutter button would not work no matter how hard I pressed it down with my index finger. In my frustration, I stepped out of the room to the corridor, and the camera worked when I took a picture of the corridor. I went back to the room, and the shutter did not work. I looked around again and it dawned on me that this was no ordinary room; it was a "stool room"—a room where black stools representing deceased chiefs of the *tɔprɛ* group are kept. You do not go to such rooms wearing shoes, or without showing any form of reverence to the ancestors; but there I was, wearing shoes and looking all dressed up. I asked the chief if he performed libation prayers to inform his forebears about my coming in to take pictures of the *tɔprɛ* drum, and he responded in the negative. So I asked him to perform libation prayers while I stepped out of the room to take off my shoes and roll up my shirt sleeves and long pants. My camera still did not work, so I asked him to call upon his forebears and have them intercede on our behalf. He grabbed a bottle of hard liquor and started another round of libation prayers by calling all of his deceased forebears in succession. As he was praying, my camera flashed twice all of a sudden, and I immediately realized that we had been given the green light to take pictures of the drum. I lifted my camera and in a quick move, without focusing, I pointed it to the drum. This time it worked! I was able to take a picture of the drum. Then I decided to focus the lens for excellent shots, but again the camera did not work. I tried without focusing, and it worked. I was able to take a couple of pictures without properly focusing the camera, but they all worked so I asked the chief to thank his forebears with another libation prayer. I was not happy with the chief for taking me to a stool room without any form of preparation, since as an Asante I know the protocol for such ritual spaces. Apparently, he did not ask me to take off my shoes out of respect due to my positionality as a university professor, and more so because I was sent by Nana Nyantakyi III who was appointed by the Asantehene. Ultimately, the culture management system at Manhyia Palace ensures that the cumulative knowledge, and the embodied knowledge of Asante-man, is not taken for granted. It has inbuilt verification procedures that guarantee that I am not the kind of person who would just take off and recklessly mishandle the knowledge that has been entrusted to me. The key to understanding and analyzing the complex knowledge presented to me is not to examine the material with preset methods designed only by the disciplines of cultural anthropology or ethnomusicology, but like McMall, Apter, Stoller, Thompson, and like-minded scholars, examining Asante indigenous knowledge and theory as embodied in and realized through lived experience. To sum up, the noted restraint in the use of a culture management system, and the resultant circuit validation, calls for a critical reassessment of the insider-outsider distinction in field research. A culture management system requires a qualitative approach to field research that recognizes indigenous theories as theories without prefixes, as in *ethno*theory, *ethno*poetics, *ethno*linguistics, and others.

Lastly, while I am keenly aware of the melodic, harmonic, and rhythmic elements of the examples I present in this book, my focus is on an in-depth analysis of the texts. To be sure, I am not against using Western notation in a descriptive graph to represent African musics, and I have done exactly that in some of my published works. However, the historical and present experience of the Asante are expressed through rhetorical devices, along with embodied performances in instrumental and song texts, dance, and visual symbols. In the words of John McCall, the texts are stylized accounts of actual events in the past and the present (2000: 55). Thus, ancient song texts of the *kete* chorus, referential poetry (*apae*), and chronicle poetry (*kwadwom*) in this volume memorialize events of historic importance, while contemporary incidents are also accounted for. By focusing entirely on textual analysis, I demonstrate how Asante performance arts—surrogate verses of ivory trumpets, flutes, drums on the one hand, and songs and dance on the other—are fundamentally based on texts. For the Asante, the frame of reference and access to musical events is obtained through texts, and we stand to gain a "profound understanding" of Asante court music and verbal arts by accessing one of the foundational resources in the musical arts (Agawu, 2016: 113). There are precedents for text-based studies in ethnomusicology. In his book *A Day for the Hunter, A Day for the Prey*, Gage Averill did not include musical transcriptions in order to engage literary scholars in cross-disciplinary discourse (Averill, 1997: xxi–xxii). Averill examines music in the context of discourse and relations of power in Haiti, presenting a substantial dose of song texts and English translations for a variety of popular songs that includes, but is not limited to, *compass* and *rara*. Lester Monts' *Dance in the Vai Sande Society* (1984), Kelly Askew's *Performing the Nation* (2002) and Thomas Turino's *Nationalists, Cosmopolitans, and Popular Music in Zimbabwe* (2000) are exemplars of text-based studies in ethnomusicology. Monts' analysis of the critical role of dance in the transition of females from adolescence to adulthood is devoid of European music notation but his analysis and conclusions are critical to our understanding of Vai society. With the exception of a reproduction of the Tanzanian National Anthem on page 183, Askew presents several texts of Tanzanian *taarab*, a genre of sung poetry, without Western notation or forms of graphic representation for sound. Similarly, Turino's critical study of "a social and style history of urban-popular music in Harare, Zimbabwe, from the 1930s to the mid-1990s" uses chord progressions and letters to represent pitches but is devoid of notation.

The chapters in this volume

My discussion of the intersections between music, lived experience, and values in Asante court music and verbal arts is grouped into six distinct but related chapters set between a prologue and an epilogue. Basing the Prologue on an event encapsulates lived experience, values, aesthetics, ideologies, philosophies, and much more, as it allows us to not only see what is done, but *how* it is done. Events assemble and reinforce lived experience and crystallize disparate creative sensibilities encoded in the complex system of ancient song texts, poetry, and instrumental texts within a single space. My narrative, however, generates a number of fascinating questions, which my discussions in the remaining chapters seek to unravel.

Chapter 2 presents the historical foundations of Asante court music and verbal arts, the continuity between the Asante and the Akan past, and the gradual and incremental development of resources for Asante court music from scratch. The history of Asante court music and verbal arts is examined through reigns, wars, and events within each reign. The last section examines the lived experience of contemporary Asante as part of a new political framework, following independence from British colonial rule. I examine the seeming lack of innovation in Asante court music in the context of the current lived experience of my interlocutors and my own views on the subject. The noticeable lack of creative impulse, new instruments, new ensembles, songs and instrumental texts, and poetry to commemorate events is due in part to the end of Asante militarism, conquests, and expansion in 1896 and 1901. These were the events and imageries that provided inspiration for innovations, but there have been new creative outlets, although less visible than in the pre-colonial era, where court musicians and poets recompose existing texts in order to recontextualize the verses and make them relevant to contemporary Asante.

Focusing on the Asante Kingdom, and particularly Manhyia Palace, in Chapters 3 to 6 I address my framing theory—the intersections between music, lived experience, and values—by examining the language and poetry of the ivory trumpets and cane flute. In Chapter 3, I begin with an overview of ivory trumpets as a group, while noting their distinctions in size from the relatively large to small types, in addition to their defining repertoires. I conclude my discussion of ivory trumpets with a considered discussion of the pervasive use of the number seven, which constitutes the number of players in each ivory trumpet group. I conclude the chapter with a contrast in the timbre and texts of the durugya flute, which technically is not an ivory trumpet but a cane flute. However, my inclusion of the latter is justified by the general reference to wind instruments in the Akan Twi as *mmɛn* (singular *abɛn*). There is no distinction between a trumpet, a horn, or a flute; they are all *mmɛn*. For the language and poetry of drums in Chapter 4, I examine texts that define the integrated rhythms of the *kete* drum ensemble and the heroic texts performed by the *fɔntɔnfrɔm, mpintin, apirede, mmedie,* and *kwantenpɔnmuta* drum and percussion ensembles. In Chapter 5, I shift my attention to rhetoric and history when I examine *kete* songs and songs performed by physicians and spiritual advisors. Finally, in Chapter 6, I examine rhetoric and history in Chronicle songs (*kwadwom*) performed by bards (*kwadwomfoɔ*) and referential poetry (*apae*) performed by members of the constabulary (*abrafoɔ*). I conclude my ethnography of the Akwasidae ceremony with an Epilogue that highlights the centrality of the musical arts in events where aspects of over three centuries of Asante history are performed. My focus on texts bears ample testimony to the use of sound-producing and musical instruments as mediating material objects that embody historical and lived experience in the past and the present, along with the conscious use of instrumental and song texts to record and memorialize historical events through the method of recalling such events during rituals, court ceremonies, funerary rites, and celebrations. Based on key issues across these chapters, I suggest that renditions of Asante socio-political and economic history that are devoid of integrated expressions in the musical and performing arts (not forgetting the visual arts) are woefully inadequate.

Notes

1 See, for instance, Nketia's contribution to the larger discussion of "Akan History and Culture" (1982).
2 For love songs in Renaissance Europe, see Emily Zazulia (2010), Giulio Ongaro (2003), Leeman L. Perkins (1999), and Don A. Monson (1995).
3 Peter Sarpong (1977) is a monograph of nubility rites for girls in Asante.
4 The reference here is Nketia (1963, 1987).
5 A.A.Y. Kyerematen (1969) lists the following functions of the Sanaahene: he collects the king's share of any payments made in the court such as thanks-offering (*aseda*); he is responsible for accounts in connection with the Sunday and Wednesday Adae Festivals; and deputizes for the king when he is unable to go himself to the three royal mausoleums at Bampenase, Bantama, and Akyeremade.
6 The *Ashanti Stool Histories* is the outcome of a project by the Institute of African Studies, University of Ghana in 1962. Fellows from the institute recorded oral histories of stools belonging to custodians of regalia objects and music ensembles for Manhyia Archives, located in the palace in Kumase but part of the institute in Accra.
7 For an interpretation of dance gestures in the *fɔntɔmfrɔm ɛkyɛm* dance suite, see Ampene and Nyantakyi III (2016: 176–179).
8 My contextual account of the Asantehene's procession expands on Kyerematen's 1969 description.
9 See Ampene and Nyantakyi III (2016).
10 I completed *Gone to the Village* in 2019.
11 Among the Akan, the seven or eight matrilineal clans are identified by their animal totems. Although a fundamentally matrilineal society, the Akan also recognize totems associated with patriclans.
12 For a fairly detailed oral history of the "descent of the Golden Stool," see Kyerematen (1966: 227–236).
13 For a detailed account of the last Anglo-Asante War, see A. Adu Boahen (2003). Ivor Agyeman-Duah (2007) is a documentary on the heroism of Nana Yaa Asantewaa and the last Anglo-Asante War. A companion book to the TV series on Yaa Asantewaa was published in 2007.
14 For a detailed description of the descent of the Gold Stool, see A.A.Y. Kyerematen's unpublished dissertation (1966: 227–241).
15 Additional books by Rattray are 1916, 1923, 1929, 1930, and 1932.
16 A culture icon in his own right, A.A.Y. Kyerematen is the founder of the Kumase Cultural Center, which is now the Center for National Culture.
17 After serving the Roman Catholic Church for over fifty years, His Grace Archbishop Peter Akwasi Sarpong retired from active service, but is as busy as ever publishing books, receiving visitors from around the world, and traveling to present lectures.
18 Closely aligned with phenomenology and dialectical relationships as theoretical constructs are Michael Bakan (1999) and Harris M. Berger (1999).
19 A recent anthology by Peggy Appiah, Kwame Anthony Appiah, and Ivor Agyemang-Duah (2007) features over 7,000 Akan proverbs.
20 Paul Stoller's (1989) monograph on the Songhay of Niger rehearses similar concepts.
21 For a general overview of Akan values, see Kwame Gyekye (1996).
22 The burial and funerary rites of Nana Afia Kobi Serwaa Ampem II was the first time in 209 years that a reigning Asante King performed the funerary rites of an Asantehemaa who was also his birth mother. She served Asanteman and Ghana for thirty-nine years (1977–2016). Born in 1905, she was 111 years old when she passed away. Ampene (2019) is a documentary of the historical burial and final funerary rites of the late Asantehemaa.
23 Over the years, a host of ethnomusicologists, including Harris Berger (1999), Mellonee Burnim (1985), Pandora Hopkins (1986), Pamela Dorn (1991), Daniel Reed

(2003), and Steven Feld (2012), to name just a handful, have successfully used the feedback technique in the field.

24 See Angela Stone-MacDonald and Ruth M. Stone 2013 for interdisciplinary examples of the Feedback Interview.

25 My discussion of cultural management systems owes a great deal to a conversation I had with Ato Quayson in November 2017 at the 60th Annual Meeting of the African Studies Association (ASA) in Chicago. I am grateful to Ato for an enlightening conversation.

26 For the history, pictures of custodians, and *tɔprɛ* drum, see Ampene and Nyantakyi III (2016: 170–173).

References

Agawu, Kofi. 2016. *The African Imagination in Music*. New York: Oxford University Press.

Agyeman, M.H.N. 1983. "Fontomfrom Music in the Adonten Traditional Areas of Akwapim Royal Instrumental Ensemble." Diploma thesis, University of Ghana.

Ampene, Kwasi. 2005. *Female Song Tradition and the Akan of Ghana: The Creative Process in Nnwonkorɔ*. Aldershot: Ashgate Publishing Ltd.

Ampene, Kwasi and Nana Kwadwo Nyantakyi III. 2016. *Engaging Modernity: Asante in the Twenty-First Century*, 2nd edition. Ann Arbor, MI: Michigan Publishing.

Anku, William. 1988. "Procedures in African Drumming: A Study of Akan/Ewe Traditions and African Drumming in Pittsburgh." PhD diss., University of Pittsburgh.

Antubam, Kofi. 1963. *Ghana's Heritage of Culture*. Leipzig, Germany: Koehler & Amelang.

Anyidoho, Akosua L. 1991. "Linguistic Parallels in Traditional Akan Appellation Poetry." *Research in African Literatures* 22 (1): 67–81.

———. 1993. "Gender and Language Use: The Case of Two Akan Verbal Art Forms." PhD diss., University of Texas, Austin.

Appiah, Peggy, Kwame Anthony Appiah, and Ivor Agyemang-Duah. 2007. *Bu Me Bɛ. Proverbs of the Akans*. Oxfordshire: Ayebia Clarke Publishing Ltd.

Apter, Andrew. 1992. *Black Critics & Kings: The Hermeneutics of Power in Yoruba Society*. Chicago: University of Chicago Press.

Arom, Simha. 1976. "The Use of Play-Back Techniques in the Study of Oral Polyphonies." *Ethnomusicology* 20 (3): 483–519.

———. 1991. *African Polyrhythm and Polyphony: Musical Structure and Methodology*. Cambridge: Cambridge University Press.

Askew, Kelly. 2002. *Performing the Nation: Swahili Music and Cultural Politics in Tanzania*. Chicago: University of Chicago Press.

Averill, Gage. 1997. *A Day for the Hunter, A Day for the Prey: Popular Music and Power in Haiti*. Chicago: University of Chicago Press.

Bakan, Michael. 1999. *Music of Death and New Creation: Experiences in the World of Balinese Gamelan Beleganjur*. Chicago: University of Chicago Press.

Bampo, Samuel O. 1990. "Mpintin Music in Akropong-Akuapim." Diploma thesis, University of Ghana.

Barbot, John. 1732. *A Description of the Coasts of North and South Guinea*. London: Messrs. Churchill.

Beecham, John. 1841. *Ashantee and the Gold Coast: Being a Sketch of the History, Social State, and Superstitions of the Inhabitants of Those Countries: With a Notice of the State and Prospects of Christianity Among Them*. London: J. Mason.

Berger, Harris M. 1999. *Metal, Rock and Jazz: Perception and the Phenomenology of Musical Experience*. Middletown, CT: Wesleyan University Press.

Boahen, A. Adu. 2003. *Yaa Asantewaa and the Asante-British War of 1900-1*. Accra, Ghana: Sub-Saharan Publishers.

Bonsu, Kenneth K. 2011. "Music and Identity: The Standpoint of Fontomfrom Music in Peki." MPhil thesis, University of Ghana.

Bosman, William. 1705. *A New and Accurate Description of the Coast of Guinea*. London: Frank Cass and Company Ltd.

Bowdich, Thomas E. 1819. *Mission from Cape Coast Castle to Ashantee: With a Statistical Account of That Kingdom, and Geographical Notices of Other Parts of the Interior of Africa*. London: John Murray and Sons.

Burnim, Mellonee. 1985. "Culture Bearer and Tradition Bearer: An Ethnomusicologist's Research on Gospel Music." *Ethnomusicology* 29 (3): 432–447.

Byron, Reginald, ed. 1995. *Music, Culture, & Experience: Selected Papers of John Blacking*. Chicago: University of Chicago Press.

Carter, William G. 1971. "The Ntahera Horn Ensemble of the Dwaben Court: An Ashanti Surrogating Medium." Master's thesis, University of California, Los Angeles.

———. 1984. "Asante Music in Old and New Juaben." PhD diss., University of California, Los Angeles.

Charry, Eric. 2000. *Mande Music: Traditional and Modern Music of the Maninka and Mandinka of Western Africa*. Chicago: University of Chicago Press.

Clayton, Martin, Byron Dueck, and Laura Leante. 2013. *Experience and Meaning in Music Performance*. New York: Oxford University Press.

Cooke, Peter. 1996. "Music in a Uganda Court." *Early Music* 24 (3): 439–452.

Cottrell, Stephen. 2004. *Professional Music-Making in London: Ethnography and Experience*. Aldershot: Ashgate Publishing Ltd.

Djedje, Jacqueline. 2008. *Fiddling in West Africa: Touching the Spirit in Fulbe, Hausa, and Dagbamba Cultures*. Bloomington, IN: Indiana University Press.

Dorn, Pamela. 1991. "Change and Ideology: The Ethnomusicology of Turkish Jewry." PhD diss., Indiana University.

Ellis, Alfred Burdon. 1887. *The Tshi-Speaking Peoples of the Gold Coast of West Africa: Their Religion, Manners, Customs, Laws, Language*. London: Chapman and Hall Ltd.

Feld, Steven. 1982. *Sound and Sentiment: Birds, Weeping, Poetics, and Song in Kaluli Expression*. Philadelphia, PA: University of Pennsylvania Press.

———. 2012. *Jazz Cosmopolitanism in Accra: Five Musical Years in Ghana*. Durham, NC: Duke University Press.

Fordwor, Kwame Donkoh. 2009. "Foreword." In *Otumfuo Ose Tutu II: The King on the Golden Stool*, edited by Kojo Yankah. Accra: Macmillan Publishers Ltd.

Freeman, R. Austin. 1898. *Travels and Life in Ashanti and Jaman*. Westminster: A. Constable & Co.

Giola, Andrea. 2016. "Passion Attendance: Becoming a 'Sensitized Practitioner' in Japanese Court Music." *Antropoligia e Teatro* 7: 243–265.

Gyekye, Kwame. 1996. *African Cultural Values: An Introduction*. Philadelphia, PA: Sankofa Publishing Company.

Harrison, LeRon James. 2017. "Gagaku in Place and Practice: A Philosophical Inquiry into the Place of Japanese Imperial Court Music in Contemporary Culture." *Asian Music* 48 (1): 4–27.

Hopkins, Pandora. 1986. *In Aural Thinking in Norway: Performance and Communication with the Harding-fele*. New York: Human Sciences Press.

Jackson, Michael D. 1982. *Allegories of the Wilderness: Ethics and Ambiguity in Kuranko Narratives*. Bloomington, IN: Indiana University Press.

———. 1989. *Paths Toward a Clearing: Radical Empiricism and Ethnographic Inquiry*. Bloomington, IN: Indiana University Press.

Kafumbe, Damascus. 2018. *Tuning the Kingdom: Kawuugulu Musical Performance, Politics, and Storytelling in Buganda*. Rochester, NY: University of Rochester Press.

Kaminski, Joseph. 2012. *Asante Ntahera Trumpets in Ghana: Culture, Tradition, and Sound Barrage*. Farnham, Surrey; Burlington, VT: Ashgate Publishing.

Kim, Hee-sun. 2012. "Performing History and Imagining the Past: Re-Contextualization of Court Ensembles in Contemporary South Korea." *The World of Music* 1 (1): 81–102.

Kubik, Gerhard. 1964. "Xylophone Playing in Southern Uganda." *The Journal of the Royal Anthropological Institute of Great Britain and Ireland* 94 (2): 138–159.

Kyerematen, A.A.Y. 1964. *Panoply of Ghana: Ornamental Art in Ghanaian Tradition and Culture*. New York: Frederick A. Praeger.

———. 1966. "Ashanti Royal Regalia: Their History and Functions." PhD diss., Oxford University.

———. 1969. *Kingship and Ceremony in Ashanti*. Accra: Buck Press Ltd.

Lam, Joseph S.C. 1995. "The Yin and Yang of Chinese Music Historiography: The Case of Confucian Ceremonial Music." *Yearbook for Traditional Music* 27: 34–51.

———. 2006. "Husong's Dashengyue, a Musical Performance of Emperorship and Officialdom." In *Emperor Huazong and Late Northern Song China: The Politics of Culture and the Culture of Politics*, edited by Patricia Buckley Ebrey and Maggie Bickford, vol. 266, 395–452. Harvard East Asian Monographs. Cambridge: Harvard University Press.

Lanxing, Hong. 1991. "Music and Dances of the Chinese Imperial Court." *Beijing Review* 33: 32–34.

Locke, David. 1990. *Drum Damba: Talking Drum Lessons*. Crown Point, IN: White Cliffs Media Company.

Maceda, José. 2001. "The Structure of Principal Court Musics of East and South East Asia." *Asian Music* 32 (2): 143–178.

Malm, William P. 1971. "Introduction." In *Gagaku: Court Music and Dance*, edited by Masataro Togi, translated by Don Kenny. New York and Tokyo: Walker, Weatherhill.

Marees, Pieter de. 1602. *Description and Historical Account of the Gold Kingdom of Guinea*. Translated from the Dutch and edited by Albert van Dantzig and Adam Jones. Oxford: Oxford University Press.

McCall, John C. 2000. *Dancing Histories: Heuristic Ethnography with the Ohafia Igbo*. Ann Arbor, MI: University of Michigan Press.

Monson, Don A. 1995. "The Troubadour's Lady Reconsidered Again." *Speculum* 70 (2): 255–274.

Monts, Lester P. 1984. "Dance in the Vai Sande Society." *African Arts* 17 (4): 53–95.

Nketia, J.H. Kwabena. 1949. *Akanfoɔ Nnwom Bi*. London: Oxford University Press.

———. 1962. "The Hocket-Technique in African Music." *Journal of the International Folk Music Council* (14): 44–52.

———. 1963. *Drumming in Akan Communities of Ghana*. London: Thomas Nelson and Sons Ltd.

———. 1969. *Funeral Dirges of the Akan People*. New York: Negro Universities Press.

———. 1971a. "Surrogate Languages of Africa." In *Current Trends in Linguistics 7*, edited by Thomas A. Sebeok, 699–732. The Hague, Netherlands: Mouton & Co., Printers.

————. 1971b. "Linguistic Aspect of Style in African Languages," In *Current Trends in Linguistics, Vol. 7, Linguistics in Sub-Saharan Africa*, edited by Thomas A. Sebeok, 733–757. The Hague, Netherlands: Mouton & Co., Printers.

————. 1982. "The Musical Traditions of the Akan." *Tarikh* 7 (2): 29, 47–59.

————. 1987. "Asante Court Music." In *The Golden Stool: Studies of the Asante Center and the Periphery*, edited by Enid Schildkrout, vol. 65, 200–208. New York: Anthropological Papers of the American Museum of Natural History.

Omojola, Bode. 2012. *Yorùbá Music in the Twentieth Century: Identity, Agency, and Performance Practice*. New York: University of Rochester Press.

Ongaro, Giulio Maria. 2003. *Music of the Renaissance*. Westport, CT: Greenwood Press.

Onwona, Osafo E. 1988. "The Music of Fontomfrom, Mpintin and Osoode in Ohum Festival of Mampong-Akwapim." Diploma thesis, University of Ghana.

Opoku, Kofi Asare. 1982. "The World View of the Akan." *Tarikh* 7 (2): 61–73.

Perkins, L. Leeman. 1999. *Music in the Age of the Renaissance*. New York: W.W. Norton & Company.

Rattary, Robert Sutherland. 1923. *Ashanti*. Oxford: The Clarendon Press.

————. 1927. *Religion and Art in Ashanti*. Oxford: The Clarendon Press.

————. 1929. *Ashanti Law and Constitution*. Oxford: The Clarendon Press.

Reed, Daniel B. 2003. *Dan Ge Performance: Masks and Music in Contemporary Côte d'Ivoire*. Bloomington, IN: Indiana University Press.

Sarpong, Peter. 1990. *The Ceremonial Horns of the Ashanti*. Accra: Sedco Press.

————. 1977. *Girls' Nubility Rites in Ashanti*. Accra and Tema: Ghana Publishing Corporation.

Stoller, Paul. 1989. *Fusion of the Worlds: An Ethnography of Possession Among the Songhay of Niger*. Chicago: University of Chicago Press.

————. 1997. *Sensuous Scholarship*. Philadelphia, PA: University of Pennsylvania Press.

Stoller, Paul, and Cheryl Olkes. 1987. *In Corcery's Shadow: A Memoir of Apprenticeship Among the Songhay of Niger*. Chicago: University of Chicago Press.

Stone, Ruth M. ed., 2000. *The Garland Handbook of African Music*. New York: Garland Publishing.

Stone, Ruth M., and Verlon L. Stone. 1981. "Event, Feedback, and Analysis: Research Media in the Study of Music Events." *Ethnomusicology* 25 (2): 215–225.

Stone-MacDonald, Angela, and Ruth M. Stone. 2013. "The Feedback Interview and Video Recording in African Research Settings." *Africa Today* 59 (4): 2–22.

Sunarto, Bambang. 2006. "Gambian Music and Literature in Javanese Court." *Asian Musicology* 8: 117–139.

Thao, Phan Thuan. 2015. "Revitalizing the Lost Instruments: Research and Reconstruction of the Bronze Bells and Stone Chimes in Vietnamese Court Music." *Asian Musicology* 25: 129–159.

Turino, Thomas. 2000. *Nationalists, Cosmopolitans, and Popular Music in Zimbabwe*. Chicago: University of Chicago Press.

Turner, Edith, William Blodgett, Singleton Kahona, and Fideli Benwa. 1992. *Experiencing Ritual: A New Interpretation of African Healing*. Philadelphia, PA: University of Pennsylvania Press.

Wade, Bonnie C. 2009. *Thinking Musically: Experiencing Music, Expressing Culture*, 2nd edition. New York: Oxford University Press.

————. 2013. *Thinking Musically: Experiencing Music, Expressing Culture*, 2nd edition. New York: Oxford University Press.

Yankah, Kwesi. 1983. "To Praise or Not to Praise the King: The Akan 'Apae' in the Context of Referential Poetry." *Research in African Literatures* 14 (3): 381–400.

Zazulia, Emily. 2010. " 'Corps contre corps,' voix contre voix: Conflicting Codes of Discourse in the Combinative Chanson." *Early Music* 38 (3): 347–359.

Videography

Agyeman-Duah, Ivor. 2007. *Yaa Asantewaa: The Heroism of an African Queen.* Accra, Ghana: Centre for Intellectual Renewal-Ghana.

Ampene, Kwasi. 2019. *Gone to the Village: Royal Funerary Rites for Asantehemaa Nana Afia Kobi Serwaa Ampem II.*

2   Asante court music in historical perspective

Nyansapɔ (Wisdom Knot: wisdom, ingenuity, intelligence). Akan Adinkra pictographic writing.

Asante is the last Akan state that came to power in the then-Gold Coast, around the late-seventeenth century, and it rapidly became one of the most powerful empires in West Africa by the nineteenth century.[1] That Asante is variously referred to in history books as a kingdom, a state, an empire, or a confederacy is indicative of the sophistication and complexity of Asanteman that resists simple categorization. By the mid-nineteenth century, through wars of conquest and expansion, Greater Asante, to borrow Ivor Wilks' label, was larger than present-day Ghana (Wilks, 1993: 203). But Asante rulers did not only concern themselves with political power, territorial expansion, or economic pursuits. It is recognized, among other things, that the growth in prestige and power associated with Asante power and sophistication was accompanied by corresponding developments in artistic creations, "which resulted in the emergence of models of cultural excellence at the courts of powerful and imaginative rulers" (Nketia, 1987: 200). Wars of conquest and expansion inspired creativity in the arts, as heroic encounters generated a large corpus of songs, instrumental texts, and poetry as records of lived experience. As observed previously, and as we shall see in the following chapters, sound-producing and musical instruments as mediating material culture were also created to commemorate events, captured as war trophies, or simply borrowed, especially from northern neighbors. During field research, court musicians, courtiers, and consultants responded to my questions by referencing reigns, wars, and events occurring within each reign. I believe Ivor Wilks found himself in a similar situation with his observations about oral histories (*abakɔsem*) in Asante. But, ever cautious and in anticipation of potential criticisms from historians for relying on oral history, Wilks cited the *Jali* (or griots) in ancient Mali, as well as Irish and Welsh bards, to validate his use of oral histories; as he came to appreciate, oral narratives can be transmitted over long periods of time (Wilks, 1993: 101–102). I have already mentioned Ɔpemsoɔ Ɔsɛe Tutu's philosophical statement, *Kɔtɔkɔ*, "you will remember me" (Example 1.1), played on his short ivory trumpet (*abɛntia*) and the creation of *kwantenpɔnmuta* drum ensemble during the reign of Ɔsɛe Asibe Bonsu (1804–1824). However, as is the case in oral narratives, while the events provide us with chronological episodes, they lack absolute dates. Since dates in Akan are not cumulative, the best possible method for recording incidents and reigns are artistic expressions. In light of the previous observations, I will examine the history of Asante court music and verbal arts within a framework of selected reigns and events. A combination of oral and written sources lead to dense narratives, but due to space constraints I examine only a few reigns, events, and wars within these broader chronological frameworks: 500 BCE–1600 CE, 1600–1680, 1680–1701, 1701–1867, 1867–1931, and 1931–present. I begin by establishing the link between Asante and the Akan past.

Akan–Asante continuum (500 BCE–1600 CE)

Akan settlements were comprised of organized towns and chiefdoms, complex agricultural and industrial installations, long-distance trade, developments in archi-tecture, expressive arts, and pictographic forms of writing commonly known as *adinkra* symbols (Anquandah, 1982a, 1982b). The Akan predominantly live in Ghana and Côte d'Ivoire, and minimally in Togo.[2] With approximately 47.5 per-cent of the total population in Ghana and 32.1 percent of the overall population in Côte d'Ivoire, they are the largest ethnic group in both countries. According to Kenya Shujaa, the outer limits of Akan settlements are bound in the east by the Volta River in Ghana and in the west by the Komoé River in the Côte d'Ivoire, while the northern and southern tips are demarcated by the Black Volta and the Atlantic Ocean, respectively (Shujaa, 2014: 30).[3] Akan groups in Ghana include the Adanse, Bono, Assen, Twifo, Akwamu, Dɛnkyira, Kwawu, Akyem, Akuapem, Sefwi, Aowin, Asante, Fante, Ahanta, and Nzema; the Abron, Baule, Anyi, and Nzema make up the groups in Côte d'Ivoire (see Figures 2.1 and 2.2 for Akan areas in Ghana and Côte d'Ivoire and a regional map of Ghana). There are a few cultural particulars and institutions that are widely shared, sometimes with slight varia-tions, among all Akan groups. The foundation of Akan social organization is based on a matrilineal system whereby one's inheritance, succession to political office, land ownership, and property is validated through the maternal line (or blood line). Every Akan belongs to one of seven or eight matrilineal exogamous clans and participates in a complex monarchical system of government made up of kings, chiefs, and corresponding *ahemaa* who, as I noted, are not necessarily the wives of chiefs.[4] Akan principles of complementarity are expressed through the dual male-female system of governance. Ɔhene (kings or chiefs) have their corresponding female counterparts, *ahemaa* (singular *ɔhemaa*), to ensure harmony, equilibrium, and social balance. The dual leadership role has its functional equivalence in the organization of musical ensembles, such as the male and female Atumpan drums. When two are used, the huge pair of *bɔmaa* drums are similarly designated as male and female drums in *fɔmtɔmfrɔm* ensembles. A week consists of seven days, and it is part of a forty-two day calendar system that is used in organizing agricultural undertakings, religious festivals, and social and political activities.[5] The calendar also provides Akan citizens with names for the soul (*kra din*) based on seven days of the week and additional names beyond the seven days, including Dapaa, Fofie, Fokuo, Fɔdwoɔ, and others. In Ghana, the Akan speak language varieties in the Twi-Fante cluster that is further divided into several mutually intelligible dialects, including Nzema, Ahanta, Sefwi, Aowin, Fante, Asante, Agona, Akuapem, Brong, and others. The dialects in Côte d'Ivoire are Baule, Anyi, and Nzema. Joseph H. Greenberg's 1963 classification listing Twi as belonging to the Kwa sub-family of the Niger-Congo has been re-classified by J. M. Stewart since 1966 as belonging to the Volta-Komoé group (Dolphyne, 1982: 35–45).[6] The new classification takes into account the Volta River in eastern Ghana and River Komoé in eastern Côte d'Ivoire. J.K. Fynn informs us that by the fifth century CE, the Akan developed agricultural industries that formed the foundations for trade in kola nuts to as far as Hausaland in Nigeria. Trade and commerce were vital to Akan economy and urbanization, as they developed techniques for mining gold and trading to the northeast and northwest with Mande traders. The Northwestern route passed through Ejura, Kintampɔ, Nsɔkɔ (referred to as Begho by the Mande), Bonduku, Kong, Wagadugu, Jenne, Timbuktu, and beyond. For the eastern corridor, the route began from the central forest to Ejura, Salaga, Yendi, San Sanne Mango, and Niamey and went further westward to Gao and eastward to Sokoto, Zaria, Kaduna, Katsina, Kano, and beyond (Fynn, 1982: 23–34).[7]

Within Akan groups, sound-producing and musical instruments, and some types of instrumental and choral singing, became institutionalized and were identified with the four-tier settlement hierarchy. The basic political unit, the state (*Ɔman*), and the chief (*Ɔmanhene*) had the largest collection of sound-producing instruments including short ivory trumpets (*mmɛntia*) and large ivory trumpets commonly known as *ntahera*, along with different sizes and shapes of drums, flutes, and pipes. Next in line are the chiefs (*Ahemfo*) of larger towns (*nkuro kɛseɛ*), who in all likelihood will have smaller ensembles than the former, while the chief (*Ɔhene*) of towns (*nkuro*) will possess a modest number of instruments and just one or two sound-producing instruments. Since the position of Village Head (*Odikro*) is not technically a chief, he has no instruments or ensembles apart from a metal gong that the town crier may use as an attention grabber on his usual rounds making announcements. The ensembles, with both sound-producing and musical instruments, became part of the heirloom (*agyapadeɛ*), and together with visual objects, body adornments of chiefs, and *ahemaa*, they became state property that was passed on from generation to generation. With the arrival of competing European nations—the Portuguese, Dutch, British, French, Germans, and Danes—along the coast, a new trade frontier opened up and spurred rapid urban and state development. Apart from coastal states, some of the Akan states that increasingly benefited from the complex trade networks were the Bono (fifteenth through eighteenth century), Akwamu (c. 1600–1730), Dɛnkyira

(c. 1660s–1690s), Adanse (c. 1500–1640), and Akyem Abuakwa (c. fifteenth century to present). An interesting development around this time is a 1629 map credited to Dutch cartographer Hans Propheet showing over twenty Akan states. A map, they say, tells a particular story and reveals the aims of the those who drew it, and in this case, the story is unquestionably about the location of gold mines in Akanland.[8] As I have previously stated, the arrival of Europeans also marked the emergence of documentary data in the form of published diaries and journal entries. A sample of these include the Portuguese Duarte Pacheco Pereira (1905); two Dutch traders, Pieter de Marees (1602) and Willem Bosman (1705); and Englishman William Towerson (1555–1556). The diaries and journals continued until the end of the nineteenth century, and I will make references to these and more in this and the following chapters.

Confirming the accounts of European merchants, the Akan themselves produced graphic images of court musicians, instruments, and royalty on diverse media, which provides us with insights into the types of instruments and the form and function of musicians and performers that existed before the advent of the Asante Kingdom. A fair number of Akan gold weights, which were developed as tools for weighing gold dust for purchasing goods and services in this period, had representations of music instruments or individuals playing instruments as motifs (Nketia, 1982: 51). There are representations of court criers (*esɛn*) striking the ubiquitous clapperless bell (*dawuro*) as an attention grabber and making public announcements. There are gold weights depicting different aspects and usages of drums, drummers in action, court trumpeters playing a side-blown ivory trumpet, and the *seperewa* harp-lute (Figure 2.3). Another object is the Akan brass treasure casket (*kuduo*), the preferred container for storing gold dust, with the lid showing a seated court trumpeter playing a side-blown ivory trumpet.[9] Excavations at ancient sites by archaeologists have produced several clay sculptures, some of which are on display at the museum in the Department of Archaeology and Heritage Studies at the University of Ghana. Excavations at Nsɔkɔ produced pieces of ivory side-blown trumpets and royal instruments used by the Bono Kingdom, with radiocarbon dating them between the sixteenth and seventeenth centuries (Anquandah, 1982b: 100–109). Funerary clay sculptures representing sixteen- or seventeenth-century court trumpeters are among the objects obtained from excavations at the royal mausoleum at Adanse Ahensan. From the same location is a seventeenth-century clan pot with a gong (*dawuro*) and manilas in high relief (Figure 2.4). Considering the location of the Akan, which is described as dense and impenetrable forest with intricate ecosystems, they demonstrated great skill and resourcefulness in exploiting their environment from the Neolithic period (2000 BCE) to the Late Iron Age (1500–1900 BCE). Given the number of powerful Akan states that existed concurrently (and still exist) or were tributaries to a neighboring Akan state, it was just a matter of time before a single and an all-powerful state would eventually emerge.[10] When it finally did, in the late seventeenth century, Asante inherited almost 2,000 years of Akan socio-political and cultural sophistication, as well as intricate and expanded trade networks. Not only did Asante inherit all of the noted developments in Akanland, but critically, they also expanded the artistic resources of Akan court music and verbal arts to an unprecedented level of sophistication up to the present day.

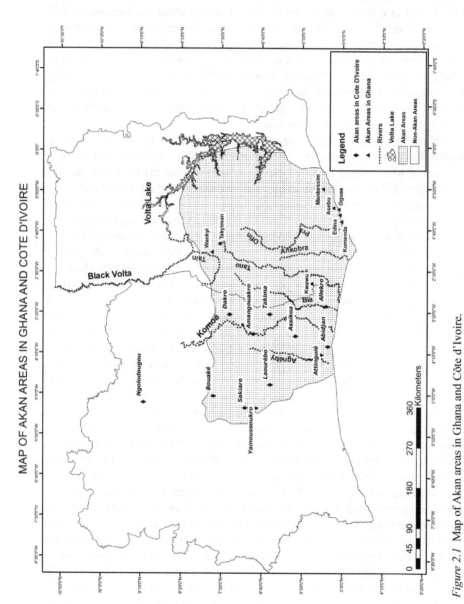

Figure 2.1 Map of Akan areas in Ghana and Côte d'Ivoire.
Source: Ben Emunah Aikins, University of Ghana, Legon.

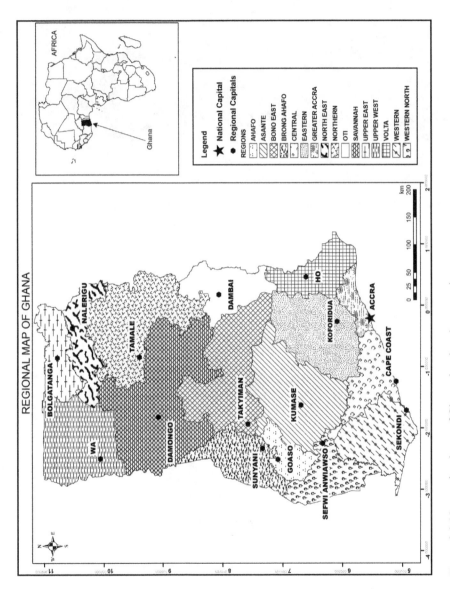

Figure 2.2 New regional map of Ghana showing sixteen regions.

Source: Ben Emunah Aikins, University of Ghana, Legon.

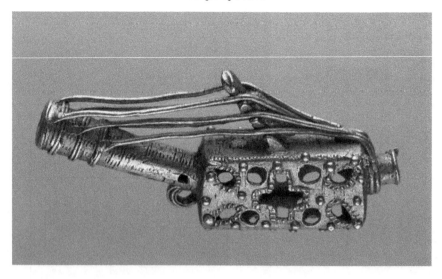

Figure 2.3 Graphic representation of Akan *seperewa* (harp-lute) as gold weight.

Source: With permission from the British Museum. Number Af1818,1114.2.

Figure 2.4 Graphic representation of Akan *dawuro* (gong) on a seventeenth-century clan
pot (*abusua kuruwa*) from Adanse Ahensan Mausoleum.

Source: With permission from the University of Ghana Department of Archaeology and Heritage
Studies Museum. Number 52/235 A.

Prelude to Asante (1600–1680)

A series of events from the early 1600s to around 1680 precipitated the creation of the Kumase state and subsequently the Asante Kingdom, but two are
particularly notable: the Kwaaman Purchase and the excesses of the Dɛnkyera
Kingdom. In his unpublished dissertation, Kyerematen describes the Kwaaman
Purchase around 1631 by Oti Akenten, who named the area Kum-ase (lit. under
the Kum tree) in reference to the location under the Kum tree that he made the
purchase. Oti Akenten relocated to the relatively fertile land with members of
his Ɔyoko matriclan from the Asumenya-Asantemanso area. He was soon joined
by heads of the Ɔyoko lineages and families from the same area, and later, also
others from Kokofu. Since they were all from the same matriclan, it was fairly
easy for them to stay united and convince the inhabitants in the area to form
a union capable of withstanding potential attacks from Dɛnkyera. Confirming
oral history, Kyerematen traces the new name of the union to the reaction of the
Dɛnkyira King Asare Boampɔnsɛm, who upon hearing of the union of Amanseε
groups, remarked in Twi, "*ɔsa nti na eyinom aka wo ho abomu*" (these people
have come together because of war). *Ɔsan nti* (because of war) led to *ɔsanti-foɔ*
(war people) and corrupted to *Asanti* or *Asante* (Kyerematen, 1966: 114–119).[11]
Despite King Boampɔnsɛm's reaction to the union of groups in Kwaaman, it
bears mentioning that crediting the etymology of the label Asante entirely to
him, as in Kyerematen's narrative, is highly questionable since Asante is a compound name of a well-known principality, Asantemanso, where members of the
lineage, as noted previously, came from. At any rate, in the 1650s, Dɛnkyera
defeated Adanse and immediately became the leading power in the central forest area. As is required for all vassal states, they paid annual tributes in addition
to sending a male member of the royal household to reside at the Dɛnkyera
court, not only as a hostage but also to study statecraft. Kyerematen (1966) and
Wilks (1993) confirm oral traditions that Oti Akenten sent one of his nephews,
Ɔsεe Tutu, to the court of King Bɔampɔnsɛm at Abankɛseεso, the capital of the
Dɛnkyera Kingdom. In no time, Ɔsεe Tutu gained a reputation at the court for
his graceful dancing, love of music, and show of valor (Kyerematen, 1966: 141).
Unfortunately, Kyerematen did not indicate the type of music, but we can safely
assume it would most likely be *bɔmaa* and *kete*, two of the most coveted royal
dances in Akan. Ɔsεe Tutu soon ran into problems with his host and eventually
had to flee to Kumase. The new chief of Kumase, Obiri Yeboa (c. 1663–1697),
who succeeded Oti Akenten when the latter passed away, hurriedly sent Ɔsεe
Tutu to the King of Takyiman in another powerful Akan state north of Kumase.
As would be expected, Ɔsεe Tutu got into more trouble, and had to flee Takyiman
and return to Kumase with several treasury items and gold. Obiri Yeboa again
sent him in another direction—this time to Akwamu, another dominant power in
Southeastern Gold Coast in the reign of King Ansa Sasraku. There are conflicting stories about how he got to Akwamu. For instance, Ivor Wilks reports that he
went in the company of Ɔkɔmfo Anɔkye (Wilks, 1993: 105). At any rate, the two
men remained in Akwamu until Obiri Yeboa's demise on the battlefield when he

invaded Dɔmaa, leading to a desperate search for his successor. The search for a successor became dire when two potential candidates declined the invitation to be enstooled. Receiving a tipoff from a stool carrier of the chief of Antoa, that Ɔsɛɛ Tutu was at the court of the Akwamu king, a delegation of five chiefs were sent to inform King Akoto of the passing of Obiri Yɛboa and to request that he return to Kumase to succeed his uncle. King Akoto obliged and presented Ɔsɛɛ Tutu with some gifts and delegated his chief executioner, Anum Asamoa, and his group to guard him on his journey back to Kumase. Several incidents occurred on their way to Kwaaman, but I have selected the few that have implications for court music and verbal arts.

Ɔsɛɛ Tutu's return

While working with descendants of Anum Asamoa, current members of the Constabulary (*Abrafoɔ*), they recounted an incident that occurred during Ɔsɛɛ Tutu's return from Akwamu to Kwaaman. The story is that Ɔsɛɛ Tutu and his men came upon a wounded elephant that had been shot by a hunter in a deep pit. A lot of people would have given up the idea of trying to recover such a huge animal from a pit, but Ɔsɛɛ Tutu encouraged his men to do just that. They were eventually able to pull the elephant from the pit with their bare hands. This incident is recorded in the referential poetry by Anum Asamoa and his group as: "if you have to lift an elephant, you lift one that lies in a pit" (*okurusono a, okukuru deɛ eda amena mu*). Example 6.9 is the full verse and analysis. The creative response of Anum Asamoa and his men set off the long tradition of members of the constabulary composing referential poetry (*apae*) to memorialize historical events. There is value in unwavering leadership, there is value in collective effort, and there is value in dreaming outside the norm.[12] After performing the funerary rites of his predecessor, Ɔsɛɛ Tutu embarked on what has been described as minor campaigns by defeating towns in close proximity to Kumase—an act seen as the beginning of his expansion strategy. The importance of these minor wars to our discussion is the acquisition of sound-producing and musical instruments, as well as the composition of chronicle and referential poetry by the bards and members of the constabulary. According to three chiefs of the Nkofe ivory-trumpet group, Nana Akwasi Assien II, Nana Kofi Owusu, and Nana Osei Kwadwo, the enemy had retreated by the time Ɔsɛɛ Tutu and his men got to Adanse Abadwam, leaving behind their ivory trumpets. They collected the trumpets, and upon their return to Kumase, Ɔsɛɛ Tutu assigned the name Nkofe to the trumpets. Nkofe, we are told, is the name of a village near the spot where they found the trumpets. Ɔsɛɛ Tutu gave the trumpets to Ta Amankwaa, a priest and spiritual advisor, for safe keeping. Since he captured these particular trumpets on the battlefield, there is a general belief that these were the original *kɔkroanya* trumpets, since they had accompanied Ɔsɛɛ Tutu to various places, including wars. Nana Tweneboa Kodua III (the Asantehene's chief of Fɔntɔmfrɔm) narrated the oral history of how the Asante captured the *bɔmmaa* drums belonging to the chief of Tafo, a major trading town at the time. According to Nana Kodua, the chief of Tafo, Ɔsafo Akonton, was alarmed as Ɔsɛɛ Tutu increased his influence in the area by waging wars with surrounding towns. He instructed his *ntahera* ivory trumpet group to play the verse *sɔre hɔ o twa, sɔre hɔ o twa* (lit. "leave this place") and for his Ɔkyerɛma to play on the *atumpan* drums: *pini do, pini do, pino do* ("move back, move back, move back") (see Kyerematen, 1966: 186–189). Not only was he defeated, but Ɔsɛɛ Tutu captured his bɔmaa and kete ensembles, and by implication Ɔsɛɛ Tutu's court assumed a higher status by possessing these two ensembles. The previous incident is recorded in Ampene and Nyantakyi III (2016: 240–243, 250–253), Nketia (1963: 121), and Wilks (1993: 107), but as a historian, Wilks' account did not reference capturing two types of drums as war trophies. Eventually, when Ɔsɛɛ Tutu turned his attention to a showdown with the Dɛnkyera, the general living conditions of tyranny under the latter played to the advantage of the former.

How Dɛnkyera made Asante (1680–1701)

The general thinking among Akan and Asante scholars is that without the excessive use of force and firm demands on citizens and vassal states, there would not have been Asante Empire as we know it today. The title of McCaskie's 2007 article, "Denkyera in the Making of Asante c. 1660–1720," reflects those sentiments. When the longest reigning monarch in Dɛnkyera, Asare Boampɔnsɛm, died around 1694, the resources of the kingdom were already stretched with wars in multiple directions: in the south with the Assen and Twifo, and in the north with the Kwaaman coalition. The impetus for expanding manpower and military resources was to control and maintain trade routes from the central forest area all the way to the coast. His successor, the overly ambitious Ntim Gyakari (*c.*1694–1701), turned out to be extremely autocratic and more exacting on his own people and, by extension, his vassal states. From the capital Abankɛseɛso to the far corners of the kingdom, Dɛnkyera citizens became disillusioned and rejected Ntim Gyakari's autocratic rule. The best way to describe the state of affairs in the Dɛnkyera of the 1890s is to turn to McCaskie's critical observation that by the time the autocrat faced potential insurgency from Ɔsɛɛ Tutu's Kwaaman coalition, "he had many enemies and few friends" (McCaskie, 2007: 2). The results are several defections from Dɛnkyera to tributary states, and as in previous instances, I will limit my discussions to those by court musicians. Out of the court musicians who sought refuge in Kwaaman, Dɛnkyerahene's principal drummer Kyerɛma Bi's defection with 1000 followers is the only one that is mentioned—and that too only in passing—in history books, including Ivor Wilks (1993: 111). Since historians are seemingly uninterested in matters involving music, Wilks did not provide us with details regarding the types of musical instruments Kyerɛma Bi brought with him. Oral history, as narrated to me by Nana Akofena Bediako II, a direct descendant and the current Akyerɛmahene (Chief of Drummers), holds that Ɔsɛɛ Tutu was impressed with Kyerɛma Bi for absconding from Dɛnkyera and taking the most followers to Kwaaman. But most importantly, he was amazed that the latter could bring a set of seventy-seven drums known as *Nkukua Mmedie*, and Amɔampɔn, the deity attached to the drums. Upon receiving them, Ɔsɛe Tutu retained Ɔkyerɛma Bi's position as the Chief of Drummers (Akyerɛmahene) at his court (see Ampene and Nyantakyi III, 2016: 232–233; Kyerematen, 1966: 201–202). With Kyerɛma Bi's defection to Kwaaman, the Bɔmaa and Sekye groups of court musicians followed suit; they deserted Abankɛseɛso and headed north to Kwaaman. According to the current Chief of *Fɔntɔmfrɔm* (*Fɔntɔmfrɔmhene*), his ancestors secretly left their village, Dɛnkyira Saam, with a huge *bɔmaa* drum and accompanying drums and reported to the court of Ɔsɛe Tutu. We may recall that they had already captured the *bɔmaa* ensemble belonging to the Chief of Tafo, thus providing the opportunity, for the first time in Akan polities, to combine two *bɔmaa* drums. The *bɔmaa* from Tafo is placed to the left of the performers and is referred to as the female drum, while the one from Dɛnkyera is the male and placed on the right-hand side of performers. With the overpowering booming sound from a combination of two large drums and accompanying drums, the newly created *bɔmaa* ensemble came to be known as *fɛntɛmfrɛm* (lit. one who swallows elephants). It is said that the extraordinary sound of the two huge *bɔmaa* drums is capable of overpowering all the variety of ensembles in a plural performance situation as in the Akwasidae Public Assembly in the Prologue. Over the centuries, *fɛntɛmfrɛm* became corrupted in the Twi language and became known as *fɔntɔmfrɔm*. It is common these days to observe two huge *bɔmaa* drums at the courts of territorial chiefs (Amanhene) in the Akan areas, but that was not the case until Ɔsɛe Tutu began using two *bɔmaa* drums in the late seventeenth century.[13] From Dɛnkyera Bɛtenase, the chief of the *sekye* drum and dance ensemble brought his family to serve the expanding court at Kwaaman. They initially sought refuge with the chief of Bantama (the Krontihene of Kumase), who in turn introduced them to the ruler who placed them under the care of Anantahene before sending them to Worakɛseɛhene, since *sekye* includes women while the Akyerɛmade group is made up of only men. In that sense, *sekye* is, technically speaking, not part of Akyerɛmade. They are presently located at Kwadaso Ohwimase near Kumase. The current chief is Nana Ɔsɛe Tutu Agyei, but since he was not available when I worked with this group, I obtained the oral history from Opanin Tawiah (who acted on his behalf) and the male and female elders of his household. Interestingly, the performance context in Dɛnkyera changed from performances for enstoolment ceremonies for territorial chiefs (Amanhene) and funerary processions to the mausoleum for the same rank of chiefs, to a new role in Kwaaman where the sekye ensemble provides music and dances to enliven rituals and ceremonies. A typical sekye performance involves lively dances suffused with sensuality that emphasize waist and pelvic dances by women. Sekye strikes a balance between the more "serious" texts of ivory trumpets, flute, drum ensembles, and the poetry of the bards and members of the constabulary.[14]

Epic showdown: Kwaaman insurgence against Dɛnkyera

Much has been written about Ɔsɛe Tutu and Kɔmfo Anɔkye's preparations for the ambitious showdown between the Kwaaman coalition and Ntim Gyakari's forces and the final defeat of the latter at Feyiase in November 1701.[15] However, there is the usual silence in historical accounts concerning the pair of *nkukuadwo* (or *nkukuadwe*) drums that Ɔkɔmfoɔ Anɔkye created to mark this event. In the summer of 2009, I met with Opanin Kwaku Ntiamoa, the chief of *nkukuadwo* (Nkuku-adwohene), who confirmed the oral narratives of the pair of drums. According to him, after the routing of Dɛnkyera forces at Feyiase, still a relatively small village even after three centuries, Anɔkye asked for two small drums to be carved for him. He coated the drums with white clay (*hyire*) to signify his personal victory for predicting Asante's triumph over Dɛnkyera. The custodians and the drums have since remained at Feyiase, from where they travel to Manhyia Palace to perform in ceremonies and rituals (see Figure 2.5).

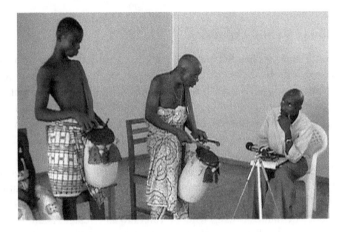

Figure 2.5 The author recording *nkukuadwe* drum texts with Opanin Kwaku Ntiamoa and his grandson. Note the white-coated drums. Summer 2011.

Source: Picture by Nana Kwame.

After the defeat of Dɛnkyera, the court musicians who sought protection in Kwaaman are the short ivory trumpeters (*mmɛntiafoɔ*). According to Nana Owusu Mran, current chief of the short ivory trumpets at Manhyia Palace, his great-uncle, Nana Ako Amaning, led his family to the victors. Ɔpemsoɔ Ɔsɛi Tutu retained his old position in Dɛnkyera as *Mmɛntiahene*, and Kɔmfo Anɔkye gave him a short trumpet and a statement to play: *Ɔsɛe Tutu wo yɛ deshee dada o* (lit. "Ɔsɛi Tutu, you are a royal from the ancient times"). This began the tradition where each succeeding Asante king creates his own short ivory trumpet and a philosophical statement or a proverb to be played behind him in processions and when formally seated on ceremonial occasions. For this reason, there are over a dozen short ivory trumpets at Manhyia Palace, whereas most Akan rulers have only one or two. I will proceed to examine selected events. Having freed themselves from the tyranny of Ntim Gyakari and Dɛnkyera, the logical step for Ɔsɛe Tutu and his spiritual advisor Ɔkɔmfoɔ Anɔkye was to build cohesion, lasting loyalty, and overriding identity among the diverse states comprising the union of states. The result was the creation of the Gold Stool as the most potent symbol of Asante soul, strength, power, and identity. Readers are referred to my discussion of sound-producing and musical instruments attached to the Gold Stool in Chapter 1. We can now state with all certainty that Ɔsɛe Tutu is officially the founder of a new state with much bigger influence than previous states in Akan polities. Due to the size of the new kingdom and its diverse states—along with the collection of sound-producing and musical instruments, music ensembles, poets, and bards— Ɔsɛe Tutu surpassed the rank of territorial chiefs. He became the founding King (Ɔpemsoɔ) of Asante. In the words of Wilks, Ɔpemsoɔ Ɔsɛe Tutu's Empire is located in the "forests of gold."[16] This area was once ruled by Adanse, well-known for creating socio-political and cultural developments in the central forest area, and later by Dɛnkyera.

Wars of conquest and expansion (1701–1867)

The eighteenth and nineteenth centuries were especially busy times for the relatively new kingdom. It was a time of conquest, expansion, and defeat at the hands of a foreign adversary—the British colonial forces. A substantial amount of literature has been produced about this momentous epoch in the history of the Asante Empire.[17] Here, I will examine the history of Asante court music and verbal arts during wars of conquest and expansion. Asantehene Opoku Ware (1720–1750), who succeeded Ɔpemsoɔ Ɔsɛe Tutu, pursued wars of conquest and alliances that succeeded in expanding Asante territory further north, northeast, and northwest to Bono, Banda, and the ancient kingdoms of Gonja and Dagbon; and south, southeast, and southwest to Akan and non-Akan settlements. Wilks (1993: 119) includes a map of modern Ghana showing what he refers to as Greater Asante with places and approximate dates.[18] Remarkably, Asante expansion spearheaded by Opoku Ware was unprecedented in the history of Akan polities. None of the powerful Akan states prior to Asante covered so much territory. Conquering two powerful northern kingdoms was unchartered territory, and Opoku Ware was honored with the title *Katakyie* (the Bold). To this end, a statue of the 15th Asantehene Opoku Ware II (1970–1999) at Suame Roundabout in Kumase has the ruler facing the wide expanse of northern territories. There are a few musical instruments, as well as chronicle and referential poetry, that memorialize the Asante experience at the time. Two separate drums associated with Opoku Ware in the eighteenth century are *bɛntɔ* and *mpebi ne nkrawiri*. Oral history in Asante has it that Opoku Ware captured the *bɛntɔ* drum ensemble during the Asante-Takyiman war in the eighteenth century (Nketia, 1963: 127, 196). From the custodians of the pair of *mpɛbi ne nkrawiri* drums, Nana Osei Kwabena (chief) and Opanin Kwame Safo, and corroborated by Kyerematen (1966: 274–277), we are told that after the defeat of Nana Ataadafinam of the Afram Plains, the drums were created to commemorate Opuku Ware's refusal to accept his share of the former's lands and treasures. The Twi word *mpɛbi* is a contraction of *me mpɛ bi* ("I don't want any") and *nkrawiri* (describes blood of the enemy streaming down the ground). *Nkukuadwo, mpebi ne nkrawiri* were used in the past as tribunal drums and were played when an accused is on trial or a war captive is about to be executed. Nketia (1963: 123–125) lists these drums under "signal drums" and describes the text and their function at the court. As we shall see in Chapter 6, one of the long poetic verses performed by the bards, *Asafo* (Example 6.3), recalls the valor, courage, and fearlessness of Opoku Ware Katakyie in the eighteenth century. Although Opoku Ware's name is not mentioned in full, the bards skillfully weave a system of metatexts that serve as identifying markers for informed listeners. For instance, the entire phrase in Line 22, *Opoku a okum sɛfoɔ, kum kwayɛfoɔ* ("Opoku who killed the savannah dwellers and the forest dwellers"), is one of several signifying codes in the poetry. Thus, *sɛfoɔ* is a contraction of *ɛsrɛmfoɔ* (savannah dwellers), while *kwayɛfoɔ* is the same as *kwayɛmfoɔ* (forest dwellers). There is value in valor, there is value in courage, and there is value in fearlessness.

As a revered ruler in the early nineteenth century, the reign of Asantehene Ɔsɛɛ Tutu Kwame, popularly known as Ɔsɛɛ Asibe Bonsu, is well documented in the oral and written history of Asante. We may recall that in 1817 it was Ɔsɛɛ Asibe Bonsu who received Bowdich in Kumase. Bowdich's description of his journey from Cape Coast to Asante is the most cited, if not for the colorful and detailed image of what he refers to as "The First Day of the Yam Custom" (Bowdich, 1819). Bowdich presents a variety of drums, including cylindrical drums with shoulder straps played on the side, with curved sticks or a combination of hand and stick techniques. There are goblet-shaped drums (perhaps *mpintin* drums) played with what seems like one or two curved sticks or a combination of hand and stick techniques. We see individuals carrying the huge *bɔmaa* drums with the skulls of defeated enemies attached, and a drummer with two sticks playing behind the carrier. There are smaller cylindrical drums, also carried on the head, but without a drummer. We see a handful of men playing long vertical flutes (or pipes) and ivory trumpeters playing only the longer and bigger variety of trumpets known as *ntahera*. The spread of ivory trumpeters in different sections of Bowdich's image is indicative of the widespread use of ivory trumpets in Asante. To the immediate right of Bowdich and his group are three flautists and a player of a gold-plated harp-lute (*seperewa*). The drawing depicts groups of people performing heroic chants (*ose* or *aho*) and accompanied by drummers or performing shouts on their own with their hands raised in the air with gyrations.[19] Even today, these heroic chants are pervasive in Asante, and are performed by Asakra or Bisa Ntiamoa groups and just about every territorial chief. To the extreme left of the image is a group (possibly Asafo groups) in similar gyration postures, waving European flags and engulfed by smoke from gun powder. Conspicuously missing in this picture are the variety of idiophones such as gongs (*nnawuro* and *adawura*) and the relatively short and small ivory trumpets (*mmɛntia*). As will be clear in the following chapters, Bowdich's graphic image is valuable in establishing, on the one hand, continuity with the Akan remote past, and on the other, continuity with the Asante present.

Ɔsɛɛ Asibe Bonsu was the first Asantehene to fight all the way to the Fante coast, and oral sources inform us that when he finally got to the coastline, he stuck his sword in the ocean and took upon himself the name of the biggest animal in the ocean, the whale. The Akan name for the whale is Bonsu, so he became known as Ɔsɛe Asibe Bonsu. In 1822, he built a new palace in Kumase with stones, modeled after the castles he saw on the coast. What follows are a few artistic records of his reign. Referential poetry (*apae*) recited by members of the constabulary (*abrafoɔ*) and cited in Chapter 6 as Example 6.9 has a line that recalls Asante wars with the Fante: *Ɔkankan Buroni se ɔpa wo kyɛw* ("the Dutch are pleading with you"); *Ɛmmfa nea wo de yɛɛ Mfante no, mfa mmɛyɛ no* ("don't treat them the same way as you did the Fante"). In the same poetry, the Asante defeat of British Governor Sir Charles MacCarthy immediately following Ɔsɛe Asibe Bonsu's passing on January 21, 1824 is recorded as: *Woakum Ɔdomanko Buroni Mankata* ("you have killed Charles MacCarthy").[20] We may recall in his initial expansion of the Kwaaman Union, Ɔsɛe Tutu captured the *bɔmaa* and *kete* ensembles belonging to the ruler of Tafo. Oral history narrated to me by the current Ketehene, Nana Agyei Boahen, is that while Ɔsɛe Tutu immediately used the *bɔmaa* drums, he kept the *kete* drums in a room. It was not until he embarked on the Gyaaman War in 1818 that Ɔsɛe Asibe Bonsu brought out the *kete* drums and had them perform for three days and three nights. He danced with Asantehemaa Nana Akosua Adoma (1809–1819) and members of the royal household, and on the third night he departed for Gyaaman. This incident triggered the tradition where after performing burial rites for a member of the royal family, succeeding Asante kings perform *kete* all night with the Asantehemaa and members of the royal household. Another event that is still performed to recall the Asante-Gyaaman War of 1818 is the dance and drum piece *Adinkra*, which is a reference to King of Gyaaman Adinkra Kwame and is performed by the *kete* and *fontɔmfrom* ensembles (see Examples 4.8 and 4.16). According to Kyerematen, it took Ɔsɛe Asibe Bonsu three years to prepare for the war with Adinkra Kwame, King of Gyaaman, and during that time, the drummers composed a piece for the *fɔmtɔmfrɔm*, *yɛ de brɛ brɛ bekum Adinkra* ("slowly but surely, we shall kill Adinkra"). True to their avowed aim, the Asante army defeated Nana Adinkra Kwame in the nineteenth century, but the piece is still performed as one of the suites of *fontɔmfrom* and *kete* ensembles (Nketia, 1963: 132). There is value in patience—as in patiently taking three years to prepare for the war with Adinkra Kwame (Kyerematen, 1966: 343–347).

For court musicians and members of ensembles in Dɛnkyera, who for various reasons could not defect to Kwaaman prior to the war, post-war conditions made it relatively easy for their relocation to a better court. Nana Kyerɛma Opong II is the current chief of the *tipre* drum ensemble, while Nana Owusu Mensah II is currently the chief of Amoakwa (ivory trumpet ensemble). The following are oral histories of their respective ensembles. During the reign of Asantehene Kwaku Dua (1834–1867), the *tipre* drum group, who were originally from Dɛnkyera Ntoam, finally arrived in Kumase after years of moving from location to location looking for a welcoming host. Although the Amoakwa group came from Dɛnkyera Nyaadoam, they were both presented to the ruler on the same day. For unexplained reasons, the Amoakwa group joined the *tipre* group when the latter performed for the ruler and the assembled elders and were able to play the drum texts on the ivory trumpets. The ruler and his elders were impressed with the spontaneous performances by the two ensembles; both were placed at the court of Asantehemaa Nana Yaa Dufie (1828–1836) or perhaps Nana Afia Sarpong (1836–1857).[21] The two ensembles have been playing together since this historic meeting, and they are now known as *Tipre ne Amoakwa*. The current chiefs of these two ensembles are direct descendants of those who migrated from the court of Dɛnkyerahene (see Examples 3.7 and 3.8). After the hostilities between the Asante and Dagbamba Kingdom, a father-son relationship developed where the Asantehene is considered to be the father and the Yaa-Naa (Dagomba king) the son. Oral history narrated by Kofi Adu-Sarhene has it that during a royal visit by the Dagbamba king, Asantehene Kwaku Dua was enthralled by the former's drummers and decided to create a similar ensemble for male royals (*Adehyemrantee*) in Kumase.[22] The Asantehene's *mpintin* ensemble dates from the reign of Kwaku Dua.

Period of instability, civil strife, defeat, and colonial domination (1867–1931)

After the passing of the 9th Asantehene, Kwaku Dua, in 1867, the kingdom entered into a long period of instability, civil wars, and the first major defeat in 1874 at the hands of the British that lasted for nearly fifty-seven years. Compared with the reigns of rulers before them, the reigns of Asantehene Kofi Kakari (1867–1874), Mensa Bonsu (1874–1883), and Kwaku Dua II (1884) were relatively short. They lasted seven years, nine years, and forty days respectively. Several monographs and journal articles have been written on this era, and readers may refer to Ivor Wilks (1975, 1993), William Tordoff (1965), and Agyemang Prempeh (2003). In 1874, Kofi Kakari was forced to abdicate the stool after the humiliating defeat by the British Colonial forces led by Sir Garnet Wolseley, in what is referred to in oral traditions as "*Sagrenti Sa*." Out of the three kings, Kwaku Dua II died of smallpox (*bropete*), after being on the Gold Stool for only forty days. Thereafter, succession disputes plunged the kingdom into a bloody three-year civil war, at the end of which the fairly young Agyemang Prɛmpɛ ascended the Gold Stool in 1888 at the age of sixteen. Also known as Kwaku Dua III, Agyemang Prɛmpɛ, as would be expected, embarked on securing the Gold Stool and restoring solidarity and unity in the kingdom almost broken apart by twenty-one years of instability, succession disputes, and civil wars. Unfortunately for Prɛmpɛ, the late nineteenth century, especially after the Berlin Conference of 1884–1885, was a period when European imperialist nations scrambled for the possession of Africa.[23] After refusing the British protectorate over the Asante kingdom, the former attacked, and Prɛmpɛ, together with several territorial chiefs and the Asantehemaa Nana Yaa Akyaa (Prɛmpɛ's mother), were arrested, sent to the Elmina Castle dungeon, then to Freetown in Sierra Leone, and finally to the far reaches of the Indian Ocean on the island nation of Seychelles. In the absence of Prɛmpɛ, the Asante Kingdom was thrown into another era of disorder for twenty-six years. From April 1900 to March 1901, one of the bloodiest and most gruesome wars in the Gold Coast took place between the British and the Asante. The Commander-in-Chief on the Asante side was the indefatigable Ɛdwesohemaa, Nana Yaa Asantewaa. Oral history refers

to it as the Yaa Asantewaa Sa, or The War for the Gold Stool. In his first authoritative book on the war, Adu Boahen lists immediate and remote causes to include
the British Governor Sir Frederick Hodgson's demand for the sacred Gold Stool
to be brought for him to sit on (Boahen, 2003). This was the last war between the
Asante and British in what has been referred to as a century of Anglo-Asante wars
(Edgerton, 1995). Nana Yaa Asantewaa was eventually captured and sent to Seychelles. In 1924, in a surprise turn of events that went against Governor Hodgson's
declaration that Agyemang Prɛmpɛ would never return to Kumase, Prɛmpɛ was
returned, not as a king of the Asante Empire but as the chief of Kumase (Boahen,
2003: 36–37). What was the artistic response to this period of instability, civil
strife, and defeat?

As much as I can tell, there are only three musical records. The first is from
the Yaa Asantewaa War, when drummers composed drum texts to commemorate
the siege of the British Fort in Kumase by the Asante forces. Nketia (1963: 30) is the
source of the text: *Buroni bɛwu abansoro do* ("the white man will die upstairs").[24]
For the second, Nana Yaa Asantewaa's bravery and leadership in the last Anglo-
Asante war is recorded in these Adowa and Nnwonkorɔ songs: *Krokrohinko e Yaa
Asantewaa, ɔbaa besia ɔda prɛmo ano e, w'ayɛ bi ama yɛn o* ("Krokrohinko, Yaa
Asantewaa, the commander of the army, you've done a lot for us"). The third musical record is the creation of a short ivory trumpet (*abɛntia*) and a statement, *Nyame
na ɛyɛɛ wo* (It's God who created you), marking the return of Agyemang Prɛmpɛ
(see Example 3.13) from Seychelles. For the most part, not much is known about
the artistic response to the period of instability and civil wars. To be sure, sound-
producing and musical instruments, musical performances, and heroic shouts (*ose*
or *ahum*) by warrior organizations (including Asakare and Bisa Ntiamoah groups)
accompanied the infantry and various divisions to war. Similarly, songs of prayers
(*mmommome*) for the safe return of loved ones from the battlefield were performed
by female members of households who were left behind. But the deafening silence,
with almost no records of music or verbal arts during the succession disputes, civil
wars, and the three defeats in 1874, 1896, and 1901 may be stunning to those unfa-
miliar with the Akan attitude towards seriously tragic events.

In the Akan world, tragic and catastrophic events are deemed unmentionable.
In a sense, a tragic event, explains Kofi Agyekum, becomes a taboo that forbids
ordinary recall in society because such recall evokes the memory of historical
events that are dangerous and unpleasant to mention (Agyekum, 2004: 317). J.K.
Fynn identifies two main reasons for declaring grave incidents taboo. First, any
private or public mention of such an event may offend the ancestors of a particular community, and secondly, it might lead to a repetition of the disaster (Fynn,
1971: 58). A tragic event is then recorded in what the Akan refer to as *Ntam* or
what Agyekum describes as "reminiscential oath" (*ibid*). In Asante, the passing
of Ɔpemsoɔ Ɔsɛe Tutu on the battlefield is a statutory Great Oath (*Ntamkɛseɛ*).
Since they reproduce social memories in several instances, even those great oaths
are uttered in coded language. For instance, just saying "I swear by the Great
Oath" (*me ka Ntamkɛseɛ*) without going into detail is enough to understand that
the individual is referring to the passing of Ɔpemsoɔ Ɔsɛe Tutu on the battlefield.

Depending on their oral history, some court ensembles possess great oaths. For instance, the great oath of the Nkofe ivory trumpet group is, "I swear by the Banda War" (*Me ka Bana Sa*). According to the chiefs of this group, a large number of trumpeters perished during the Asante-Banda war (c. 1770), while several surviving members died of smallpox; as a result, this incident is a taboo, unmentionable for the Nkofe group.[25] For Akan rulers, thorough investigations precede the mentioning of the Great Oath, and in the past, offenses related to the oath were punishable by death. In recent times, it has led to the destoolment of chiefs in Asante while citizens face steep fines, in addition to a prescribed number of sheep for cleansing rituals to restore order. In the past, chiefs and citizens have sworn upon the great oath before embarking on war with an adversary. It is obvious from the previous discussions that, although the period of instability, civil wars, and defeats are well-known, creative artists at the courts did not record the incidents in music and poetry for the simple reason that they might offend the ancestors or the tragic event may happen again. The period of instability, civil strife, and defeats fall into the Akan understanding of taboos—unmentionables that could only be recalled by invoking the Great Oath (*Ntamkɛseɛ*).

Another setback for court music and verbal arts occurred during the twenty-eight-year exile of Agyemang Prɛmpɛ. We may recall that Asante court music and verbal arts are integral to the political, religious, and judicial functions of the state and, as a result, the absence of a reigning monarch—the central political figure—implies a total absence of supporting infrastructure for the performance arts. The situation is all the more dire for Asante court musicians and poets who do not, as a matter of tradition, perform for patrons outside the court, since court music and poetry is not for entertainment. Unlike the *jali* in the Mali Empire and the *Lunsi* and *goje* performers in the Dagomba Kingdom, who could easily find professional outlets and patrons outside the court system, Asante (and Akan) court musicians and poets lack performance contexts outside the palace. The absence of Agyeman Prɛmpɛ seriously affected the socio-political order, including the creation and performance of music and poetry. Similar situations occurred in the Buganda Kingdom in Uganda during the exile of the *kabaka*. Speaking specifically on the Kawuugulu, Damascus Kafumbe reports that the absence of a reigning *kabaka* rendered Kawuugulu inactive (Kafumbe, 2018: xxvi–xxvii, 8). Peter Cooke made similar observations about the kingdom, that when the royal compound of the *kabaka* was attacked and burned down by Ugandan government forces in 1966, surviving musicians fled, vowing never to play again until the king is returned (Cooke, 1996: 450). Although we have no records of such comments from court musicians in Asante, it bears emphasizing that the exile of Agyeman Prɛmpɛ meant that there was no ruler to lead religious rites linked to the forty-two day Akan calendar, no public assemblies, no annual festivals or convocations of chiefs, no judicial meetings, and no social contexts requiring artistic performances. It was in this socio-political, religious, and artistic vacuum created by Prɛmpɛ's absence that Robert Sutherland Rattray conducted his anthropological field research in Asante in the early twentieth century and published his trilogy: *Ashanti* (1923), *Religion and Art in Ashanti* (1927), and *Ashanti Law and Constitution* (1929). In the conditions set forth for his repatriation, Prɛmpɛ returned to Kumase, initially as a private citizen and two years later as the Head Chief of Kumase, thus further negating opportunities for music and performance. Prɛmpɛ was working on restoring the union of the states when he passed away on May 12, 1931, marking thirty-five years without court music and verbal arts.

Restoration of Asante confederacy and the new political framework (1931–present)

Otumfoɔ Sir Ɔsɛe Agyemang Prɛmpɛ II (Kwame Kyeretwie or Prɛmpɛ II) succeeded and immediately continued from where his predecessor left off. His philosophical statement for his newly carved short ivory trumpet (*abɛntia*) was *atoto yɛ sane* (we shall untie all tangled threads). True to his word, on Thursday, January 31, 1935 the Asante Confederacy was reestablished in a historical ceremony in Kumase (see Example 3.14). According to a report written by Isaac T.A. Wallace-Johnson, the event featured the full complement of Asante court music and verbal arts—performance arts that had been absent for thirty-nine years, almost four decades (Wallace-Joohnson, 1935: 111–138).[26] The "Procession of the National Stool and Stool Properties of the Ashanti Nation. . . (ibid: 129)," had all the trappings of prototypical royal processions involving the Asantehene. My ethnographic description of Akwasidae Public Assembly in the Prologue and the 2014 Asanteman Adaekɛsee and Convocation of Chiefs at the Baba Yara Sports Stadium in Kumase bear striking resemblance to the 1935 event. In a marked continuity with the past, Wallace-Johnson's description of the royal procession is in three broad sections: the Advance Group, Stools or the Gold Stool Group, and the Asantehene's Group.[27] For our purposes, I will list only the sound-producing and musical instruments in all three groups, taking care to preserve Wallace-Johnson's descriptions without editing:

> **Advance Group:** *Ketefuo* (Kete Players), Nkontwimafuo (Long Horn Blowers), Nkofefuo (Owam Horn Blowers), Ntakyirafuo (Ntaherafuo, Elephant Tusk Horn Blowers), Mbirifuo (Ordinary Horn Blowers), Prempe (Drums), and Asranponhene (Drums).
>
> **Gold Stool Group:** Sika Sankuo (Golden Native Concertinas), Asankutwini (Set of Musical Instruments/Players of), Kwantinponmuta (Gold Musical Instruments-Players of), Nkukuadwifuo (Drummers), Abrafuo (Balladists and Executioners), Mpebi-ne-Nkrawiri (Drums).
>
> **Asantehene's Group:** Kwadwumfuo (Balladists), Mpintinkafuo (State Drummers), Amani (Drums-Ordinary), Mbentiaheynfuo (Golden and Silver Horns, Blowers of), Bento (Drums-Ordinary), Fontomfrom (Native Drums-State), Amoakwa (Other kinds of Musical Instruments, Native-Players of) (Wallace-Johnson, 1935: 126).

Additionally, Wallace-Johnson's account mentions the throbbing sounds of "Ashanti drums" that could be "heard from every section of Kumasi" as early as four a.m. (ibid: 120–121). The procession of chiefs, he continues, began as early as six a.m., and although he did not mention the accompanying processional music, those familiar with Akan festivals know very well that music is integral to royal processions. After the inspection of the Guard of Honor by His Excellency Sir Arnold Hodson, the Governor and Commander-in-Chief of the Gold Coast, Wallace-Johnson records that "Ashanti drummers beat the 'Ashanti Welcome.'" Given the previous situation, how were the vast resources of Asante court music and verbal arts activated in a comparatively short time after thirty-nine years? Unlike the publication detailing the extent of negotiations and transactions that led to the momentous event marking the restoration of the confederacy, there are no such documents about courtiers, custodians, or stool regalia including the material culture of music and poets. However, for those familiar with courtiers and custodians of tangible and intangible regalia, including musical instruments, it is acknowledged that with the exception of a few court musicians, instruments, and regalia objects that are kept in the palace, the vast majority of musical instruments are kept with custodians who live in scattered villages throughout the kingdom. In that case, looting and burning Kumase and the palace, as the British did in 1874, could not potentially wipe out the performance arts. Further, and as previously stated, Asante court music and verbal arts are integral to the social and political order. Most rituals, festivals, and ceremonies begin and end with music, thus making recall relatively easy. Guided by contextual usage, it is possible for oral traditions to persist based on the kind of music or instrument required for specific rituals.

Prɛmpɛ II reigned from 1931 to 1970, for a total of thirty-five years. It was a tumultuous time in the Gold Coast. Resistance to colonial rule was well under way, and despite the agitation for an independent Asante state, central leadership made a bold decision to join neighboring chiefdoms to form a single unified state. The British Gold Coast gained its independence in 1957 with a new nation state, Ghana, and a constitution that acknowledged but also undermined pre-colonial political systems. Asante was demarcated as one of the sixteen administrative regions in the Republic of Ghana and referred to as Asante Region (or Ashanti Region). However, Asanteman Council covers more than the confines of a single administrative region, with approximately seventy Traditional Council Areas. Forty out of the seventy areas are in the Asante Region, while the remaining thirty areas are spread across six regions including Ahafo, Bono, Bono East, Eastern, Oti, and Asante (Figures 2.2. and 2.6). Otumfoɔ Opoku Ware II succeeded Prɛmpɛ II, reigning from 1970–1999 and continuing the peaceful integration of the kingdom, even as the new nation entered into a period of political and economic instability. The 16th occupant of the Gold Stool, Otumfoɔ Ɔsɛe Tutu II, was enstooled on April 26, 1999; it had been eighty-four years since the Asante Confederacy was restored. See Appendix A for a list of Asante kings and Asantehemaa and Appendix B for the Genealogy of Asante Kings and Asantehemaa. With a central political figure occupying the Gold Stool, the religious, judicial, and socio-political order was assured, but what about the lived experience of the court musicians and poets who were my interlocutors? If the era of warfare, territorial conquests, and expansion provided imagery and resources for artistic creations, what would happen during peaceful times? Would Asante court music become a legacy of the pre-colonial past? Would there be a stagnation in creativity or a noticeable loss of items or musical repertoire? I will devote the last section of this chapter to these issues.

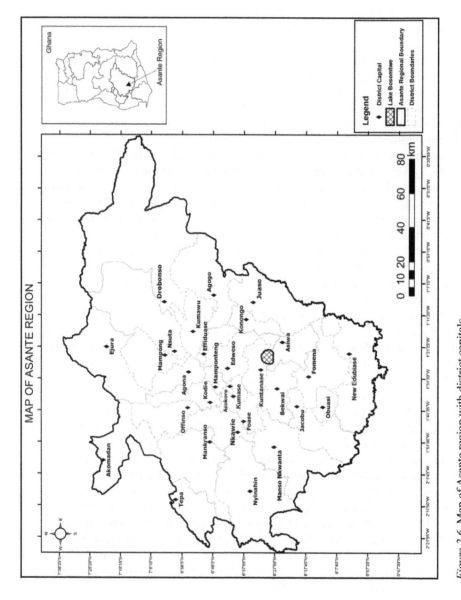

Figure 2.6 Map of Asante region with district capitals.

Source: Ben Emunah Aikins, University of Ghana, Legon.

Current experience of my interlocutors

As discussed in Chapter 1, my rationale for selecting Manhyia Palace as the site for the present work is due to the largest collection of visual and performing arts in all Akan polities and, arguably, Ghana. Additionally, I have established marked continuity between Asante and the Akan past, thus making it possible to determine the link between the musical resources in post-colonial Asante with pre-colonial Asante. There is no question that the end of Asante militarism, conquest, and expansion—initially in 1896 and finally in 1901—and the integration of the kingdom into the new political framework of independent Ghana in 1957 comes with new challenges. In order to assess these, it is helpful to cast our minds back to the formative years of the kingdom. My historical account of Asante court music and verbal arts did not identify the extant lists of instruments, court music ensembles, and verbal arts, or a repertoire list of each ensemble or solo instrument; rather, there was a gradual buildup that began with the expansionist activities of Ɔpemsoɔ Ɔsɛe Tutu. Further, defections of royal musicians from Dɛnkyera prior to the Asante-Dɛnkyera War, and especially after the defeat of the latter, brought about an exponential increase in the size and repertoire of Asante court music and verbal arts. Additional buildup in the eighteenth and nineteenth centuries by succeeding rulers show an incremental upsurge in court music resources. The grandeur of the Asantehene's court is due to the extensive collection of music ensembles and performance arts and, crucially, the resources to retain such a large retinue of courtiers. Custodians as well as court musicians and poets were given large tracts of lands to settle on and to farm. With lands to cultivate and manage, some heads of families and chiefs of ensembles founded villages and later towns (Asɔkwa, Nkukuabooho and others). Situated within a new political setup with a national government responsible for creating a national identity, Nketia rightly points to a drying up of sources that inspire musical creativity and poetic imagination (Nketia, 1987: 207). There are two ways of assessing the nature of challenges facing Asante court music today: a lack of innovation and no new additions to the repertoire. Similarly, there are two ways of understanding the current artistic response, and that is for court musicians to recompose existing repertoire to commemorate landmark events, or reach out to embodied collective memory to stage landmark events, including the burial and final funerary rites for the late Asantehemaa.

Apart from the noted creation of short ivory trumpets and philosophical statements for Agyeman Prɛmpɛ in 1924, Prɛmpɛ II in 1931, and Opoku Ware II in 1970, no new ensembles or solo instruments have been created to memorialize events. Crucially, a number of sound-producing instruments and ensembles are either missing or have ceased to exist. The list of missing instruments includes, but is not limited to, the six-string harp lute (*seperewa*), the *prɛmpɛ* drum, the *etwie* (friction drum), the *bɛntɔ* drum ensemble, *sankutwene* (drums), *mmɔdwemmɔdwe, sɔkɔbɛn, asisibɛn* (ivory trumpets), and an ensemble of pipes (*mmɛn*) in the *kete* ensemble. Currently, the entire supporting drums are missing from the Asantehene Fɔntɔmfrɔm ensemble.[28] Exceptions are two gold-plated harp lutes (*seperewa*) that are part of the regalia objects of the Gold Stool (see Ampene and Nyantakyi III: 218–219), which are performed outside the royal court. Since the 1990s, Osei Korankye led the revival of *seperewa*, when Nketia invited him to join the staff of the International Center for African Music and Dance (ICAMD). He is now a member of faculty in the Music Department at the University of Ghana. As far back as 1953, Nketia brought similar observations to Prɛmpɛ II, who initially thought his *fɔntɔmfrɔm* ensemble was intact until he realized some supporting drums were missing. While he immediately corrected the omission, it seems that we have come full circle with regards to the supporting drums. One of the most affected areas of court music and poetry is the issue of dwindling repertoire. A large corpus of repertoire is fast diminishing at an alarming rate. In his pioneering field research in the early 1950s, before Ghana's independence, Nketia observed the loss of *fɔntɔmfrɔm* oath swearing (*akantam*) pieces. Out of about eighty proverbs, Nketia reported hearing a limited number of just three or four, which performers repeated over and over.

Several decades down the line, the situation is no different: based on my experience, the royal drummers at Manhyia are capable of playing only six *akantem* pieces. Similarly, Nana Akwasi Amponim, chief of the Kɔkroanya ivory trumpet ensemble, informed me that in the past they had over 300 instrumental verses in their repertoire, but they were only able to play about twelve for me to record. It bears noting that the loss of repertoire is not limited to just the *kɔkroanya* group, but is found across the board. All ivory trumpet groups, the *durugya* cane flute, chronicle songs (*kwadwom*), *apae*, and all court music are seriously affected. Despite the noted challenges, it is not all gloomy when it comes to recomposing and recontextualizing existing repertoire, rendering ancient pieces relevant to contemporary experience. A contemporary experience of historical proportions in recent memory is the 2017 burial and final funerary rites of the late Asantehemaa Nana Afua Kobi Sɛɛwaa Ampem II. On November 14, 2016, Nana Afia Kobi passed on (or went to the village, as we say in Asante) at the age of 111 years old. As Asantehemaa, she served Asanteman and Ghana for thirty-nine years from 1977–2016. Due to a complex system of matrilineal inheritance, the burial and final funerary rites of the late Asantehemaa, in January and December of 2017, was the first time in 209 years that a reigning Asantehene performed the funerary rites of an Asantehemaa who was also his birth mother. The last one was in 1809, when Ɔsɛe Asibe Bonsu performed the funerary rites for Konadu Yiadɔm, his mother and Asantehemaa from 1768–1809. Besides a few passing references by Bowdich (1819) and Wilks (1993, 1975), to the best of my knowledge there is no documentary record of the nature and extent of Konadu Yiadɔm's funerary rites. However, the combination of oral traditions, political authority, and national unity with the visual, musical, and performance arts during the collective mourning of the late Asantehemaa is unprecedented in over a generation. Without recourse to written documents, how did the Asante recall the complex rituals involved? There may be several answers, but one is the embodied experience—continuity with the past—that I have cited on numerous occasions in this volume and the contextual relevance of oral traditions in Asante. In terms of continuity with the past, the final funerary rites were staged as a battle with an imaginary enemy—death. Seven out of the fifteen-day funerary rites held between December 1–15, 2017 recalled activities associated with the declaration of war against an adversary, as in the time of conquests and expansion. Friday, December 1, was Dapaakan on the

Akan calendar, and just as they consulted with Kɔmfo Anɔkye before the Asante-Denkyera War of 1701, Asante priests from all corners of the kingdom performed priestly dances (*Akɔm*) to pray for a successful event. Saturday, December 2 was *Dapaa*, and while musical performances continued, it was a day for preparation in anticipation of the momentous event. Sunday, December 3 was Akwasidae, but due to the pending final funerary rites of the Asantehemaa, it was celebrated as *Kuntunkunidae*. Gold jewelry, *kente* cloths, and brightly colored cloths were discarded for the dark *kuntunkuni* cloth. It was a day for territorial chiefs who double as commanders of units in their territories and Kumase chiefs (Abrɛmpɔn) and their retinue to converge on Dwabrem to verify if there was truly crisis in the kingdom. Having confirmed the nature of crisis—the passing of the Asantehemaa—they all return to prepare for an imaginary war with death (*baamoa wuo*). On Monday, December 4, Adaedwoada, the Asantehene, wore the Great War Tunic (*Batakarikɛseɛ*) as the Commander-in-Chief and led the divisions and units from Kumase, also wearing a *batakri* war dress, marching from the Pampaso Stool House through downtown Kumase to Manhyia Bɔnmu, a natural forest reserve behind the palace, for an encounter with death. The ritual firing of guns known as *atrane* or *trane*, to the total view of the newly enstooled Asantehemaa, has the entrapments of all the militancy and heroism we could possibly imagine. Leading their divisions and units on Tuesday, December 5 were territorial chiefs decked out in the *batakari* war dress going to the battlefront to perform the ritual firing of guns. The seemingly perfect coordination of multifaceted activities made it seem as though they had been thoroughly rehearsed over weeks, but this was the result of embodied experience and a contextual manifestation of purely oral traditions. The collective expression of grief defined by a complex mix of dance, song, and drumming is the current experience of Asante and of my interlocutors, the court musicians and poets, in a constant dramatization of the Asante historical past.

In one of the feedback sessions with Opanin Kofi Fofie, a leading cantor (or bard) of Chronicle singers (*kwadwom kandifoɔ*), he shared with me how he and his brother Opanin Kwame Ɔboɔ recomposed Lines 19–21 in Example 6.1 in 1999 with the stool name, in addition to identifying the parents of the newly enstooled king, Ɔsee Tutu II. Similarly, in Example 6.2, the beginning phrase in Line 10, Ɔsɛe Tutu, is a substitution for the name of the immediate past ruler, Opoku Ware II. As I observed in connection with compositional processes in *nnwonkorɔ*, names or nominals are variable formulaic phrases in songs and instrumental texts and subject to manipulations for recomposition and text substitutions (Ampene, 2005: 51–126). In that sense, songs and instrumental texts, as well as the poetry of bards and referential poetry, have inbuilt mechanisms to recompose variable formulaic phrases in existing pieces in order to recontextualize the songs, instrumental texts, and poetry for contemporary audiences and experiences. A case in point is the performance of what we might call a short version of the Long Verse (*Nnwontene*) by the bards when the Asantehene delivered the keynote address on September 13, 2019 at the United Nations High Level Forum on Culture and Peace in New York. Example 2.1 is the transcription of the performance at the United Nations; following that, I will compare with Example 6.1 for a fuller appreciation of artistic response to contemporary situations.

Example 2.1 Nnwontene (Long Verse), Kwadwom at the United Nations (September 13, 2019).

1. Ɔsagyefo gunwa gu ase o
2. Okuru Asante Naadu e kasa nge
3. Kɔtɔkɔhene kasa e
4. Krɔbeahene kasa nge
5. Mere ma wo Krobea ayirifi anwoma ne kɔtɔkɔ nge
6. Asante atwa ne tiri o Twum o Kyampɔn noforo nge
7. Asante asiesie bo Sumantete e
8. Krɔbea Asante Naadu e kasa nge
9. Ɔsεε Tutu e memmɔ wo dinwe awisi o
10. Hwan na ɔbε nya sε Kantinkyire Boakye Dankwa ne Sεεwaa Ampem Sikabɔɔ ba no woɔ
11. Obi nyaa saa bi anka ɔbεyε bi
12. Εmaanu Atia Dufie ba e Demirefi e kasa nge
13. Kyerewaa ne ntɔfe mmɔdwe e nge
14. Odoforo dadeε Twum o Kyampɔn noforobo nge
15. Ɔsεε Tutu e me mmɔ wo dinwe awisi o
16. Wo pεn so na wo de aniεden ne nkabom kyekyeree w'Asanteman nyinaa
17. Obi nyaa saa bi anka ɔbεyε bi
18. Brago Abakan nana e Frimpɔn o damirifua Awisi
19. Meremawo Juaben do Adakwa Yiadɔm nge
20. Ɔsεε Tutu e me mmɔ wo dinwe awisi o
21. Wo pεn so na wo de nkabom ne asomdwe baa wo Asanteman mu ne Ghanaman nyinaa
22. Obi nyaa saa bi anka ɔbεyε bi
23. Ɔsagyefo gu nwa gu ase nge
24. Okuru Asante Naadu e kasa nge

Lead and Response
25. Okuru bedi atɔprεba demirefi su nna nyane awo
26. Dɔmaako Sakyi asono aworobεn

English Translation
1. Ɔsagyefo let's be formally seated
2. Okuru Asante Naadu speak
3. Kɔtɔkɔhene speak
4. Krɔbeahene speak
5. I am greeting you as the overall king of Kɔtɔkɔ
6. Asante has beheaded Twum Kyampɔn noforobo
7. Asante has fortified itself with the charm Sumantete
8. Krɔbea Asante Naadu kasa
9. Ɔsεε Tutu, I do not mention your name in vain
10. Who will not enjoy being the song of Kantinkyire Boakye Dankwa and Sεεwaa Ampem the gold nugget
11. Had someone gotten this privilege, the one would brag
12. The son of Εmaanu Atia Dufie Demirefi speak
13. The grandchild of Kyerewaa and Ntofe mmɔgye
14. Odoforo deadeε Twum Kyampɔn noforobo
15. Ɔsεε Tutu, I do not mention your name in vain
16. It is during your reign that you used bravery and unity to found the Asante Kingdom
17. Had someone gotten this privilege, the one would brag
18. Grandchild of Brago Abakan, condolences
19. I am greeting you, Adarkwa Yiadɔm of Dwaben
20. Ɔsεε Tutu, I do not mention your name in vain
21. It is your reign that has brought unity and peace to Asanteman and the whole of Ghana
22. Had someone gotten this privilege, the one would brag
23. Ɔsagyefo let's be formally seated
24. Okuru Asante Naadu speak

Lead and Response
25. Demirefi, the song of Okuru is performing atɔprε, wail and wake up
26. Dɔmaan Sakyi, the elephant's tusk trumpet

Due to time constraints at such a global forum, the previous performance is twenty-six lines long, as compared to the sixty lines in Examples 6.1. While Lines 1–4, 8, and similar phrases in the poetry are meant to awaken the ruler from his sleep, the same lines in the previous example implore the ruler to speak. Lines 16 and 21 in the performance at the United Nations is totally different, featuring textual substitutions reflecting the theme of the Asantehene's keynote address, Culture and Peace. There are times when large portions of song texts are recomposed in order to serve as records of current events, as exemplified by the *nnwonkɔrɔ* song, Naa Konadu Hemaa, performed on February 6, 2017, the day the ruler appointed his older sister to succeed the late Asantehemaa with the stool name Nana Konadu Yiadom III.

Example 2.2 Naa Konadu Hemaa, Manhyia Tete Nnwonkɔrɔ.

Twi Text	*English Translation*
Lead	**Lead**
1. Ɔhemaa	Ɔhemaa
2. Naa Konadu hemaa	Nana Konadu hemaa
3. Kɔtɔkɔhemaa	Queen of Porcupines
4. Naa Konadu hemaa	Nana Konadu hemaa
5. Yɛ ma wo akwaaba o	We welcome you
6. Nana e	Grandmother
7. Naa Sɛɛ Tutu de onua bi aba	Nana Ɔsɛɛ Tutu has given us his sister
8. Yɛ frɛ no Naa Konadu o	Her name is Nana Konadu o
Chorus	**Chorus**
9. Ɔhemaa	Ɔhemaa
10. Naa Konadu hemaa	Nana Konadu hemaa
11. Kɔtɔkɔhemaa	Queen of Porcupines
12. Naa Konadu hemaa	Nana Konadu hemaa
13. Yɛ ma wo akwaaba o	We welcome you
14. Nana e	Grandmother
15. Naa Sɛɛ Tutu de onua bi aba	Nana Ɔsɛɛ Tutu has given us his sister
16. Yɛ frɛ no Naa Konadu o	Her name is Nana Konadu o

Considering the historical perspective of Asante court music and verbal arts outlined in this chapter, it is not hard to imagine the type of cultural dynamism sustaining Asante from the seventeenth century to the present time—a period of about 400 years. One of the remarkable aspects of Asante sophistication is the recognizable evidence of historical, socio-cultural, and political continuity with, first, the Akan past, and second, the Asante past. Critical to the exponential development of court music and verbal arts in Asante are the wars of conquest and expansion that inspired creativity in the musical and performative arts. Instruments were acquired as war trophies, while defections of court musicians from the once-powerful Dɛnkyera kingdom enriched the resources of the relatively new kingdom. In line with Akan notions of tragic and catastrophic events, taboos, and great oaths, there is an utmost silence in the creative impulse during a period of instability, civil strife, and defeat, for fear of recurrence or offending ancestors. Court musicians and poets ceased to perform for almost four decades, from Agyeman Prεmpε's exile and return to the restoration of the Asante Confederacy. Remarkably, there was a huge turnout of Asante court music and verbal arts during the event, marking the restoration of the confederacy in Kumase. Currently, Asante is part of a relatively new nation-state, thus ending militarism and conquest— two activities that seem to have provided the bulk of inspiration for musical and performative arts. There is a considerable lack of innovations in peace time, and the Asante court has lost a fair number of musical instruments and ensembles, while a large corpus of repertoire is dwindling at a rapid pace. However, a new outlet for innovation in Asante court music and verbal arts is the recomposition of existing texts—both instrumental and songs—to recontextualize and make past lived experiences relevant to contemporary audiences, or to memorialize current experience, as in the performance of the bards at the United Nations or the recomposition of *nnwonkoro* songs following the appointment of a new Asantehemaa. Having examined the historical relevance of Asante court music and verbal arts, I turn my attention to instrumental texts and how they provide the basis for our understanding of lived and current experience in Asante.

Notes

1 Ivor Wilks (1993) and T.C. McCaskie (1995) provide a comprehensive overview of the literature in historical studies. Osei Kwadwo (2000, 1994) are valuable and may be used as textbooks for high schools.
2 Kwasi Konadu (2014) is a collection of oral, historical, and archaeological literature on the Akan. In 1982, the Nigerian Historical Society published a special interdisciplinary volume on "Akan History and Culture" in the journal *Tarikh* with Ghanaian historian John Kofi Fynn as the Guest Editor.
3 My brief overview of the Akan owes a great deal to Kenya Shujaa's chapter in Kwasi Konadu (2014).
4 Akan clans (*Abusua*) and corresponding totems are *Asona* (crow), *Bretuo* (leopard), *Ɔyoko* (hawk), *Aduana* (dog), *Ɛkoɔna* (bull), *Agona* (parrot), *Asakyiri* (vulture), and *Asenie* (bat).
5 Osafo K. Osei (1997) is a comprehensive study of the Akan calendar. Eight days in some places stems from beginning on the day of, instead of the day after. For instance, seven days from Monday would ideally begin from Tuesday to Monday, not Monday to Monday.
6 See Joseph H. Greenberg (1966).
7 J.K. Fynn (1982) includes a concise discussion of Akan trade networks.
8 The map is reproduced in James Anquandah (1982a: 90), while a redrawn and revised version by Rebecca Warren is published in Kwasi Konadu (2014: xv).
9 Ray Silverman (1983) includes a detailed discussion of the form and function of Akan *kuduo*.
10 See James Anquandah (1982a, 1982b).
11 Ivor Wilks' version of the Kwaaman Purchase (1993: 100–103) is based on oral history dictated in exile by Asantehene Agyeman Prεmpε in 1907.
12 The oral history by members of the Constabulary is confirmed by Kyerematen (1966), page 153.
13 See Ampene and Nyantakyi III (2016: 250–253).
14 See Ampene and Nyantakyi III (2016: 234–239), for a description of *sekye*, instruments, and dances.

15 Basing his account on oral traditions, Kyerematen (1966: 196–214), is more detailed; for historical accounts, see Ivor Wilks (1993: 109–1212), and the entire article by McCaskie (2007).
16 Ivor Wilks titled his book *Forests of Gold* (1993).
17 A casual list include T.C. McCaskie (1995), Larry W. Yarrak (1990), J.K. Fynn (1971), Ivor Wilks (1975, 1993), and Robert B. Edgerton (1995).
18 John K. Fynn (1971) is an in-depth account of Opoku Ware's reign.
19 Kwasi Ampene (2019: 191–205) is a brief critique of Bowdich's colorful image and the notion of iconography as absolute data.
20 See Ivor Wilks (1993: 331) for an account of some of the aggressive policies of Governor Sir Charles MacCarthy.
21 For an oral history and pictures of members of ensemble, see Ampene and Nyantakyi III (2016: 208–211, 224–225).
22 In another version of the oral history of *mpintin* drums, Nketia (1963: 120) credits Dɛnkyera King Asare Boa Ampɔnsɛm with the introduction of *mpintin* drums to Akanland. It is plausible that by the mid-seventeenth century, Akan states had interactions with their northern neighbors through trade, and it is possible that they had begun to adopt some of the instruments from the north.
23 M.E. Chamberlain (2010) and Barbara Harlow and Mia Carter, editors (2003) are two out of a larger trove of literature on the subject of Europe's scramble for possession of Africa.
24 A. Adu Boahen (2003: 78–92) provides a historical account of the siege of Kumase fort.
25 See Ampene and Nyantakyi III (2016).
26 Isaac Theophilus Akunna Wallace-Johnson was a Sierra Leonean journalist, activist, and politician who lived in Ghana and was the founder and editor of *The West African Sentinel*. We may recall the looting and burning of the palace in Kumase following the crushing defeat in 1874. In 1896, several regalia objects, including sound-producing and musical instruments, were taken from the palace to Britain—some are kept in the British Museum in London, but the vast majority of items are kept in the Armed Forces Museum in Edinburgh, Scotland.
27 See Ampene and Nyantakyi III (2016: 31–40).
28 Nketia (1963: 136) has a full list of instruments in the *fontɔmfrom* ensemble.

References

Agyekum, Kofi. 2004. "'Reminiscential Oath' Taboo in Akan." *Language in Society* 33 (3): 317–342.
Ampene, Kwasi. 2005. *Female Song Tradition and the Akan of Ghana: The Creative Process in Nnwonkorɔ*. Aldershot: Ashgate Publishing Ltd.
———. 2019. "Iconography, Documentary Evidence, Continuity, and Akan Musical Expressions Before the 15th Century." *Ghana Studies* 22: 191–205.
Ampene, Kwasi, and Nana Kwadwo Nyantakyi III. 2016. *Engaging Modernity: Asante in the Twenty-First Century*, 2nd edition. Ann Arbor, MI: Michigan Publishing.
Anquandah, James. 1982a. *Rediscovering Ghana's Past*. Accra: Sedco Publishing Ltd, and Harlow, Essex: Longman Group Ltd.
———. 1982b. "The Archaeological Evidence for the Emergence of Akan Civilization." *Tarikh* 7 (2): 9–21, 26.
Boahen, A. Adu. 2003. *Yaa Asantewaa and the Asante-British War of 1900–1*. Edited with editor's note by Emmanuel Akyempong. Accra: Sub-Saharan Publishers.
Bosman, William. 1705. *A New and Accurate Description of the Coast of Guinea*. London: Frank Cass and Company Ltd.

Bowdich, Thomas E. 1819. *Mission from Cape Coast Castle to Ashantee: With a Statistical Account of that Kingdom, and Geographical Notices of Other Parts of the Interior of Africa*. London: John Murray and Sons.

Chamberlain, M.E. 2010. *The Scramble for Africa*. Harlow and New York: Longman Press.

Cooke, Peter. 1996. "Music in a Uganda Court." *Early Music* 24 (3): 439–452.

Dolphyne, Florence Abena. 1982. "Akan Language Patterns and Development." *Tarikh* 7 (2): 26, 35–45.

Edgerton, Robert. 1995. *The Fall of the Asante Empire: The Hundred-Year War for Africa's Gold Coast*. New York: The Fee Press.

Fynn, John Kofi. 1971. *Asante and Its Neighbours 1700–1807*. Evanston, IL: Northwestern University Press.

———. 1982. "Trade and Politics in Akanland." *Tarikh* 7 (2): 23–34, 26.

Greenberg, Joseph H. 1966. *The Languages of Africa*. Bloomington, IN: Indiana University Press.

Harlow, Barbara, and Mia Carter, eds. 2003. *The Scramble for Africa*. Durham, NC: Duke University Press.

Kafumbe, Damascus. 2018. *Tuning the Kingdom: Kawuugulu Musical Performance, Politics, and Storytelling in Buganda*. Rochester, NY: University of Rochester Press.

Konadu, Kwasi. ed. 2014. *The Akan People: A Documentary History*. Princeton: Markus Werner Publishers.

Kyerematen, A.A.Y. 1966. "Ashanti Royal Regalia: Their History and Functions." PhD diss., Oxford University.

Marees, Pieter de. 1602. *Description and Historical Account of the Gold Kingdom of Guinea*. Translated from the Dutch and edited by Albert van Dantzig and Adam Jones. Oxford: Oxford University Press.

McCaskie, T.C. 1995. *State and Society in Pre-Colonial Asante*. Cambridge; New York: Cambridge University Press.

———. 2007. "Denkyira in the Making of Asante c. 1660–1720." *Journal of African History* 48: 1–25.

Nketia, J.H. Kwabena. 1963. *Drumming in Akan Communities of Ghana*. London: Thomas Nelson and Sons Ltd.

———. 1982. "The Musical Traditions of the Akan." *Tarikh* 7 (2): 26, 47–59.

———. 1987. "Asante Court Music." In *The Golden Stool: Studies of the Asante Center and the Periphery*, edited by Enid Schildkrout, vol. 65. New York: American Museum of Natural History.

Osei, Kwadwo. 1994. *An Outline of Asante History*, part 1, 2nd edition. Wiamoase, Ashanti: Osei Kwadwo Enterprise.

———. 2000. *An Outline of Asante History*, part 2, vol. 1. Buokrom, Kumasi: Cita Press Ltd.

Osei, Osafo K. 1997. *Discourse on Akan Perpetual Calendar (For Religious Ceremonies and Festivals*. Accra, Ghana: Domak Press Ltd.

Pereira, Duarte Pacheco. 1905. *Esmerald de Situ Orbi*. Edited by Critica annotada por Augusto Epiphanio da Silva Dias. Lisboa, Protugal: Sociedade de Geographia de Lisboa.

Prempeh I, Nana Agyeman. 2003. *The History of Ashanti Kings and the Whole Country Itself and Other Writings*. Edited by A. Adu Boahen *et al*. Oxford and New York: Oxford University Press.

Rattray, Robert Sutherland. 1923. *Ashanti*. Oxford: The Clarendon Press.

———. 1927. *Religion and Art in Ashanti*. Oxford: The Clarendon Press.

———. 1929. *Ashanti Law and Constitution*. Oxford: The Clarendon Press.

Shujaa, Kenya. 2014. "Akan Cultural History: An Overview." In *The Akan People: A Documentary History*, edited by Kwasi Konadu, 29–88. Princeton: Markus Wiener Publishers.

Silverman, Raymond. 1983. "Akan Kuduo: Form and Function." In *Akan Transformations Problems: Problems in Ghanaian Art History*, edited by Doran H. Ross and Timothy F. Garrard, vol. 21. Los Angeles, CA: UCLA Museum of Cultural History Monograph Series.

Tordoff, William. 1965. *Ashanti Under the Prempehs 1888–1935*. London: Oxford University Press.

Towerson, William. 1555–1556. "First and Second Voyage." In *The Akan People: A Documentary History*, edited by Kwasi Konadu, 327–330. Princeton: Markus Wiener Publishers.

Wallace-Johnson, Isaac T.A. 1935. *Papers Relating to the Restoration of Ashanti Confederacy and a Full and Illustration Report of the Proceedings of the Restoration of the Ashanti Confederacy*. Kumasi: Educational Press and Manufactures.

Warren, Rebecca. 2014. "Revised Version of 1629 Akan Map." In *The Akan People: A Documentary History*, edited by Kwasi Konadu. Princeton: Markus Wiener Publishers.

Wilks, Ivor. 1975. *Asante in the Nineteenth Century: The Structure and Evolution of a Political Order*. Cambridge: Cambridge University Press.

———. 1993. *Forests of Gold: Essays on the Akan and the Kingdom of Asante*. Athens, OH: Ohio University Press.

Yarrak, Larry W. 1990. *Asante and the Dutch 1774–1873*. Oxford: The Clarendon Press.

3 The language and poetry of ivory trumpets and *durugya* flute

Akoben (War Trumpet: embodies bravery, gallantry, courage). Akan Adinkra pictographic writing.

I address my framing theory—the intersections between music, lived experience, and values—by examining the language and poetry of ivory trumpets and the *durugya* flute. I focus in Chapters 3 to 6 entirely on textual analysis to demonstrate how Asante performative arts—drumming, singing, and dancing—become intelligible to participants whose frame of reference and access to the music is through texts. The language and poetry of ivory trumpets and the *durugya* flute are embedded in a sophisticated system of surrogate speech, defined by Joseph Kaminski as "spoken tonal texts recited from the vibrating lips of the performer" (2012: 13). Like many other languages in Africa, the Akan Twi language is tonal, consisting of two pitches—low and high—thus making it possible for the tones in Twi to be reproduced on a sound-producing or musical instrument. It bears emphasizing that, contrary to popular belief, instrumental speech surrogates are not limited to drums, but include all classes of musical instruments extant in Africa. As a result, analyses of instrumental texts lead to the appreciation of "the deep-seated rhetorical functions" embodied in court music ensembles (Bokor, 2014: 166). In the case of the Akan and Asante, journal entries by European explorers and traders hint at the practice of instrumental surrogate speech in the eighteenth century. Bosman (1705) and Barbot (1732) describe the practice, while later observers including Bowdich (1819), Beecham (1841), and Freeman (1898) confirm the observations of those who came before them with reports that the natives were able to converse by means of their flutes. Based on our knowledge of musical continuity with the Akan past in Chapter 2, the practice predates the arrival of Europeans in the fifteenth century.

The Akan practice of using ivory trumpets to send coded messages between settlements and farmlands in the early iron age (500 BCE–500 CE) were transformed into symbolic codes and instrumental speech in the days of migrations, conquests, and warfare in the middle and late Iron Age (500–1500 and 1500–1900 CE).[1] Although the call to arms were mostly sounded on drums, ivory trumpets invariably accompanied the infantry to the battlefield—a situation that was not lost on Bowdich (1819) when he observed that coded sentences were immediately recognized by Asante soldiers and some of the people. As in the case of war drums, ivory trumpets (plural, *mmɛn*; singular, *abɛn*) gained their reputation as war trumpets (*akobɛn*) and were visually encoded in Adinkra pictographic writing to signify heroic ideals. A wooden carving of a short ivory trumpet placed on top of large umbrellas (*bɛnkyinyɛ*) of chiefs not only conveys militarism but also indicates the role of ivory trumpets in sending coded messages on the battlefield.

At the National Heroes Park in Kingston, Jamaica, a monument to the powerful and remarkable eighteenth-century leader of the Jamaican Maroons, Queen Nanny, is represented by a sculpture of what is known as *Abeng*, interpreted as the horn and placed on top of a tall metal pole. Nanny's monument is said to reproduce the sound of *abeng*, a sound-producing instrument used by Nanny and her soldiers similarly to its Akan usage, for sounding coded signals and esoteric texts. When I visited Heroes Park during my first visit to Kingston in 2014 in the company of my friend Clayton Brown, the heroic militancy and the ancestral link of Nanny and her brothers Quao (Kwaw), Cudjoe (Kwadwo), and Accompong (Akyampɔn) undeniably connected their origins to the Akan of present-day Ghana (see Figure 3.1 – *Akobɛn*).[2]

As stylized accounts of actual events in the past and the present, the precedence for text-based studies in ethnomusicology include Gage Averill (1997), Kelly Askew (2002), and Thomas Turino (2000), to name just a few. I begin with an overview of ivory trumpet groups, followed by an in-depth discussion of seven different ivory trumpet ensembles and an analysis of selected texts. The ivory trumpets are named in the Twi language in the following order: *ntahera,*

Figure 3.1   Akobɛn (the war trumpet; embodies bravery, gallantry, and courage): a representation of an ivory trumpet in Adinkra pictographic writing.

kɔkroanya, nkɔntwema, amoakwa, nkrawobɛn, nkɔfe, mmɛntia, and *kɔtononko* as a single group. Since the *tipre* drums and percussion ensemble is combined with the *amoakwa* and *nkrawoben* ivory trumpets to form a single orchestra, *Tipre ne Amoakwa,* I include *tipre* in this section as well. The pervasive use of the number seven as a defining number for each group of ivory trumpets (except *mmɛntia* and *kɔtononko*) is thoroughly considered with regard to Akan notions of spirituality and perfection in numbers. I conclude the chapter with contrasting timbre and texts of the *durugya* flute, which is technically not an ivory trumpet but a cane flute. However, my inclusion of the latter is justified by the general reference to wind instruments in the Akan Twi as *mmɛn* (singular *abɛn*). There is no distinction between a trumpet, a horn, or a flute; they are all *mmɛn*.

Ivory trumpets (*Asɔkwa*)

Ivory trumpets featured prominently in my ethnographic description of Akwasi-dae Public Assembly in the Prologue. The various ivory trumpet groups are recognized as a unit (*fekuo*), and at the Manhyia Palace, the unit is known as *Asɔkwa* (loosely translated as trumpets) or *Asɔkwafoɔ* (trumpeters). The trumpets are further clustered with drums to form the larger umbrella group *Asɔkwa ne Akyerɛmade* (Trumpets and Drums). *Asɔkwa* is the Twi word for the hornbill, and the designation suggests a metaphorical equivalence, according to the Akan, of the cries of the hornbill to the sounds of the trumpets. The different groups have corresponding chiefs and elders, but they are collectively under Ɔkyeame Boakye Yam, a ranking member of Asantehene's Royal Spokespersons. A key component of Akan states is the widespread use of ivory trumpets of a variety of shapes and sizes made exclusively from elephant tusks. Due to its natural bore, animal horns and elephant tusks are most likely to be some of the earliest sound-producing instruments created by the Akan. Fortunately for our purposes, the widespread use of ivory trumpets in present-day Asante is a mark of unprecedented cultural continuity with the past, accounting for certain levels of transformation. In the days of warfare and territorial conquests, ivory trumpets gained their reputation as war trumpets (*akobɛn*), since they preceded fighting units while sounding coded messages as signals for action or inaction. In a conversation with the Asantehene's *Nnomuahene* Nana Akwasi Assien II in the summer of 2009, he recounted some of the tactics several units of the infantry used in connection with the trumpets. Asante war formation, recalled Nana Akwasi Assien II, is a three-pronged attack from the right flank, the center, and the left flank. Signals by trumpeters alert the right flank, for instance, to rise up and shoot, move forward, or retreat. Some of the messages include: it is okay to move forward (*anim yɛ*), it is not okay to move forward (*anim nyɛ*), bend down (*mo nkoto*), rise up (*mo mpɛgya mo mu*), retreat (*monsan mo akyi*), and others. In addition to providing signals, the trumpets were used to wage psychological warfare where, upon hearing the combined sounds, enemy combatants would desert or flee because they imagined a large army to be upon them. Due to such a mis-judgment by adversaries, we are told that the Asante infantry won quite a few battles without resistance. In the past, the combined sound of several ivory trumpet groups not only scared enemy soldiers but also animals and bugs in the forest. The sound is said to ruffle bees' nests, sending them in the opposite direction to attack enemy soldiers. In the time of territorial conquests, talismans (*nsɛbɛ*) were attached to some of the trumpets, and it is said that the sound directed bees to attack enemy soldiers ahead of the Asante infantry. In addition to other sound-producing instruments in the court, ivory trumpets are used as indexes of power, and in the past, several wars were won or lost just by capturing the ivory trumpets belonging to an adversary. For instance, Kyerɛ Wo Mmɛn (Show Us Your Trumpets), a favorite piece by the *nkontwema* group, is meant to elevate the Asantehene above his adversaries. Example 3.9 is the full text and analysis.

I would like to correct three potential misconceptions about the ivory trumpets in this study. First, the widely used English term "horns" is misleading since they are made from elephant tusks, which are technically teeth, while horns are projections on the heads of animals. Joseph Kaminski provides technical reasons for why we cannot refer to these sound-producing instruments as horns (Kaminski, 2012: 12). Second, the Akan terms *abɛn* (singular) and *mmɛn* (plural) do not distinguish between a trumpet, horn, or flute, as they are all referred to as *mmɛn*. In order to recognize the agency of Akan forebears who have critical reasons for creating the Twi taxonomy, it is most helpful to use the Akan nomenclature, as in *abɛn* (singular) or *mmɛn* (plural), and the names of each trumpet group, as in *Nkofe, Ntahera, Kɔkroanya, Nkontwema*, and others—or, with much reservation, the English term "trumpet." Third, the players use the ivory trumpets to *speak* in place of the human voice and spoken word, thereby imitating the tonal inflections or pitches of the Twi language.[3] In the *Ceremonial Horns of the Ashanti*, Peter Akwasi Sarpong is explicit that the "player uses the horn to speak" and "the horns are not musical instruments" (Sarpong, 1990: 1). In light of Sarpong's statements and their usages in Asante, it is most accurate to consider the ivory trumpets as *sound-producing instruments* instead of "musical" instruments.[4] All trumpets have a rectangular lip-receiver (embouchure) chiseled into the concave side near the narrow end. It is critical for the trumpet carver, according to Kaminski, to cut the lip-receiver "at the point where the tip of the tusk ceases to be solid and the [natural] bore of the tube begins" (Kaminski, 2012: 14). The technique of producing sound on ivory trumpets is recognized by the Akan with the word *hyɛn*. In that sense, the players are also referred to as *mmɛnhyɛnfoɔ*. I shall now turn my attention to two ivory trumpet groups, *ntahera* and *kɔkroanya*.

Ntahera and *kɔkroanya*

The multi-sited fieldwork of Joseph Kamiski in Kumase, Ɛdweso, Dɔmaa-Ahenkro, and Dɛnkyera points to the widespread use of *ntahera* groups in Akan states prior to the founding of Asante (Kaminski, 2012: 16).[5] Although they have different histories and chiefs and come from different locales in the kingdom, my justification for discussing *ntahera* and *kɔkroanya* together is that they share the same repertoire due to some incidents, as well as for historical reasons. *Kɔkroanya* suffered from several years of disuse following the disruption of political, social, and economic life during Asantehene Agyeman Prɛmpɛ's twenty-nine years of exile. Upon his return, the king revived the group and asked the *ntahera* group to teach the *kɔkroanya* group the former's repertoire. In the 1950s, the *ntahera* also had some challenges, and it was members of the *kɔkroanya* group who taught them the repertoire. The *ntahera* and *kɔkroanya* ensembles consistently feature at celebratory events, as well as funerals and court ceremonies.

Ntahera

As narrated by the current chief of *ntahera*, Nana Poku Bosompem II, the oral history of Ntahera holds that Ɔpemsoɔ Ɔsɛe Tutu (c. 1680–1719) created his group as part of his three-year preparation for the Dɛnkyera War. Seven days after commanding the Gold Stool from the sky, Kɔmfo Anɔkye created *Ntahera Bɔaman* (destroyer of nations) for the *ntahera* chief to carry with him to war. Contrary to Joseph Kaminski's historical account, *ntahera* did not descend from the heavens with the Gold Stool in 1697 (Kaminski, 2012: 18). It is one of the recurring errors in the oral and written histories of regalia objects that we have corrected in Ampene and Nyantakyi III (2016). The players of *ntahera* lived in Manhyia Palace together with other courtiers until the reign of Opoku Ware Katakyie. After creating the *Dadeɛsoaba* stool, the king asked the *Dadeɛsoabahene* to give the *ntahera* group a

Figure 3.2 Members of Ntahera in a procession during Akwasidae Public Assembly in Kumase, July 30, 2017.

Source: Picture by author.

place to stay. The group relocated to Dekyɛmso, but when the Ntaherahene, Nana Kwame Bosompem, found a piece of land close to Lake Bosomtwe, they asked the king for that land. After consultation with the *Edwesohene* and *Boɔntɛmhene*, the land was released to Nana Bosompem and his *ntahera* group. Now, *Kokrobiko* is the home of the *ntahera* group, and the present Head of Village (*Dikuro*), Nana Agyekum Tuffour, is a member of the *ntahera* group. Before going to war and after performing a special ritual, the chief would remove the cowrie shells (*sedeɛ*) from inside the *Boaman* and place them in the lead trumpet (*sesee*) to be played in the direction of enemy soldiers. We are informed that the spiritually potent sound mass of the *ntahera* is able to rustle bees and other dangerous animals to attack their enemies ahead of the Asante infantry (see Figure 3.2). Presently, *Ntahera Boaman* is rarely brought out, since these are peaceful times, but rituals are performed for it on special occasions including the forty-two-day Adae cycle. As members of the *ntahera* will say: "it is an old lady who does not travel. We go to bid her farewell before we travel" (*ɛyɛ abrewa, ɛntu kwan. Sɛ yɛ kɔ na y'akɔ akɔ kra no*). Two deities attached to the *ntahera* stools in *Kokrobiko* are *Boabɔduru* and *Afena*.

Kɔkroanya

Kɔkrɔanya, writes Peter Sarpong, is a compound word and comes from *kɔkwan a ɛnya* (literally, does not travel without).[6] True to its name, the Asantehene rarely leaves it behind on his official duties during state ceremonies, when he attends funerals, or on his official travels in Ghana and abroad. Members of the *kɔkrɔanya* group came to Kumase from Dɛnkyera Dwokwaa during Asantehene Opoku Ware's time (1720–1750). The current chief of Kɔkroanya, Nana Akwasi Boadi Amponim, informed us that Nana Gyakari, who was the head of the family at the time, realized that the only female member of his lineage, Akosua Darkwaa, could not bear children, and that could have potential consequences for the future of his matrilineage. In his search for a solution to this situation, Nana Gyakari was advised to go to Kumase where it was likely they would find the solution to his sister's barrenness. He traveled to Kumase with his sister and a maidservant. After meeting with Opoku Ware, the Asantehene asked his uncle, the Nsutahene, to give them a place to live. Nsutahene gave them a piece of land at Nsuta Amoaman; however, his decision to marry Akosua Darkwaa created a misunderstanding between him and Nana Gyakari that led to the beheading of their maidservant. When Nana Gyakari informed Opoku Ware about the incident, he summoned his uncle, but it was too late; the harm had already been done. In order to keep them close to him, Opoku Ware decided to create *kɔkrɔanya* ivory trumpets for Nana Gyakari and his family. In my description of the Akwasidae procession, the *kɔkrɔanya* group preceded the Stool Group. Since they were royals (*adehyeɛ*) at Dwokwaa, they could always go to the king directly without going through an intermediary; they did not have to lower their cloths when they were in his presence and performing their duties. Akosua Darkwaa later had three children, Ɔbasɛm, Manu, and Mansa, whose descendants are the rightful heirs to the *kɔkrɔnya* stool and succession is on a rotational basis. Nana Gyakari was the first chief, while the present chief, Nana Akwasi Boadi Amponim, is a descendant of Mansa.

Figure 3.3 Kɔkroanya ivory trumpets, summer 2009.
Source: Picture by Author.

The seven trumpets that constitute each group of *ntahera* and *kɔkrɔanya* ensembles are divided into four sections. The secteions are one *sesee* (the sayer), two *afrɛ* (callers), three *agyesoa* (responders), and one *bɔsoɔ* (the reinforcer). In addition to in-depth conversations and recordings of repertoire, I have several separate recordings with each ensemble documenting their participation in ceremonies including the Akwasidae Public Assembly that I referenced in the Prologue. As I noted in my methodology, I also engaged in feedback conversations by playing previously recorded events for them to provide their input for further analysis. All of the text in a performance unit is numbered for easy reference in the analysis. Spoken text is labelled *abee*, while text performed on the lead trumpet is labelled *sesee*, and together with the two *afrɛ* (callers), are aligned to the left. Responses by three *agyesoa* and *bɔsoɔ* trumpets are indented to the right to suggest the performance procedure and the internal configuration of call and response. After the initial call by the lead trumpet, the *sesee* player joins *afrɛ* (the caller) for the call phrases, which are always aligned to the left. Each example is followed by textual analysis.

Example 3.1 Kankane Pɛ Twie Ayɛ (The Civet Cat Will Like to Be the Leopard): *kɔkroanya* (ivory trumpets).

Abee (spoken) by Nana Akwasi Boadi Amponim (Kɔkroanyahene)	
1. Kankane pɛ twie ayɛ wanya	The civet cat couldn't be like the leopard
2. Kankane pɛ twie ayɛ wanya	The civet cat couldn't be like the leopard
3. Hwan na ɔtesɛ wo Agyeman	Who is like you Agyeman?
4. Hwan na ɔtesɛ wo Agyeman	Who is like you Agyeman?
5. Kankane pɛ twie ayɛ wanya	The civet cat couldn't be like the leopard
6. Hwan na ɔtesɛ wo	Who is like you?
7. Hwan na ɔtesɛ wo Ɔsɛe Tutu	Who is like you Ɔsɛe Tutu?

Seseɛ (trumpet surrogate speech) *Mmranee* (praise poetry)	*Seseɛ* (trumpet surrogate speech) *Mmranee* (praise poetry)
8. Adeɛ kɔkye a	When the day breaks
9. Ɛkɔ kye me wɔ Sɛkyerɛ o	I was in Sɛkyerɛ when the day breaks
10. Enwunu kɔ dwo a	When the night falls
11. Ɛkɔ dwo me wɔ Sɛkyerɛ o	I was in Sɛkyerɛ when the night falls
12. Ɔsɛkyerɛhene ne hwan?	Who is the chief of Sɛkyerɛ?
13. Ɔsɛkyerɛhene ne Kwame Ante Bosompem	Kwame Ante Bosompem is the chief of Sɛkyerɛ
14. Ɔsɛkyerɛ popuro	Ɔsɛkyerɛ popuro
15. Ɔsɛkyerɛ Akuamoa	Akuamoa of Sɛkyerɛ
16. Krɔbea Asante Kɔtɔkɔhene	Krɔbea Asante Kɔtɔkɔhene
17. Yɛ bɛnom Buroni biribi	We are thirsty for the Whiteman's drink
18. To	To
19. Taa to taa to to	Taa to taa to to
20. To to	To to
21. Kankane pɛ twie ayɛ	The civet cat will like to be like the leopard
Afrɛ (two afrɛ)	*Afrɛ* (two *afrɛ*)
22. Paa	It's true
Agyesoa/bɔsoɔ	*Agyesoa/bɔsoɔ*
23. Wanya	He couldn't
Afrɛ (two *afrɛ*)	*Afrɛ*
24. Paa	It's true
Agyesoa/bɔsoɔ	*Agyesoa/bɔsoɔ*
25. Wanya	He couldn't
Afrɛ (two *afrɛ*)	*Afrɛ*
26. Paa	It's true
Agyesoa/bɔsoɔ	*Agyesoa/bɔsoɔ*
27. Wanya	He couldn't
Afrɛ (two *afrɛ*)	*Afrɛ*
28. Paa	It's true
Agyesoa/bɔsoɔ	*Agyesoa/bɔsoɔ*
29. Wanya	He couldn't
Afrɛ (two *afrɛ*)	*Afrɛ*
30. Paa	It's true
Agyesoa/bɔsoɔ	*Agyesoa/bɔsoɔ*
31. Wanya	He couldn't
Afrɛ (two *afrɛ*)	*Afrɛ*
32. Paa	It's true
Agyesoa/bɔsoɔ	*Agyesoa/bɔsoɔ*
33. Wanya	He couldn't
Afrɛ (two *afrɛ*)	*Afrɛ*
34. Paa	It's true
Agyesoa/bɔsoɔ	*Agyesoa/bɔsoɔ*
35. Wanya	He couldn't
Afrɛ seseɛ	*Afrɛ sesɛɛ*
36. Paa puuuuuuuuuuu	It's true puuuuuuuuuuu
Agyesoa/bosoɔ	*Agyesoa/bosoɔ*
37. Wanya	He couldn't
Afrɛ	*Afrɛ*
38. Paa	It's true
Agyesoa/bɔsoɔ	*Agyesoa/bɔsoɔ*
39. Wanya	He couldn't
Seseɛ/afrɛ	*Seseɛ/afrɛ*
40. Paa paa paaaaaaa	Paa paa paaaaaaa

The African civet cat (*kankane*), with its black and white markings, bears a striking resemblance to the leopard. The performer-composers deride the wishful thinking on the part of the civet cat that it can ever achieve the status of the leopard, the king of the forest. There is value in being who we are without making false claims about what we cannot possibly be. The metaphoric allusion in the verbally intoned *abeɛ* by Nana Amponim becomes clear if we consider that out of the several territorial chiefs (*Amanhene*) in Asanteman, there is only one king, and that is the Asante king. No matter the circumstances, there can never be more than one king. The previous example is instructive on several levels, and I will unpack it by first examining it at the global level. The verse begins with seven lines of spoken poetry, *abeɛ*, by the chief of the *kɔkrɔanya* trumpet group, Nana Amponim. This section expresses the main theme that the civet cat cannot equal the leopard. The spoken word is *ɔkankane*, with the initial particle *ɔ* elided in this poetic verse, resulting in *kankane*. The leading trumpeter, Kwasi Bosompem, playing the *seseɛ*, takes over from Nana Amponim and sends us far afield with a different theme for his praise poetry (*mmranee*) that doubles as a speech surrogate mechanism on the trumpet. It is not until the last phrase of his verse, Line 21, that he re-introduces the initial theme as a signifier for the remaining trumpets, two *afrɛ*, three *agyesoa*, and one *bɔsoɔ* to join him on a seemingly never-ending journey of cyclical responses. There are over forty verses of cyclical performance on the audio, but I present only twenty for our purposes. The previous example is overlaid with a composition-in-performance by the *seseɛ* that I shall discuss shortly.

At the micro level, the *abeɛ* section from Lines 1–7 is heavily weighted on the parallel repetition of whole linear units to emphasize the importance of the main theme. Line 1 is immediately repeated in Line 2. Lines 3 and 4 strategically introduce the addressive *Agyeman* as an end phrase. It is possible that *Agyeman* is a reference to either Asantehene Agyeman Prɛmpɛ (1888–1931) or Asantehene Ɔseɛ Agyeman Prɛmpɛ II (1931–1970).[7] At any rate, it is likely this title can be treated as a variable formulaic phrase that can be recomposed with the stool names of past or reigning kings. Lines 5–7 recap the message by strategically placing the name of the current king, Ɔseɛ Tutu, as the end phrase in order to prompt the *seseɛ* player to take over from him. The praise verse (*mmranee*) by the *seseɛ* player is a masterful manipulation of instrumental speech surrogacy and a parallel repetition of linear units, unlike the just-completed verbal component from Lines 1–7. Here, parallel repetition involves the repetition of the end phrase *kɔkye a* in Line 8 and as the beginning phrase, *(Ɛ)kɔ kye*, in Line 9. The end phrase *kɔ dwo* in Line 10 begins the phrase in Line 11 as *(Ɛ)kɔ dwo*. The end phrase in Line 11, *Sɛkyerɛ*, is a crucial marker in the *seseɛ*'s surrogate phrase in the sense that it establishes a location or a place of abode in the kingdom. Sɛkyerɛ covers a wide area of large urban centers and seats of territorial chiefs, including Effiduase, Asante Mampɔn, and Agona. Lines 12–15 present the parallel repetition of *Ɔsɛkyerɛ* with different end phrases set up in the following order: *hwan, Kwame Ante Bosompem, popuro,* and *Akuamoa*. All four lines begin with the particle *Ɔ* affixed to *Sɛkyerɛ*, thus creating a prosodic effect that leads to the name cluster *Krɔbea Asante Kɔtɔkɔhene* in Line 16. The sound structure of the multisyllabic *Ɔ-sɛ-kye-rɛ-he-ne* in Lines 12 and 13 is not lost on listeners of this ancient verse. The entire linear unit in Line 17 is dramatically different from the preceding lines, since it redirects the verse from praise to making a special request for imported alcoholic drinks on behalf of the *kɔkrɔanya* group. The request for alcoholic drinks is a commentary on the current experience of the trumpeters, who might be thirsty from long hours of court ceremonies but need to articulate the need for refreshments by way of instrumental speech. The request is immediately followed by calling the rest of the group to action with the non-lexical prompters from Lines 18–20 and the lexical prompter that re-introduced the main theme in Line 21.[8]

The call-and-response dialogue is triggered by two distinct prompters—first, in Line 21 by the *sesee* player, and second, by the two *afrɛ* players in Line 22 as *Paa*—that tempt us to consider these two gestures as separate calls. It only makes sense if we interpret it globally as an aspect of hocket apparatus that spreads a single sentence to all four sections of the group. Here is the phrase in spoken Twi: *Kankane pɛ etwie ayɛ ampa wanya.* The Twi word for the leopard is *etwie*, and it is represented here with the first syllable *e* elided, while the sounded *afrɛ* call *Paa* is a contraction of *ampa*, with the first two syllables elided but the particle *a* added to it, resulting in *paa*. The cyclical call and response phrases generated by the two *afrɛ* without the *sesee* are quite distinct from the norm, where the *sesee* joins *afrɛ* in leading the dialog. This procedure frees up the *sesee* player and thus allows him to engage in composition-in-performance, or what is commonly labelled as improvisation. We might consider the first as his idea of *playing* with non-lexical rhythms by manipulating the thumbhole to produce the *pu*, low pitch, when his thumb is covering the hole and *pa*, the high pitch, when the thumb hole is opened. The resultant rhythm is described in Twi as *ɔde gyegye ho*, meaning he is guiding the cyclical repetition of phrases by two *afrɛ*, on the one hand, and three *agyesoa* and one *bɔsoɔ* phrases on the other.

Example 3.2 Lead Trumpeter's Composition-in-Performance (Non-Lexical Texts).

---

pu pa pu pa/pu pa pu pa/pu pu pu pa/pu pu pu pa/pu pa pu pa

The Seseɛ phrase in Line 36, *puuuuuuuuuuuu*, described by the trumpeters as *otu abɛn no mu* (metaphorically, he is clearing the inside of the trumpet), serves as a prompt that he is about to end the cyclical verse. After two calls by *afrɛ* and the same number of responses by *agyesoa* and *bɔsoɔ*, the *sesee* and two *afrɛ* sound the concluding gesture in Line 40 together and briefly sustain the third *paaaaaa* with a swell. The next example presents us with different sets of rhetorical devices.

Example 3.3 Abosomanketrε (The Chameleon), *Kɔkroanya* (Ivory Trumpets).

Abeε (spoken) by Kwaky Ofori Mensah

1. Abosomankere foro nyina   The chameleon climbs the silk-cotton tree
2. Sane nyina   Descends the silk-cotton tree
3. Ne nsa nhyia   Its arms do not encircle the tree
4. Ne nan nhyia   Its legs do not encircle the tree
5. Ɔte kɔhwee a   When it falls down
6. Asaase de no mmrase   The earth consoles it
7. Asaase de no mrase mrase aberaw   The earth consoles and consoles it
8. Mo mma yɛnkɔyi Katakyie ayε o   Let's go and congratulate the gallant one
9. Ɔkɔ yε akyε o   For he has been away for a long time
10. Bɔfodɔmsuro   A hunter feared by multitudes

Seseε (Ɔkwan) honam sin   ***Seseε (Ɔkwan) honam sin***

11. To   To
12. Taa to taa to to   Taa to taa to to
13. To to   To to
14. Bremueeeee   Bremueeeee
    Agyesoa/bɔsoɔ   ***Agyesoa/bɔsoɔ***
15. Yee   Yee
Seseε/afrε   ***Seseε/afrε***
16. Bremueeeee   Bremueeeee
    Agyesoa/bɔsoɔ   ***Agyesoa/bɔsoɔ***
17. Yee   Yee
Seseε/afrε   ***Seseε/afrε***
18. Bremueeeee   Bremueeeee
    Agyesoa/bɔsoɔ   ***Agyesoa/bɔsoɔ***
19. Yee   Yee
Seseε/afrε   ***Seseε/afrε***
20. Bremueeeee   Bremueeeee
    Agyesoa/bɔsoɔ   ***Agyesoa/bɔsoɔ***
21. Yee   Yee
Seseε/afrε   ***Seseε/afrε***
22. Brem   Brem

We may recall in Example 3.1 that the *seseε* player made a request for alcoholic drinks in Line 16. *Abosomanketere* (the chameleon) is a classic example of the type of poetry that the Ntahera and Kɔkroanya groups may perform by way of instrumental surrogacy to communicate their gratitude to the ruler for responding to their request for refreshments in a timely manner. One of the hallmarks of instrumental surrogacy is that an expression of gratitude is channeled through elegant texts performed on an ivory trumpet rather than the spoken texts of regular discourse. Instead of sounding *yε da wo ase o* (we thank you), we have ten lines of *abeε*, a verbal performance by Kwaku Ofori Mensah who plays the *bɔsoɔ* trumpet in the group, followed by what they refer to as *Honam Sin*, or *Nam Sin* for short. When the *seseε* player calls the group to action using the prompt *to* without sounding a verse of praise poetry, they refer to that performance as *honam sin*. There are several reasons why the *seseε* may decide to limit his verses to *honam sin*. Performers may be tired due to the long hours of court ceremonies or national events, and they need to conserve energy for the duration of the event.

Additionally, depending on the demands of a particular program, there may be situations where they need short verses to keep the program moving along. After the prompt, the *seseɛ* player calls for the group to perform *Ɔsansa* ("The Hawk").

The metaphoric allusion to the efforts of the chameleon in the previous example is indeed touching. The tiny chameleon is motivated to succeed against all odds by climbing the humongous silk-cotton tree without being able to encircle the tree with his arms or legs. It is an accomplishment that comes with extreme risks, and it is not surprising that sometimes the chameleon misses its step and falls to the ground (Line 5). With its bountiful presence and motherly love, the earth provides the only comfort for the unfortunate chameleon (Lines 6–7). The emotional dilemma of the chameleon is the frame of reference for their own situation. The *kɔkrɔanya* group may try to face the challenges of life themselves, but like the chameleon, they are unable to succeed without the support of the ruler. Obviously, Example 3.3 is a long-winded method of expressing gratitude. Kwaku Ofori plays with parallel repetition and the sound structure of end phrases *nyina* and *nhyia*, first in Lines 1–2 and then Lines 3–4. The prosody of the end phrases is quite remarkable in showing the resourcefulness of Akan poets for adjusting *(o)nyina* by deleting the first letter and making it rhyme with *nhyia*. Lines 8–9 are directives for all the members of *kɔkrɔanya* to go and express their gratitude to their overlord for taking care of their needs. The multisyllabic *bɔfodɔmsuro* in Line 10 is a contraction of *ɔbɔfoɔ a ɛdɔm suro no* (a hunter feared by the multitudes) as an attribute of the ruler and a preferred conclusion to the spoken verse. The dialogic interplay between the sections from Lines 11–22 follows a familiar architectural framework, where calls are issued by the *seseɛ* and *afrɛ* and the responses lie squarely with the *agyesoa* and *bɔsoɔ*. Remarkably, the previous verse lacks the usual signifying code by the *seseɛ* that he is about to end, while the ending gesture in Line 22 is very short and the first of its kind in our analysis. Indeed, there is value in motivation to succeed against all odds, and there is value in expressing gratitude. The next example recalls the Asante-Banda War in the eighteenth century.

Example 3.4 Ɛnteɛrɛ Kasanpren ("A Name"): *kɔkrɔanya* (ivory trumpets).

Abeɛ (spoken) by Nana Akwasi Boadi Amponim

1. Mekɔɔ musuyie ɔhene adware me	I went for removal of mischief and the chief has cleansed me
2. Mekɔɔ musuyie a ɔhene adware me	I went for removal of mischief and the chief has cleansed me
3. Nteɛrɛ Kasanpren, asuo yiri a na yɛfrɛ me	Nteɛrɛ Kasanpren, they call me when the river is flooded
4. Nteɛrɛ kasanpren, asuo yiri a na yɛfrɛ kɔkrɔanya	Nteɛrɛ Kasanpren, they call Kɔkrɔanya when the river is flooded
Seseɛ	
5. Abɛn sɔ me mu ɛ	Abɛn, help me
6. To taa to taa to to	To taa to taa to to
7. To to	To to

(Continued)

Example 3.4 (Continued)

Sesεε	
8. Ntεεrε ee	Ntεεrε ee
Agyesoa/bɔsɔɔ	**Agyesoa/bɔsɔɔ**
9. Yee	Yee
Sesεε/afrε	**Sesεε/afrε**
10. Paa	Paa
Agyesoa/bɔsɔɔ	**Agyesoa/bɔsɔɔ**
11. Yee	Yee
Sesεε/afrε	**Sesεε/afrε**
12. Pa pa	Pa pa
Agyesoa/bɔsɔɔ	**Agyesoa/bɔsɔɔ**
13. Yee	Yee
Sesεε/afrε	**Sesεε/afrε**
14. Paa	Paa
Agyesoa/bɔsɔɔ	**Agyesoa/bɔsɔɔ**
15. Yee	Yee
Sesεε/afrε	**Sesεε/afrε**
16. Paa puuuuuuuu	Paa puuuuuuuu
Agyesoa/bɔsɔɔ	**Agyesoa/bɔsɔɔ**
17. Yee	Yee
Sesεε/afrε	**Sesεε/afrε**
17. Paaaaaaa	Paaaaaaa

Another version of a short call (*honam sin*) by the *sesεε* player, the historical impetus for the previous verse is the Asante-Banda War (or Bana Sa) that took place around 1770 with the powerful and fearful Worosa, the king of Banda.[9] Through processes of linear repetition of whole units (Lines 1–2, 3–4), the *kɔkrɔanya* groups are comparing their selfless dedication to the ideals of the kingdom to that of *ntεεrε*, a metaphoric reference to someone whom everyone calls upon, or a dependable individual in times of crisis. Interpretation may be situated in specific events, and how it was performed for *ntεεrε* may be attributed to the ruler, or in other situations to the *kɔkroanya* and *ntahera* groups, as the reference to *kɔkrɔanya* in Line 4 depicts. The signal to end is sounded by the *sesεε* player in Line 16, and after a single response in Line 17, the *sesεε* and *afrε* conclude the verse (Line 18) with a contraction of *ampa* (truly) by eliding the first two syllables (*am*)*pa* and extending the last syllable, resulting in *paaaaaa*.

Nkɔntwema

Compared with *ntahera* and *kɔkrɔanya*, the *nkɔntwema* ivory trumpets are relatively small in size and the only group whose timbre is closer to *mmεntia* (short trumpets). The identifying marker (*ahyεnso*) is the coarse camel blanket (*nsaa*) that is wrapped around each instrument (see Figure 3.4). The seven *nkɔntwema* trumpets are grouped into four sections as follows: one *sesεε* (the sayer), two *afrε* (callers), three *agyesoa* (responders), and one *bɔsɔɔ* (reinforcer). In processions, they are usually behind members of the Treasury (*Afotosanfoɔ*) and are the first

Figure 3.4 Nkɔntwema ivory trumpets, summer 2009.
Source: Picture by author.

ivory trumpet group in any given procession to herald the imminent approach of the ruler. *Nkɔntwema* literally translates to "don't go and bring trouble" and refers to the peaceful nature of this group in the sense that they are not troublemakers. Narrating their oral history, Nana Owusu Ansah, the Chief of Nkɔntwema, said their elders escaped from Kyebi to Kumase just before one of the Asante-Akyem Abuakwa wars, probably during Opoku Ware's time, to seek refuge and protection. They settled at Dɛnkyɛmenaso when they first arrived in Kumase. At that time, Dɛnkyɛmenaso was under Ntotoyɛhene, who doubled as the Akyeamehene (chief of the royal spokespersons and diplomats). From Dɛnkyɛmenaso, they also lived at Amoana and then finally settled in their present location at Fankyen-ebra near Kumase. Originally, they used bamboo stems to construct these sound-producing instruments until the ruler gave them elephant tusks (*asonse*).

In addition to serving as *Asɔkwafoɔ*, they were responsible for building fences around the palace and supplying the palace with firewood for cooking. As with all of the *Asɔkwafoɔ*, my first meeting with the *Nkɔntwemafoɔ* was on July 16, 2009 at the Manhyia Palace. Led by their chief Nana Owusu Ansah, we had a lengthy conversation about the history of *nkɔtwema*, in addition to recording the repertoire. I have since observed and recorded the group perform in a variety of court events, including Akwasidae and funerary rites, as well as taken my transcriptions back to them for corrections and clarification. Sarpong presents eleven verses (1990: 26–31) that are reproduced in Joseph Kaminski's book in the Appendix (2012: 169–172). Here are two transcriptions and analysis of their surrogate verses that I recorded in our first meeting.

Example 3.5 Boafo Ako Ako (Boafo Who Fights and Fights), *Nkɔntwema* (ivory trumpets).

Sesee	***Sesee***
1. Mo nsɔ mu o	Hold your trumpets
2. Boafo ako ako	Boafo who fights and fights
3. Ɔhene nante brɛ brɛ brɛ	The king walks majestically
Afrɛ	***Afrɛ***
4. Paa pa	Yes indeed
Sesee/agyesoa/bɔsoɔ	*Sesee/agyesoa/bɔsoɔ*
5. Sɛ	Truly
Afrɛ	**Afrɛ**
6. Paa pa	Yes indeed
Sesee/agyesoa/bɔsoɔ	*Sesee/agyesoa/bɔsoɔ*
7. Sɛ	Truly
Afrɛ	***Afrɛ***
8. Paa pa	Yes indeed
Sesee/agyesoa/bɔsoɔ	*Sesee/agyesoa/bɔsoɔ*
9. Sɛ sɛɛ sɛɛ sɛ	Truly, truly truly truly
Afrɛ	***Afrɛ***
10. Paa pa	Yes indeed
Sesee/agyesoa/bɔsoɔ	*Sesee/agyesoa/bɔsoɔ*
11. Sɛ	Truly
Afrɛ	***Afrɛ***
12. Paa pa	Yes indeed
Sesee/agyesoa/bɔsoɔ	*Sesee/agyesoa/bɔsoɔ*
13. Sɛ	Truly
Afrɛ	***Afrɛ***
14. Paa pa	Yes indeed
Sesee/agyesoa/bɔsoɔ	*Sesee/agyesoa/bɔsoɔ*
15. Sɛ sɛɛ sɛɛ sɛ	Truly, truly truly truly
Afrɛ	***Afrɛ***
16. Paa pa	Yes indeed
Sesee/agyesoa/bɔsoɔ	*Sesee/agyesoa/bɔsoɔ*
17. Sɛ	Truly
Afrɛ	***Afrɛ***
18. Paa pa	Yes indeed
Sesee/agyesoa/bɔsoɔ	*Sesee/agyesoa/bɔsoɔ*
19. Sɛ	Truly
Afrɛ	***Afrɛ***
20. Paa pa	Yes indeed
Sesee/agyesoa/bɔsoɔ	*Sesee/agyesoa/bɔsoɔ*
21. Sɛ sɛɛ sɛɛ sɛ	Truly, truly truly truly
Afrɛ/sesee	***Afrɛ/sesee***
22. Paa pa Puuuuuuu	Yes indeed Puuuuuuu
Sesee/agyesoa/bɔsoɔ	*Sesee/agyesoa/bɔsoɔ*
23. Sɛ	Truly
Afrɛ	***Afrɛ***
24. Paa pa	Yes indeed
Sesee/agyesoa/bɔsoɔ	*Sesee/agyesoa/bɔsoɔ*
25. Sɛ	Truly
Afrɛ	***Afrɛ***
26. Paa pa	Yes indeed
Sesee/agyesoa/bɔsoɔ	*Sesee/agyesoa/bɔsoɔ*
27. Sɛ sɛɛ sɛɛ sɛ	Truly, truly truly truly
Sesee/afrɛ	***Sesee/afrɛ***
28. Paaaaaaa	Indeed

The previous example is a favorite verse of the *nkɔntwema* group that is typically sounded when the ruler is walking in a procession like the one I described in the Prologue. As an individual who bears the burden of the state on his shoulders, the ruler walks slowly and majestically. His responsibility to his subjects is represented by the metaphoric allusion and attribute of a restless warrior, *Boafo ako ako ako* ("Boafo who fights and fights") in Line 2. For those who understand instrumental surrogacy, it makes sense that one cannot walk briskly if they are carrying a heavy load. A distinctive feature of *nkɔntwema* is that the procedure for assigning surrogate roles within the four sections is totally different from the trumpet ensembles we have discussed so far. The call to action, *mo nsɔ mu o* ("hold your trumpets"), is given by *sesee* player Kwaku Afodoɔ in Line 1, followed by two linear lines with the reduplication of end phrases *ako ako* in Line 2 and *brɛ brɛ brɛ* in Line 3. Instead of joining forces with the *afrɛ* players, the *sesee* links up with one *bɔsoɔ* and three *agyesoa* players to complete the hocket phrase that is triggered by the two *afrɛ* players. The two-word phrase *ampa sɛ* ("truly indeed," or "it is true") goes through processes of deleting and adding particles, guided by the hocket mechanism and resulting in *(am)Paa (am)pa sɛ*. The overall architectural design demonstrates four periods marked by the formulaic phrase *sɛ sɛɛ sɛɛ sɛ* in Lines 9, 15, 21, and 27. As a result, we can safely identify an introduction from Lines 1–3, the four periods, and an appendix marked by the concluding gesture in Line 28. Note that the *sesee* player finally joins the two *afrɛ* players to sound the concluding phrase.

Example 3.6 Kyerɛ Wo Mmɛn ("Show Your Trumpets"): *Nkɔntwema* (ivory trumpets).

Sesee	*Sesee*
1. Mo nsɔ mu o	Hold your trumpets
2. Nipa ɔne wo sɛ	A chief who claims your status
3. Kyerɛ wo mmɛn	He should show his trumpets
4. Kyerɛ wo dɔm	He should show his people
Afrɛ	*Afrɛ*
5. Kyerɛ wo dɔm	Show your people
Sesee/agyesoa/bɔsoɔ	*Sesee/agyesoa/bɔsoɔ*
6. Ampaa sɛ	Yes indeed
Afrɛ	*Afrɛ*
7. Kyerɛ wo mmɛn mmɛn mmɛn	Show your trumpets, trumpets, trumpets
Sesee/agyesoa/bɔsoɔ	*Sesee/agyesoa/bɔsoɔ*
8. Ampaa sɛ	Yes indeed
Afrɛ	*Afrɛ*
9. Kyerɛ wo dɔm	Show your people
Sesee/agyesoa/bɔsoɔ	*Sesee/agyesoa/bɔsoɔ*
10. Ampaa sɛ	Yes indeed
Afrɛ	*Afrɛ*
11. Kyerɛ wo mmɛn mmɛn mmɛn	Show your trumpets, trumpets, trumpets
Sesee/agyesoa/bɔsoɔ	*Sesee/agyesoa/bɔsoɔ*
12. Ampaa sɛ	Yes indeed

(Continued)

Example 3.6 (Continued)

Afrɛ	*Afrɛ*
13. Kyerɛ wo dɔm	Show your people
Seseɛ/agyesoa/bɔsoɔ	***Seseɛ/agyesoa/bɔsoɔ***
14. Ampaa sɛ	Yes indeed
Afrɛ	*Afrɛ*
15. Kyerɛ wo mmɛn mmɛn mmɛn	Show your trumpets, trumpets, trumpets
Seseɛ/agyesoa/bɔsoɔ	***Seseɛ/agyesoa/bɔsoɔ***
16. Ampaa sɛ	Yes indeed
Afrɛ	*Afrɛ*
17. Kyerɛ wo dɔm	Show your people
Seseɛ/agyesoa/bɔsoɔ	***Seseɛ/agyesoa/bɔsoɔ***
18. Ampaa sɛ	Yes indeed
Afrɛ	*Afrɛ*
19. Kyerɛ wo mmɛn mmɛn mmɛn	Show your trumpets, trumpets, trumpets
Seseɛ/agyesoa/bɔsoɔ	***Seseɛ/agyesoa/bɔsoɔ***
20. Ampaa sɛ	Yes indeed
Afrɛ/seseɛ	**Afrɛ/seseɛ**
21. Kyerɛ wo dɔm Puuuuuuu	Kyerɛ wo dɔm Puuuuuuu
Seseɛ/agyesoa/bɔsoɔ	***Seseɛ/agyesoa/bɔsoɔ***
22. Ampaa sɛ	Yes indeed
Seseɛ/afrɛ	**Seseɛ/afrɛ**
23. Kyerɛ wo dɔɔɔɔɔm	Show your people

With slight variation, similar organizational procedures in Example 3.5 operate in the previous example. For instance, the four-line introductory verse by the *seseɛ* player includes the usual call to action in Line 1, followed by the main theme from Lines 2–4. The main theme includes the parallel repetition of two linear lines with the same beginning phrases, *kyerɛ* in Lines 3 and 4, and different end-phrases, *mmɛn* (trumpets) in Line 3 and *dɔm* (multitude) in Line 4. Further, the two *afrɛ* are on their own, while the *seseɛ* team up with the three *agyesoa* and one *bɔsoɔ* in the repeated phrase *ampaa sɛ*, until the concluding phrase when the *seseɛ* player joins the two *afrɛ* to sound the concluding gesture in Line 23. As I have previously noted, this verse is typically performed by the *nkɔntwema* to reinforce the ruler's political authority, which is marked by the number of ivory trumpets at his court and the multitude (*ɛdɔm*) that he commands. Compare the single-syllable phrase *dɔm*, which is sounded by the *afrɛ* in Lines 5, 9, 13, 17, and 21, with *mmɛn mmɛn mmɛn* in Lines 7, 11, 15, and 19—the former refers to a large crowd (in a sense, a multitude), while the latter refers to trumpets. A combination of perhaps thousands or millions of people in a kingdom, and several varieties of *mmɛn*, indexes the power and authority of rulers. There is value in numbers, and the ability to retain all the different groups of *Asɔkwafoɔ* in the kingdom speaks volumes about the power of the Asantehene. I shall now turn my attention to *Tipre ne Amoakwa*, the only orchestra at Manhyia Palace that combines drums and percussion with ivory trumpets. Although *tipre* is made up of drums and percussion, I include them in this section because they combine forces with the *amoakwa* and *nkrawobɛn* ivory trumpets to form the *Tipre ne Amoakwa* ensemble.

Tipre ne Amoakwa

In the past, the *Tipre ne Amoakwa* orchestra included *nkrawobɛn, mmɔdwemmɔdwe*, and *patuda* ivory trumpets, but the last two are not part of the current ensemble. It is the Asantehemaa's orchestra, and as stated in the previous section, it is the only orchestra that combines ivory trumpets, drums, and percussion instruments. It is one of the largest orchestras in Manhyia Palace. Additionally, this is the only ivory trumpet group that performs for dancers, although dancing is restricted to the Asantehemaa, members of the royal family, and the young maidens in the *ɔhemaa*'s court (*mmɔdwoafoɔ*). The drums and percussion involve a pair of *atumpan* and one *kwadum* drum played with two curved sticks (*nkonta*). A smaller drum called by its onomatoepoeic sound, *penpa*, and *kyɛnkyɛn*, two hand-held cymbals also known by their onomatoepoeic sound, complete the ensemble. All five groups in the orchestra have corresponding chiefs, as in *Tiprehene, Amoakwahene, Nkrawobɛnhene, Mmɔdwemmɔdwehene*, and *Patudahene*. Unlike other court ensembles, they do not go to war; rather, they remain with the Asantehemaa when the ruler and the Asante soldiers are on the battlefield and accompany the women of the royal household as they sing songs of exhilaration (*mmommome*). Sometimes, the trumpets will play without the drums, and that is referred to as *mmɛnten*.

According to Nana Owusu Mensah II, the Chief of Amoakwa (Amoakwahene), his forebears were originally from Dɛnkyera Nyaadoam and sought refuge in Kumase around the same time as the *tipre* group, when they were both presented to the ruler. Strangely for all present, the *Amoakwa* group joined the *tipre* group when the latter performed, and in addition to playing drum texts on their trumpets, they were able to improvise and support the drums. Predictably, the ruler was so impressed with this orchestra that he placed them under the care of Dadeɛsoabahene and later asked them to join the Asantehemaa's court. In processions, they perform behind her including when she is carried in her palanquin (*Seko*). *Nkrawobɛn* is derived from the red felt *nkrawoɔ* that covers the seven trumpets. The red felt is also the identifying marker (*ahyɛnso*) for that particular trumpet (Figure 3.5). Apart from black tape wrapped around the entire tusk of the *sesee* and other tapes partially wrapped around the remaining six trumpets to prevent wear and tear, the *Amoakwa* uses the bare tusks without an identifying cloth (Figures 3.5, 3.6, and 3.7). Although the *tipre* consists of drums and percussion, I include a picture here since it is central to this ensemble, as its name implies.

Figure 3.5 Six members of the Amoakwa ivory trumpet group with the Chief, Nana Owusu
        Agyei Mensah II, summer 2011 at Manhyia Palace.

Source: Picture by author.

Figure 3.6 Five members of Nkrawoben ivory trumpet group with Ama Serwaa (Patuda
        Obaapanin, seated left) and Opanin Yaw Sekyere (Patudadikro, seated right),
        summer 2011, Manhyia Palace.

Source: Picture by author.

Figure 3.7 Nana Kyerema Opong II, the Chief of Tipre, and his group without the metal cymbal (*kyenkyen*). The instruments are a pair of *atumpan* drums (played by K. Amankwaa), *kwadum* (played by Kwadwo Fori), and *petia* (played by Akwasi Gyamfi, standing in the middle), summer 2011.

Source: Picture by author.

I worked with the *Tipre ne Amoakwa* ensemble and its corresponding chiefs, Nana Kyerema Opong II and Nana Owusu Agyei Mensah II, at the palace in the summer of 2009 and 2011. However, I did not work with the *mmɔdwemmɔdwe* and *patuda* groups, nor did I observe the instruments in any court ceremonies. Although the Head of Patuda village, Opanin Yaw Sekyere, was with us during my conversations with the group, I did not see the trumpet. However, I saw a picture of *mmɔdwemmɔdwe* in the British Museum when I did archival and library research in London in November of 2016. The two examples that follow are from my recordings in the summer of 2011, and in response to the hocket framework, my textual representations are organized differently from the preceding examples. I have labeled each line with a bold letter, as in **A**, **B**, **C**, and **D**, and each line should be read separately and horizontally from left to right before moving on to the next letter. Thus, we begin with **A**, and from left to right we move on to **B**, and then similarly to the next letter, until we complete the cycle and return to **A**. With space limitations, the text is a partial transcription followed by a partial transcription of drums and percussion accompaniment (*tipre*).

Example 3.7 *Nana Wo Yε* (Nana You Are Generous), *Tipre ne Amoakwa* (Ivory Trumpets,
Drums, and Percussion).

Sesɛɛ			*Sesɛɛ*		

1. Nana e Nana e   Nana, Nana
2. Yɛn huu bi da   We've never seen this before
3. Wo yɛ   You are generous
4. Wo yɛ pa pa pa pa paaa pa   You are truly generous
5. Nana wo yɛ   Nana you are generous
6. Wo yɛ   You are generous
7. Wo yɛ paa paa pa   You are truly generous

A. Sesɛɛ	*Afrɛ*	*Sesɛɛ*	*Afrɛ*	*Sesɛɛ*	*Afrɛ*	
Nana wo	yɛ	wo	yɛ	wo	yɛ	paa paa pa
		Agyesoa/bɔsoɔ				
B. Sesɛɛ	*Afrɛ*	Paa pa	*Afrɛ*	paa pa	*Afrɛ*	paa paa pa
		Sesɛɛ		*Sesɛɛ*		
Nana wo	yɛ	wo	yɛ	wo	yɛ	paa paa pa
		Agyesoa/bɔsoɔ				
C. Sesɛɛ	*Afrɛ*	Paa pa	*Afrɛ*	paa pa	*Afrɛ*	paa paa pa
		Sesɛɛ		*Sesɛɛ*		
Nana wo	yɛ	wo	yɛ	wo	yɛ	paa paa pa
		Agyesoa/bɔsoɔ				
		Paa pa		paa pa		paa paa pa
D. Sesɛɛ	*Afrɛ*	*Sesɛɛ*	*Afrɛ*	*Sesɛɛ*	*Afrɛ*	
Nana wo	yɛ	wo	yɛ	wo	yɛ	paa paa pa
		Agyesoa/bɔsoɔ		paa pa		paa paa pa
		Paa pa				

Tipre
Kyɛnkyɛn
*   *   *   *   *   *   *   *   *   *

A. *Atumpan*
Nokware nokware kronkron kronkron nokware nokware   kronkron kronkron
    Akwadum
    Firi   firi   firi tete firi   firi
Akwadum
Firi tete

B. *Atumpan*
        Nokware nokware   kronkron kronkron   Nokware nokware
    Akwadum
            firi   firi   firi tete Firi

C. *Atumpan*
    kronkron kronkron
Akwadum
firi   firi tete
Penpa
Pen pa pen pa pen pa pen pa etc

Signal to end
sesɛɛ
Tatan tatan tatan trrrrrrr

Example 3.7 is a classic verse by the *Tipre ne Amoakwa* orchestra that comments on the generous and compassionate character of the Asantehemaa, for there is value in a generous and compassionate leader. Although the two ivory trumpets, *amoakwa* and *nkrawobɛn*, are each played in groups of seven with the noted four sections, the overall structure portrays an expansive architecture and multi-circular progression. Kwadwo Appiakubi begins the performance by sounding seven lines on his lead trumpet (*seseɛ*), which spells out the main theme of the verse.[10] We can relate the sounding of Lines 1–4 by Appiakubi to the praises by the *ntahera* or *kɔkrɔanya seseɛ* players. This is followed by the phrases in Lines 5–7, which set the formula for the ensuing hocket apparatus for the words *Nana wo yɛ paa* ("Nana, you are truly generous"), labeled with letters **A**, **B**, **C**, and **D**. The seseɛ is assigned *Nana wo*, afrɛ continuous with the single syllable *yɛ*, while the Agyesoa and Bɔsoɔ complete the sentence with *paa pa*.[11] The end of the sentence coincides with the repetition of *wo* by the sesee. For a fuller grasp of the hocket formula, we should think in terms of a cyclical progression, where **A** flows seamlessly into **B**, **B** into **C**, **C** into **D**, **D** into **A**, and so forth. The end of **D** is not necessarily the end of the performance, for as in the case of all court ensembles, the duration of a performance unit is determined by several factors, including, but not limited to, the type of ceremony or ritual and the goal of the performance. The parallel repetition of linear phrases, especially the beginning phrase *wo yɛ* in Lines 3, 4, 6, and 7, serves to emphasize the main theme.

The drums and percussion (*tipre*) use different texts to affirm the initial submission by the ivory trumpets that the *ɔhemaa* is kind. Here is the actual sentence in Twi: *(Ɛyɛ) nokware, (e)firi tete kronkron*, which literally translates into English as "it is true, from the ancient times, true and pure." In parenthesis are the phrase and particle that were elided in the drum text. The *kyɛnkyɛn*, represented by asterisks in the previous example, are played on the downbeat throughout the performance, while the first syllable *pen* coincides with the downbeat of *kyɛnkyɛn*, with the second syllable *pa* on the upbeat. The resulting juxtaposition of multitexts within the *amoakwa* and *nkrawobɛn*, and between the trumpets, drums, and percussion, is an outstanding expression of artistry grounded in the Akan imagination, which includes circular mappings of musical expressions. Added to the previous artistry are symbolic gestures of the dancers, which I will briefly examine in the next example. The *amoakwa seseɛ* player, who seems to be the ultimate leader of the orchestra, plays the signal to end the verse with the gesture *Tatan tatan tatan trrrrrrr*, followed by what seems like a repetition of the syllable *papapapapa* on the trumpets and a roll on the drums.

Example 3.8 Kukubɛnkuo (Something Big, Strong, and Heavy)-Tipre ne Amoakwa (Ivory Trumpets, Drums, and Percussion).

Seseɛ

1. Mo wɔ hɔ?	Are you all present?
2. Mmaa e	Ladies
3. Adekɛseɛ	Something big
4. Kukubɛnkuo	Something big, strong, and heavy
5. Me pɛ deɛ ɛso na ma'goro ano	I want something big to play with
6. Ano paa paa pa	To play with it

Seseɛ

Me pɛ deɛ so na ma'goro ano

    Agyesoa/bɔsoɔ

       Ɛyɛ   ɛyɛ

       Afrɛ

       Ɛyɛ paa paa pa

           Seseɛ

           Me pɛ deɛ so na ma'goro ano

              Agyesoa/bɔsoɔ

              Ɛyɛ   ɛyɛ

              Afrɛ

              Ɛyɛ paa paa pa

Tipre (drum and percussion) *kyɛnkyɛn*

*   *   *   *   *   *   *   *** Atumpan**

Me pɛ deɛ so na ma'goro no, ɛyɛ paa paa pa

Akwadum

Me pɛ deɛ   ma'goro no * *   *   *   *   **Penpa**

Pen pa pen pa pen pa pen pa pen pa pen pa

The relative brevity of the previous verse, compared with the previous example, is one of the few light, jovial, and sensual verses performed in the Asantehemaa's court. The text is repeated several times, and depending on the performance event, it may last for half-an-hour or more. Its suggestive and multisyllabic text, *kukubenkuo*, is the Akan poetic equivalent of the visual phallus, which is combined with exaggerated costumes and dance gestures in order to strike a balance between the mostly intense court ceremonies and rituals with some lighthearted performances. For the costumes, the women usually tie pillows around their waists, covering them with printed wraps tied under their armpits—a close resemblance to the *adɔsoa* costume by female dancers who combine *kente* cloth with gold jewelry and precious beads. The dance gestures for *kukubenkuo* are quite suggestive, as the women and maidens raise their fisted right hands with support from their left hands under their elbows. When dancing, they move their fisted right hands from left to right, or forward and backward, to signify the type of *kukubenkuo* they would like to play with—that is, something big, strong, and heavy, as in Line 4. Acting as master of ceremony, Appiakubi begins his surrogate speech by establishing that the ladies are all present and excited (Lines 1–2). Similar to our first example, Lines 5–6 establish the hocket apparatus for the rest of the ensemble. The spoken phrase is *Me pɛ deɛ (ɛ)so na ma'goro ano, ɛyɛ ampa*—literally, "I want something big to play with it." This time, the *atumpan* drums play the same repeated phrase as the *sesee*, while the *akwadum* breaks up the phrase. The *kyenkyen* and *penpa* parts are the same as before. It bears emphasizing that, apart from the *amoakwa* and *nkrawoben* trumpets that constitute the *Tipre ne Amoakwa* orchestra, all of the ivory trumpets function as instrumental speech surrogates that are sounded in place of spoken language.

Nkofe

Peter Akwasi Sarpong's introductory book *Ceremonial Horns of the Ashanti* includes snippets of information on *nkofe*, in addition to texts of thirteen verses and English translations (Sarpong, 1990). Joseph Kaminski's monograph on the Asantehene's *ntahera* ivory trumpet group attempts to expand on Sarpong's work, but his discussion of the etymology of the Twi word *nkofe* is inadequate. Kaminski's assertion that the Gã word *koN* for horn and *fe*, meaning to blow, as the sources of the Twi word, *nkofe*, is highly questionable. Additionally, his historical account of *nkofe*, although it identifies King Ɔsee Kwadwo with the origins of *nkofe*, and later Ɔpemsoɔ Ɔsee Tutu, lacks historical accuracy (Kaminski, 2012: 100–102). My discussion that follows seeks to address these kinds of recurring inaccuracies in the oral and written history of the *nkofe* ivory trumpet group. I recorded the oral history of *nkofe* by three chiefs: Nana Kofi Owusu (Chief of Nkofe), Nana Akwasi Essien II (Nnomuahene), and Nana Osei Kwadwo (Abɛnbɛnhene). According to all three, there is the original history and the relatively modern history of *nkofe*. The former began with the early years of the kingdom, when Ɔpemsoɔ Ɔsee Tutu captured the original trumpets in one of his first wars with the Akyem at Adanse Abadwam during the reign of Ɔkyehene Kuntunkununku.[12] Oral traditions hold that by the time Ɔsee Tutu and his men got to Adanse Abadwam, the Akyem had retreated, leaving behind their ivory trumpets. The king and his men collected the trumpets, and when they got to Kumase, he assigned the name *nkofe* to the trumpets. We are also told that Nkofe is the name of a village near the spot where they found the trumpets, and there may be symbolic reasons for picking this name. Ɔsee Tutu gave the trumpets to Ta Amankwaa, a priest and one of his spiritual advisors at the time, for safekeeping. Since Ɔsee Tutu fought and captured the *nkofe*, they made sure that no other chief could possess similar trumpets as part of their regalia. In fact, there is a general belief that these trumpets were the original *kɔkroanya* ivory trumpets, since they accompanied Ɔsee Tutu to various places including the battlefield.[13]

However, the *nkofe* as we know them today were reconstituted by the 4th Asantehene, Ɔsee Kwadwo (Ɔko Awia, "he fights in broad daylight"), who reigned from 1764–1777. Oral accounts of this latter history link it to the Asante-Banda War that I referenced in connection to the *ntahera* and *kɔkroanya* groups. For the Banda War, Asantehene Ɔsee Kwadwo elected the chief of Dadeɛsoaba (Dadeɛsoabahene) to lead the Asante army. King Worosa showed up with a formidable army, and although the Asante eventually defeated him, beheaded him, and brought his decapitated head to Kumase, several of the Asante infantry perished.

As in past wars, Dadeɛsoabahene thought Worosa's army would take to their heels if they heard the blaring sounds of the *asɔkwafoɔ* (ivory trumpeters), so he sent all of the ivory trumpeters ahead of the infantry. When things got worse, several of the trumpeters perished. Some of them returned with just one surviving trumpeter, others with none, and others with two or three trumpeters. Since the immediate environment surrounding Banda was relatively new to the Asante, and they were not immune to diseases in this area, they suffered severe casualties from diseases such as chickenpox (*bropete*). Those who were seriously affected by diseases were left behind and eventually intermarried to the extent that the *Nkofe Fekuo* now trace some of their family members to Banda Adadeɛm.

Understandably, Ɔsee Kwadwo was not happy about the loss of his cherished trumpeters, so he asked them to form a single group, took them away from Dadeɛsoabahene, and placed them in the care of one of his senior spokespersons, Ɔkyeame Boakye Yam. Although all seven chiefs who formed the newly reconstituted group kept their autonomy, the Asantehene gave them a neutral name, *nkofe*, with the chief of Ta Amankwaa's stool as the head of the group (*fekutire*) and Nkofehene. The seven chiefs are: 1) the *Abɛnbɛnhene* (chief of *abɛnbɛn*), whose actual name is *Abamoo Abɛn*; 2) *Nnomuahene* (chief of *nnomuammɛn*), a corruption and contraction of *ɛdɔm mmoano abɛn*, which is the trumpet sounded to gather the masses or soldiers; 3) *Ankaasemmɛnhene* (chief of *ankaase* trumpets); 4) *Akyeremademmɛnhene* (chief of *akyeremade* trumpets); 5) *Adwensɔdwensɔhenemmɛn* (chief of urinal); 6) *Gyaamanmmɛnhene* (chief of *gyaaman* trumpets); and 7) *Edwaasemmɛnhene* (chief of *edwaase* trumpets). The home of Nkofehene's stool, Ta Amankwaa, is situated in Atraman near Kumase, but Asantehene Ɔsee Kwadwo settled the newly formed *Nkofe Fekuo* at Adadeɛm, which is also near Kumase. According to the *Nkofehene*, they chose the name Adadeɛm in reference to the town in Banda where most of their kinsmen perished, while those who were left behind but survived the outbreak of chickenpox lived on. Following the war, the losses and bitter experiences with diseases became the great oath (*ntamkɛseɛ*) of the Nkofe group, which is: *Me ka Bana sa* ("I swear by the Banda War").[14]

Apart from its relatively large size compared to similar types in Akan, and even at Manhyia Palace, the physical description of all the ivory trumpets are similar to *nkofe*. They are side-blown, have rectangular lip receivers, and the sound is produced by vibrating the lips. The only difference is that the lead trumpet, *seseɛ*, is slightly smaller than the rest to enable the player to play long verses of surrogate speech. Similar to the *asikabɛn* and all short trumpets (*mmɛntia*), a round hole is drilled into the apex of the lead trumpet for the player to use similar methods of manipulation for speech surrogacy, while the remaining members of the group have just the rectangular lip receiver in addition to the open end. The *nkofe* uses a fixed number of seven players that is further divided into four sections, namely, one *seseɛ* (lead trumpeter), one *afrɛ* (caller), four *agyesoa* (responders), and one *bɔsoɔ* (reinforcer). The *bɔsoɔ* trumpet is bigger than the rest of the trumpets, and, when played individually or collectively, they produce a woody sound (Figure 3.8).

Figure 3.8 The author recording the Nkofe group with two chiefs, Nana Osei Kwadwo (the Abɛnbɛnhene) and Nana Kwaku Agyare II (Gyaamanmmɛnhene). Ash Town, Kumase, January 29, 2017.

Source: Picture by Nana Kwame.

In the Appendix of his monograph, Kaminski republished Sarpong's thirteen verses (*ibid*, 174–177), and although they include English translations, he, like Sarpong, did not analyze the texts. For our purposes, I shall present two verses from my field recordings and follow them with textual analysis. The call and response procedure is similar to the performance framework by *ntahera/kɔkroanya* and *nkɔntwema*, where the call or lead phrases are aligned to the left while the response phrases are indented.

Example 3.9 Awisia Gyae Su (Orphan, Stop Wailing), *Nkofe* (Ivory Trumpets).

Seseɛ	*Seseɛ*
1. Mo nsɔ mu o	Hold your trumpets
2. Awisia gyae su, gyae su	Orphan stop wailing, stop wailing
3. Owuo yi firi tete tete	For death has been in existence since ancient times
Agyesoa **and** *bɔsoɔ*	
4. Aane aane aane aane	Indeed, indeed, indeed, indeed
Afrɛ	
5. Pa pa pa	It's true, it's true, it's true

(Continued)

Example 3.9 (Continued)

Sesɛɛ	Sesɛɛ
Sesɛɛ/afrɛ	
6. Firi tete tete	It's from ancient ancient times
Agyesoa and bɔsoɔ	
7. Aane aane aane aane	Indeed, indeed, indeed, indeed
Sesɛɛ and *afrɛ*	
8. Pa pa Firi tete tete	It's true, it's true from ancient times
Agyesoa and bɔsoɔ	
9. Aane aane aane aane	Indeed, indeed, indeed, indeed
Sesɛɛ and *afrɛ*	
10. Pa pa Firi tete tete	It's true, it's true from ancient times
Agyesoa and bɔsoɔ	
11. Aane aane aane aane	Indeed, indeed, indeed, indeed
Sesɛɛ and *afrɛ*	
12. Pa pa Firi tete tete	It's true, it's true from ancient times
Agyesoa and bɔsoɔ	
13. Aane aane aane aane	Indeed, indeed, indeed, indeed
Sesɛɛ and *afrɛ*	
14. Pa pa Firi tete tete	It's true, it's true from ancient times
Agyesoa and bɔsoɔ	
15. Aane aane aane aane	Indeed, indeed, indeed, indeed
Sesɛɛ and *afrɛ*	
16. Pa pa Firi tete tete	It's true, it's true from ancient times
Agyesoa and bɔsoɔ	
18. Aane aane aane aane	Indeed, indeed, indeed, indeed
Sesɛɛ and *afrɛ*	
19. Pa pa Firi tete tete	It's true, it's true from ancient times
Agyesoa and bɔsoɔ	
20. Aane aane aane aane	Indeed, indeed, indeed, indeed
Sesɛɛ and *afrɛ*	
21. Pa pa Firi tete tete	It's true, it's true from ancient times
Agyesoa and bɔsoɔ	
22. Aane aane aane aane	Indeed, indeed, indeed, indeed
Sesɛɛ and *afrɛ*	
23. Pa pa Firi tete tete.	It's true, it's true from ancient times
Agyesoa and bɔsoɔ	
24. Aane aane aane aane	Indeed, indeed, indeed, indeed
Sesɛɛ and *afrɛ*	
25. Puuuuuuuu Firi tete tete	Puuuuuuuuu from ancient times
Agyesoa and bɔsoɔ	
26. Aane aane aane aane	It's true, it's true from ancient times
Sesɛɛ and *afrɛ*	
27. Pa pa Firi tete oooooooo	Indeed, indeed from ancient times

Apart from separate meetings and observations of performances during ceremonies and rituals, I met the *nkofe* group for feedback conversations on January 29, 2017, ten days following the intensive grand funerary and burial rites for the late Asantehemaa.[15] It was no surprise that they performed the previous verse first, since we were all recovering from the burial rites of the previous week. As in the case of all performing ensembles in the court, ivory trumpets are sounded in times of bereavement to console the king and the people, and that is precisely the basis for the previous verse.[16] A way of expressing sympathy with the king and the royal family and consoling them, the *nkofe* group is sharing a well-known Akan experience and reflection on death: that death is said to be from the beginning of time, and this is not the first or the last time we are facing the wrath of death. As the lead trumpet of the ensemble, the *sesee* trumpeter plays Lines 1–3 alone. He initially calls his group to be ready in Line 1, and then establishes the main theme in Lines 2 and 3. The repetition of end phrases in Lines 2 and 3 are fairly emphatic: it is *gyae su, gyae su* ("stop wailing, stop wailing") in Line 2 and *tete tete* ("ancient times, ancient times") in Line 3. The beginning phrase *awisia*, "an orphan," strikes an unforgettable chord with the ruler since he lost his father, Nana Kwame Boakye-Dankwa, right after his enstoolment in 1999 and then his mother in 2016. *Awisiaa Gyae Su* ("Orphan, Stop Wailing") is a short verse, but the performance architecture is fairly elaborate and includes mechanics of repetition and a quasi-hocket rendition resulting in twenty-seven lines. In its simplest form, the text is: *Efiri tete tete aane ampa, ampa aane* ("it is from ancient times, yes indeed, indeed yes") that is distributed throughout the performance. The *sesee* and *afrɛ* initiate the calls, while four *agyesoa* and one *bosoɔ* combine forces to respond. Techniques of elision apply to two words: *firi*, in the medial position in Line 3 and all the recurring places in the verse, and *pa*, in Line 5 and all the recurring points. In the former, the three-syllable word *e-fi-ri* is reduced to two by suppressing the initial syllable *e*. In the latter, the initial syllable in *am-pa* is also omitted, resulting in *pa pa pa* instead of *ampa ampa ampa*. The beginning phrase in Line 25, *puuuuuuu*, replaces the *pa pa* sounded by the *sesee* as a non-lexical prompter for the group that they are about to conclude the verse. After one cycle of the response phrase by Agyesoa and Bosoɔ, the *sesee* and *afrɛ* conclude the verse by substituting the end repeated phrase *tete* with a long particle, *o*.

Example 3.10 Hwan Na Ɔde Ne Man? ("Who Owns the State?"): *Nkofe* (ivory trumpets).

Sesee/mmranee Nana Kwaku Agyare II (*Gyaamanmmɛnhene*)

1. Ɔsebereso adwera Sɛe	Ɔsebereso adwera Sɛe
2. Ɔsee kronkron	Ɔsɛe, true and pure
3. Abrankɛse Twumasi Ampɔnsɛm	Twumasi Ampɔnsɛm of Abrankɛse
4. Owusu Panin ba Ɔsee Tutu e	Ɔsɛe Tutu, the son of Owusu Panin
5. Daasebrɛ	Endless gratitude
6. Mo nsɔ mu oo	Hold your trumpets
7. Hwan na ɔde ne man?	Who owns the state?
8. Ɔsee Tutu a ɔde ne man	It is Ɔsɛe Tutu who owns his state
9. Ɔde n'ahenie yi firi tete o	His reign dates from the ancient times
10. Yee, Kokofu Sɛe Tutu a,	It's Ɔsɛe Tutu of Kokofu
11. Ɔhen Panin e	The eldest king
12. Asanteman gyinaɛ o	Asanteman flourished
13. Nana de w'ahenɛe yi firi tete o	Nana, his reign dates from the ancient times
14. Hwan na ɔde ne man?	Who owns the state?

(*Continued*)

Example 3.10 (Continued)

Seseɛ/mmranee Nana Kwaku Agyare II (*Gyaamanmmenhene*)

15. Ɔsɛe Tutu a ɔde ne man   It is Ɔsɛe Tutu who owns his state
  16. **Afrɛ:** Aane aane   Aane aane
  17. **Agyesoa/bɔsoɔ:** Paa, paa   Paa, paa
  18. **Afrɛ:** Aane   Aane

Seseɛ

19. Kokofu Sɛe Tutu a   It 's Ɔsɛe Tutu of Kokofu
20. Ɔhen panin e   The eldest king
  21. **Afrɛ:** Aane aane   Aaane aane
  22. **Agyesoa/bɔsoɔ:** Paa, paa   Paa, paa
  22. **Afrɛ:** Aane   Aane

Seseɛ

23. Asanteman gyinaɛ o   Asanteman flourished
  24. **Afrɛ:** Aane aane   Aane aane
  25. **Agyesoa/bɔsoɔ:** Paa, paa   Paa, paa
  26. **Seseɛ/afrɛ:** Aane eeeeee   Aane eeeeee

The previous example is made up of two sets of praise poetry (*mmranee*), sounded entirely by the *seseɛ* player, with no time spared in establishing Ɔpemsoɔ Ɔsɛe Tutu as the one addressed in this verse. Set One is from Lines 1–6, while Set Two is from Lines 7–13; sandwiched between the two sets is Line 6, which is a prompter (or a call to action) for the trumpeters. Usually such a prompter is immediately followed by a call phrase by the *seseɛ* for the rest of the group to respond, but in this instance, he decided to embark on praise poetry that lasted for seven lines from Line 7–13. A much wider range of texts are deployed in this speech surrogacy. Lines 1 and 2 are praises, while Lines 3 and 4 establish the paternity of Ɔpemsoɔ Ɔsɛe Tutu and the location of a village. Twumasi Ampɔnsem, according to Kyerematen, was the maternal grandfather of Kɔmfo Anɔkye, who is the younger sibling of Ɔsɛe Tutu's father *Owusu Panin*, who was the chief of Abrankɛse Nyameani. The beginning phrase in Line 3, *Abrankɛse*, is then understood in the previous context as Twumasi Ampɔnsem who hails from Abrankɛse. Typical of Akan eulogies, this section is concluded with words of gratitude, *daasebrɛ* in Line 5, for we are forever indebted to Ɔsɛe Tutu due to his sacrifices for Asanteman. Line 7 begins with a question that is immediately answered in Line 8, which triggers a distinct theme for Set Two—that Ɔpemsoɔ Ɔsɛe Tutu owns the state. and his reign and leadership traits can be traced to ancient times. As in Set One, there is a reference to the locale Kokofu in Line 10. Oral history has it that the founder of the kingdom belongs to the Ɔyɔko family that relocated from Kokofu to Kwaaman. It has been established that Ɔpemsoɔ Ɔsɛe Tutu was born at Kokofu Anyinam, and his birthplace features prominently in songs, drum poetry, and the verses of ivory trumpets, as evident in the previous *nkofe* verse. The surrogate speech in Set Two is propelled by literary devices including the parallel repetition of end phrases, as in *ɔde ne man*, framed as a question in Lines 7 and 14 and *ɔde ne man*, framed as an answer in Lines 8 and 15. Another repetition of an end phrase at a distance is *firi tete o* in Lines 9 and 13. Elided particles of the beginning syllable are *(Ɔ)Sɛe* in Lines 1, 10, and 19; *(Ɔ)man* in Lines 8, 14, and 15; *(am)Paa* in Lines 17, 22, and 25; and the suppression of the end syllable *Ɔhen(e)* in Lines 11 and 20.

Mmɛntia

Because the first *abɛntia, asikabɛn* (gold trumpet), is kept in the stool room, the *mmɛntiafoɔ* (short trumpeters) are the only trumpeters who take part in stool-room rituals. When the morning worship on Sunday Adae is over, it is the *mmɛntiafoɔ* who play the trumpets to signal to courtiers that the ritual is over and the Asantehene will soon join the Public Assembly. Similar to all the ivory trumpets in Akan that are made from the elephant tusk, *abɛntia* is a side-blown trumpet. All short trumpets have a round hole that is drilled into the apex, which the player covers with his right thumb, and through processes of manipulation (opening and closing), he is able to vary the speech tone (Figure 3.9).

Figure 3.9 Two *mmɛntia* players, Yaw Antwi Boasiako (right) and Kwamena Opoku (left) performing behind the Asantehene when he is formally seated. Awukudae ceremony at Manhyia Palace, Kumase, January 25, 2017.

Source: Picture by author.

The verses of *mmɛntia* are relatively short philosophical statements or proverbs described as epigrams, and as a result, I present six examples of philosophical statements sounded on *mmɛntia* during all kinds of events—celebratory or grief-ridden—including the Akwasidae Public Assembly that I described in the Prologue. I will follow each example with a historicized textual analysis in line with my position that the sounding of *mmɛntia* in a present-day Akwasidae Public Assembly bears testimony to historical markers that are socially maintained over time. In his previously referenced book, Akwasi Sarpong listed a glossary of fourteen examples of *mmɛntia* texts and their English translations, as well as the name of the reigning king who provided the epigram (Sarpong, 1990: 18–20). Joseph Kaminski reproduced Akwasi Sarpong's list in the Appendix of his 2012 publication (Kaminski,

2012: 164–165). I expand the framework by presenting the epigrams in chronological order and following each statement with a critical historical and textual analysis,
as well as performance procedures. My discussion corrects the historical inaccuracies in Kaminski's analysis and rhetorical devices in the texts (*ibid*, 120–124).
I have already discussed the first philosophical statement by Ɔpemsoɔ Osei Tutu in
connection with my theoretical framework in Chapter 1. The logical next step is to
examine the statement provided by Opoku Ware. Yaw Antwi Boasiako, Kwamena
Opoku, Kwame Kumi, and Kwaku Owusu performed all the *mmɛntia* verses for
me in 2009 and 2011, unless otherwise stated. Unlike the sections in the previous
groups of ivory trumpeters, there are only two sections in the short trumpet group—
the lead (*ntosoɔ*) and the rest of the group that responds (*agyesoɔ*).

Example 3.11 Kɔtɔkɔ Poku (Opoku Ware Katakyie): *mmɛntia* (short ivory trumpets).

Ntosoɔ (leader)	**Ntosoɔ (leader)**
1. Kɔtɔkɔ Poku e	Poku the crested porcupine
Agyesoɔ (response)	**Agyesoɔ (response)**
2. Kɔtɔkɔ Poku e	Poku the crested porcupine
3. Kɔtɔkɔ Poku e	Poku the crested porcupine
4. Kɔtɔkɔ Poku e	Poku the crested porcupine
5. Asante Kɔtɔkɔ Poku e	Asante Poku the crested porcupine
Leader and response	**Leader and response**
6. Asante Kɔtɔkɔ Poku e	Asante Poku the crested porcupine

Opoku Ware (1720–1750) succeeded Ɔsɛe Tutu, and shortly thereafter dispelled
all rumors that the demise of the latter would be the end of the relatively new kingdom. To the utmost surprise of many doubters, Opoku Ware, reports Kyerematen,
consolidated and extended Asante's sphere of influence by conquering and annexing
several powerful states, including Akyem Kotoku, Sehwi, Wassa, Bodwesɛanwo,
Takyiman, Gyaaman, Gonja, Dagbon, and areas in the Afram Plains.[17] For
these successes and more, his subjects added *Katakyie* ("the courageous") to
his name. He added new items to the regalia, the most notable of which was the
extensive use of gold and gold-cast symbols on regalia.[18] As we might imagine, conquests essentially translate into economic prosperity, and the reference to Asante as
the Kingdom of Gold began from Opoku Ware's time. As in the case with his predecessor, Opoku Ware requested a short ivory trumpet from the carvers and gave them
the statement included in the previous example to play for him. For the first time,
we have two short trumpets, and as is typical in African musical organization, they
engage in dialogic call-response format. The lead trumpet, *ntosoɔ*, plays a phrase for
the second trumpeter to respond to by repeating the entire linear phrase, and after
two repetitions, the leader inserts *Asante* as the beginning phrase in Line 5, which is
immediately repeated by both the leader and responding trumpet in Line 6 to conclude the verse. Depending on the occasion and number of trumpeters, there may be
more than a single responder. *Kɔtɔkɔ Poku* can be interpreted as "the brave and all-
conquering Poku" or "Poku of Asante," as I have noted previously that the crested
porcupine is interchangeable with Asante as a people. It is one and the same with the
larger implication and recognition that there is value in courage and heroism.

Example 3.12 Kɔtɔnonko (Go and Fight Him), *Abɛntia* (Short Ivory Trumpet)
    by Opanin Yaw Sarfo.

Kɔtononko o	Go and fight him
Kɔtononko o	Go and fight him
Kɔtononko o	Go and fight him

Kɔtononko

Kɔtononko is the poetic contraction of the normal spoken sentence *kɔ na wo ne no nkɔ ko* ("go and fight with him/her"). The *no* in the sentence is gender neutral, but I have translated it as *him* assuming that only men engaged in warfare in those days. As I have noted before, the players of short trumpets are always behind the ruler, and during ceremonies the player will play *kɔtononko* intermittently. Each performance involves repeating the epigram three times. In 2011, I recorded Opanin Yaw Sarfo, who had been playing the *kɔtononkɔ* short trumpet since 1967. Yaw Sarfo and the chief of the previously named trumpet, Nana Akwasi Boateng II (*Kɔtononkohene*), are both located at Pankrono Atafoa, and I recorded the oral history of this unique instrument from them. As the newly enstooled Asantehene and the 7th occupant of the Gold Stool, King Ɔsɛe Asibe Bonsu (1800–1823) asked the instrument-makers for a new short trumpet. He gave it to the *mmɛntiafoɔ* and asked them to play *kɔtononko* as his epigram (Figure 3.10). His promise to the chiefs and elders of the kingdom was that he would consolidate territorial gains and add new states to the kingdom.

Figure 3.10 Opanin Yaw Sarfo with his ivory trumpet, Kɔtononko, in the playing position. Manhyia Palace, January 16, 2017.

Source: Picture by author.

Ɔsɛe Asibe Bonsu's extraordinary accomplishments in forging a strong and loyal kingdom are comparable to those of Ɔpemsoɔ Ɔsɛe Tutu and Opoku Ware. His personal sword, Kyerematen reports, was made to rank next to that of Opoku Ware's Mpɔnpɔnsuo sword.[19] His real name was Ɔsɛe Asibe or Ɔsɛe Tutu Kwame, but he added Bonsu after he defeated a combined army of Fante States, and upon inquiring about the most powerful animal in the ocean, he was told that it was *bonsu* (the whale), so he added Bonsu to his name and became known as Ɔsɛe Asibe Bonsu. Impressed with his accomplishments all the way from Kumase to the Fante coast of Anomabo, the Asante also referred to him as Ɔsɛe Bonsu *a ɔbɔɔ hyɛn* ("Ɔsɛe Bonsu who builds the canoe"). Sticking with his chosen epigram, Ɔsɛe Asibe Bonsu successfully repressed all uprisings within the kingdom, including those of the Asene, Fante, Akyem Abuakwa, Akyem Kotoku, Akwapem, Gyaaman, and several coastal states, earning him the honorific *ɔko kyere ahene* ("he fights to capture kings"). With this brief comment about Ɔsɛe Bonsu, it is understandable why he created the short trumpet and its epigram *kɔtononko*. As a brief side note, his reign is well-documented in written records, as Europeans were well entrenched in the then-Gold Coast by the nineteenth century. As mentioned in Chapter 2, he was the first Asante king to receive British trade representatives from the African Company led by Thomas E. Bowdich in 1817, which was followed three years later in 1820 by receiving an envoy of the British Government, Joseph Dupuis, who established the first diplomatic relations between the two kingdoms. In what has become a classic text, but not devoid of essentialized characterizations, Bowdich recorded his travel to the kingdom and his reception in vivid detail, and to this day, his text represents comprehensive insights into the Asante Kingdom in the early nineteenth century.[20]

Example 3.13 Nyame Na Yɛɛ Wo (It Was God Who Created You), *Mmɛntia* (Short Ivory Trumpets).

***Ntosoɔ* (leader)**	***Ntosoɔ* (leader)**
1. Nyame na ɛyɛɛ wo	It's God who created you
***Agyesoɔ* (response)**	***Agyesoɔ* (response)**
2. Nyame na ɛyɛɛ wo	It's God who created you
3. Nyame na ɛyɛɛ wo	It's God who created you
4. Nyame na ɛyɛɛ wo	It's God who created you
5. Agyeman e	Agyeman
Leader and response	**Leader and response**
6. Nyame na ɛyɛɛ wo	It's God who created you

The tumultuous reign of Agyeman Prɛmpɛ (1888–1931), who is fondly called Akwasi Prɛmpɛ and was the 13th occupant of the Gold Stool, is well documented by historians, and I covered it briefly in Chapter 2.[21] According to Nana Owusu Mran (*Mmɛntiahene*, chief of short trumpeters), it was during the welcome ceremonies for Agyeman Prɛmpɛ in 1924 that the late Ɔpanin Kwaku Frimpɔn, a member of the *mmɛntiahyɛnfoɔ*, remarked at the time that Prɛmpɛ is in excellent shape, considering the hardships he went through in addition to having endured a twenty-eight-year absence from his kingdom. Ɔpanin Frimpɔn concluded that it was truly God who created King Prɛmpɛ, and expressed his sentiment as an epigram on the short trumpet. As had been the practice since antiquity, they carved a new trumpet to represent that event and observation. Like previous examples, similar processes of linear repetition and interactive call-response play are activated here. After four lines of repetition, the addressive Agyemang Prɛmpɛ is finally identified in Line 5. The addressive in Line 5 has the dual role of signifying to the trumpeters that they should all sound Line 6 as the concluding phrase. Structurally, we notice a scheme where the name of the addressive is mentioned in the penultimate phrase, followed by the concluding phrase that is sounded by all the short trumpeters together.

Example 3.14 Atoto Yɛ Sane (We Are Untying Knots), *Mmɛntia* (Short Ivory Trumpets).

Ntosoɔ (leader)	*Ntosoɔ* (leader)
1. Atoto yɛ sane	We are untying tangled threads
Agyesoɔ (response)	*Agyesoɔ* (response)
2. Atoto yɛ sane	We are untying tangled threads
3. Atoto yɛ sane	We are untying tangled threads
4. Atoto yɛ sane	We are untying tangled threads
5. Ɔsɛe e	Ɔsɛe e
6. Ɔsɛe e	Ɔsɛe e
7. Ɔsɛe Agyeman e	Ɔsɛe Agyeman
Leader and response	**Leader and response**
8. Atoto yɛ sane	We are untying tangled threads

The previous philosophical statement encapsulates Otumfoɔ Sir Ɔsɛe Agyeman Prɛmpɛ II's main goal for his thirty-nine-year reign. He pledged to the chiefs and people of Asanteman during his enstoolment in 1931 that he would disentangle all the knots and divisions in the kingdom and restore the union of states that had been dispersed. His praise name was Kwame Kyeretwie, "Kwame who captures the leopard with his bare hands." Born in 1892, his childhood was marked by the total disintegration of the Asante Kingdom, following, as I noted previously and elsewhere, the eventual defeat of the kingdom by the British. Continuing from where his predecessor left off, Prɛmpɛ II began his reign as chief of Kumase and ended in 1970 as the Asantehene (Asante king). On January 31, 1935, he finally succeeded in re-establishing a substantial number of states and subsequently restoring the Asante Kingdom with an official act by the British Colonial government.[22] The previous statement (Example 3.14) metaphorically describes the daunting task of not only untying several strands of politically tangled threads but also includes recovering one of the largest pieces of tangible and intangible stool regalia in Sub-Saharan Africa. The recovery includes the visual and performing arts, the social and economic order, and the religious and philosophical worldview, ensuring peaceful coexistence and a multitude of tasks. His eventual success in the previous mission is the reason why the visual and performing arts have continued to historicize the Asante past and present. It bears observing that, similar to his forebears, Prɛmpɛ II's activities in his thirty-nine-year reign demand courage, diplomacy, strategic planning, and bravery to accomplish such daunting tasks. In 1947, he was awarded a Knighthood of the British Empire (KBE) and became known as Otumfoɔ Sir Ɔsɛɛ Agyeman Prɛmpɛ II. In addition to all of this, he succeeded in steering his kingdom on the right course by living peacefully with the rest of the independent kingdoms in the Gold Coast, which resulted in the founding of a new nation state, Ghana, in 1957, with Kwame Nkrumah as the first president. As in the previous statements, Example 3.14 uses noted procedures by the *mmɛntia*, including the dialogic interactive structure and two repetitions of the statement followed by releasing the name of the addressive. They hinted at the first name *Ɔsɛɛ* in Line 6, but since there are several past kings with that first name, they added the middle name *Agyeman* in Line 7 to remove any doubt about which of the Ɔsɛɛs they were referring to. They finally concluded the verse with the archetypal repetition of the statement in Line 8 by all the *mmɛnita*: there is value in courage, diplomacy, and strategic planning.

Example 3.15 Wo Maame Wɔ Hen? ("Where is Your Mother?"): *Mmɛntia* (short ivory trumpets).

Ntosoɔ (leader)	*Ntosoɔ* (leader)
1. Wo maame wɔ he?	Where is your mother?
Agyesoɔ (response)	*Agyesoɔ* (response)
2. Wo maame wɔ he?	Where is your mother?
3. Wo maame wɔ he?	Where is your mother?
4. Wo maame wɔ he?	Where is your mother?
5. Opoku Katakyie	Opoku Katakyie
Ntosoɔ/agyesoɔ	*Ntosoɔ/agyesoɔ*
6. Wo maame wɔ he?	Where is your mother?

The 15th occupant of the Gold Stool, Otumfoɔ Opoku Ware II, contributed the previous statement to the ever-expanding short trumpets and repertoire, which indicates the crucial factor of matrilineal identity in Asante. Like his predecessors in the twentieth century, he was born in 1919 when the kingdom and royal family were in disarray, witnessed the restoration of the kingdom, and grew up during the pro-independence movements and eventual coming of age of the new nation of Ghana in 1957. He continued to consolidate the achievements of his predecessors in forging a long-lasting Asante unity within a new nation state, and for that reason he is seen as one of the most peaceful kings in modern times. One of his regrets was that his mother passed away and was not around to observe his enstoolment ceremony and enjoy the fruits of her labor as the mother of a king. In remembrance of his mother, he requested a short trumpet from the carvers, gave it to the *mmɛntiafoɔ*, and asked them to play the previous statement for him. I have previously alluded to the praise name, *Katakyie*, of the first Opoku Ware, and because he chose Opoku Ware as his stool name, he became Opoku Ware II with the same praise name. The poetic devices are the same as the previous example's. After the usual repetition from Lines 1–4, the addressive is identified with the phrase *Opoku Katakyie* in Line 5, followed by the concluding phrase in Line 6.

Example 3.16 Wo Yɛ Dehye Dada ("You Are a Royal from the Beginning of Time"): *Abɛntia* (short ivory trumpet).

Leader

1. Wo yɛ dehye dada o	You are a royal from the beginning of time
2. Wo yɛ dehye dada o	You are a royal from the beginning of time
3. Ɔsɛe e	Ɔsɛe e
4. Ɔsɛe Tutu e	Ɔsɛe Tutu e
5. Wo yɛ dehye dadadadadadada	You are a royal from the beginning of time

The previous statement is performed on *asikabɛn* (the gold trumpet), the first short trumpet associated with Ɔpemsoɔ Ɔsɛe Tutu, but I am going to connect it to the reign of the present ruler, Otumfoɔ Ɔsɛe Tutu II. As the 16th occupant of the Gold Stool, he chose the name of the founder of the kingdom, Ɔsɛe Tutu, for his stool name. Although he has added a substantial number of items to the regalia, including the performing and visual arts, he is yet to create a new trumpet and a statement for the short trumpeters. Instead of a new trumpet and a philosophical statement, he has embraced the previous epigram that Kɔmfo Anɔkye created for Ɔpemsoɔ Ɔsɛe Tutu more than 300 years ago. His reasoning is that, as his name implies, he is Ɔsɛe Tutu Ababio (literally, Ɔsɛe Tutu has returned) so he does not need a new short horn or a statement. We are twenty years into his reign, and the trumpeters still perform the previous statement for him. What is not certain is if he might change his mind, or if an incident will inspire a statement from him. Until then, this is going to be his statement for the *mmɛntiafoɔ*. In order to maintain the tradition where only one player is responsible for performing the *asikabɛn*, the previous epigram is performed on a single short trumpet at all times, even if several short trumpeters are available. The repetition of linear units is a defining performance feature in *mmɛntia*. Lines 1–2 present linear repetition, while Lines 3–4 present the addressive by announcing the first or proper name *Ɔsɛe*. The last name is added to the first name, as in *Ɔsɛe Tutu* in Line 4, in order to offset the apparent ambiguity in stating only the first name of the addressive; for, as I previously noted, there are several kings with Ɔsɛe as their first name. As the penultimate phrase, the full name in Line 4 is a prompt for those informed that he is going to sound the concluding phrase in Line 5, which is a repetition of Lines 1 and 2 with multiple duplication on the syllable *dada*. End particles *o* in Lines 1–2 and *e* in Lines 3–4 are literary devices meant to give the phrases additional prominence. Lines 1 and 2 are sustained longer than Lines 3 and 4. In the former phrases, the end particles add a higher pitch to the otherwise repeated low pitch in the two-syllable *dada*. Lastly, the end particle *o* follows the type of noun that represents an idea, while *e* is appended to the type of noun that identifies a name. The multiple duplications of the end phrase *dadadadadadada* in Line 5 confers an aesthetic accent and intensifier to the two-syllable word.

All territorial and high-ranking chiefs owe at least one *abεntia* as part of the stool regalia, in addition to a philosophical statement or a proverb that succeeding chiefs inherit and maintain. Instead of preserving the inherited statements, succeeding Asante kings are expected to create an entirely new short trumpet as well as their philosophical statement. As a result, there are over a dozen short trumpets and several epigrams that are part of the heritage of stool regalia associated with the Asante king. It appears that there are two types of *mmεntia*: regular and irregular. The regular type of *mmεntia* is the relatively short and small type, as the suffix *-tia*, meaning "short," implies. The shorter trumpets produce a reedy sound with a wider distribution in Akan areas. The irregular types are slightly bigger than the regular one, in addition to producing a slightly lower sonority. They are only located at Manhyia Palace, and they include kɔtononko ("Go and Fight Him"), sɔkɔbεn (elephant trumpet), asesebεn (speaking trumpet), and mmɔdwemmɔdwe (jaw trumpet). While I worked with the *Kɔtononkɔ* player in 2011, I have not seen or heard the other types performed. It appears that in *Ceremonial Horns of the Ashanti*, Akwasi Sarpong has a picture of seven *mmεntia* that shows different sizes and shapes, and it is likely that both types were in use in the 1970s and 1980s when he did his research (Sarpong, 1990: 5). As part of my multi-sited research, I spent two weeks in Britain from November 19 to December 3, 2016, and spent time in the British Museum and Library in London, along with other locations both inside and outside London. The British Museum has the *mmɔdwemmɔdwe* type of *abεntia* in its collection.

Significance of the number seven

There is no denying the pervasive use of the number seven in any branch of Asante (and Akan) discourse, and my present book is no exception. I am in the third chapter, and I am sure that I have referenced seven in various ways, both directly and indirectly, including the use of seven trumpets in each ivory trumpet group.[23] The Akan worldview and philosophy confers perfection to the number seven because it is comprised of a combination of the numbers three and four. These philosophical reflections are demonstrated in practical terms in a sophisticated number of ways. To begin with, the Akan proto-religious and agricultural calendar (*asranaa*) that I mentioned in the previous chapters has seven days in a week, which means that the notion of eight days (*nnawɔtwe*) is a modern misrepresentation. The first day is a reference point in order to compute the days in a week. That is, if we select Monday as our starting point, then we count from Tuesday to Monday for a total of seven days. With regard to matrilineal groupings, the Akan recognize seven major groups, and the naming of eight matrilineages or clans began with R.S. Rattray's 1923 publication on the subject, which from all indications was based on misinformation. For instance, seven clay bowls representing the foundational Akan clans (*abusua*) are placed at the entrance to the sacred forest at Asantemanso (see for instance, Shujaa, 2014: 69). In its simplest form, the matrilineages are Aduana, Asona, Asenee, Asakyiri, Bretuo, Ɔyoko, and Ɛkoɔna.[24] Further, the Akan transferred the notion of perfection to the development of towns and urban centers. According to Anquandah, the famous trading town of Nsɔkɔ had seven suburbs (1982a: 96–98).

The concept of seven as a perfect spiritual force has led the Akan to consider multiples of seven to be a symbolic aggregate. Here are selected examples: *Nkukua Mmedie* consists of seventy-seven drums, but the great Priest Kɔmfo Anɔkye ordained that they should not play all seventy-seven drums in a single ceremony (see Figure 4.6). After the descent of the Gold Stool on the faithful Friday, Kɔmfo Anɔkye is said to have listed seventy-seven injunctions to regulate moral and religious conduct of the people (Kyerematen, 1966: 235). Ɔpemsoɔ Ɔsɛe Tutu is recognized for embarking on seventy-seven wars, and while the exact numbers may not be known, the Akan method of articulating a perfect endeavor is to assign multiples of the perfect number to Anɔkye's injunctions or Ɔsɛe Tutu's wars. The size of urbanized centers that usually serve as capitals of Akan states is distinguished by the number of suburbs; Takyiman, Kumase, Asantemanso, and Abankɛsɛɛso in Dɛnkyera all had seventy-seven suburbs. For instance, the Asante refer to several suburbs in the capital as *Kumase abrɔnoo aduoson nson* ("the seventy-seven suburbs of Kumase"). Kenya Shujaa reports further multiples of seven at Bono Manso and Adansemanso, with each having 177 streets (Shujaa, 2014: 51). Essentially, seventy-seven may be more symbolic than real in many situations, since the goal is to identify with the spiritually perfect number. The Akan notion of seventy-seven (or 177) is a way of expressing several suburbs. At the beginning of this section, I stated that the number seven is perfect because it is made up of three and four. Let me unpack Akan notions of these two numbers by first examining the number three. Three is spiritually linked to the three foundational elements of creation—the Court Crier, the Creator's Drummer, and the Executioner.

Significance of the number three

A brief synopsis of the prevalence of three in the Akan worldview and philosophy is as follows. The representation of the Tree of God (*Nyame Dua*) is a three-pronged abstraction that, in the past, was fixed in a compound house to hold an earthenware pot to collect rain (*Nyankonsuo*, God's rain) for washing the face three times in the morning.[25] In times of distress, grief, or national tragedy, the Asante king sits on cushions with his back propped against a modeled *Nyame Dua* ("God's Tree") to express his reliance on the Supreme Being for spiritual fortitude in order to go through a physically challenging time.[26] Three concentric circles embody the highest conception and expression of all Akan Adinkra pictographic writing, and not surprisingly, it is called *Adinkrahene* ("King of Adinkra"). That the consummate symbol representing the highest creative impulse is the boundless and limitless symbol of the universe is a deeper reflection of Akan experience and social values. The Akan hearth (*mokyea*) consists of three clay mounds in the form of a tripod, either with two sides connected and one side open, or with all three sides open. Cooking for the entire household is done on the hearth. Three gifts of the same or different objects imply *ɔdɔnsa*, which literally means that love is never exhausted, just as creation will never be exhausted. My last example is that the name Mɛnsa (also spelled as Mensah) is given to a third-born son, while a third-born daughter is Mansa (also spelled as Mansah). The Akan saying is *kuro biara Mɛnsa wɔ mu* ("there is an individual named Mɛnsa or Mansa in every town"). The Akan will tell you that it is no coincidence that individuals named Mɛnsa or Mansa are unique, enthusiastic, and wise, as exemplified by the cultural activist John Mensah Sarbah (affectionately called Kofi Mensah) in the colonial Gold Coast.[27] Mensah Sarbah's cultural activism and his leadership in the Aborigines' Rights Protection Society, founded in 1897, paved the way for Ghana's independence from British Colonial rule. As in the case of multiples of seven, the Akan ascribe spiritual attributes to multiples of three. One of the methods of mitigating potentially sanctioned words in formal discourse, especially in public, is to precede a statement with *sebɛ sɛbe o mpreaduasa*—roughly translated as "apologies, apologies thirty times," after which the speaker is tacitly allowed to utter politically incorrect words without facing the wrath of legal summons or ridicule by the elders.[28] There is also recognition of a woman who takes care of not only her own children, but children from other homes, with the Akan saying: *ɔno na wa'wo abaduasa nso ɔgye abayɛn.* That is, "she has given birth to thirty children, yet she still raises additional children."

As we can imagine, our unpacking of seven as a spiritually perfect number in Akan will be incomplete unless we interpret the number four and its multiples. As I previously mentioned in this chapter, the funeral and burial of the late Asantehemaa Afia Kobi Sɛwaa Ampem II lasted for four days, from Monday, January 16 to Thursday, January 19, 2017.[29] The Akan calendar (*Asranaa*) is calculated with the foundational knowledge of nine cycles of forty days in a year. Technically, the six weeks that comprise a cycle is forty-two days, but the Akan refer to the total number of days as *adaduanan* (forty days).[30] The Akan developed a calendar as a guide for agricultural pursuits, to mark special days for performing certain rituals, and to point to the remote origins for the use of the numbers three, four, and seven. This method of aggregating numbers is no different from multiples of seven and three, with their ambiguous designation, but does point to a worldview and philosophy that strives for the perfect order. Giving birth to several children is symbolically aggregated to mean thirty, or embarking on several wars of expansion is reckoned as seventy-seven wars, and so forth. In addition to the seventh-day ritual for a deceased person, the fortieth and eightieth days after someone's passing were in the past adhered to as part of post-burial remembrances. Ultimately, the Akan worldview and spiritual life is ordered in threes, fours, and sevens, for there is value in spiritually perfect numbers. It is the collective Akan experience in identifying with the spiritual order and a perfect universe comprised of the perfect number seven that inform the selection of seven ivory trumpets in each group. I will now turn my attention to the cane flute, *durugya*. As I mentioned in my opening paragraph, the *durugya* is not part of the ivory trumpet groups (*asɔkwafoɔ*), but as an aerophone, I am placing it here for the sake of convenience.

Durugya

The hauntingly mournful tone of *durugya* (cane flute) is not only unique but also distinct, as it is the only aerophone made out of the stem of a cane (*demire*) and because it is limited in its distribution in Akan courts. A different type of flute, *atɛntɛbɛn*, however, was relatively widespread in Akan communities as part of ensembles that combined drums and voices or played by themselves in a group. The former were called *atɛntɛ*, while the latter were referred to simply as pipes.[31] The *durugya* is usually twenty-four inches long, while the *atɛntɛbɛn* is usually half the length of the *durugya* and mainly made from a cane stem. When making the *durugya* flute, they remove the soft tissue from inside the cane and four finger holes are carved in front from approximately a third of the way down. The index and middle fingers of the left hand correspond to the two holes on top, while the index and the middle fingers of the right hand are for the two lower holes. The embouchure at one end makes it possible to play in a transverse or vertical position. In order to prevent the cane from decaying easily from saliva, almost a third of the flute is covered with black felt from the mouthpiece down. There is a small hole slightly below the embouchure that is covered with mirlitons or spider membrane (*afafa*) for a buzzing sound. The opening at the end is decorated with a sponge-like raffia (*ɛdoa*) that is made to hang as an extension of the flute (Figure 3.11). *Duru-gya* (literally, "I'll get there before you") is a compound word that essentially means that doors are readily opened for the *durugya* player while others are prevented from entering.

Figure 3.11 Kwadwo Agyemang (left) and Kwaku Gyabaah (right) holding the *durugya* flute. Manhyia Palace, January 19, 2017.

Source: Picture by author.

The modern history of *durugya* at Manhyia Palace parallels almost a century of active service on the part of the late chief of *durugya*, Nana Yaw Opoku Mensah. In 2009, Nana Yaw Mensah shared with me how he acquired his skills and eventually became the chief of *durugya*. It all began in 1924 during a welcome gathering to celebrate the return of Asantehene Agyemang Prɛmpɛ from his exile in Seychelles. At the ceremony, the Kukuomhene had a *durugya* player in his procession, and when he got to where Prɛmpɛ was sitting, those around him pointed to the *durugya*, saying, "Nana, here is one of your flutes." In a conversation with the *Kukuomhene*, the Asantehene informed him that he would like to reestablish the *durugya* in his court. The *Kukuomhene* indicated his willingness to teach anyone from the Asantehene's court, if they were prepared to travel with him to Kukuom after the ceremony. Nana Yaw Mensah, then in his teens, volunteered to go. After a year of studying with an expert in Kukuom, he returned to Kumase, where he has been playing for the court for over eight decades. Before retiring in 2005, Nana Yaw Mensah served four kings: Agyeman Prɛmpɛ, Ɔsɛe Agyeman Prɛmpɛ II, Opoku Ware II, and the present king, Ɔsɛe Tutu II. Nana Yaw Mensah passed away on April 15, 2016, and his family estimates he was over 120 years old. His two grandchildren, Kwadwo Agyemang and Kwaku Gyabaah, are now serving the court as *durugya* flutists (*durugyakafoɔ*). In the Asantehene's court, *durugya* is mostly played solo, and in some cases as a duet with a singer. As a solo instrument, the player, together with *mmɛntia* (short ivory trumpets) and the bards (*kwadwomfoɔ*), stands behind the king so that he may hear the flute and the bards. Through its poetic verses, and by way of instrumental surrogate speech, the *durugya* recounts history in addition to regular praise poetry. In addition to speech mode, the *durugya* sometimes plays music, so strictly speaking it can and does play music. In a sense, there are two types of *durugya* playing: *ayan* (loosely, poetry) and *nnwom* (songs or metered music). Like drum poetry, *ayan* is performed by way of instrumental surrogacy and adheres to speech contours and stylized Twi, while the latter refers to the singing or a more melodic rendition of poetic texts. Since he had retired, I recorded Nana Yaw Mensah in 2009 and 2011 at his home in Sepɛ Owusu Ansa, a suburb of Kumase.

Example 3.17 Mama me Homene so (I Have Stirred Myself), *Durugya* (Cane Flute).

	English Translation
1. M'ama me homene so	1. I have stirred myself
2. M'ama me homene so	2. I have stirred myself
3. M'ama me homene so	3. I have stirred myself
4. Ɔdomankoma kyerɛma sɛ	4. The Creator's Drummer says
5. W'ama ne homene so	5. He as stirred himself
6. Ɔdomankoma kyerɛma sɛ	6. The Creator's Drummer says
7. W'ama ne homene so	7. He has stirred himself
8. Akyaa se Amoa Wusu Ansa	8. Akyaa's Dad Amoawusu Ansa
9. Ɔsɛi Tutu Daasebrɛ	9. Ɔsɛe Tutu our benefactor
10. Akyaa se Amoa Wusu Ansa	10. Akyaa's Dad Amoa Wusu Ansa
11. Ɔsɛi Tutu Kantinka	11. Ɔsɛe Tutu the valiant one

	English Translation
12. Ɔsɛi Tutu Daasebrɛ e	12. Ɔsɛe Tutu our benefactor
13. Okumanin	13. Killer of pythons
14. Ɔdomankoma Kyerɛma sɛ	14. The Creator's Drummer says
15. M'ama ne homene so	15. He has roused himself for action
16. M'ama me homene so ɔkorɔntɔ	16. I have stirred myself ɔkorɔntɔ
17. M'ama me homene so apem bɛba	17. I have stirred myself for thousand will come
18. M'ama me homene so ɔdɛɛfoɔ ba	18. I have stirred myself our benefactor's child
19. Akyaa se Amoa Wusu Ansa	19. Akyaa's Dad Amoa Wusu Ansa
20. Ɔsɛe Tutu Daasebrɛ	20. Ɔsɛe Tutu our benefactor
21. Akyaa se Amoa Wusu Ansa	21. Akyaa's Dad Amoa Wusu Ansa
22. Ɔsɛe Tutu Kantinka	22. Ɔsɛe Tutu the valiant one
23. Ɔsɛe Tutu Daasebrɛ e	23. Ɔsɛe Tutu our benefactor
24. Okumanini	24. Killer of pythons
25. Ɔdomankoma Kyerɛma se	25. The Creator's Drummer says
26. W'ma ne homene so	26. He has stirred himself

With the aid of an embouchure and four finger holes, the *durugya* flute is capable of playing fairly long verses, placing it squarely in the category of surrogate instruments that communicate by what Kwabena Nketia has referred to as speech mode (Nketia, 1971: 699–732).[32] In the *durugya*'s repertoire, the previous example is designated as *ayan*. Thus, it is poetry played with the flute, as opposed to drum poetry (*ayan*) performed by the Creator's Drummer (*Ɔkyerɛma*) on the pair of *atumpan* drums. In the process, the *durugya* flutist aligns his verse with the Akan concept of creation, whereas the Creator's Drummer is the embodiment of knowledge in an orderly universe.

The mechanism of instrumental speech that is used in place of spoken language is not lost on the Akan, as they refer to the *durugya* player as *durugyakani* (*durugya-ka-ni*)—literally, "one who speaks (ka) with/through the *durugya*." A major characteristic of the previous *durugya* verse is the parallel repetition of linear units. Line 1 is repeated three times (Lines 1–3) to stress to the gathering that the *durugya* is ready for action. The relatively low tone of the *durugya* is not suitable for processions, and it is only when the king is formerly seated in state that the player joins the bards (*kwadwomfoɔ*) and players of short trumpets (*mmɛntiafoɔ*) behind him. So, after a period of inactivity, he has arisen and is fired up for action. He invokes the attributes of the Creator's Drummer (*Ɔdomankoma Kyerɛma*) as his entry point in Line 4, as well as in a series of repetitions in Lines 6, 14, and 25. The aforementioned lines, however, are supported by the linear phrases immediately following in Lines 7, 15, and 26. A particularly interesting feature of the parallel repetition of linear units is that the beginning phrases, *m'ama* ("I have") in Lines 1–3, are substituted with *w'ama* ("he has") in Lines 5, 7, and 26, thus transforming the statement from the first-person to the second-person pronoun. If we consider the three foundational elements of creation, then it is understandable why Nana Yaw Mensah would invoke Akan values associated with the

Creator's Drummer to justify his participation in the event. Consequentially, he is aligning his *durugya* poetry with that of the Creator's Drummer, for it embodies knowledge.

After consolidating his participation in the ceremony, he resorts to an addressive, Ɔsɛe Tutu, as the focus of his verse in Lines 9, 11–12, 20, and 22–23. We may recall that Ɔsɛe Tutu established the foundations of the Asante Kingdom in the late seventeenth to early eighteenth centuries, while the stool name of the present ruler is Ɔsɛe Tutu II. This temporal link is not by accident; Ɔsɛe Tutu (the founder) may be long gone, but he lives on in the current ruler. In a series of parallel repetitions, Ɔsɛe Tutu's name is followed by his traits, which are drawn from a palate of stock expressions but strategically placed at the end of linear units. The traits are *daasebrɛ* in Lines 9, 20, and 23, and *kantinka* in Lines 11 and 22. The first end pattern, *daasebrɛ*, is an expression for an individual who deserves everlasting praise, for, among others, Ɔsɛe Tutu defeated and annexed several Akan States in order to establish the kingdom. The bravery of the king is also expressed as *kantinka* ("the valiant one"). Although the multisyllabic phrase *okumanini*, in Lines 13 and 24, is part of the traits and hence a stock expression, it is not conceived of as an end pattern in a parallel repetition. *Okumanini* translates as "the killer of pythons" and denotes indomitable power or fearlessness. For these attributes, the Creator's Drummer, represented by the *durugya* player, has stirred himself up to play his *durugya* poetry—*ayan*.

Lines 16–18 are statements that dwell on parallel repetitions of linear units with stock expressions as end patterns: *ɔkorɔntɔ* in Line 16 is an archetypal Akan response to greetings and is presented here as a sign of admiration that one may have for the greeter. *Apem bɛ ba* in Line 17 is the symbolic axiom during the inter-war years that referenced the quills of the porcupine (*kɔtɔkɔ* in Twi) for heroism. If you kill a thousand Asante soldiers, a thousand will immediately replace those killed. For the previous deeds, Asante kings (dead or alive) are the benefactors of the living, hence the expression *ɔdɛefoɔba* in Line 18. The historical names in Lines 8, 10, 19, and 21 are quite obscure apart from knowledge that the entire linear unit is an interpolation that seems to break the monotony of parallel repetitions. Further, we need to account for the end particle *e*, which is appended to the addressives in Lines 12 and 23. Pitches of end particles are sustained longer than the other phrases and draw attention to the phrases to which they are attached. Although repeated throughout the verse, the concluding phrases in Lines 25–26 impart a sense of closure to the performance. At the global level, it appears that a tripartite structural scheme guiding the delivery of this characteristically *durugya* verse is probable. Section 1 includes Lines 1–7 that activates the *durugya* player's participation in a ceremony with self-serving proclamation, Section 2 is made up of Lines 8–15 that emphasize addressives and attributes, and finally, Section 3 involves Lines 16–26, which concentrate on greetings. This brings us to our final *durugya* verse, Example 3.18, which, although similar in terms of poetic mechanisms, is the *nnwom* (song) type.

Example 3.18 Ɔwea Kwaduampɔn Kyerefoɔ (The Tree Bear), *Durugya* (Cane Flute).

1. Ɔwea e Kwaduampɔn e	1. The Tree Bear
2. W'ano asɛm kyɛn wo o	2. Your utterances are greater than you
3. Ɔwea e Kwaduampɔn	3. The Tree Bear
4. W'ano asɛm kyɛn wo.	4. Your utterances are greater than you
5. Ɔwea Kwaduampɔn Kyerefoɔ ɔdedua e	5. The Tree Bear
6. Ɔwea Kwaduampɔn Kyerefoɔ ɔdedua e	6. The Tree Bear
7. Ɔwea e bra o Kwaduampɔn e	7. Come the Tree Bear
8. W'ano asɛm kyɛn wo o	8. Your utterances are greater than you
9. W'ano asɛm kyɛn wo.	9. Your utterances are greater than you
10. Ɔwea e Kwaduampɔn e	10. The Tree Bear
11. W'ano asɛm kyɛn wo o	11. Your utterances are greater than you
12. Ɔwea e Kwaduampɔn e	12. The Tree Bear
13. W'ano asɛm kyɛn wo.	13. Your utterances are greater than you
14. Ɔwea Kwaduampɔn Kyerefoɔ ɔdedua e	14. The Tree Bear
15. Ɔwea Kwaduampɔn Kyerefoɔ ɔdedua e	15. The Tree Bear
16. Ɔwea e bra o Kwaduampɔn e	16. Come the Tree Bear
17. W'ano asɛm kyɛn wo o	17. Your utterances are greater than you
18. W'ano asɛm kyɛn wo.	18. Your utterances are greater than you

The parallel repetition of linear units in the previous example are meant to caution enemies of the state, or individuals in society who refuse to heed advice, that their eventual demise is their own doing. The tree bear (*ɔwea*) is notorious for crying out loud in the forest at night. For nearby animals whose lives are in danger due to the excessive noise, there is no feeling of sympathy; for instead of heeding advice to be quiet or even to relocate to another abode, the tree bear is instead dug in with his cries. The graphic imagery of uncompromising behavior is represented by the end phrase *ɔdɛdua* in Lines 5–6 and 14–15. Although a single word with three syllables, *ɔ-de-dua* describes how the tree bear is fastened to the tree, despite attempts to convince it to leave a particular tree and relocate to another, with the median phrase *bra o* in Lines 7 and 16. *Bra o* literally means "come," but in this context it is intended to communicate feelings of concern in the short and long term for the potential consequences of uncompromising behavior. Compared to Example 3.17, the pitch of the end particle *e* in Lines 1, 5, 6, 14, and 15 are held longer, while Lines 5, 6, 14, and 15 represent relatively long linear phrases in the verse. The previous verse can be broken down into four segments. Lines 1–4 represent the first segment, whereby the sense of repose is signified by the end phrase *wo* in Line 4 without the particle *o*, as in Line 2, to convey a sense of temporary reprieve. The second segment is from Lines 5–9 with similar devices that render the temporary rest easy to comprehend, since Line 8 is repeated in Line 9 without the particle *o*. Lines 10–13 represent the third segment, but it is the exact repetition of the first segment, while the fourth segment, Lines 14–18, is a repetition of the second segment. In practice, both *durugya* verses can be extended longer or shortened more than I have presented here, bearing in mind that the contingencies of rituals or ceremonies determine these factors.

As suggested in Chapter 1, lived and historical experience as well as current experience in Asante court music and verbal arts are expressed in the language and poetry of ivory trumpets and *durugya* flute. Instrumental texts in Example 3.1 highlight the reigns of Agyeman Prɛmpɛ, Prɛmpɛ II, the architect and founder of the kingdom, Ɔsɛe Tutu, and the current Asantehene, Ɔsɛe Tutu II. Depending on our interpretation, the name of the founder recalls lived experience in the past while that of the reigning king signifies contemporary experience, including that of my interlocutors. Example 3.4 alludes to the Asante-Banda War (*Bana Sa*) that took place around 1770, while part of the oral history of the *nkofe* ivory trumpet group is linked to the same war. Example 3.10 establishes the paternity of Ɔpemsoɔ Ɔsɛe Tutu and his spiritual advisor, Ɔkɔmfoɔ Anɔkye, along with the birthplace of the former, Kokofu Anyinam. The recurring texts of short trumpets (*mmɛntia*) are direct in providing us with philosophical statements of Ɔpemsoɔ Ɔsɛe Tutu and the reigning kings; Opoku Ware, Ɔsɛe Asibe Bonsu, Agyeman Prɛmpɛ, and Prɛmpɛ II, and Opoku Ware II. In addition to nominals, locations and places are critical in oral discourse. *Sɛkyerɛ* still exist in Asante, and the historical reference is not by accident. Imagery in the Asante landscape provides abundant inspiration for the creative impulse. The civet cat (*kankane*), chameleon (*abosomaketerɛ*), silk-cotton tree (*onyina*), and tree bear (*ɔwea*) are metaphors for real-life situations. Recalling Reginald Byron's quote in Chapter 1, the value of the surrogate texts in this chapter stems from their ability to express the Asante historical experience. In the final analysis, there is value in recognizing authority by not making false claims (Example 3.1), there is value in the motivation to succeed at all costs, there is value in bravery and patience, and there is value in expressing gratitude (Example 3.3). There is also value in a compassionate and generous leader (Example 3.7). As key components of oral history, the language and poetry of ivory trumpets and *durugya* flute are records of reigns, wars, and events, which, while lacking absolute dates, use the powerful medium of performance arts in order to be transmitted for millennia—in the forty-two day Akwasidae Public Assembly, in times of celebration, and in periods of crisis or collective mourning—in a grand continuum of history.

Notes

1 These three broad phases of Akan socio-political and cultural development are from Shujaa (2014: 33).
2 Note the similarity in the name of the trumpet or horn, *abɛn*, among the Akan of West Africa.
3 See, for instance, Florence Dolphyne, 1982: 35–46.
4 Margaret Trowell and K.P. Waschman (1953) provide one of the early usages of the term "sound instruments" to describe similar objects in Uganda. The technique of using sound-producing instruments for signals or in place of the human voice has generated a fair amount of literature, with Kwabena Nketia (1962) and his student William G. Carter (1971, 1984) standing out as specialized studies. Taking a similar approach to the works of Nketia and Woodson are Joseph Kaminski's journal articles (2008, 2015) and his eventual monograph (2012). Kaminski provides us with critical descriptions of Akan ivory trumpets by adding the Greek terms *cheilophones* (literally, lip sound) or *cheilophonetic*, which focus on a vibrating-lip technique for sound production. For, it is the "surrogate-speaking lip," continues Kaminski, "rather than the vocal chords, that vibrate through the tusk to produce word-tone" (2012: 11).

5 In addition to the locations Kaminski visited, there are *ntahera* groups in Takyiman, Dwaben, Nsuta, Kokofu, Asante Mampong, Bekwai, Agogo, and other principalities.

6 See Peter Sarpong (1990: 3).

7 See William Tardoff (1965) and Nana Agyeman Prempeh I (2003).

8 It bears noting that it is instances of deviation from the usual norm of praise poetry, such as those noted in Line 17, that inform Kwesi Yankah's argument that the general reference to all oral poetry in Africa as "praise poetry" is problematic, especially if we consider factors that inspired the verses in the first place (Yankah, 1983: 381–384). For Yankah, oral poetry is a "megagenre" at best, and he prefers the somewhat neutral designation "referential poetry" over the commonplace designation of praise poetry. In the case of the *kɔkrɔanya* group, it may well be that the long hours characterizing court ceremonies, coupled with humid temperatures, lead to sweating and dehydration. As a result, they need some type of refreshments, which can be any form of liquid, from water to liquor. However, as I have noted, in formal situations the trumpeters only speak by way of their sound-producing instruments. The only way to place such a request is to tactically throw in a line to draw attention to their needs when they know the king is listening to their surrogate verses. In order to avoid repeated requests that may take up several lines of verse from the *sesee* player, the king is likely to send them the drinks immediately.

9 A gold-cast symbol of King Worosa's head is attached to one of the Asomfomfena swords, referred to as *Worosa Ti* (Worasa's Head). See Ampene and Nyantakyi III (2016: 161).

10 Of all the *sesee* players I have encountered, Kwadwo Apiakubi is one of the most prolific performer-composers at the court. He never repeated his *mmrane*, no matter how hard I tried to pin him down to a single line of thought to allow me to transcribe his surrogate speech.

11 The hocket technique performed on sound-producing and musical instruments is widespread across Africa, including flutes, xylophones, horns and trumpets. See, for instance, Nketia (1962).

12 Ampene and Nyantakyi III (2016: 202–205) provide additional information on Nkofe.

13 See, for instance, Akwasi Sarpong (1990).

14 Kofi Agyekum (2004) offers a detailed discussion of *ntam*.

15 Nana Afia Kobi Sɛɛwaa Ampem II went to the village on November 7, 2016. The four-day event took place from Monday, January 16 to Thursday, January 19, 2017 to enable the Asante, the Akan, and Ghanaians, in particular, and along with guests from around the world in general, to file past her body and pay their last respects. As one of the court ensembles at Manhyia Palace, the *nkofe* group participated daily in the funerary rites. I went to Ghana from January 11 to February 4, 2017 to join my countrymen in celebrating the life of our illustrious Asantehemaa, and I but stayed on to gather additional materials related to the burial rituals, as well as to interact further with courtiers for this and future monographs. *Gone to the Village* is a film by Kwasi Ampene (2019) that chronicles the crucial role of female leaders in the social and political life of Asante over the past 500 years. The documentary is a fusion of oral traditions, political authority, and national unity with the visual, musical, and performative arts of Asante.

16 See Sarpong (1990: 10) for instrumental texts of *nkofe*. See also Kaminski's Appendix (2012).

17 For Opoku Ware's parentage and birth, and his wars of conquests and expansion, see Kyerematen's unpublished dissertation (1966: 250–282).

18 See Ampene and Nyantakyi III (2016: 21) for the incident that led Opoku Ware to cover regalia objects with gold.

19 See Kyerematen (1966: 339–350).

20 For accounts of Ɔsɛe Asibe Bonsu's reign, see Thomas Bowdich (1819), Joseph Dupuis (1824), and Ivor Wilks (1975).

21 For a detailed account of Agyeman Prɛmpɛ and his successor Ɔsɛe Agyeman Prɛmpɛ II, see Wiliam Tordoff (1965).

22 Most of the documents associated with the restoration can be found in Wallace-Johnson (1935).

23 Prior to his field research in Kumase that resulted in his dissertation and a monograph on the *Asante Ntahera,* Kaminski informs us that he met with the French scholar Simha Arom in Paris, and the latter asked Kaminski to find out why the ensembles used seven trumpets. Arom is a well-known scholar of the Banda Linda horn traditions in the Central African Republic. My discussion of the number seven expands on Kaminski's findings (Kaminski, 2012: xx–xxi).

24 A.A.Y. Kyerematen (1966: 62–74) confirms that there were seven original matriclans.

25 A.A.Y. Kyerematen discusses the notion of threefold in Asante (1966: 47–51).

26 See Ampene and Nyantakyi III (2016: 258–259) for a picture and a description of God's Tree as part of the Asantehene's regalia.

27 Mensah Sarbah co-founded the Aborigines' Rights Protection Society with J.W. de Graft-Johnson, J.W. Sey, J.P. Brown, and J.E. Casely Hayford.

28 Agyekum (2008) includes a detailed discussion of Akan greetings.

29 The choice of days, Monday to Thursday, has spiritual and symbolic meaning, but due to space limitations, I will examine the issues involved with those days in another paper.

30 For a detailed interpretation of the Akan calendar, see Osafo K. Osei (1997).

31 In his search for an alternative to European Missionary Hymnody and Classical music, Ephraim Amu transformed the *atenteben* (bamboo flute) from its Akan enclave to a national instrument by extending the melodic range while incorporating diatonic tuning. Adventurous artists including Nana Danso Abeam, Sammy Nukpese of Roots Anabo fame, Dela Abotri, and others extended the melodic range to include chromatic notes. Bowdich's (1819) graphic representation of a convocation of chiefs, headed by the Asantehene Ɔsɛe Asibe Bonsu, has a group of court musicians playing what look to be pipes.

32 My analysis of the *durugya* and all the earophones in this section owe a great deal to Nketia's 1971 groundbreaking article on surrogate speech in Africa.

References

Agyekum, Kofi. 2004. " 'Reminiscential Oath' Taboo in Akan." *Language in Society* 33 (3): 317–342.

———. 2008. "The Pragmatics of Akan Greetings." *Discourse Studies* 10 (4): 493–516.

Ampene, Kwasi, and Nana Kwadwo Nyantakyi III. 2016. *Engaging Modernity: Asante in the Twenty-First Century*, 2nd edition. Ann Arbor, MI: Michigan Publishing.

Anquandah, James. 1982a. *Rediscovering Ghana's Past.* Accra: Sedco Publishing Ltd, and Harlow, Essex: Longman Group Ltd.

Askew, Kelly. 2002. *Performing the Nation: Swahili Music and Cultural Politics in Tanzania.* Chicago: University of Chicago Press.

Averill, Gage. 1997. *A Day for the Hunter, a Day for the Prey: Popular Music and Power in Haiti.* Chicago: University of Chicago Press.

Barbot, John. 1732. "A Description of the Coast of North and South Guinea." In *Churchills Voyages.* London: Messrs. Churchill.

Beecham, John. 1841. *Ashantee and the Gold Coast: Being a Sketch of the History, Social State, and Superstitions of the Inhabitants of Those Countires: With a Notice of the State and Prospects of Christianity Among Them.* London: J. Mason.

Bokor, Michael J.K. 2014. "When the Drum Speaks: The Rhetoric of Motion, Emotion, and Action in African Societies." *A Journal of History of Rhetoric* 32 (2): 165–194.

Bosman, William. 1705. *A New and Accurate Description of the Coast of Guinea.* London: Frank Cass and Company Ltd.

Bowdich, Thomas E. 1819. *Mission from Cape Coast Castle to Ashantee: With a Statistical Account of that Kingdom, and Geographical Notices of Other Parts of the Interior of Africa.* London: John Murray and Sons.

Carter, William G. 1971. "The Ntahera Horn Ensemble of the Dwaben Court: An Ashanti Surrogating Medium." Master's thesis, University of California, Los Angeles.

———. 1984. "Asante Music in Old and New Juaben." PhD diss., University of California, Los Angeles.

Dolphyne, Florence Abena. 1982. "Akan Language Patterns and Development." *Tarikh* 7 (2): 26, 35–45.

Dupuis, Joseph. 1824. *Journal of a Residence in Ashantee*. London: H. Colburn.

Freeman, R. Austin. 1898. *Travels and Life in Ashanti and Jaman*. Westminster: A. Constable & Co.

Kaminski, Joseph. 2008. "Surrogate Speech of Asante Ivory Trumpeters in Ghana." *Yearbook for Traditional Music* 40 (40): 117–135.

———. 2012. *Asante Ntahera Trumpets in Ghana: Culture, Tradition, and Sound Barrage*. Farnham, Surrey; Burlington, VT: Ashgate Publishing Ltd.

———. 2015. "Nketia's Influence in Ntahera Hocket and Surrogate Speech Analyses." In *Discourses in African Musicology: J.H. Kwabena Nketia Festschrift*, edited by Kwasi Ampene, Akosua A. Ampofo, Godwin K. Adjei, and Albert K. Awedoba, 56–74. Ann Arbor, MI: Michigan Publishing.

Kyerematen, A.A.Y. 1966. "Ashanti Royal Regalia: Their History and Functions." PhD diss., Oxford University.

Nketia, J.H. Kwabena. 1962. "The Hocket-Technique in African Music." *Journal of the International Folk Music Council* 14: 44–52.

———. 1971. "Surrogate Languages of Africa." In *Current Trends in Linguistics*, edited by Thomas A. Sebeok. The Hague, Netherlands: Mouton & Co., Printers.

Osei, Osafo K. 1997. *Discourse on Akan Perpetual Calendar*. Accra: Domak Press Ltd.

Prempeh I, Nana Agyeman. 2003. *The History of Ashanti Kings and the Whole Country Itself and Other Writings*. Edited by A. Adu Boahen *et al*. Oxford and New York: Oxford University Press.

Sarpong, Peter Kwasi. 1990. *The Ceremonial Horns of the Ashanti*. Accra: Sedco Press.

Shujaa, Kenya. 2014. "Akan Cultural History: An Overview." In *The Akan People: A Documentary History*, edited by Kwasi Konadu, 29–88. Princeton: Markus Wiener Publishers.

Tardoff, William. 1965. *Ashanti Under the Prempehs 1888–1935*. London: Oxford University Press.

Trowell, Margaret, and Klaus P. Waschman. 1953. *Tribal Crafts of Uganda*. London and New York: Oxford University Press.

Turino, Thomas. 2000. *Nationalists, Cosmopolitans, and Popular Music in Zimbabwe*. Chicago: University of Chicago Press.

Wallace-Johnson, Isaac T.A. 1935. *Papers Relating to the Restoration of Ashanti Confederacy and A Full and Illustration Report of the Proceedings of the Restoration of the Ashanti Confederacy*. Kumase, Ghana: Educational Press and Manufactures.

Wilks, Ivor. 1975. *Asante in the Nineteenth Century: The Structure and Evolution of a Political Order*. Cambridge: Cambridge University Press.

Yankah, Kwesi. 1983. "To Praise or Not to Praise the King: The Akan 'Apae' in the Context of Referential Poetry." *Research in African Literatures* 14 (3): 381–400.

Filmography

Gone to the Village: Royal Funerary Rites for Asantehemaa Nana Afia Kobi Serwaa Ampem II. Produced by Kwasi Ampene, Executive Producer, Lester P. Monts. 2019. Ann Arbor, Michigan.

4 The language and poetry of drums

Adinkrahene (represents greatness, appeal, and leadership): Akan Adinkra pictographic writing. Captures the boundlessness of nature, the earth, the ocean, and the sky, and the continuous renewal of resources in the natural order.

Based on another medium of instrumental texts, the language and poetry of drums is a continuation of the key issues in Chapter 3. Like ivory trumpets, a variety of drums featured prominently in my ethnographic description of the Akwasidae Public Assembly in the Prologue. In Chapter 2, I demonstrated how wars of conquest and expansion inspired creativity in music, as heroic encounters generated a large corpus of song and instrumental texts, as well as poetry. As mediating material culture, sound-producing and musical instruments were created to memorialize events, captured as war trophies, or borrowed from neighbors. I pointed to the relationship between the hierarchical structure of Akan chieftaincy and the ownership of drums as indexes of power. Similar to ivory trumpets, drum language operates in a sophisticated system of surrogate speech whereby spoken language is replicated on a variety of drums. For Modesto Amegago, an accomplished drummer and scholar, drumming as a mode of communication is accomplished by the formulaic use of language or text (Amegago, 2015: 76–95). Referring to the music and dance of *Adzogbo* among the southern Ewe speakers in Ghana and Togo, David Locke describes a performance scheme whereby sequences of dance movements are introduced by spoken or sung texts and then reproduced in the rhythms of the leading drum (Locke, 1981: 25). In a study among the Banda Linda in the Central African Republic, Simha Arom is of the view that the language of drums "constitute semiotic systems whose rules generally concern both language and music" (Arom, 2007: 1). As we shall see in this chapter, the widespread use of sound-producing and musical instruments for surrogate speech performances include short repeated signals and imitations of spoken language. Within these two modes of signal and speech performance, drums are used to send messages, make announcements, play invocations, offer prayers, play proverbs and eulogies, or sound emergency alarms.[1] As in the case of ivory trumpets, drums were a vital part of warfare, conquest, and expansion, and the notion of war drums or a war drum is due to their sending coded messages for the infantry and regular messages within and outside of settlements.

At the Asantehene's court, the variety of drums and drum ensembles are known as *akyerɛmade* (loosely, "drums place") or *akyerɛmadefoɔ* ("drummers"). As I stated in Chapter 3, they are grouped together with ivory trumpets and referred to as *asɔkwa ne akyerɛmade* (loosely, "trumpets and drums"). Similar to the trumpeters, each drum ensemble has its own chief and elders, but collectively they are under the *Anantahene*, Baafoɔ Agyei Fosu Twitwikwa. I begin with a general overview of Akan and Asante drums, followed by an in-depth discussion and analysis of texts from eight groups, including *kete, fɔntɔmfrɔm, mpintin, apirede, mmedie, kwantenpɔnmuta, nkukuadwe,* and *nsumangorɔ*. Although I discuss a ninth group, *sekye*, I did not include the texts since the leading drummer was quite old. Of the eight, *kete, fɔntɔmfrɔm, apirede, nsumangorɔ,* and *sekye* are drum and dance ensembles; and, while *kete* features chorus for special events, singing is ever-present in *nsumangoro*. *Mpintin, mmedie,* and *kwantenpɔnmuta* ensembles are essential to processions, and while the pair of *nkukuadwe* drums features prominently in processions, they are mainly tribunal drums.

Akyerɛmade (drums)

Unlike animal horns or ivory trumpets with natural bore, the technique of drum-making in Africa is much more complex than we could possibly imagine.[2] From the wooden shell to the leather membrane, the Akan drum is made up of several materials, and even by today's standards it requires extraordinary skill for drum carvers to create a single drum. For the shell of the drum, drum carvers with special skills identify the *cordia platythyrsa* (*tweneboa or tweneduro* tree) and perform a ritual to propitiate the spirit of the tree before cutting it down. Having cut out the preferred size and length of the desired shell, they peel the log and hollow the inside to the required shape. In the past, elephant ears (*ɛsono aso*) and the duyker skin (*ɔtwe nhoma*) were used as drum heads, but currently most drum-carvers have settled on the less-durable skins of the cow, goat, or sheep. The *ɔfɛma* tree is used for drum pegs, while the vines used as ropes to attach the leather membrane to the drum shell are obtained from the *obua* or *obofunu* tree—though it is becoming increasingly common for drum carvers to use manufactured ropes. Sometimes a type of cane known as *ɛyeɛ* is used for the same purpose. For durable drumsticks, they use the *ɔfɛma* tree. With exceptions for drums made for the tourist market in urban centers and cities, another ritual is performed on a completed drum.

The general name in Twi for all of the drums in Akan, *twene*, is taken from the first two syllables of the *tweneboa* or *tweneduro* tree. Because it took centuries for the Akan to finally identify the *tweneboa* tree as the ideal material for a drum shell, they remained indebted to this singular tree, as exemplified by the following invocations to the spirit of the tree as an expression of gratitude. The text is from Nketia (1963: 6).[3]

Example 4.1 Tweneboa Kodua: drum poetry (*ayan*) expressing gratitude to the *tweneboa* tree.

Tweneboa Akwa	Wood of the drum, Tweneboa Akwa
Tweneboa Kodua	Wood of the drum, Tweneboa Kodua
Kodua Tweneduro	Wood of the drum, Kodua Tweneduro
Tweneduro, wokɔɔ baabi a	Cedar wood, if you have been away
Merefrɛ wo; yɛse bra	I am calling you; they say come
Meresua, momma menhu	I am learning, let me succeed

In terms of construction, shape, and size, two types of drums are used in Akan-land: open drums with a leather skin covering the head, which have an opening at one end, and closed drums with single- or double-headed drums without an open-ing at the end (Nketia, 1963: 4–16). Open drums are quintessential Akan drums, while closed drums are historically cultural adaptations from northern neighbors, as described in Chapter 2. There are two types of open drums in Akan: the smaller, barreled-shaped types known as *nkukua* (or *nkukuwa*) and bottled-shaped drums known as *apentema*. With noted continuity with the past, *nkukua* drums played with straight sticks are still used in Akan areas and have a variety of names and functions, such as *etwie* (friction drums), *sikakua* (gold drum), *nkukuadwe* (or *nkukuadwo*), and *mmedie*. As its name implies, the drum shell of *sikakua* is cov-ered with gold leaf (the Akan word for gold is *sika*), and as noted previously, this drum is part of the regalia of the Gold Stool. There are comparatively big-ger, barrel-shaped drums known as *twenesini* (literally, short drums). Examples of *twenesini* are *mpebi ne nkrawiri, kwadum, twenenini, twenebedeɛ* or *kusukurum* in *apirede* ensembles, *adukurogya*, and several varieties of *asafo* drums. Arguably, the largest drums in West Africa are the barrel-shaped drums known as *twenekɛseɛ* (big drum) or *bɔmaa*, which, as noted in Chapter 2, became known as *fɔntɔmfrɔm* from the time of Ɔpemsoɔ Ɔsɛe Tutu. On the other hand, *apentema* represents the relatively small bottle-shaped drums, which are played with the hands; however, the bigger version, the pair of *atumpan* drums, are played with two carved sticks (*nkonta*).

Since closed drums are adaptations from the Dagbamba kingdom (see Chap-ter 2), they are limited in distribution across Akan areas; but at the same time, gourd drums (*mpintintoa*), hourglass-shaped drums (*donno* or *dɔnka*), and long cylindrical drums (*gyamadudu*) together constitute one of the leading ensembles in processional music at the court. The bigger version of the hourglass-shaped drum (*dɔnka*) is one of the supporting drums in *fɔntɔmfrɔm*, while two medium-sized versions of the same drum are tied together and used in the *kete* ensemble as twin drums (*donnota*). The *donno* is also used in *sekye* drum and dance ensembles and in popular bands such as *adowa*. Osekye (also known as *atɛntɛ*) and *sanga* are versions of *gyamadudu* drums. Nketia's classic text identifies three modes of drumming: signal, speech, and dance. All three modes rely on language to convey a message or to communicate collective sentiments, and that explains my focus on the language and poetry of drums in this section. The noted three modes of

drumming are not limited to Akan or Asante traditions, and drum texts or languages are complex systems of communication in sub-Saharan Africa. Some of
the relevant literature includes Bode Omojola (2012), Nketia (1971: 699–732),
Akin Euba (1991), David Locke (1990, 1998), and Kofi Agawu (1995).

Kete

As with ensembles in Akan and other areas in Africa, the name *kete* may refer
to the drum ensemble, dance, chorus, or all of the above. It may also simply
refer to any one of the dance suites or all of the dances collectively. Of all the
court music and ensembles, the drumming and rhythms of *kete* have attracted the
most scholarly inquiry and a significant body of texts. We may begin with R.S.
Rattray (1927), Kwabena Nketia (1963), James Keotting (1970), William Anku
(1988), Emmanuel Cudjoe (2015), and Ben Paulden (2015, 2017). Like most
court ensembles, *kete* ensembles were present in several Akan polities before the
founding of the Asante Empire. We may recall in Chapter 2 that by the fifteenth
century, Tafo—a major urban and trading center—and similar places in established kingdoms, including Dɛnkyera, Adanse, Akyem, and as far as Akwamu,
had *kete* drum ensembles. The current list of *kete* ensembles in Akan areas is
quite extensive, and readers are referred to Ben Paulding's unpublished master's
thesis.[4] For the Asantehene's *kete*, it is said that Ɔpemsoɔ Ɔsɛɛ Tutu seized the
kete drums from the Tafohene, Nana Ketekyire, following his defeat. The drums
were initially kept in a room in the palace until the night before Ɔsɛɛ Asibe Bonsu,
the 7th Asantehene, embarked on the Gyaman War in 1818. In the words of Nana
Agyei Boahen, Chief of *kete* (*Ketehene*), Ɔsɛɛ Bonsu's spiritual advisors informed
him that he would not live beyond three years following his triumph over King
Adinkra Kofi of Gyaaman. They gave him the option of either staying home or
going to war. Ɔsɛɛ Bonsu (sometimes referred to as Ɔsɛɛ Bonsu Panin or Ɔsɛɛ
Bonsu Ɔbɔɔ Hyɛn) chose the war option, along with its potential consequences.
Before leaving for the war, however, he staged performances of *kete* for three days
and three nights and danced with the Asantehemaa, his wives (*aheneyerenom*),
and members of the royal household. Ɔsɛɛ Bonsu's actions set in motion the tradition where successive kings perform throughout the night with the *kete* orchestra
after the internment of a member of the royal family at Brɛman. Oral traditions
have it that the *kete* orchestra represents the dilemma of the ruler, and in recognition of that, the drums are covered with a red-and-black-checkered cloth design
that projects crises, matters of grave consequences, and grief. Thus, *kete* is well
marked for funerary rites, although like most Akan ensembles they also feature
prominently in festivals where the focus is on celebration. The red-and-black-
checkered design is restricted to the Asantehene's *kete* drums, and to date, those
colors identify the Asantehene *kete* drum ensemble (Figure 4.1).

In several areas it is now a common practice to limit the *kete* orchestra to just
the drum ensemble, but the Asantehene's grand *kete* orchestra consists of a large
chorus involving the Asantehemaa, royal wives of past kings (*aheneyerenom*),
the drum ensemble, and long vertical flutes described as pipes (*atɛntɛbɛn*).[5] The

Figure 4.1 The Asantehene *kete* drums covered with the red-and-black checkered cloth. From left to right: *kwadum* (leading drum), played with two curved sticks (*nkonta*); *petia*, played with two curved sticks; *apentema*, played with both hands; small, medium, and tall *aburukua* drums. played with two straight sticks; two joined armpit drums, *donnota*, played with a curved stick; a container rattle with the seeds inside, *ntorowa*; and the boat-shaped metal idiophone, *adawura*.

pipes are currently missing from the Asantehene *kete* orchestra, and thus we are left with the drum and chorus. The present practice, whereby territorial chiefs maintain just the drum ensemble, may be due to the expense that comes with maintaining a large orchestra. It may well be that the cost of maintaining such a large orchestra—drum ensemble, chorus, and pipes—is not tenable for most chiefs, and as a result, they tend to settle on only the drum ensemble. Currently, most *kete* groups maintain the core drums—*kwadum, apentema, petia, aburukua, dondo, adawura*, and *ntorowa*—but the Asantehene's drum ensemble is expanded to include the following: *kwadum*, the leading drum is the biggest with low sonority and played with two curved sticks (*nkonta*); *petia*, which is shorter and also played with two curved sticks; *asppentenma* and *abrema* drums, which are bottle-shaped, taller than *petia*, and played with both hands; three different sizes of *aburukua*, which are played with two strait sticks; *donnota*, two joined *donno* drums (*ta* means twins, so "twin *donno*"); and a gourd rattle (*ntorowa*), usually played by a female member and *adawura* (a big boat-shaped metal bell, see Figure 1). Interestingly, *kete* is the only court ensemble that incorporates a rattle in addition to a female player.[6] When I recorded the Asantehene's *kete* in the summer of 2009, they had a chorus of about thirty women with the late Asantehemaa, Nana Afia Kobi Serwaa Ampem II, presiding over it. *Kete* involves thirteen or more suites of dances that are associated with historical events and guide the selection of pieces for particular situations. For instance, Nketia states that *Yɛtu Mpɔ* ("We Are Digging Gold") is appropriate for processions and the preferred piece to play behind Asante chiefs when they are going to greet the Asantehene, for the latter occupies the Gold Stool. *Kete* performances involving the chorus are restricted to *mmaadae* (Adae for women) in the inner space of the palace, which is not opened to the general public. The only public performance that I am aware of is a concert of Asante music and dance that was organized at the Center for National Culture (CNC) in Kumase as part of the Silver Jubilee celebration of Otumfoɔ Opoku Ware II in 1995.[7] During the events marking the 2004 Adaekɛseɛ (also marking the fifth anniversary of the reign of Otumfoɔ Ɔsɛe Tutu II), the Asantehene and Asantehemaa performed with members of the *kete* chorus at the Center for National Culture (CNC) in Kumase. The last public occasion that I am aware of was the 2009 Adaekɛseɛ, when the Asantehene staged a similar performance at the Center for National Culture. I will first of all begin with the instrumental texts of thirteen dances.

Kete drum texts

In the summer of 2011, I recorded thirteen pieces under the supervision of Nana Agyei Boahen, chief of the Asantehene's *kete* (*Ketehene*), with only the drum ensemble without the chorus. The pieces are *Kete Tene, Nisuo Bekume, Dankwadwam, Abɔfoɔ, Ɔyaa, Apɛntɛm, Adaban, Adinkra Kofi, Kwame Dogo, Antrefo, Me Mpɛ Asɛm, Yɛ Tu Mpɔ, and Mmorosa.*[8] It is worth pointing out that the following list does not follow any performance format, since the type of event determines the choice of dance suite to be performed as well as the duration of particular pieces. Six different bell patterns (*topoi*) are featured in the thirteen dance suites listed previously.[9] The first type appears twice in *Kete Tene* and *Me Mpɛ Asɛm* (Examples 4.2 and 4.12); the second pattern appears three times in *Nisuo Bekume, Dankwadwam, and Adaban* (Examples 4.3, 4.4, and 4.8); the third appears five times in *Abɔfoɔ, Adinkra Kofi, Kwame Dogo, Antrefo, and Mmorosa* (4.5, 4.9, 4.10. 4.11, and 4.14); the fourth appears in *Ɔyaa* (Example 4.6); the fifth appears in *Apɛntɛm* (Example 4.7); and the sixth and final bell pattern appears in *Yɛ Tu Mpɔ* (Example 4.13).[10] The cyclical rattle and *dondota* rhythm patterns stay the same throughout all of the thirteen dance suites, and they are identified by the assigned mnemonics. Unlike the dialogic call and response framework between the *atumpan* and *bɔmaa* drums in *fɔntɔmfrɔm* ensemble, the architectural framework in *kete* is based on an astounding system of multipart drumming fundamentally grounded in cyclical motion. The exception is *Adaban* (Example 4.8), where the *kwadum* on the one hand, and the *apentema* and *petia* on the other hand, intermittently engage in call and response. The overall texts of *kete* dance suites highlight multipart texture with independent drum texts that should be read horizontally at all times. The bell pattern (*adawura*) is the reference point and all the individual drum parts are transcribed with particular attention to their entry point. In that case, I have separated the first phrase of the cyclical bell pattern from the second phrase to demonstrate the entry point for the rattle, the supporting, and lead drums. For instance, in Example 4.2, the *ntorowa, donnota, aburukuwa, apentema* and *kwadum* begin at the first stroke of the bell pattern, while the *petia* begins on the sixth attack point of the bell pattern.

Example 4.2 Kete Tene, Asantehene *kete* drum ensemble.

Adawura
Ken ke ke ken ke ken ka   Ken ke ke ken ke ken ka Ken ke ke ken ke ken ka
                                       Ntorowa
                                       Sa sa sa sa Sa sa sa sa Sa sa sa sa Sa sa sa sa Sa sa sa sa Sa sa sa sa
                                       Dondota
                                       Ketewa kɛseɛ ketewa kɛseɛ ketewa kɛseɛ ketewa kɛseɛ
                                       Aburukuwa
                                       Yɛ nie yɛ nie yɛ nie yɛ nie yɛ nie yɛ nie yɛ nie
                                       Apentema
                                       Yɛ nie yɛ nie yɛ nie yɛ nie yɛ nie yɛ nie yɛ nie
                            Petia
                                       Nkanto nkanto nkanto nkanto nkanto nkanto nkanto (Nka ntam nto)
                                       Kwadum (lead drum)
                                       Nana ya'tena ase, Nana ya'tena ase, Nana ya'tenase
English Translation, *adawura*:
Ken ke ke ken ke ken ka Ken ke ke ken ke ken ka Ken ke ke ken ke ken ka
                                       Ntorowa
                                       Sa sa sa sa Sa sa sa sa Sa sa sa sa Sa sa sa sa
                                       Dondota
                                       Small big small big small big, small big, small big
                                       Aburukuwa
                                       Here we are here we are here we are here we are
                                       Apentema
                                       Here we are here we are here we are here we are
                            Petia
                                       Don't invoke a taboo and lie
                                       Kwadum
                                       Nana we are seated, Nana we are seated, Nana we are seated

---

Kete Tene is typically performed to accompany the chorus when the king is formally seated during *Mmaadae*. The preferred songs are *Wa'tenase, Bonsu Panin ma mo atena* ("He is Seated, Bonsu Panin is Seated"), or *Ɔhene Bra* ("King Come"). The *topos* begins and ends on the upbeat and underscores seven attack points with two contrasting pitches and rhythms: *Ken* is longer than *ka*. The *Aburukua* and *Apentema* drummers join forces to affirm the presence of participants by sounding the phrase, "here we are." The contrasting timbre that results in the use of two straight sticks on the *aburukua* drum, and the palm technique on the *apentema*, is not lost on participants. In the mix of all the excitement, the *petia* drummer throws in a word of caution to all participants to avoid missteps or loose talk with the contraction, *nkanto*, but its full meaning is *nka ntam nto* ("don't invoke or utter the great oath under false pretext").[11] With its deep sonority, the *kwadum* player wraps up the integrated texts with a resounding message to the king that they are all seated and ready for the evening's event.

Example 4.3 Nisuo Bekume ("Tears Will Kill Me"): Asantehene *kete* ensemble.

Adawura:

Ken ke ken ka Ken ke ken ka Ken ke ken ka Ken ke ken ka Ken ke ken ka

Ntorowa

Sa sa sa sa Sa sa sa sa Sa sa sa sa Sa sa sa sa Sa sa sa sa

Dondota

Ketewa kɛseɛ ketewa kɛseɛ ketewa kɛseɛ ketewa kɛseɛ ketewa kɛseɛ

Aburukuwa

Nana kafra, Nana kafra, Nana kafra, Nana kafra, Nana kafra, Nana kafra

Apentema

Menkɔ nisuo bekume, menkɔ nisuo bekume, menkɔ nisuo bekume

Petia

Gyae su gyae su gyae su gyae su gyae su gyae su gyae su

Kwadum

Mo nyae mma yɛn ka, mo nyae mma yɛn nka, mo nyae mma yɛn nka ka ka ka ka

Variation: Mo mmra mo mmra nisuo bekume, Mo mmra mo mmra nisuo bekume

English Translation
Adawura:

Ken ke ken ka Ken ke ken ka Ken ke ken ka Ken ke ken ka Ken ke ken ka

Ntorowa

Sa sa sa sa Sa sa sa sa Sa sa sa sa Sa sa sa sa

Dondota

Small big small big small big, small big, small big

Aburukuwa

Nana apologies Nana apologies Nana apologies

Apentema

I won't go, tears will kill me, I won't go, tears will kill me

Petia

Stop crying stop crying stop crying stop crying stop crying

Kwadum

Allow us to speak allow us to speak, say it say it say it

Variation: Come come, I'll die from crying, Come come, I'll die from crying

---

The implicit meaning of shedding tears endlessly due to the pain of death makes the previous dance suite, *Nisuo Bekume*, appropriate for funerary rites, especially during wake-keeping and all of the pre-burial rites immediately preceding internment. Deep-seated grief is expressed in the extraordinarily dense multipart drum texts and the never-ending cyclical motion that is the power and driving force in this *kete* drumming. The *topos* begins on the upbeat but ends on the downbeat, thus displaying a sense of departure and return. The first attack point of the bell is the entering point for the *ntorowa* (rattle) and the *aburukuwa* drums, while the entry point for *apentema, petia,* and *kwadum* (the leading drum) drums coincide with the fourth attack point of the bell. While the *aburukua* player is expressing sympathy, "Nana apologies," the *appentenma* drummer is sounding the sentiment that becomes the title of this piece, *Menkɔ, nisuo bekume* ("I won't go, tears will kill me"): that is, I will perhaps die from dehydration from shedding endless tears. The *petia* drummer urges the bereaved to stop crying: *gyae su* ("stop crying"). All the while, the lead drummer on *kwa-dum* anticipates the cathartic effect of bellowing out one's grief by sounding *mo nyae mma yɛnka* ("allow us to speak"). In other words, they will feel better if they are able to voice their pain. The lead drummer invokes a communal ethos in mourning, with the strategic placement of *yɛn* ("us") toward the end of the phrase, in addition to playing the single syllable *ka* ("say") five times by means of a single stroke for emphasis, and as a way of artistically filling up the space within the same phrase, or as a bridge to sounding the second theme. The beginning phrase, *mo*, is yet another mechanism for highlighting a communal code in the grieving process, thus inviting members of the community to join the bereaved family and share grief; for, as the Akan will say, *baanu so a ɛmmia* ("a single carrier of a load feels it more than two or more").

Example 4.4 Dakwadwam: Asantehene *kete* ensemble.

Adawura:
Ken ke ken ka Ken ke ken ka Ken ke ken ka Ken ke ken ka Ken ke ken ka
Ntorowa
Sa sa sa sa Sa sa sa sa Sa sa sa sa Sa sa sa sa Sa sa sa sa Sa sa sa sa
Dondota
Ketewa kɛseɛ ketewa kɛseɛ ketewa kɛseɛ ketewa kɛseɛ ketewa kɛseɛ
Aburukuwa
Mo mmɛ sa mo mmɛ sa mo mmɛ sa mo mmɛ sa mo mmɛ sa
Apentema
Mo mmɛ sa mo mmɛ sa mo mmɛ sa mo mmɛ sa mo mmɛ sa
2nd Theme: Animuonyam nka hene, animuonyam nka hene
Pɛtia
Nana mo Nana mo Nana mo Nana mo Nana mo, Nana mo
Kwadum (Lead Drum)
Mo nka mma me mo nka mma me gyae gyae gyae, monka mma me monka mma me mommra mmɛtie

English Translation
Adawura:
Ken ke ken ka Ken ke ken ka Ken ke ken ka Ken ke ken ka Ken ke ken ka
Ntorowa
Sa sa sa sa Sa sa sa sa Sa sa sa sa Sa sa sa sa Sa sa sa sa Sa sa sa sa
Dondota
Ketewa kɛseɛ ketewa kɛseɛ ketewa kɛseɛ ketewa kɛseɛ
Aburukuwa
Come and dance come and dance come and dance come and dance
Apentema
Come and dance come and dance come and dance come and dance
2nd Theme: Glory to our king glory to our king glory to our king
Petia
Congratulations Nana Congratulations Nana Congratulations Nana
Kwadum
Proclaim it for me, stop stop stop, Proclaim it for me, Proclaim it for me, Come and listen

Dakwadwam is performed during *mmaadae* for the royal family and the wives of past kings to dance, particularly when the Asantehene is formally seated at the event. Once again, the *aburukuwa* and *apentema* drummers join forces to invite the previously named individuals to come and express themselves with dance: *Mo mmɛ sa* ("come and dance"). Occasionally, the *apentema* drummer disengages from his alliance with *aburikuwa* to play a second theme to glorify the Asantehene. Along the same lines, the *petia* drummer seems to applaud the ruler with *Nana mo* ("congratulations") for successfully presiding over another Adae Public Assembly. For his part, the lead drummer is encouraging all to proclaim the collective sentiments: *mo nka mma me* ("proclaim it for me"). As stated previously, communal participation is projected with the end phrase *na mommra mmɛtie* ("come and listen").

Unlike the celebratory focus in *Dakwadwam,* the *kete abɔfoɔ* dance captures all of the metaphoric allusions in the expression and value of hunters in Asante. Like

---

Example 4.5 Abɔfoɔ (Hunter's Dance), Asantehene *kete* ensemble.

Adawura

Ken keken ken   Ken keken ken Ken keken ken Ken keken ken
                      Ntorowa
                      Sa sasa sa Sa sasa sa Sa sasa sa Sa sasa sa Sa sasa sa
                      Dondota
                      Ketewa kɛseɛ ketewa kɛseɛ ketewa kɛseɛ ketewa kɛseɛ
                      Aburukuwa
                      Ketekete ketekete ketekete ketekete ketekete ketekete
                 Apentema
              Ɔhene wɔhe? Bra ha, Ɔhene wɔhe? Bra ha, Ɔhene wɔhe? Bra ha
                      Petia
              Me a na me pɛ, me a na me pɛ, me a na me pɛ me a na me pɛ
                      ***Kwadum* (lead drum)**
              Ɔhene mo Ɔhene mo Ɔhene mo Ɔhene mo Ɔhene mo Ɔhene mo

English Translation
***Adawura*:**
              Ken keken ken Ken keken ken Ken keken ken Ken keken ken
              Ntorowa
              Sa sasa sa Sa sasa sa Sa sasa sa Sa sasa sa Sa sasa sa
              Dondota
              Little by little little by little little by little little by little little by little
              Aburukuwa
              Very small very small very small very small very small very small
           Apentema
              Where is the king? Come here Where is the king? Come here Where is the king? Come here
              Petia
              It's my fault it's my fault it's my fault it's my fault it's my fault it's my fault
              ***Kwadum* (lead drum)**
              Congratulations king congratulations king congratulations king congratulations king

---

other African groups, hunting animals is not a sport, particularly when it is done at night and lasts as little as a day or potentially as much as a few months. The longer hunters stay in the forest, the greater their need for temporary shelter to rest and to smoke and preserve the game before sending it to the village or town. It is known that most of the shelters eventually became villages, towns, or even cities. Considering the thick and sometimes impenetrable forest in Akanland, hunters are considered brave individuals with special skills for monitoring and pursuing animals in the tropical forest. Hunting in Asante demands extreme patience. Through constant interaction with wild animals and foliage, hunters acquire knowledge of herbal medicine, and they are well-known as herbalists. *Abɔfoɔ* is a popular dance suite that is performed for the ruler when the masses want to communicate values of patience, bravery, strength, firmness, and persistence to him. For his part, the ruler conveys grave matters to his subjects during funerary rites, when he dances *kete abɔfoɔ* while wearing a special tunic (*batakari*) and the *nimo* hat, and also dances with a gun and a sword. Writing in the 1960s, Nketia reports that in the past, *kete abɔfoɔ* was performed before a chief presiding over an important shrine or a chief whose town was associated with a famous priest. The four attack points of the *topos* are set in motion with an upbeat and the last attack point ending on the downbeat. The beginning of the bell pattern (the first attack point) marks the entry point for *ntorowa*, *donnota*, and *aburukuwa*; the *apentema* entry is on the fourth attack point; although they express different texts, the *petia* and *kwadum* (the lead drum) begin at the end of the fourth attack point, thus filling the space between the end of the bell cycle and the beginning of another bell cycle.

In order for the ruler to resolve known challenges, he needs to move in little steps, as indicated by the *aburukuwa* drum text *ketekete* ("little by little"). The *apentema* reinforces the need for leadership or direction, *ɔhene wɔhe? Bra ha* ("where is the king? Come here"), to ensure collective success in overcoming hardships. For the *petia*, imaginary foes should blame themselves if they are overpowered, *me a na me pɛ* ("it's my fault"), and perhaps the enemy was overpowered, for the leading drummer plays the recurring two phrases, *Ɔhene mo*, congratulating the ruler throughout a performance.

Ɔyaa, Example 4.6, is a light-hearted dance meant to enliven the mood of participants and to provide contrast to ritual-based dances like *abɔfoɔ* or *adaban*. It is usually performed to welcome the ruler to the *mmaadae*, and we gather that it was the favorite of most royals and wives of past kings, as they would hit the dance floor the moment they heard this piece. The *topos* is close to the *akatape* that usually accompany vocal ensembles such as *adowa* and *nnwonkorɔ*. The *topos*, *Ken kekren ke ken*, is in two parts: antecedent and consequent phrases. The antecedent phrase, *Ken kekren*, sets the piece in motion, while the antecedent phrase, *ke ken*, brings some sort of closure to the motion. The *aburukuwa* drummer begins the integrated texts with a request to make a statement—*monyae mame nka* ("let me say it")—while the *apentema* drummer offers encouragement to the dancers, *mo mo bra bra* ("well done, come come"). The *petia* drummer cautions the dancers not to engage in excessive dance gestures that are not socially acceptable with the phrase *Nana mpɛ* ("Nana will not like it"). Finally,

Example 4.6 Ɔyaa: Asantehene *kete* ensemble.

Adawura
Ken kekren ke ken Ken kekren ke ken Ken kekren ke ken
Ntorowa
Sa sasa sa Sa sasa sa Sa sasa sa Sa sasa sa Sa sasa sa
Dondota
Ketewa kɛseɛ ketewa kɛseɛ ketewa kɛseɛ ketewa kɛseɛ
Aburukuwa
Monyae mame nka (na) mɛka Monyae mame nka (na) mɛka
Apentema
Mo mo bra bra Mo mo bra bra Mo mo bra bra Mo mo bra bra
Petia
Nana mpɛ Nana mpɛ Nana mpɛ Nana mpɛ Nana mpɛ Nana mpɛ
Kwadum (lead drum)
Me pɛ deɛ ɔbɛba abɛsene, deɛ ɔbɛba abɛ sene, Me pɛ deɛ ɔbɛba abɛsene, deɛ ɔbɛba abɛsene

English Translation
Adawura
Ken kekren ke ken Ken kekren ke ken Ken kekren ke ken
Ntorowa
Sa sasa sa Sa sasa sa Sa sasa sa Sa sasa sa Sa sasa sa
Dondota
Small big small big small big small big small big small big
Aburukuwa
Let me say it for I'll say it let me say it for I'll say it let me say it for I'll say it
Apentema
Well done well done come come well done well done come come
Petia
Nana will not like it Nana will not like it Nana will not like it Nana will not like it
Kwadum (lead drum)
I'm looking for who will pass by, I'm looking for who will pass by, I'm looking for who will pass by

---

the lead drummer dares those who are not expected to take part in this exclusive dance to join at their own peril.

Apɛntɛm, Example 4.7, is sometimes referred to as *apɛntɛ*, and as its name implies, it reminds participants and the general public that the ruler does not hurry or walk fast during processions. Although it is one of the featured dance suites, *apɛntɛm* is usually performed behind the Asantehene when he is walking or being carried in a palanquin during funerary processions. Compared with *ɔyaa*, *apɛntɛm* has a moderate tempo, but like the same dance suite, the bell pattern is organized around an antecedent motion-generated phrase and immediately followed by a consequent phrase that concludes the motion. The integrated drum texts embody the ideal for the ruler to walk in majesty, as the *abukuruwa* drummer cautions him not to rush with *gidi gidi nyɛ* ("rushing is not good"). The *apentema* drummer affirms the previous statement with the phrase *mo nyae* ("stop it"), while the *petia* drummer plays the emphatic text *brɛ brɛ* ("slowly, slowly"). The leading drummer on *kwadum* generates a series of pronouncements—*kaaho kɔ, kaaho ma yɛnkɔ,*

Example 4.7 Apɛntɛm ("Not in a Hurry"): Asantehene *kete* ensemble.

Adawura
Ke ken ke ken ken kankara   Ke ken ke ken ken kankara Ke ken ke ken ken kankara
    Ntorowa
    Sa sa sa Sa sa sa Sa sa sa Sa sa sa Sa sa sa Sa sa sa Sa sa sa
    Sa sa sa Sa sa sa Sa sa sa
    Dondota
    Ketewa kɛseɛ ketewa kɛseɛ ketewa kɛseɛ ketewa kɛseɛ
    ketewa kɛseɛ ketewa kɛseɛ
  Aburukuwa
  Gidi gidi nyɛ, mo nyae mma me nka Gidi gidi nyɛ, mo nyae mma
  me nka
    Apentema
    Mo nyae, mo nyae, Sɛ ɛyɛ ampa a mo nyae Sɛ ɛyɛ ampa a
    mo nyae, Mo nyae, mo nyae
    Petia
    Brɛ brɛ brɛ brɛ brɛ Brɛ brɛ brɛ brɛ brɛ Brɛ brɛ brɛ brɛ brɛ
    Brɛ brɛ brɛ brɛ brɛ
    Kwadum (lead drum)
    Kaaho kɔ Kaaho kɔ Kaaho kɔ Kaaho ma yɛnkɔ Yɛmpɛ
    ntɛm ma yɛnkɔ

English Translation
Adawura
Ke ken ke ken ken kankara   Ke ken ke ken ken kankara Ke ken ke ken ken kankara
    Ntorowa
    Sa sa sa Sa sa sa Sa sa sa Sa sa sa Sa sa sa Sa sa sa Sa sa sa
    Sa sa sa Sa sa sa Sa sa sa
    Dondota
    Small big small big small big small big small big small big
  Aburukuwa
  Rushing is not good, let me say it, rushing is not good, let me say
  it, rushing is not good, let me say it
    Apentema
    Stop it, stop it, stop it if it's true, stop it if it's true, stop it
    stop it if it's true, stop it if it's true
    Petia
    Slowly slowly slowly slowly slowly slowly slowly slowly
    slowly slowly
    Kwadum
    Hurry and go hurry and go hurry and go, hurry and let's go,
    we are not in a hurry, let's go

---

yɛmpɛntɛm ma yɛnkɔ—from the spoken word *kaa wo ho ma yɛnkɔ, yɛmpɛntɛm* ("hurry and let's go, we are not in a hurry"). *Kaaho* is a contraction of *kaa wo ho*, and it is meant to reiterate the theme of this piece: there is value in patience.

Although the tempo is considerably moderate, *kete adaban*, Example 4.8 describes the characteristically fast-paced dance movements. The fast-paced dance is described in Twi as *ɔte adaban*, which is distinct from the priestly dance by the same name. In the past, *adaban* was considered to be a dance for members of the constabulary who carried out the executions of criminals or war captives. Sometimes

Example 4.8 Adaban: Asantehene *kete* ensemble.

Adawura
Ken ke ken ka Ken ke   ken ka Ken ke ken ka Ken ke ken ka Ken ke ken ka
        Ntorowa
        Sa sasa sa Sa sasa sa Sa sasa sa Sa sasa sa Sa sasa sa Sa sasa
        sa Sa sasa sa Sa sasa sa
        Dondota
        Ketewa kɛseɛ ketewa kɛseɛ ketewa kɛseɛ ketewa kɛseɛ ketewa
        kɛseɛ ketewa kɛseɛ
        Aburukuwa
        Ɔnie ɔnie ɔnie ɔnie ɔnie ɔnie ɔnie ɔnie ɔnie ɔnie ɔnie ɔnie ɔnie
        ɔnie ɔnie ɔnie ɔnie ɔnie ɔnie
        Apentema
        Wei fata wei fata wei fata wei fata wei fata wei fata. . . . ampa   ampa
        Petia
        Wei fata wei fata wei fata wei fata wei fata wei fata. . . . ampa   ampa
        Kwadum (lead drum)
        Wei fata wei fata wei fata, Ɛsompa dabia mo mmɛ som Ɛsompa
        dabia mo mmɛ som

English Translation
Adawura
Ken ke ken ka   Ken ke ken ka Ken ke ken ka Ken ke ken ka Ken ke ken ka
        Ntorowa
        Sa sasa sa Sa sasa sa Sa sasa sa Sa sasa sa Sa sasa sa Sa sasa
        sa Sa sasa sa Sa sasa sa
        Dondota
        Small big small big small big small big small big small big
        small big small big
        Aburukuwa
        There he/she is there he/she is there he/she is there he/she is there
        he/she is
        Apentema
        He/she deserves it he/she deserves it he/she deserves it   truly
        Petia
        He/she deserves it he/she deserves it he/she deserves it   truly
        Kwadum (lead drum)
        He/she deserves it he/she deserves it, Extraordinary service come
        and serve every day

---

it is confused with *tɔprɛ* or *atɔprɛ*, a type of execution drumming that was preceded with severe torture by another branch of the constabulary referred to as *tɔprɛfoɔ*. Quite distinct from the *kete* drum ensemble, the main drum is referred to as *tɔprɛ twene*, as opposed to *kwadum* in *kete*.[12] Currently, *adaban* is usually performed behind the Asante king during funerary processions, particularly when he is carried in a palanquin while holding a gun and sword as his props. In those events, the drummers will perform *adaban* until the procession is over and the ruler is brought down from the palanquin. As stated previously, this is one of the few pieces where the lead drummer on *kwadum* intermittently engages in dialogue with the *apentema* and *petia* drummers. Initially, all three drums play the same text, *wei fata* ("he deserves it")—that is, an imaginary victim deserves capital punishment. After a while, the lead drummer on *kwadum* disengages from the joint proclamation to play a text, *εsompa dabia mo mmε som* ("extraordinary service, come and serve everyday"), yielding a combined response from the *apentema* and *petia* drummers: *ampa* ("truly!"). In the meantime, the *aburukuwa* drummer repeats the single phrase *ɔnie* ("there he/she is") throughout the multi-text architectural scheme.

Example 4.9 Adinkra Kofi, Asantehene *kete* ensemble.

Adawura
Ken keken ken   Ken keken ken Ken keken ken Ken keken ken Ken keken ken
                 Ntorowa
                 Sa sasa sa Sa sasa sa Sa sasa sa Sa sasa sa Sa sasa sa Sa sasa sa Sa sasa sa Sa sasa sa
                 Dondota
                 Ketewa kεseε ketewa kεseε ketewa kεseε ketewa kεseε ketewa kεseε ketewa kεseε
          Aburukuwa
          Brε brε brε brε brε bεkum Adinkra Brε brε brε brε brε bεkum Adinkra
          Apentema
          Brε brε brε brε brε bεkum Adinkra Brε brε brε brε brε bεkum Adinkra
          Petia
          Brε brε brε brε brε bεkum Adinkra Brε brε brε brε brε bεkum Adinkra
          Kwadum (lead drum)
          Sε wo pε o Sε won pε o, yε bεkum Adinkra
Variation 1: Kaa wo ho ε kaa wo ho ε, (yε) bεkum Adinkra
Variation 2: Ɔmpε o ɔmpε o, bekum Adinkra

Ebglish Translation
Adawura
Ken keken ke   Ken keken ke Ken keken ke Ken keken ke Ken keken ke Ken keken ke
                Ntorowa
                Sa sasa sa Sa sasa sa Sa sasa sa Sa sasa sa Sa sasa sa Sa sasa sa Sa sasa sa Sa sasa sa
                Dondota
                Small big small big small big small big small big small big small big small big
          Aburukuwa (two straight sticks)
          Slowly slowly slowly slowly slowly, will kill Adinkra, slowly slowly slowly slowly slowly will kill Adinkra
          Apentema (hands, palm technique)
          Slowly slowly slowly slowy slowly, will kill Adinkra, slowly slowly slowly slowly slowly will kill Adinkra
          Petia (two *nkonta*, curved sticks)
          Slowly slowly slowly slowly slowly, will kill Adinkra, slowly slowly slowly slowly slowly will kill Adinkra
          Kwadum
          Whether you like it or not, we shall kill Adinkra
Variation 1: Hurry up hurry up, we shall kill Adinkra
Variation 2: Like it or not, we shall kill Adinkra

Adinkra Kofi is the *kete* version of the same historical piece performed by members of the *fɔntɔmfrɔm* ensemble under the title *akantam* ("oath swearing"). It is an example of intertextual mappings in Asante court music and verbal arts, where variants of pieces with the same historical referents are performed across genres. The distinction between the call-and-response architectural scheme in *fɔntɔmfrɔm* and the simultaneous and cyclical multipart drum texts in kete are all the more apparent in *Adinkra Kofi*. The powerful and combined forces of *aburukuwa, apentema,* and *petia* drummers all playing the same text to intensely demonstrate the resolve of the Asante is quite remarkable. The drum texts for the previous three drums are *brɛ brɛ brɛ brɛ brɛ bɛkum Adinkra* ("slowly slowly will kill Adinkra"). The spoken word in Twi is *yɛ de brɛ brɛ, yɛ bekum Adinkra* ("slowly but surely, we shall kill Adinkra"). The drum texts are without the beginning phrase *yɛ de* or the median phrase *yɛ*. The leading *kwadum* drummer is fairly busy as he alternates between the three themes: the first is *sɛ wo pɛ o, sɛ won pɛ o, yɛ bɛkum Adinkra* ("whether you like it or not, we shall kill Adinkra"); the second is *kaa wo ho ɛ* ("hurry up hurry up, we shall kill Adinkra"); and the third is *ɔpɛ o ɔmpɛ o, bɛkum Adinkra* ("like it or not, we shall kill Adinkra"). The single syllable *yɛ*, which is supposed to be in the median position, is deleted from the phrase. Due to the historicized reckoning of this particular dance suite, it is the piece performed behind the Asantehene when he is walking in a procession from the outskirts of Brɛman to the mausoleum for Remembrance Day Rituals. For the same historical understanding, Nketia reports that if *Adinkra Kofi* is played in the wrong context, it may lead to trouble, a quarrel, or even a fight (Nketia, 1963: 132). He goes on to state that in the past, *Adinkra* was performed in honor of chiefs for their military accomplishments, or it may be performed when an adversary is in the immediate area where the ruler is formally seated.

Example 4.10 Kwame Dogo: Asantehene *kete* ensemble.

Adawura
Ken keken ken   Ken keken ken Ken keken ken Ken keken ken Ken keken ken
Ntorowa
Sa sasa sa Sa sasa sa Sa sasa sa Sa sasa sa Sa sasa sa Sa sasa sa Sa sasa sa Sa sasa sa
Dondota
Ketewa kɛsɛɛ ketewa kɛsɛɛ ketewa kɛsɛɛ ketewa kɛsɛɛ ketewa kɛsɛɛ ketewa kɛsɛɛ
Aburukuwa
Kwame Dog Kwame Dogo Kwame Dog Kwame Dogo Kwame Dog Kwame Dogo
Apentema
Akwoa yi yɛ tenten Akwoa yi yɛ tenten Akwoa yi yɛ tenten Akwoa yi yɛ tenten
Petia
Kwame Dogo . . . Kwame Dogo . . . Kwame Dogo Kwame Dogo Kwame Dogo . . . Kwame Dogo . . .
Kwadum (lead drum)
Kwame Dogo . . . Kwame Dogo . . . Kwame Dogo . . . Kwame wo yɛ tenten kwa

(*Continued*)

Example 4.10 (Continued)

English Translation
Adawura
Ken keken ken   Ken keken ken Ken keken ken Ken keken ken Ken keken ken
                Ntorowa
                Sa sasa sa Sa sasa sa Sa sasa sa Sa sasa sa Sa sasa sa Sa sasa sa Sa sasa
                sa Sa sasa sa
                Dondota
                Small big small big small big small big small big small big small big
                small big
        Aburukuwa
        Kwame Dogo, Kwame Dogo, Kwame Dogo, Kwame Dogo, Kwame Dogo
        Kwame Dogo
        Apentema
        The man is tall the man is tall the man is tall the man is tall the man is tall
        Petia
        Kwame Dogo . . . Kwame Dogo . . . Kwame Dogo Kwame Dogo Kwame
        Dogo . . . Kwame Dogo . . .
        Kwadum (lead drum)
        Kwame Dogo . . . Kwame Dogo . . . Kwame Dogo . . . Kwame you are tall
        for nothing

Kwame Dogo, Example 4.10, is not restricted to any event, and as a result, it could be performed at any time. The main theme is Kwame's height that gives him visibility at all times, but he is unable to take advantage of it, as indicated by the *kwadum* lead drummer's last phrase, *Kwame wo yɛ tenten kwa* ("Kwame, you are tall for nothing").

Example 4.11 Antrefo ("One Who Doesn't Listen to Advice"): Asantehene *kete* ensemble.

Adawura
Ken keken ken   Ken keken ken Ken keken ken Ken keken ken Ken keken ken
                Ntorowa
                Sa sasa sa Sa sasa sa Sa sasa sa Sa sasa sa Sa sasa sa Sa sasa sa Sa sasa
                sa Sa sasa sa
                Dondota
                Ketewa kɛsee ketewa kɛsee ketewa kɛsee ketewa kɛsee ketewa kɛsee
                ketewa kɛsee
        Aburukuwa
        Kɔgye wo ba Kɔgye wo ba Kɔgye wo ba Kɔgye wo ba Kɔgye wo ba Kɔgye
        wo ba
        Apentema
        Dede kwa kwa Dede kwa kwa Dede kwa kwa De de kwa kwa De de kwa
        kwa De de kwa kwa
        Petia
        Gyae mano nkɔ Gyae mano nkɔ Gyae mano nkɔ Gyae mano nkɔ Gyae mano
        nkɔ Gyae mano nkɔ
        Kwadum (lead drum)
        Brɛ brɛ bɛgye wo ba Brɛ brɛ bɛgye wo ba Brɛ brɛ bɛgye wo ba Brɛ brɛ bɛgye
        wo ba

English Translation
Adawura
Ken keken ke   Ken keken ke Ken keken ke Ken keken ke Ken keken ke Ken keken ke
            Ntorowa
            Sa sasa sa Sa sasa sa Sa sasa sa Sa sasa sa Sa sasa sa Sa sasa sa Sa sasa
            sa Sa sasa sa
            Dondota
            Small big small big small big small big small big small big small big
            small big
        Aburukuwa (two straight sticks)
        Go for your child go for your child go for your child go for your child
        Apentema (hands, palm technique)
        You are making noise for nothing you are making noise for nothing
        Petia (two *nkonta*, curved sticks)
        Let him/her go let him/her go let him/her go let him/her go let him/her go
        Kwadum
        Slowly slowly come for your child slowly slowly come for your child

Antrefo, Example 4.11, refers to an individual who is averse to advice and can be compared with *Adaban*, since the outcome of such behavior might have led to executions in the past, or in peaceful times, to a fine in sheep or something else. *Antrefo* can be performed in the same events as *Adaban*. The *aburukua* drummer is the instigator here, as he directs an imaginary troublemaker *Kɔgye wo ba* (go for your child or a valuable possession), while the *apentema* player confirms that he is only making noise for nothing, *de de kwa*. The *petia* player mockingly encourages the troublemaker to go forward, *gyae mano nkɔ* ("let him go"), while the *kwadum* lead drummer provides the required advice without guarantee that if the protagonist plans well, he will be able to go for his child or retrieve his valuable asset.

Example 4.12 Mpɛ Asɛm (Do Not Court Trouble), Asantehene *kete* ensemble.

Adawura
Ken ke ke ken ke ken ka   Ken ke ke ken ke ken ka Ken ke ke ken ke ken ka
            Ntorowa
            Sa sa sa sa Sa sa sa sa Sa sa sa sa Sa sa sa sa Sa sa sa sa Sa sa
            sa sa
            Dondota
            Ketewa kɛseɛ ketewa kɛseɛ ketewa kɛseɛ ketewa kɛseɛ ketewa
            kɛseɛ ketewa kɛseɛ
        Aburukuwa
        Mo nyae mo nyae ma no nka Mo nyae mo nyae ma no nka Mo
        nyae mo nyae ma no nka
    Apentema
    Ɔhene de hene, bra bra Ɔhene de hene, bra bra Ɔhene de hene, bra bra Ɔhene
    de hene, bra bra
    Petia
    Mo nyae mo nyae ma no nka Mo nyae mo nyae ma no nka Mo nyae mo nyae
    ma no nka

(Continued)

Example 4.12 (Continued)

Kwadum (lead drum)
Ɔhenepɔn bra Ɔhenepɔn bra Ɔhenepɔn bra Ɔhenepɔn bra
Variation 1: Ɔkɛseɛ bra bra bra, Ɔhenepɔn bra
Variation 2: Ɔhene bra Ɔhene bra Ɔhene bra

English Translation
Adawura
Ken ke ke ken ke ken ka   Ken ke ke ken ke ken ka Ken ke ke ken ke ken ka
                           Ntorowa
                           Sa sa sa sa Sa sa sa sa Sa sa sa sa Sa sa sa sa
                           Dondota
                           Small big small big small big small big small big small big
                           small big small big
                           Aburukuwa
                           Leave him leave him alone to say it leave him leave him alone to
                           say it
                Apentema
                Our king deserves to be king our king deserves to be king, come come our king
                deserves to be king, come come
                Petia
                Leave him leave him alone to say it leave him leave him alone to say it
                Kwadum
                Mighty king come mighty king come mighty king come mighty king come
Variation 1: The great one come, mighty king come
Variation 2: Our lord come, our lord come, our lord come

Me Mpɛ Asɛm or *Mpɛ Asɛm* ("I do not court trouble" or "do not court trouble")
Example 4.12, is one of the dance suites that can be performed at all kinds of
events. According to Nketia (1963: 130), the integrated drum texts are meant to
project the power of the ruler and to warn potential adversaries. For the first time,
the main theme articulated by the *apentema* player, *Ɔhene de hene, bra bra* ("the
king deserves to be king, come come"), is sandwiched between the *aburukuwa*
and *petia* drummers who are sounding a warning with a unified voice: *mo nyae mo
nyae ma no nka* ("leave him, leave him alone to say it"). Once again, the lead *kwadum* drummer is busy with three thematic areas expressed as "mighty king come,"
"the great one come," and "our lord come," which are played interchangeably.

Example 4.13 Yɛ Tu Mpɔ ("We Are Digging Gold"): Asantehene *kete* ensemble.

Adawura:
Ken ken ke ken   Ken ken ke ken Ken ken ke ken Ken ken ke ken Ken ken ke ken
                  Ntorowa
                  Sa sasa sa Sa sasa sa Sa sasa sa Sa sasa sa Sa sasa sa Sa sasa sa Sa sasa
                  sa Sa sasa sa
                  Donnota
                  Ketewa kɛseɛ ketewa kɛseɛ ketewa kɛseɛ ketewa kɛseɛ
                  Aburukuwa
                  Ampa ampa ampa ampa ampa ampa ampa ampa ampa ampa ampa ampa
                  ampa

Apentema
Ampa sɛ Ampa sɛ Ampa sɛ Ampa sɛ Ampa sɛ Ampa sɛ Ampa sɛ Ampa sɛ
Petia
Ampa ampa ampa ampa ampa ampa ampa ampa ampa ampa ampa ampa ampa ampa
Kwadum
Ka Kaa ho ma yɛnkɔ ɛ ka kaa ho ma yɛnkɔ ɛ ka kaa ho ma yɛnkɔ ɛ, Nana ɛba, Kaa ho ma yɛnkɔ ɛ

English Translation

Adawura:
Ken ken ke ken   Ken ken ke ken Ken ken ke ken Ken ken ke ken Ken ken ke ken
Ntorowa
Sa sasa sa Sa sasa sa Sa sasa sa Sa sasa sa Sa sasa sa Sa sasa sa Sa sasa sa Sa sasa sa
Donnota
Small big small big small big small big small big small big small big small
Aburukuwa
True true true true true true true true true true true true true true true true true true
Apentema
Truly truly truly truly truly truly truly truly truly truly truly truly truly truly truly truly
Petia
True true true true true true true true true true true true true true true true
Kwadum
Hurry and let's go Hurry and let's go Hurry and let's go, Nana is coming, Hurry and let's go

Yɛ Tu Mpɔ ("We Are Digging Gold") is usually performed behind the ruler after the evening's *mmaadae* when he is retiring to his private residence. Due to the reference to gold, Nketia reports that in Asante, it is the most suitable piece to play behind territorial chiefs who are on their way to greet the Asantehene, since he is the occupant of the Gold Stool (Nketia, 1963: 129). Similar to Example 4.12, the main text *ampa sɛ* ("truly indeed") played on the *apentema* is sandwiched between the combined voices of *aburukuwa* and *petia*, as they repeat the single phrase *ampa* ("true"). For his part, the lead drummer on *kwadum* urges the entire ensemble on with the phrase *kaa ho ma yɛnkɔ ɛ* ("hurry and let's go"), repeated three times and followed by *Nana ɛba* ("Nana is coming"), in a recurring fashion.

Example 4.14 Mmorosa ("Alcoholic Beverages"): Asantehene *kete* ensemble.

Adawura
Ken keken ken   Ken keken ken Ken keken ken Ken keken ken Ken keken ken
           Ntorowa
           Sa sasa sa Sa sasa sa Sa sasa sa Sa sasa sa Sa sasa sa Sa sasa sa Sa sasa
           sa Sa sasa sa
           Dondota
           Ketewa kɛseɛ ketewa kɛseɛ ketewa kɛseɛ ketewa kɛseɛ ketewa kɛseɛ
           ketewa kɛseɛ
           Aburukuwa
           Wo nso wo ne hwan? Wo nso wo ne hwan? Wo nso wo ne hwan? Wo nso
           wo ne hwan?
           Apentema
           Panin kwa kwa kwa? Panin kwa kwa kwa? Panin kwa kwa kwa? Panin kwa
           kwa kwa?
           Petia
           Wo nso wo ne hwan? Wo nso wo ne hwan? Wo nso wo ne hwan? Wo nso
           wo ne hwan?
           Kwadum (lead drum)
           Brɛ brɛ panin bra Brɛ brɛ panin bra Brɛ brɛ panin bra Brɛ brɛ panin bra
           Variation 1: Panin bra panin bra panin bra

English Translation
Adawura
Ken keken ke   Ken keken ke Ken keken ke Ken keken ke Ken keken ke Ken keken ke
           Ntorowa
           Sa sasa sa Sa sasa sa Sa sasa sa Sa sasa sa Sa sasa sa Sa sasa sa Sa sasa
           sa Sa sasa sa
           Dondota
           Small big small big small big small big small big small big small big
           small big
           Aburukuwa
           Who do you think you are? Who do you think you are? Who do you think
           you are?
           Apentema
           Just an elder? Just an elder? Just an elder? Just an elder? Just an elder? Just
           an elder?
           Petia
           Who do you think you are? Who do you think you are? Who do you think
           you are?
           Kwadum (lead drum)
           Slowly slowly elder come slowly slowly elder come slowly slowly elder
           come
Variation: Elder come Elder come Elder come

Finally, the last dance suite, *Mmorosa*, refers to a time in the *mmaadae* when the ruler personally serves palm wine (*nsafufuo*) to participants. It is a time when members of the *kete* chorus perform one of their favorite songs, *Okura Mmoraso* ("He is Serving Alcoholic Drinks"). Similar to Example 4.6, *Mmorosa* is a lighthearted dance that essentially invigorates participants from the long day of activities. The multipart architectural framework is similar to *Me mpe Asɛm* and *Yɛ Tu Mpɔ*, as the texts of the *apentema* player, *panin kwa?* ("just an elder?"), are crammed in the middle of the unified voices of the *aburukuwa* and *petia* phrase *won so wo ne hwan?* ("who do you think you are?"). The *kwadum* phrases "slowly, slowly elder come" and "elder come, elder come" are quite reassuring, and we can imagine excited participants having fun with drumming, singing, and dancing—a true celebration of *mmaadae*. We shall now turn our attention to the language and poetry of the Asantehene *fɔntɔmfrɔm* Ensemble.

Fɔntɔmfrɔm

One of the tallest and largest drums in Akanland is *bɔmmaa*, and the associated court ensemble and dances are referred to by the same name. As I discussed in Chapter 2, *bɔmmaa* has been part of Akan court ensembles, and particularly that of territorial chiefs (*Amanhene*) and kings, for centuries, and thus preceded the founding of the Asante Kingdom. Further, I revealed how the huge cylindrical drum was initially called *twenekɛseɛ, bɔmmaa*, and then, finally, *fɛntɛmfrɛm*. My historical account examined how the founder and architect of the kingdom obtained his drums from Tafo and Dɛnkyera. The *bɔmmaa* from Dɛnkyera is slightly larger with deep sonority, representing the male drum, while the relatively smaller *bɔmmaa* from Tafo with a higher sonority is the female drum. In performance, the male *bɔmmaa* is placed to the right, while the female *bɔmmaa* drum is stationed to the left. A drummer is assigned to each drum, and the drums are played with two large curved sticks (*nkonta*). The unusually booming sound that results from the combination of two *bɔmmaa* drums and the accompanying drums became known as *fɛntɛmfrɛm* (literally, "one who swallows elephants"). The implications are that, in a plural performance environment, the booming sounds of the two huge *bɔmmaa* drums are said to "swallow" the sound of all the variety of ensembles. The name *fɛntɛmfrɛm* somehow became corrupted in the Twi language over the years and became known as *fɔntɔmfrɔm*. As is the case with names of ensembles, *fɔntɔmfrɔm* is now the widely used term and has replaced the original *fɛntɛmfrɛm*. It is now common for territorial or divisional chiefs to own two *bɔmaa* drums, but in the past, it was only the Asantehene who used the two huge drums as part of his *fɔntɔmfrɔm* ensemble. In 1963, J.H. Kwabena Nketia listed the full ensemble, consisting of mainly drums, in the following order: two *bɔmmaa*, a pair of *atumpan, adukurogya* (or *adedemma*), *paso, brɛnko, appentemma, nnɔnka* (big squeeze drums), and two large gongs (*nnawuro*). Apart from the *dɔnka*, most of the accompanying drums are missing from the current ensemble at Manhyia Palace, thus resulting in two *bɔmaa*, a pair of *atumpan*, one *dɔnka*, and three large gongs (*nnawuro*; see Figure 4.2).

It is, however, encouraging for the Center for National Culture in Kumase to use all the accompanying drums listed by Nketia. Unlike the players of *nkukuammedie*, who replicate the tonal and rhythmic patterns of the Akan Twi language on their drums without the usual constraints of a *topos* or a timeline, *fɔntɔmfrɔm* dance suites are driven by *topoi* that identify each dance suite in addition to having a bearing on the drum text. The Asantehene's Fɔntɔmfrɔm Ensemble's two chiefs, the Creator's Drummer (*Ɔdomankoma Kyerɛma*), is the chief of the pair of *atumpan* drums. He is also referred to as *Atumpakani* (loosely, the one who "speaks" with the *atumpan* drums). The remaining drums and percussion instruments have their own chiefs. The twin brothers,

Figure 4.2 The Asantehene Fɔntɔmfrɔm ensemble. A pair of *atumpan* drums partly covered with white cloth and played with two curved sticks (*nkonta*); a pair of
huge *bɔmaa* drums partially covered with *nsaa kente* cloths, played with larger
curved sticks; an armpit drum (*dɔnka*), covered with a cloth with leopard skin
patterns; and two (out of three) large gongs (*dawuro*).

Kwabena Atta Panin and Kakra, informed me that in the 1950s, the *fɔntɔmfrɔm* orchestra lost their original *atumpan* drummer, and when they could not find a successor,
they made a special request to the Asantehene Agyeman Prɛmpɛ II to permit Kyerɛma
Pong (affectionately called Kyirifufuo) to join and play with them. Kyerɛma Pong
joined the *fɔntɔmfrɔm* ensemble, but he retained his position and autonomy as the
Atumpakahene and the *Ɔdomankoma Kyerɛma* (the Divine Drummer). Until his death
in 1999, Kyerɛma Pong combined all of the duties of the Principal Court Drummer
(*Ɔdomankoma Kyerɛma/Atumpakani*) with that of the *fɔntɔmfrɔm* ensemble.

   Fɔntɔmfrɔm ensemble represents all that is heroic in Asante culture and, as the saying goes, it projects militancy (*animsɛm* or *mmɛnsɛm*) in all performing situations. In
the inter-war years, it was performed behind the Asantehene on his way to and from
the battlefield. It is performed during the enstoolment and installation of a new king;
in particular, one of the suites, *atrane* or *trane*, is performed during the symbolic firing of a gun by a newly enstooled king in the presence of the Asantehemaa to indicate
his readiness and willingness, like his forebears, to protect the kingdom until his last
breath. Further, *fɔntɔmfrɔm* is performed in precessions during the periodic Akwasidae Public Assembly or the Asanteman Adaekɛseɛ (the Grand Adae that is celebrated
every five years). Additionally, *fɔntɔmfrɔm* is performed during annual remembrance

rites (*Brɛman Ɛsomkɛseɛ*) or *Kuntunkunidae*, funerary rites for members of the royal family, territorial chiefs, and higher-ranked Kumase chiefs (*abrempɔn*). The usual playing position is to place all drums on the ground, with the *bɔmmaa* tilted slightly towards the players to allow the sound to escape from the end, while the *atumpan* drums are placed on a stand with the membrane facing the dancers. The *dɔnka* is placed under the armpit to enable the player to squeeze the strings to vary the pitch while striking the membrane with a curved stick. Carrying the *bɔmaa* and *atumpan* drums on the head and playing behind chiefs during processions are essential parts of the previously-named situations (see cover picture). There are five main suites of dances—*Atoprɛtia, Naawea, Akantam, Ɛkyɛm*, and *Trane*—with identifiable sub-themes in three out of four of them. There is no particular order for performing the dances, as the context determines the choice of dance suite, order of performance, and duration of each piece. Ɛkyɛm is a dance suite strictly for the shield bearers while *Trane* is performed for the symbolic firing of gun by the Asantehene. I noted in Chapter 2 that with the exception of the *dɔnka*, all of the supporting drums—*adukurogya* (or *adedemma*), *paso, brɛnko*, and *apentema*—are missing from the Asantehene's Fɔntɔmfrɔm Ensemble. As a mark of contemporary experience, it is now possible to recover the missing drums because the Center for National Culture (the CNC) in Kumase performs with the full complement of the ensemble. Given this situation, my textual transcription of the language and poetry of the fɔntɔmfrɔm ensemble is limited to the gong (dawuro), atumpan, and two bɔmaa drums. I will begin with drum texts of *Atoprɛtia*, follow with *Naawea*, and conclude with *Akantam*.

Atoprɛtia, Example 4.15, is a war dance that was historically performed before or on the way to war. The heroic militancy is evident from the props, as the Asantehene dances with a gun in his left hand and the Mpɔnpɔnsɔn sword in his right hand, or with just a gun if he is being carried in a palanquin. Thus the music and dance of *atoprɛtia* is very serious and intense. In peaceful times, death has replaced wars as the invincible but formidable foe that constantly engages the living in an arduous battle we cannot seem to win. As the Akan will say, *owuo ne yɛ ko* (death is at war with us). The entire drum text in the previous example engages a call and response framework at the global level between the atumpan drummer and the two *bɔmaa* drummers to broadcast to the general public how they conquered town, after town, after town. The atumpan drummer calls the gong players, Adawura Kofi, to rise up for action from Lines 1–4 and then establishes the *topos* that not only sets the tempo but also identifies the type of dance suite in Line 5. The two Bɔmaa drummers join the ensemble with the recurring phrase *bra, bra, bra* (come, come, come), which may well be a hold pattern meant to encourage the ruler to come forward with the gun and sword for the dance. They will sustain the hold pattern until they receive a call, *Yeeeee*, from the atumpan drummer in Line 7. Although the bɔmaa drums repeat the same phrase, *Y'akye Odikuro* (literally, we have captured the head of town or a chief) from Lines 8–26, they are not referring to the same event or chief that has been conquered; rather, they signify successive encounters in different locations at different times. The non-lexical phrase, *gede gede gede*, in Line 27 is a symbolic description of fighting on the battlefield that goes on as long as it takes the atumpan drummer to initiate a call, as in Line 28, for the bɔmaa to respond as before. Prɛmpɛ in Lines 11, 17, 19, 23, 25, 32, 38, 40, 44, and 46 recalls the historical achievements of the 13th and 14th kings, Agyeman Prɛmpɛ (1888–1931) and Ɔsɛɛ Agyeman Prɛmpɛ II (1931–1970). With remarkable vision and statesmanship,

Example 4.15 Atopretia, Asanthene fɔntɔmfrɔm ensemble.

Atumpan
1. Adawura Kofi
2. Ma wo homene so ɛ
3. Ɔdomankoma Kyerɛma
4. Ma wo homene so ɛ
5. Keken ken, keken ken, keken ken, keken ken
   Bɔmaa
   6. Bra bra bra bra bra bra bra bra bra
Atumpan
7. Yeeeee
      8. Y'akye Odikuro
9. Ma 'nka?
      10. Y'akye Odikuro
11. Prɛmpɛ
      12. Y'akye Odikuro
13. Yeeeee
      14. Y'akye Odikuro
15. Ma 'nka?
      16. Y'akye Odikuro
17. Prɛmpɛ
      18. Yɛkura kuram
19. Prɛmpɛ
      20. Yɛkura kuram
21. Monka
      22. Yɛkura kuram
23. Prɛmpɛ
      24. Y'akye Odikuro
25. Prɛmpɛ
      26. Y'akye Odikuro
      27. Gede gede gede gede gede gege gede gede gede gede gede gede gede gede gede
28. Yeeeee
      29. Y'akye Odikuro
30. Mannka?
      31. Y'akye Odikuro
32. Prɛmpɛ
      33. Y'akye Odikuro
34. Yeeeee
      35. Y'akye Odikuro
36. Ma 'nka?
      37. Y'akye Odikuro
38. Prɛmpɛ
      39. Yɛkura kuram
40. Prɛmpɛ
      41. Yɛkura kuram
42. Monka
      43. Yɛkura kuram
44. Prɛmpɛ
      45. Y'akye Odikuro
46. Prɛmpɛ
      47. Y'akye Odikuro

English Translation
Atumpan
1. Adawura Kofi (gong)
2. Gear yourself up
3. The Creator's drummer
4. Gear yourself up
5. Keken ken keken ken, keken ken keken ken
   Bɔmaa
   6. Come, come, come, come, come, come, come, come, come, come, come,
Atumpan
7. Yeeee
   8. Odikuro has been captured
9. Didn't I predict it?
   10. Odikuro has been captured
11. Didn't I predict it?
   12. Odikuro has been captured
13. Prempɛ
   14. Odikuro has been captured
15. Yeeee
   16. Odikuro has been captured
17. Didn't I predict it?
   18. Odikuro has been captured
19. Prempɛ
   20. We cling to it
21. Prempɛ
   22. We cling to it
23. Say it
   24. We cling to it
25. Prempɛ
   26. Odikuro has been captured
27. Prempɛ
   28. Odikuro has been captured
   29. Gede gede gede gede gede gege gede gede gede gede gede gede gede gede
30. Yeeee
   31. Odikuro has been captured
32. Didn't I predict it?
   33. Odikuro has been captured
34. Didn't I predict it?
   35. Odikuro has been captured
36. Prempɛ
   37. Odikuro has been captured
38. Yeeee
   39. Odikuro has been captured
40. Didn't I predict it?
   41. Odikuro has been captured
42. Prempɛ
   43. We cling to it
44. Prempɛ
   45. We cling to it
46. Say it
   47. We cling to it
48. Prempɛ
   59. Odikuro has been captured
50. Prempɛ
   51. Odikuro has been captured

both rulers developed outstanding solutions to the tumultuous times that characterized the period of extensive colonization in West Africa. The restoration of Asanteman in the colonial Gold Coast in 1935 would have been impossible but for the vision and resilience of the previously-named kings. The rationale behind the repeated phrase, *Yɛkuram yɛkuram*, from Lines 18–22 becomes clear when it is related to the endeavors of both kings. Taken at the literal level, we cling to it, is a solemn pledge by the citizens to their forebears that they will hold on to and protect the enduring institutions that their forebears established for them. In other words, they will not allow the sacrifices of both rulers to go in vain. The solemn declaration transitions into a dramatization of the battlefield with its sonic representation on the bɔmaa drums by the non-lexical phrase *gede gede gede* in Line 27. Atoprɛtia is performed until the atumpan drummer initiates a new *topos*, thus introducing another dance suite, *Naawea*, which is the basis for my next discussion.

Example 4.16 Naawea-Asantehene fɔntɔmfrɔm ensemble.

Atumpan
1. Adawura Kofi
2. Ma wo homene so ɛ
3. Ken keken ken, ken keken ken, ke keken ken
4. Yee!
    Bɔmaa
    5. Ɔhene ko, Ɔhene nnwane
6. Yee!
    7. Ɔhene ko, Ɔhene nnwane
8. Yee!
    9. Ɔhene ko, Ɔhene nnwane
10. Yirefi Fredua
    11. Ɔhene ko, Ɔhene nnwane
12. Boafo akoako
    13. Ɔhene ko, Ɔhene nnwane
14. Kɔtɔkɔhene
    15. Ɔhene ko, Ɔhene nnwane
16. Kɔtɔkɔheneba
    17. Ɔhene ko, Ɔhene nnwane
18. Yiadɔm Boakye Berempɔnba
    19. Ɔhene ko, Ɔhene nnwane
20. Ampem Bɔakuroba
    21. Ɔhene ko, Ɔhene nnwane

Variation
Atumpan
1. Yee!
    Bɔmaa
    2. Ɔhene ko, Ɔhene dwane
3. Yee!
    4. Ɔhene ko, Ɔhene dwane
5. Yee!
    6. Ɔhene ko, Ɔhene dwane
7. Yirefi Fredua
    8. Ɔhene ko, Ɔhene dwane
9. Boafo akoako
    10. Ɔhene ko, Ɔhene dwane etc

English Translation
Atumpan
1. Adawura Kofi
2. Arise!
3. Ke ken ken ken, ke ken ken ken, ke ken ken ken
4. Yee!
    Bɔmaa
    5. The king fights, the king does not flee
6. Yee!
    7. The king fights, the king does not flee
8. Yee!
    9. The king fights, the king does not flee
10. Yirefi Fredua
    11. The king fights, the king does not flee
12. Boafo fights and fights
    13. The king fights, the king does not flee
14. King of Kɔtɔkɔ
    15. The king fights, the king does not flee
16. The son of the king of Kɔtɔkɔ
    17. The king fights, the king does not flee
18. Yiamdɔm Boakye Berempɔnba
    19. The king fights, the king does not flee
20. Ampem Bɔakuroba
    21. The king fights, the king does not flee

Variation
Atumpan
1. Yee!
    Bɔmaa
    2. The king fights, a king/chief flee
3. Yee!
    4. The king fights, a king/chief flee
5. Yee!
    6. The king fights, a king/chief flee
7. We are from Fredua
    8. The king fights, a king/chief flee
9. Boafo fights and fights
    10. The king fights, a king/chief flee

Sub-Theme. Kuakua Anisuo

Atumpan	Bɔmaa Berima (Male)	Bɔmaa Obaa (Female)
1. Bra	da hɔ	Na wo bɛhu
2. Bra	da hɔ	Na wo bɛhu
3. Bra bra bra	da hɔ, da hɔ, da hɔ	Na wobɛhu, Na wobɛhu, Na wobɛhu

English Translation

Atumpan	Bɔmaa Bɛrima (Male)	Bɔmaa Obaa (Female)
1. Come	wait	and you will see what will happen
2. Come	wait	and you will see what will happen
3. come, come, come	wait, wait, wait	and you will see what will happen
		and you will see what will happen
		and you will see what will happen

The ominous undercurrent that is the hallmark of *atopretia* is rectified with celebration in *naawea*, resulting in two contrasting ends of a spectrum. The former is
performed at a relatively slow tempo, while the latter is fast. In performance situations, *atopretia* is invariably followed by *naawea*. If *atopretia* is performed on the
way to the battlefield, *naawea* is the dance that is performed on the way back from
a successful war campaign. In that sense, a return from the battlefield without the
celebratory performance of *naawea* is indicative of a dreaded outcome. Similarly,
atopretia is performed when the Asantehene is on his way to pay his last respects
to a deceased chief or member of the royal family; that is, he is metaphorically on
his way to war. *Naawea* is performed on his way back from viewing the body. The
signal to change from *atopretia* to *naawea* is given by the atumpan drummer in
Lines 1–2, as members of the ensemble will stop abruptly the moment they hear
the signal. Similar to the formal architecture in *atopretia*, the recurring phrase
of the two *bomaa* drums—*the king fights, the king does not flee*—is a declaration that they rely on the ruler to protect them as well as to defend them. As the
Commander-in-Chief, he leads by example but not from a distance. The active
participation of Asante rulers in conflicts bring into sharp focus the Akan proverb:
"if a chief declines to fight or lead a war his subjects flee" (*odehyeɛ anko a, akoa
dwane*). As noted in the previous example, the recurring *bomaa* phrase from Lines
5–21 entails diverse war situations and several different battle scenarios.

It is during the repeated *bomaa* phrases (cyclical in effect) that the Ɔkyerɛma
playing the atumpan drums momentarily disengages from the call-and-response
framework to sound the strong appellations (*abodin*) and by-names (*mmrane*) of
either the Asantehene, the dancer, a chief, or to call upon a chief to join the dance
space. In the previous example, Lines 10, 12, 14, 16, 18, and 20 sourced out referential poetry in praise of the king. Thus King of Kɔtɔkɔ, the son of the King of Kɔtɔkɔ,
in addition to being a reference to the king's parentage, is also the name of his father
in Line 18 (Yiadɔm Boakye Berempɔnba) and his mother, the late Asantehemaa
Nana Afia Kobi Sɛɛwaa Ampem II, who is represented by her last name *Ampem*
and her strong appellation, *Boakuroba*. Depending on the situation, sometimes the
bomaa recomposes the recurring phrase *Ɔhene ko, Ɔhene nnwane* (The king fights,
the king does not flee) by replacing it with *Ɔhene ko, Ɔhene dwane* (The king fights,
a king/chief flees). A variation on the first theme, the recomposed phrase implies
that, since the king stood firm and fought, the enemy took to his heels. In other
words, there is value in strong and unwavering leadership. In the days of territorial
expansion and conquests, *Akantam* (Oath Swearing) was performed for territorial
chiefs (*Amanhene*) who doubled as commanders of their divisions to reaffirm their
royalty to the Gold Stool before embarking on war. There is usually a verbal component when the chiefs swear by invoking the Great Oath (*Ntam Kɛseɛ*) of Asanteman
to the Asantehene before they go to the battlefield. The following *Akantam* dance
suite is a non-verbal constituent of the verbally intoned Great Oath.

Akantam, Example 4.17, is fundamentally based on proverbs. Kwabena Nketia's 1953 anthology of drum poetry, *Ayan*, includes seventy-seven verses that
he collected in the Akan areas in the colonial era and immediately following
independence in the early 1960s (Nketia, 1974: 95–114). Akantam is generally

Example 4.17 Adinkra (Akantam, Oath Swearing Dance), Center for National Culture fɔntɔmfrɔm ensemble, Kumase.

Atumpan
1. Adawura
2. Ma wo homene so ɛ
3. Ken ke ken ken ken ka, ken ke ken ken ken ka, ken ke ken ken ken ka
   Bɔmaa
   4. Gruuuuuuuuuuuuuuuuuuuu
   5. bra bra bra bra bra bra
6. Yɛde brɛbrɛ bɛkum Adinkra
   7. Boafo akoako
8. Yɛde brɛbrɛ bɛkum Adinkra
   9. Boafo akoako
10. Yɛdeɛ yɛde brɛbrɛ bekum Adinkra
    11. Boafo akoako
12. Sono akura sono akura
    Atumpan and Bɔmaa
    13. Sono abotokura
    14. Sono akurapa
    15. Sono akura kronkron kronkron
    16. Bediako, Bediako, Bediako, Bediako, Bediako
    Bɔmaa
    17. Bra bra
    18. Bra bra
Repeat Line 6-18

English Translation
Atumpan
1. Adawura
2. Arise!
3. Ken ke ken ken, ken ke ken ken, ken ke ken ken
   Bɔmaa
   4. Gruuuuuuuuuuuuuuuuuuuu
   5. Bra bra Bra bra bra bra
Atumpan
6. Gradually, we shall kill Adinkra
   7. Boafo always fighting/the fighter's fighter
8. Gradually, we shall kill Adinkra
   9. Boafo always fighting/the fighter's fighter
10. As for us, we shall gruadually kill Adinkra
    11. Boafo always fighting/the fighter's fighter
12. There is a difference between a mouse and a mouse
Atumpan and Bɔmaa
    13. There is a difference between a stripped mouse
    14. There a difference between a shrewd mouse
    15. There is a difference between a real mouse
    16. Bediako, Bediako, Bediako, Bediako, Bediako ken ke

Repeat Line 6-16 as needed.

performed at a medium tempo. The title of the piece is named for the powerful and newly enstooled king of Gyaaman, Nana Adinkra, who was reported to have made a replica of the Gold Stool for his kingdom. Asantehene Ɔsɛe Asibe Bonsu (1800–1823) prevailed upon Nana Adinkra to surrender the stool peacefully to him. Adinkra eventually surrendered the stool to emissaries of the Asantehene, led by Kwame Butuakwa. He later changed his mind and sent soldiers to go after them, but they failed to retrieve the stool. Nana Adinkra's only option was to prepare for war while the Asante did not underestimate his resolve. It took three years for the eventual showdown between the two foes, but in the intervening years before the war, Asante drummers composed the previous phrase, *yɛ de brɛbrɛ bekum Adinkra* (slowly but surely, we shall kill Adinkra), which advocates patience as a virtue. The Asante defeated Nana Adinkra, brought him to Kumase, made a gold effigy of his decapitated head, and attached it to the base of the Gold Stool. There is more to this single phrase than it seems. By the time of this encounter, the Asante were keenly aware of extraordinary developments in the expressive arts in the great state of Gyaaman. Not only had the Gyaaman developed an effective political system, but they had also created an impressive array of visual arts in the form of woodcarvings and textiles. In that sense, "capture" is not only restricted to the physical act of seizing King Adinkra, but it also recognizes that, slowly but surely, the Asante shall learn skills of creativity in the visual and performing arts from the Gyaaman. In fact, several of his craftsmen were brought to Kumase to continue practicing their crafts. There is certainly value in patience.

As in the previous examples, the message is propelled by the interactive play of call and response between the atumpan and the two bɔmaa drums. That the long-term goals and determination of the Asante do not allow any state to reduce the sacredness of the Gold Stool by making a replica is clear from Lines 6–16. The first is a collective will that is projected in the beginning phrase *yɛde* (we shall) in Lines 6 and 8, while the second begins with the pickup phrase *yɛdeɛ* (as for us) in Line 10. In that sense, the Ɔkyerema (the Creator's Drummer) personalizes the message for the Asantehene since he is the Commander-in-Chief. Line 12 delves into metaphoric allusion and compares the house mouse with the mouse in the forest by using the prosody in the Twi language to construct a memorable phrase, *sono akura sono akura* (there is a difference between a mouse and a mouse). The first phrase, *sono*, is the Akan word *ɛsono*, with the first letter (ɛ) elided in the drum text. The collective sounding of the phrases from Lines 13–16 is suggestive of several soldiers chanting, which is marked by two brief, non-sounded pauses at the end of Lines 13 and 14 that contrast with the continuous sounding of Lines 15–16. Another interpretation is the parallel comparison between a mouse and mouse in the antecedent phrase in Line 12 and three collective responses from Lines 13–16 to ground the initial agitation in Line 12. At the end of the collective sounding of phrases, the two bɔmaa drums resume another hold pattern (Lines 17–18) while waiting for a call from the atumpan drummer. The piece is repeated from Lines 6–18 until the atumpan drummer initiates a new piece. The next example is tied to Akan settlements, migration, and religious philosophy that recognize the natural order as created by the Supreme Being (Onyankopɔn).

Example 4.18 Ɔkwan Twareɛ Asuo (The Path Crosses the River. Akantam-Oath Swearing Dance)-Asantehene Fɔntɔmfrɔm Ensemble.

Atumpan
1. Ɔkwan tware asuo
2. Asuo tware ɔkwan
   Bɔmaa
   3. Ɔpanin ne hwan?
4. Ɔkwan tware asuo
5. Asuo tware ɔkwan?
   6. Ɔpanin ne hwan?
   Atumpan and Bɔmaa
   7. Yɛbɔɔ kwan no kɔtoo asuo no
   8. Asuo no firi tete
   9. Ɔdomankoma bɔɔ adeɛ
   10. Kronkron Tano, Brefi Tano
   11. Agya Kwaante e
   12. Woama Bosom Pra adi afaseɛ
   13. Ɔwea damirifa, damirifa, damirifa, damirima, damirifa

English Translation
Atumpan
1. The path crosses the river
2. The river crosses the path
   Bɔmaa
   3. Who is the elder?
4. The path crosses the river
5. The river crosses the path
   6. Who is the elder?
   Atumpan and Bɔmaa
   7. We created the path and met the river
   8. The river is from ancient times
   9. The creator created things
   10. Tano the holy one, Brefi Tano
   11. Agya Kwaante e
   12. You have compelled Pra to eat water yam
   13. The tree bear condolence, condolence, condolence, condolence, condolence

Akans are very concerned with constructing harmonious relationships with their immediate environments, including, but not limited to, the sky, earth, oceans and rivers, and the forest. For those familiar with the Akan physical landscape, there are a profusion of streams and rivers straddling Akan settlements, with some of the major rivers including Ankobra, Birem, Offin, Pra, Tano, and the Volta. The river deity of the Asante is River Tano. Centuries of reflection by the Akan about the resources of rivers led to the understanding that rivers are from God, the Creator of all things, and that in their search for food and shelter, human beings created the path and met the river. The path is constructed by physical beings, but the river is one of the spiritual manifestations of God on earth. It is this existential experience that is expressed by the Ɔdmankoma Kyerɛma (the Divine Drummer) in the previous dance suite. Additionally, it is a constant reminder for the Asante to praise and thank the Supreme Being for providing us with rivers to sustain us on earth. There is value in a harmonious relationship with the environment.

Dialogue between the atumpan and bɔmaa drums is configured in a riddle. The atumpan initiates the riddle in Lines 1 and 2, while the bɔmaa rounds it up with the question in Line 3. After repeating the riddle (Lines 4–5), the atumpan and bɔmaa join forces to deliver answers: we (humans) created the path and met the river (Line 7), but the river is from antiquity (Line 8). It bears repeating that, in Line 9, they acknowledge God (the Creator of all things) as the source of the river. Line 10 then reinforces the belief that the Asante river deity Tano is truly holy, and then qualifies it with the by-name *Brefi Tano*. Line 11 is a name, while Line 12 calls on River Pra with the name deity (Bosom-Pra). It is a bad omen to drop water yam in the River Pra. The Creator's drummer anticipates the imbalance in the natural order that would occur if they were to touch or drop water yam in the Pra River. The last phrase is continuous with the apparently bad picture, when the drummer offers condolences to the people by alluding to the tree bear (*ɔwea*). According to the Asante, the lonely tree bear always brings attention to itself when it cries intermittently in the night and unknowingly leads the hunter to follow the sound of its cries to its location, hence also facing its fate. That explains the expression of condolences after the name of the tree bear is cited. Another version of the predicament of the lonely tree bear is the story of how it lost its once-beautiful tail when several women admired it, and in the process of showering praises on it, an unknown assailant chopped off its beautiful tail and ran away with it. The latter version is usually performed by *nnwonkorɔ* and *adowa* groups. We shall now consider the language and poetry of mpintin ensemble.

Mpintin

Mpintin is a compound word derived from the Akan word *pene* (literally, push/pushing) and *tene*, the second syllable in *san-tene* that describes a procession. Like fɔntɔmfrɔm or kete, mpintin refers to the drums, music, or both. Essentially, the mpintin ensemble provides music for court processions, ceremonies, and festivals. It is literally meant to push the king forward if he is walking or being carried in a palanquin. Nketia describes the music of mpintin as boisterous, gay, and lighthearted (Nketia, 1963: 134). Taken as a whole, the mpintin ensemble is quite unique on four levels. First, it is one of the few ensembles where the *topos* (timeline) is assigned to a drum—a fairly small donno (squeeze drum)—instead of the ubiquitous metal bell. None of the varieties of rattles are included in the ensemble. Second, despite the primacy of *topos*, mpintin drum patterns are not for dancing, but strictly meant for processions, as I indicated previously. Third, all the instruments in the ensemble are not originally Asante (or Akan) drums; rather, they originated from Dagbamba, the northern neighbors of Asante, and are indicative of cultural interactions between the two kingdoms. I recounted how the Asante adapted the mpintin ensemble during the reign of Asantehene Kwaku Dua in Chapter 2. Although the Asantehene asked male members of the royal family—nephews, cousins, grandchildren, and sons, including those of past kings—to constitute the drummers (*mpintinkafoɔ*), he selected Nana Kwaku Owusu, a courtier but not a royal, to be the presiding chief (*Mpintinkafoɔhene*). Another version of the origins of the *mpintin* ensemble in Akan is Nketia, who traces it to the "seventh king of Denkyira, Nana Boa Amponsɛm" (1963: 120).

In the Asantehene's court, the instrumental music of *mpintin* is considered lively or, in the words of Nketia, "boisterous and gay" (Nketia, 1963: 134). As a result, it is performed on celebratory occasions such as the Akwasidae that I alluded to in the Prologue, or during state visits of dignitaries. The Asantehene's *mpintin* ensemble is never performed during funerary rites, but for historical purposes, the only exception is the funerary rites involving Kumase Adontenhene where the Asantehene may participate with the *mpintin* ensemble. The drums are exclusively closed types, and, apart from the single *Donno Dawuro*, there is no fixed number of drums because the size of the ensemble is determined by the number of drums and players available for events. In terms of physical appearance, there are three different sizes of donno, with the smallest playing the time line, two different sizes of *mpintintoa* (large-sized gourds; the largest of which is referred to as *saawisie*), and the large and cylindrical *gyamadudu* drum.[13] While the different sizes of donno and gyamadudu have leather on both ends, making them double-headed, the large-sized gourds are single-headed drums with leather covering only one side. When performing, *donno* drums are placed under the armpit and played with curved sticks, while the large-sized gourd drums are attached to a pair of braces and hung over each shoulder to position them on the belly, where they are played with both hands. A sling is attached to the *gyamadudu* to enable the player to hang it on his left shoulder while playing with a slightly bigger stick. All of the instruments are played while standing or walking in processions. Nketia identifies three major pitches that correspond with the sizes of *donno* drums: the *dawuro* and *ntwaamu donno* are smaller with higher pitches, followed by the medium *agyesowa donno* (responders) with relatively middle pitches, while the larger *dɔnka* (Pl. nnɔnka), which is the leading drum, has lower sonority (Nketia, 1963: 14–15). On the other hand, the sound of the medium-sized *mpintintoa* can be described as medium-pitch, while the larger *mpintintoa*, known in Asante as *saawisie*, produces relatively lower pitches. The *gyamadudu* cylindrical drum provides the lowest sonority, which grounds the sound of the mpintin ensemble. All of the drums are covered with a light cloth. The cyclical topos is assigned to the smallest drum, *donno dawuro*, while two *ntwamu donno* respond with a counter pattern. There is no fixed number for the *Agyesoa donno* (responding drums), and at any given time there may be two, four, or more, depending on the number of players available. Additional rhythm patterns are played on *mpintintoa* and *saawisie*. As in the responding squeeze drums, there are no restrictions on the number of large-sized gourds, and, as a result, there may be four *mpintintoa* and two *saawisie*, or more of each at any given time (Figure 4.3).

Besides recording ceremonies involving the *mpintin* ensemble, I worked with the drummers in the summers of 2009 and 2011. Opanin Kofi Adu-Sarhene deputized for Nana Kwaku Owusu II, the *mpintin* chief, who was recuperating from a

Figure 4.3 Mpintin ensemble performing processional music behind the Asantehene in
     Akwasidae public assembly. Four *mpintinto* and four armpit drums are visible
     in the picture, July 17, 2016.

Source: Picture by author.

short illness. The repertoire of the *mpintin* ensemble consists of two basic pieces:
ɛfɔm (earth/ground) and *ɛsoro* (above/up), and for those familiar with the noted
pieces, they can discern if the procession is moving forward or if it is at a stand-
still. *Ɛfɔm* is performed when the Asantehene is walking in a procession, while
ɛsoro is performed when he is carried in a palanquin. There are two types of *ɛfɔm*:
ntientia and tenten. Ntientia are short, repeated phrases that allow the performers
to conserve their energy when there is a pause in the procession, or if the Asantehene is taking brief pauses to bid farewell to his subjects by shaking hands after
an event. There are times when the king will pause to listen to the messages of the
ivory trumpets or to acknowledge the invocation of the *mmedie* drums, and that
will call for these short repeated phrases. *Tenten* refers to long, recurring phrases
meant to literally push the Asantehene forward when he is walking majestically in
a procession. In those instances, his steps are timed to correspond to the rhythmic
patterns of the *mpintintoa*, with the umbrella carriers (*kyinyɛkyimfoɔ*) also lifting
the huge umbrellas (*bɛnkyinyɛ*) up and down in synchrony with the rhythm patterns. The only piece that is performed when the Asantehene is being carried in a
palanquin is appropriately referred to as *Ɛsoro* (Above or Up). Nketia refers to the
ɛfɔm pieces as *akyea* (describes the manner of walking), while the piece played
behind the palanquin is *aten*, when there is a need to hurry (Nketia, 1963: 134).

Example 4.19 Ɛfɔm-Ntientia (On the Ground, Short Version (Standing)), Asantehene mpintin ensemble.

Donno Dawuro
Biribi ba biribi Biribi ba biribi Biribi ba biribi Biribi ba biribi Biribi ba biribi (biribi ɛreba
Dawuro Ntwaamu
    brɛbrɛ   brɛbrɛ   brɛbrɛ   brɛbrɛ
Dɔnka
Gyataba nante   Gyataba nante   Gyataba nante   Gyataba nante

Mpintintoa
    brɛbrɛ   brɛbrɛ   brɛbrɛ   brɛbrɛ
Saawisie
    brɛbrɛ ssh   bre bre sshh   brɛbrɛ sshh   brɛbrɛ sshh
Gyamadudu
Brɛ brɛ brɛbrɛ   Brɛ brɛ   brɛbrɛ   Brɛ brɛ

Dɔnka Variations
1. Ɔhene kyea/Na wo yɛ kyɛkyerɛ kyɛkyerɛ
2. Gyataba ɛba, Gyataba ɛba, Gyataba ɛba
3. Me yɛ dehyemapa/Me bɔ dondo/Ɔsee duom ma yɛnkɔ ɛ

English Translation
Donno Dawuro
Biribi ba biribi Biribi ba biribi Biribi ba biribi Biribi ba biribi Biribi ba biribi (biribi ɛreba
Dawuro Ntwaamu
    Slowly   Slowly   Slowly   Slowly
Dɔnka
Lion cub walks Lion cub walks Lion cub walks Lion cub walks

Mpintintoa
    Slowly   Slowly   Slowly   Slowly
Saawisie
    Slowly ssh   Slowly sshh   Slowly sshh   Slowly sshh
Gyamadudu
Slow slow slowly   Slow slow   slowly   Slow slow

Dɔnka Variations
1. The King is greeting/But you are not ready
2. The son of lion is coming, the son of lion is coming, the son of lion is coming
3. I am a true royal/I play donno/Ɔsee let's go

Examples 4.19 and 4.20 are performed as a single piece. The former, *Ntientia* (Short Phrases) fluidly moves to *Tenten* (Long Phrases) and then back to the Short Phrases without a break. The drum patterns in *mpintin* straddles the call-and-response and multipart architectural frameworks in fɔntɔnfrɔm and kete, respectively. The text of Donno Dawuro, the timeline, literally translates as "something is coming, something"—that is, the ruler is coming. Seven syllables of the Twi text, Biribi ba biribi, are played with five attack points with a sense of an antecedent

Example 4.20 Ɛfɔm-Tenten (On the Ground, Long Version (Walking)), Asantehene mpintin ensemble.

Donno Dawuro
Biribi ba biribi Biribi ba biribi Biribi ba biribi Biribi ba biribi Biribi ba biribi (biribi ɛreba
Dawuro Ntwaamu
 brebre brebre brebre brebre brebre brebre brebre brebre rebre brebre brebre
Dɔnka
Me yɛ dehyemapa Me bɔ dondo Me yɛ dehyemapa Me bɔ dondo Me yɛ dehyemapa Me
bɔ dondo
Mpintintoa
 brebre brebre brebre brebre brebre brebre brebre brebre rebre brebre brebre
Saawisie
 brebre ssh bre bre sshh brebre sshh brebre sshh brebre ssh bre bre sshh brebre

Gyamadudu
Bre bre brebre bre Bre bre brebre bre Bre bre brebre bre Bre bre brebre bre

Dɔnka Variations
1. Ɔhene kyea/Na wo yɛ kyɛkyere kyɛkyerɛ
2. Gyataba ɛba, Gyataba ɛba, Gyataba ɛba
3. Ɔsee duom ma yɛnkɔ ɛ

English Translation

Donno Dawuro
Biribi ba biribi Biribi ba biribi Biribi ba biribi Biribi ba biribi Biribi ba biribi (biribi ɛreba
Dawuro Ntwaamu
 brebre brebre brebre brebre brebre brebre brebre brebre rebre brebre brebre
Dɔnka
Me yɛ dehyemapa Me bɔ dondo Me yɛ dehyemapa Me bɔ dondo Me yɛ dehyemapa Me
bɔ dondo
Mpintin Ntoa
 brebre brebre brebre brebre brebre brebre brebre brebre rebre brebre brebre
Saawisie
 brebre ssh bre bre sshh brebre sshh brebre sshh brebre ssh bre bre sshh brebre

Gyamadudu
Bre bre brebre bre Bre bre brebre bre Bre bre brebre bre Bre bre brebre bre

---

phrase made up of three attack points that is rounded off with a consequent phrase
made up of two attack points. It is performed as Biri-bi ba bi-bi, where two syllables, biri, are given a single stroke. It is worth noting that the phrase Biribi ba
(something is coming), without mentioning the name of what is actually coming,
confers something strange, fearful, and mysterious in reference to the ruler. The
remaining drum patterns of Dawuro Ntwaamu, Dɔnka, Mpintintoa, Saawisie, and
Gyamadudu are overlaid with a hocket arrangement, whereby the phrase *Gyataba
nante brebre* is distributed among the previous drums and cyclically performed
for as long as the Asantehene is standing and greeting his subjects. As the lead
drum, the Dɔnka player is assigned the two phrases, Gyataba nante (the lion cub

walks), while Dawuro Ntwaamu and the remaining drums conclude the phrase with brɛbrɛ (slowly). The non-lexical ssh that is tagged on the concluding phrase is created by rubbing both hands on the drum head of the *saawisie* gourd drums, and it is meant to describe the sound of the ruler's sandals. The Gyamadudu's part is slightly different, with the integrated texts *brɛ brɛ brɛbrɛ* (slow slow, slowly). The repeated rhythm pattern of accompanying drums provides a stable base for the Dɔnka player to introduce a variety of themes and text substitutions. For instance, *Me yɛ dehye mapa* (I'm a true royal) replaces *Gyataba nante* (the lion cub walks), followed by the phrase *Me bɔ donno* (I play donno). In practice, the lead donno drummer repeats all of these phrases as long as he can, or he can follow "I'm a true royal" with "I play donno." After a while, he may play *Ɔsee duom ma yɛnkɔ ɛ* (Ɔsee let's go) as a coded communication for the Asantehene to move on. The transition to the second type, Tenten (long, recurring phrases), in Example 4.20 is very swift and happens the moment the king begins to walk. The drum texts and patterns are the same as Example 4.19, except there are no pauses between the phrases, resulting in *Brɛbrɛ brɛbrɛ brɛbrɛ* (slowly slowly slowly).

Example 4.21 Ɛsoro (Above Riding in Palanquin), Asantehene 3.

Dawuro Donno
Biribi ba biribi Biribi ba biribi Biribi ba biribi Biribi ba biribi Biribi ba biribi (biribi ɛreba
Dawuro Ntwaamu
Somu somu somu   Somu somu somu   Somu somu somu
Dɔnka
    Ɔwɔ soro ɔwɔ soro ɔwɔ soro som ma yɛnkɔ   Ɔwɔ soro ɔwɔ soro ɔwɔ soro som ma yɛnkɔ
Mptintintoa
    Brɛ brɛ brɛ brɛ brɛ   Brɛ brɛ brɛ brɛ brɛ
Saawisie
    Brɛ brɛ brɛ brɛ brɛ   Brɛ brɛ brɛ brɛ brɛ
Variation: Biribi ba Biribi ba   Brɛ brɛ brɛ brɛ brɛ
Gyamadudu
    Brɛ brɛ brɛ brɛ brɛ   Brɛ brɛ brɛ brɛ brɛ

English Translation

Dawuro Donno
Biribi ba biribi Biribi ba biribi Biribi ba biribi Biribi ba biribi Biribi ba biribi (biribi ɛreba
Dawuro Ntwaamu
Hold it hold it hold it   Hold it hold it hold it   Hold it hold it hold it
Dɔnka
He is up he is up he is up hold it and let's go   He is up he is up he is up hold it and let's go
Mptintintoa
    Slow slow slow slow slow   Slow slow slow slow slow
Saawisie
    Slow slow slow slow slow   Slow slow slow slow slow
Variation: Something is coming   Slow slow slow slow slow
Gyamadudu
    Slow slow slow slow slow   Slow slow slow slow slow

The bell pattern is the same as the previous examples, but the Dawuro Ntwaamu, on the one hand, and Mpintintoa, Saawisie, and Gyamadudu, on the other, are engaged in a quasi-hocket arrangement. The Twi words are *Somu brɛbrɛ* (Hold it carefully), which is distributed by having the Dawuro Ntwaamu reduplicate three times, as in Somu somu somu (Hold it hold it hold it), while the noted drummers respond "carefully" five times. Unlike Example 4.19, *Brɛbrɛ* here means carefully. Occasionally, the Saawisie drummer disengages from the collective text to introduce *Biribi ba biribi* (Something is coming, something) as a variation on the main theme, brɛbrɛ (carefully). The lead drummer on Dɔnka announces to the participants of an event that the Asantehene is truly riding the palanquin by using the phrase "He is up" three times and, on the fourth time, adding: "hold it (the palanquin) and let's go." *Som* (hold it) in the phrase is a contraction of the Twi word *so mu*. The signal to end the two types of pieces is the same, and it is given with three strokes by the Dɔnka in a non-lexical gesture as *gen gen gen*, followed by two drum strokes, *gengen*, by all of the drummers. I would like to conclude my discussion of *mpintin* by referencing Nketia's work on the same subject. It appears that the drum texts recorded by Nketia published in 1963 are totally different from what I have presented here (Nketia, 1963: 134–136). Unlike the fɔntɔmfrɔm and kete drum texts that display marked continuity, it seems that the integrated drum texts of the *mpintin* ensemble might have changed over time because the older generation were not able to adequately pass on the drum texts to the younger generation, or perhaps the younger generation felt the need to create new texts in response to contemporary demands.

Apirede

As in the previous drum ensembles, Apirede refers to the drums, music, or both. In my discussion of the Gold Stool in Chapter 2, I pointed to the apirede as one of the musical ensembles attached to the revered object. According to Nana Kwabena Poku (Apiredehene), Ɔkɔmfoɔ Anɔkye created the apirede drums on the same Friday (Fofie on the Akan calendar) that he brought the Gold Stool from the heavens. That of the apirede, we are told, happened later in the evening. Nana Poku is of the view that it is the apirede that defines the power (*tumi*) of the Gold Stool. The original apirede drums are in the stool room, and they are only used in rituals related to the Gold Stool, meaning that what we normally see outside during events are replicas of the originals. All of the four drums comprising the apirede ensemble are covered with camel blankets (*nsaa*) from the Sahel Region in Africa. The largest drum is known as *twenenini* (male drum), and it is played with a pair of curved sticks (*nkonta*). The female drum (*twenebedeɛ*) is slightly smaller than the male drum, and it is played with a single straight stick. *Atɛtaa* is the same height as the male drum but smaller and played with a straight stick. The fourth drum is *akukua*, and as its name implies, it is shorter like most of the *nkukua* drums that I previously described. *Akukua* is played with two straight sticks. The membrane—the drum head—is made out of elephant ears and is

Figure 4.4 Members of the Apirede ensemble performing inside the Pampaso Stool House while the Asantehene was being garbed in the great war tunic (*batakarikɛseɛ*). Kwabena Tuffuor playing the male drum (*twene nini*) with two curved sticks; next is the female drum (*twene bedeɛ*); *akukua* is the smallest drum in the ensemble; the slightly tall drum is *atɛtaa*; and the third person after *atɛtaa* is playing the stick clappers (*abaa dawuro*). December 4, 2017.

Source: Picture by author.

known to be highly durable and last for decades. Unlike the usual bells or metal gongs commonly found in Akan ensembles, wooden clappers known in Twi as *Abaadawuro* provide the *topos* (timeline) in apirede. In the inter-war years, they used the bones of human hands, but these were replaced with wooden clappers during peaceful times.

Before the Gold Stool is brought out as part of a procession or ceremony, the Apiredehene and his group play a set piece three times, and then the Nkonwasoafoɔ (stool carriers) lift the Gold Stool up and carry it on the nape of his neck. Since it is linked with stools, its position in a procession is the Stool Group, right after the Gold Stool or in the absence of the latter, the apirede is placed in the same spot behind the Asantehene's chair. Depending on the occasion, apirede provides music in a restricted and controlled space inside the palace. Participation is highly restricted to the extent that royals are even not permitted to dance to *apirede*. Apart from the king, only those who are identified as Asekanfoɔ (those with *sɛpɔ* knifes) or those with *anadwosekan* (lit. night knifes) are allowed to dance. They

Example 4.22 Ɔsɛɛ Tutu Yɛ Bɛɛma (Ɔsɛɛ Tutu Is Truly a Man), Asantehene apirede
ensemble.

Abaadawuro
ka   Sɛɛ Tutu (yɛ) bɛɛma Sɛɛ Tutu (yɛ) bɛɛma Sɛɛ Tutu (yɛ) bɛɛma Sɛɛ Tutu (yɛ) bɛɛma
Atɛtaa
Mo mma mo homene so Mo mma mo homene so Mo mma mo homene so
Akukua
Sɛɛ Tu kronkron Sɛɛ Tu kronkron Sɛɛ Tu kronkron Sɛɛ Tu kronkron Sɛɛ Tu kronkron

Variations:
1. Nana Sɛɛ Tutu Nana Sɛɛ Tutu Nana Sɛɛ Tutu yɛ bɛɛma Nana Sɛɛ Tutu yɛ bɛɛma
2. Ampa ampa ampa yɛ bɛɛma

Twenenini
Sɛɛ Tu yɛ bɛɛma   Sɛɛ Tu yɛ bɛɛma   Sɛɛ tu yɛ bɛɛma   Sɛɛ Tu yɛ bɛɛma
Twenebedeɛ
              Ampa   ampa   ampa   ampa

Variation 1
Twenenini
Sɛɛ Tutu, mahu mogya nsuswan   Sɛɛ Tutu, mahu mogya nsuswan
Twenebedeɛ: Ampa ampa ampa   Ampa ampa ampa

Variation 2
Twenenini
Ɔsɛɛ Tutu Apirede, mahu mogya nsuswan
Twenebedeɛ: **Ampa ampa ampa**

Variation 3:
Twenenini
Ɔsɛɛ Tutu Apirede me suro hwan?   Ɔsɛɛ Tutu Apirede me suro hwan?
Twenebedeɛ
              Ampa ampa ampa

Signal to End
Twenenini: Ken ken ken ka

English Translation
Abaadawuro
ka   Sɛɛ Tutu (yɛ) bɛɛma Sɛɛ Tutu (yɛ) bɛɛma Sɛɛ Tutu (yɛ) bɛɛma Sɛɛ Tutu (yɛ) bɛɛma
Atɛtaa
Rise up and let's go Rise up and let's go Rise up and let's go Rise up and let's go
Akukua
Sɛɛ Tu is holy Sɛɛ Tu is holy Sɛɛ Tu is holy Sɛɛ Tu is holy Sɛɛ Tu is holy Sɛɛ Tu is holy

Variations:
1. Nana Sɛɛ Tutu Nana Sɛɛ Tutu Nana Sɛɛ Tutu is truly a man Nana Sɛɛ Tutu is truly a man
2. Truly truly truly he is a man
Twenenini
Sɛɛ Tutu is truly a man   Sɛɛ Tutu is truly a man   Sɛɛ Tutu yɛ bɛɛma
Twenebedeɛ
              Truly   Truly   Truly

Variation 1
Twenenini
Sɛe Tutu, I've seen blood flowing like it is flooding
Twenebedeɛ: **Truly, truly, truly**   Indeed, Indeed, Indeed

Variation 2
Twenenini
Ɔsɛe Tutu Apirede, I've seen blood flowing like it is flooding
Twenebedeɛ: **Truly, truly, truly**

Variation 3:
Twenenini
Ɔsɛe Tutu Apirede whom shall I fear?   Ɔsɛe Tutu Apirede whom shall I fear?

Twenebedeɛ
                              Truly, truly, truly

Signal to End
Twenenini: Ken ken ken ka

---

include the Abrafoɔ, Dɛɛboɔsohene, Hyiawuhene, and Manwerehene. Those without *sɛpɔ* knifes but allowed to dance are the Apiredehene, since he is the chief of the ensemble, and the *Nkonwasoafoɔhene* (chief stool carrier). The Asantehene dances with his *sɛpɔ* knife, *Kum Abrempɔn* (killer of chiefs), while the others dance with their *sɛpɔ* knifes exposed from the pouch. Unlike kete or fɔntɔmfrɔm ensembles that have several dance suites, the Apirede has a single piece and the integrated texts are Ɔsɛe Tutu Yɛ Bɛɛma (Ɔsɛe Tutu is Truly a Man), which is grounded in a cyclical motion with intermittent variation by the Twenenini and Twenebedeɛ drummers. In addition to court ceremonies, I recorded the Apirede ensemble in 2009, 2011, and 2017.[14]

A performance unit of Apirede, Example 4.22, is set in motion with the prompter *ka*, a single hit that is played by striking the wood clappers (*abaadawuro*) together as a heads up for the performers to be ready. The player of the wood clappers then establishes the *topos* by articulating three cycles of the single line verse, *Sɛe Tutu (yɛ) bɛɛma*, at which point the drums—*atɛtaa, akukua, twenebedeɛ,* and *twenenini*—join in that order. Similar to *mpintin* where donno dawuro articulates the bell pattern with five attack points, in addition to expressing antecedent and consequent phrases, the attack points within the *topos* are generated from six syllables: Sɛe Tu-tu (yɛ) bɛɛ-ma, which is a contraction of *Ɔsɛe Tutu yɛ Ɔbɛrima*. The parenthesis around (*yɛ*) implies a silent non-articulated text. The architectural framework in apirede is quite unique, as the integrated patterns of three instruments— *Abaadawuro, Atɛtaa, and Akukua*—project a dense texture with contrasting timbres. The Akukua drummer's part is not stable, as he engages in text substitutions now and then. Concurrently, the two big drums, Twenenini and Twenebedeɛ, engage in an interactive call-and-response framework that lightens the texture with spaces between the call and response drums. In order to break the monotony, the drummer of the male drum intermittently disengages from the initial interactive phrases to introduce new phrases in the call, while the response phrases remain the same. We are presented with three types of textual recompositions: *Ɔsee Tutu mahu mogya nsusuane* (Ɔsee Tutu, I've seen blood flowing like it is flooding); *Ɔsee Tutu Apirede, mahu mogya nsusuane* (Ɔsee Tutu's Apirede, I've seen blood flowing like it is flooding); and *Ɔsee Tutu Apirede me suro hwan?* (Ɔsee Tutu's Apirede, who shall I fear?). The first two are metaphoric allusions to battle scenes in the past when several adversaries perished at the hands of Asante soldiers. The drummer of the female drum's (*twenebedee*) response to each of the previous variations is the emphatic and repetition of "*truly*" three times. The signal to end a performance unit is given by the Twenenini (male drummer) with the expansive and non-lexical text *Ken ken ken ka*, and the remaining members of the ensemble joining him on *ken ka*. Similar to most court ensembles, it is the combination of extraordinarily dense multipart drum texts, interactive structures generated by the call-and-response parts, and the seemingly never-ending cyclical motion that is the power and driving force in Apirede performance. Although I have observed the Apirede in diverse court events including Akwasidae, Adaekesee, and several processions in January and December 2017, I saw them perform nonstop for up to two hours during the Burial and Final Funerary Rites for the late Asantehemaa, Nana Afia Kobi Seewaa Ampem II.

Mmedie

Unlike fɔntɔmfrɔm and kete ensembles, not much is known about the *mmedie* (*nkukuwammedie*) drums. The oral history of mmedie drums are discussed in Chapter 2. Although there are seventy-seven drums in all, Ɔkɔmfoɔ Anɔkye ordained that they should never present nor play all seventy-seven at the same time.

As I stated in Chapter 2, the relatively small drums are known as *nkukua* and, as court drums, they are covered with *nsaa* (camel blanket). The players are referred to as Nkukuafoɔ, but most people mistakenly referred to the drums as *tumi* (power) due to the drum text they perform (see Figure 4.5). The lead drum, Panten, is slightly bigger and higher than the rest of the drums. Panten is played with two curved sticks (*nkonta*), while the remaining drums are played with two straight sticks. During processions, the drums are strategically positioned near the doorless entrance around the corner from Nhyiayem in the Efikeseem courtyard. As soon as the king appears at Nhyiayem, either in the *Apakan* (palanquin) or walking, the Nkukuafoɔ will play the mmedie drums to invoke spiritual powers from the Creator for the king. They will begin, Example 4.23, with the Panten (lead drum) initiating the call, followed by the rest of the responding drums.

The phrase is repeated three times, and at the end of the third phrase, the Asantehene acknowledges the drummers by nodding his head in appreciation, which is followed with hand gestures that include waving his right hand forward and backward. Fortified with spiritual powers from above, the Asantehene then proceeds to the gathering. With spiritual powers from God, he will be able to face adversaries or challenges that may come his way during the day's proceedings.

Figure 4.5 A set of *mmedie* drums invoking power from God for the Asantehene as he
emerges from the inner chambers of the palace for Akwasidae public assembly
at the palace grounds (*Bogyaweε*), July 5, 2015.

Source: Picture by author.

Example 4.23 Tumi (Power), Asantehene Nkukuammedie.

Panten (Lead drum): Tumi, tumi, tumi (power, power, power)
Nkukuammedie (Response drums): Bra, bra, bra, bra, bra, bra, bra, bra, bra, bra (come,
  come, come, come, come, come, come, come, come, come)

Panten (Lead drum): Tumi, tumi, tumi (power, power, power)
Nkukuammedie (Response drums): Bra, bra, bra, bra, bra, bra, bra, bra, bra, bra (come,
  come, come, come, come, come, come, come, come, come)

Panten (Lead drum): Tumi, tumi, tumi (power, power, power)
Nkukuammedie (Response drums): Bra, bra, bra, bra, bra, bra, bra, bra, bra, bra (come,
  come, come, come, come, come, come, come, come, come)

The act of invoking powers from the Creator above for the Asanthene is known
as *yegu no mmedie*, and it is said that *ye gu no mmedie aduasa; yegu no mmedie
aduosonson nson* (literally, we are covering him with spiritual powers thirty times
or seventy-seven times).[15] The process is repeated during recessions when the
ruler is returning from the gathering. He stops as soon as he gets to where the

Nkukuammedie are positioned, listens to what they have to say, acknowledges the drummers as before, and then moves on. The implications of the foregoing is that the presence of a set of *nkukuammedie* drums at any event recalls the history of how the forebears of present Akyeremahene Nana Akofena Bediako II relocated from Denkyera to Kumase in the late seventeenth century. It has been socially maintained for over 300 years by its usage and active role in Public Assemblies such as Akwasidae, court ceremonies, funerary rites, and a variety of ceremonies. There is value in the spiritual protection from God, the Creator of all things.

Kwantenpɔnmuta

Similar to nkukuammedie drums, and in spite of the visible presence in proces-sions and court ceremonies, the *kwantenpɔnmuta* ensemble is hardly known beyond the confines of Manhyia Palace. I discussed the oral account of the inci-dent that inspired the creation of this ensemble in Chapter 2 (see Figure 1.1). Kwantenpɔnmuta is the only drum ensemble that is part of *Patomfoɔ* (or *Patom Fekuo*), and as a result, it is not under the Anantehene. In the absence of older men in the family, Bodede Ɔbaapanin Nana Konadu Brayie II is the presumptive elder of the group until such a time when one of the males in her family is old enough to be enstooled as the chief of the group. In the past, they played kwantenpɔnmuta and danced when chiefs and elders were gathered to signal the imminent arrival of the Asantehene. In those instances, they would enter the gathering, play and dance briefly, return to wait for the ruler's procession, and then take their right-ful place behind the *Nsɛneefoɔ* (Court Criers). The dance is basically a display of heroism (*animsɛm*) and involves jumping up high and making one or two turns before landing on the ground. The instruments include one *adawura* (boat-shaped bell), *dawuruta* (double-clapperless bell), one *aburukuwa* drum, one *donno* drum, and two *kwantenpɔnmuta* drums that are relatively big armpit drums. In addition to recording them in ceremonies and rituals, I worked with them in 2009 and 2011. Like *nkukuamedie*, they have a single piece in their repertoire, as in the next example.

The integrated rhythm patterns in Example 4.24 are based entirely on the multi-syllabic phrase *Kwan-ten-pɔn-mu—ta*, a graphic description of surprisingly chanc-ing upon a trail in a thick forest after weeks of losing one's way. The previous phrase is subject to cyclical manipulation during a performance, and it is performed as long as the procession or recession of the ruler is taking place. It encapsulates a sense of relief, joy, and celebration. Despite its relational connection with dance, as mentioned previously, the bell pattern is not based on the usual *topos* that we asso-ciate with Asante music; instead, the bell plays the same non-lexical phrase, *ye ye*, in unison with the donno. A performance unit by the Kwantenpɔnmuta ensemble projects two distinct sections: an Introduction Gesture and the Main Line. Only two kwantenpɔnmuta drums and the aburukuwa play the first section in a quasi-hocket mode, where kwantenpɔnmuta 1 and the aburukuwa drums sound four out of the five syllables, as in *kwantenpɔnmu*, while the kwantenpɔnmuta 2 drum

Example 4.24 *Kwantenpɔnmuta*, Asantehene Kwantenpɔnmuta ensemble.

---

1. Introduction Gesture

Kwantenpɔnmuta 1
Kwantenpɔnmu   Kwantenpɔnmu   Kwantenpɔnmu   Kwantenpɔnmu   Kwantenpɔnmu
Kwantenpɔnmuta 2
        ta   ta   ta   ta
Aburukuwa   Kwantenpɔnmu   Kwantenpɔnmu   Kwantenpɔnmu   Kwantenpɔnmu

Donno

Adawura

2. Main Line

Kwantenpɔnmuta 1
Kwantenpɔnmuta   Kwantenpɔnmuta   Kwantenpɔnmuta
Kwantenpɔnmuta 2
Kwantenpɔnmuta   Kwantenpɔnmuta   Kwantenpɔnmuta
Aburukuwa
Kwantenpɔnmuta bra bra   Kwantenpɔnmuta bra bra   Kwantenpɔnmuta bra bra
Donno
      Ye ye   ye ye   ye ye
Adawura
      Ye ye   ye ye   ye ye

---

rounds up the phrase with the last syllable, *ta*. The previous format is repeated for a while until the Kwantenpɔnmuta 1 drum seamlessly plays the Main Line, at which point the Kwantenpɔnmuta 2 and *aburukuwa* drums join in a collective sounding of the entire phrase, Kwantenpɔnmuta. In the repeated multipart texts, the donno and *adawura* join forces to fill the space between each sounding of the multisyllabic phrase with *ye ye*. Interestingly, the *aburukuwa* fills up the same space with *bra bra* (come come), which completes the call by the ruler for his soldiers to join him.

Nkukuadwe (Nkukuadwo)

As we discussed in Chapter 2, and similar to Nkukuammedie, this name implies relatively small drums, *nkukua*, with *dwe* appended to it. I discussed how Kɔmfo Anɔkye created the pair of nkukuadwe drums to commemorate the Asante defeat of Dɛnkyera in 1701 in Chapter 2. The drum head is made of elephant ear and is connected to pegs that tune it and keep the leather in place. Three rectangular metal jingles (*akasaa*) with metal rings are attached to the rims of each drum (see Figure 2.5). When the drum heads are struck with a pair of drum sticks, the vibrations of the metal jingles and rings expand to achieve a mass of sound. As musical instruments, the pair of *nkukuadwe* drums physically mark the previous historical event, and, as a result, their use in processions in the recurring Akwasi-dae Public Assemblics or court ceremonies recall that momentous history. The drums are kept at Feyiase to this day, and for court ceremonies the custodians travel to Manhyia Palace with the pair of drums in order to perform their duty. As we shall soon discover, the content of drum texts performed by *nkukuadwe* drummers is mediated by the historical defeat of Dɛnkyera at Feyiase, and, as a result, the texts allude to heroism and bravery, or as we say in Twi: *ntwene no ka animsɛm.*

Each drum is played with a pair of fairly large drumsticks that have short-ened curved sides. Each drum has a shoulder strap made of red felt cloth, and for the playing position, the shoulder strap is hung on the left shoulder. It is worth mentioning that in the past, they were used together with Mpebi ne Nkrawiri (another pair of drums) as tribunal drums and sounded into the night to signal the execution of a criminal or a war captive. Both drums are considered to be male because masculinity is associated with executions or capital punishment. They play relatively short verses. Further, Nkukuadwe drums are part of the plural performance soundscape at the periodic Akwasi-dae ceremony and all court ceremonies. In peaceful times, in the absence of territorial conquests and capital punishment, nkukuadwe are performed as part of royal funerary rites. That explains the rationale for the following drum text, which is performed in order to protect members of the constabulary (the *Abrafoɔ*) from the ghost or spirit (*sasa*) of those executed. We say in Twi: *ɔko ne ho sasa* (literally, he is protecting himself from *sasa*). I recorded the fol-lowing two examples in the summers of 2009 and 2011 in the inner court of Manhyia Palace.

Example 4.25 Ɔsɛe Tutu, A Pair of Nkukuadwe Drums.

Twi Text	English Translation
Lead Drum	**Lead Drum**
1. Ɔsɛe Tutu	Ɔsɛe Tutu
Response Drum	**Response Drum**
2. Ɔsɛe Tutu	Ɔsɛe Tutu
3. Wo ho baabi yɛ dum	Part of your body is the silk cotton tree
4. Wo ho baabi yɛ dum	Part of your body is the silk cotton tree
5. Wo ho baabi yɛ dan	Part of your body is the dan tree
6. Wo ho baabi yɛ dan	Part of your body is the dan tree
7. Wo ho baabi yɛ fɛntɛmfrɛm	Part of your body swallow elephants
8. Wo ho baabi yɛ fɛntɛmfrɛm	Part of your body swallow elephants
9. Ɔsɛe Tutu	Ɔsɛe Tutu
10. Ɔsɛe Tutu	Ɔsɛe Tutu
11. Wo ho baabi yɛ kakapenpen	Part of your body breaks easily
12. Wo ho baabi yɛ kakapenpen	Part of your body breaks easily
13. Sɔre kɔka ma yɛn kɔ ɛ	Rise, give command and let's go to war
Lead and Response Drums	**Lead and Response Drums**
14. Sɔre kɔka ma yɛn kɔ ɛ	Rise, give command and let's go to war

Example 4.26 Ɔbɛn Twerefoɔ (The Brave Fighter)- A pair of Nkukuadwe drums.

1. Lead Drum: Ɔbɛn Twerefoɔ a ne ho bɔn atoduro
2. Response Drum: Ɔbɛn Twerefoɔ a ne ho bɔn atoduro
3. Lead Drum: Ɔbɛn Twerefoɔ a ne ho bɔn atoduro
4. Lead and Response Drums: Ɔbɛn Twerefoɔ a ne ho bɔn atoduro

English Translation
1. Lead Drum: Ɔbɛn Twerefoɔ whose body smells of gunpowder
2. Response Drum: Ɔbɛn Twerefoɔ whose body smells of gunpowder
3. Lead Drum: Ɔbɛn Twerefoɔ whose body smells of gunpowder
4. Lead and Reasponse Drums: Ɔbɛn Twerefoɔ whose body smells of gunpowder

The performing procedure is such that the Response Drum repeats verbatim the entire phrase played by the Lead Drum, but the end phrase is played by both drums. In his drum text, Opanin Ntiamoa strikes a comparison between the strength of the ruler with that of the *odum* (milicia regia) and *ɔdan* trees (Lines 3–6)—which are strong, durable, and impossible for termites or fungus to destroy—and the *kakapenpen* tree (Lines 11–12), which has branches that can be broken easily with minimum effort. In times of need, one cannot depend or lean on the *kakapenpen* because it breaks easily. Pairing the strong and indestructible with the weak is the focus of the previous verse. The end phrase, *Fɛntɛmfrɛm*, in Lines 7–8, is an additional proclamation that the ruler is like the waterlogged mud that easily swallows elephants. As a single line that is repeated four times throughout the performance procedure noted previously, Example 4.25 is one of the shortest verses performed by the pair of nkukuadwe drums. Example 4.26, Ɔbɛn Twerefoɔ, references Asante kings, and the opening phrase is intended to instill fears in imagined adversaries that Ɔpemsoɔ Osei Tutu, who defeated several states, smells of gunpowder at all times. In that sense, successive kings are brave fighters who are always ready to defend the kingdom no matter the time of day.

Drum and percussion accompaniment in priestly dance (Nsumangorɔ)

Nsumangorɔ has several connotations. It describes a special ritual restricted to the Asantehene, the Nsumankwaahene and some chiefs listed in connection with the apirede ensemble. It also refers to the songs, dances, and drum and percussion accompaniments. I will examine the integrated drum texts in this section and the song texts in Chapter 5. A total of four instrumentalists provide the accompaniment for this type of priestly dance. The instruments consist of three differently sized large gongs identified as *Dawurokan* (First Bell), *Dawuro Ntwaamu* (the Bell that Crosses), *Dawurokɛsee* (the Biggest Bell), and the *Kwadum* drum (the same type of lead drum in kete ensembles). The only difference in the playing technique is that, in kete, the *kwadum* player uses two curved sticks (*nkonta*) while the drummer in the priestly dance uses two straight sticks (Figure 4.6).

The architectural framework in the instrumental accompaniment (Example 4.27) is based on a multipart organization grounded in cyclical motion. The player

Figure 4.6 The drummer and percussionists in Nsumangorɔ are Kwadwo Brenya (*dawuro-kan*, first gong), Kwame Appiah (kwadum, leading drum), Kwaku Mensah Baawua (*dawuro ntwaamu*, the crossing gong) and Atta Poku Panin (*dawuro adikan*, first gong), December 13, 2017. Nsumankwaa Palace, Kumase.

Source: Picture by author.

Example 4.27 Drum and Percussion Texts in Nsumangorɔ (Priestly Dance).

Dawurokan
Mo mra mo mmɛ hwɛ yɛn no Mo mra mo mmɛ hwɛ yɛn no Mo mra mo mmɛ hwɛ yɛn no
    Mo mra mo mmɛ hwɛ yɛn no
Dawuro Ntwaamu
                            Wa ba wa ba wa ba wa ba wa ba wa ba wa ba wa ba wa ba
Dawurokɛseɛ
                                        Onie onie ɔnoara
onie ɔnoara onie Onie onie ɔnoara onie onie onie onie onie onie onie
Kwadwum
Gyina mu ye gyina mu ye gyina mu ye me se gyina mu ye Gyina mu ye gyina mu ye
    gyina mu ye me se gyina mu ye (deɛ wo gyina no, timtim. na wo gyina ɔhene anim

English Translation
Dawurokan
Come and see us Come and see us Come and see us Come and see us
Dawuro Ntwaamu
                            He is here he is here he is here he is here he is
here he is here he is here he is here
Dawurokɛseɛ
                                        There he is there
he is he himself is here there he is he himself is here there he is there he is he himself is
here there he is there he is there he is there he is there he is there he is
Kwadwum
Stand firm stand firm I say stand firm stand firm stand firm I say stand firm

of the First Bell establishes the *topos* with a high-pitched timbre that is meant to invite members of the community to come and participate in the event. The timeline is fast-paced in the style of priestly dances (*Akɔm*). The seven syllables forecast seven attack points, with a unique $1 + 1 + 2 + 1 + 1 + 1$ feature. The *dawuro ntwaamu* alerts participants that the king has joined the event, while the Biggest Bell affirms that he is really here. The *kwadum* drummer offers a word of caution for all participants to stand firm, as they are dancing with the king. Combined with singing, instrumental accompaniment, dancing, ululation, and other vocal utterances for several hours, not only are nsumangorɔ performances intense and animated, they also involve an assessment of spiritual fortitude of participants. Do not take part in *nsumangorɔ* if you are not spiritually and physically strong.

Sekye

The Sekye ensemble is quite unique in the sense that it combines drums with a large group of dancers from both sexes. I discussed what caused them to flee Dɛnkyera to Kwaaman and additional issues in Chapter 2. Since the ensemble includes women, but members of Akyerɛmade are all male, Sekye is, technically speaking, not part of Akyerɛmade. Sekye, as an ensemble, is quite distinct from *fɔntɔmfrɔm*, which is for dances, but they do not have their own dancers as part of the ensemble. The only similarity with fɔntɔmfrɔm is that *sekye* do not have a chorus of singers. Sekye and Mpintin drums are two ensembles at the Asantehene's court with direct links to the northern neighbors of the Asante, although as I previously noted, the historical source of mpintin orchestral, the Dagbon, is well known through oral history. Four out of the five drums are cylindrical in shape, as well as double-headed with strings attached to both ends for tuning and keeping the membrane in place.[16] The leading drum in Sekye is called *Twene Kɛseɛ* (big drum), and as its name implies, it is the biggest cylindrical drum in the ensemble. It is followed by two smaller cylindrical drums known as *sekye twene mma* (children of sekye drums), which are referred to as *ntwaamu* (crossing drums) and *anigye* (happy drum). There is also donno (squeeze drum) and *apentema*, the only Akan drum in Sekye with the usual bottle-shaped design and pegs as the tuning mechanisms. The drums are accompanied by *adawura* (boat-shaped metal idiophone) and *ntorowa* (gourd rattle; Figure 4.7).

Like the previous ensembles, the custodians bolted from Dɛnkyera Bɛtenase with the sekye drums, and all of the cylindrical drums, are covered with red felt cloths, while the *apentema* and *donno* are not covered. All cylindrical drums in the ensemble come with shoulder straps that are hung on the left shoulder during the performance. Readymade for processions, they are played with two straight sticks, while the *apentema* is usually carried on the shoulder or placed between the legs and played with both hands, slightly tilted forward to allow sound to escape from the lower end. The performing context in Dɛnkyera is quite differ-ent from the case of Kumase. In Dɛnkyera, it was performed for the installation of Amanhene (Divisional Chiefs), and it was significant in royal funerary rites including the procession to the mausoleum for internment. In the Asante king's court, the music and dance of Sekye is primarily to enliven rituals and ceremonies in order to create a balance between the more "serious" varieties of instrumental texts and light entertainment. The dances of Sekye are lively and mocking, with

Figure 4.7 Instrumental accompaniment in *sekye* involves *twenekesee* (a large two-sided
cylindrical drum), two *sekye twene mma* (children of *sekye* drums), two small
two-sided cylindrical drums (*ntwaamu*, the crossing drum, and *anigye*, happy
drum), *dondo* (armpit drum), *ntorowa* (container rattle, not in the picture), and
aduwra (boat-shaped iron bell).

leanings toward sensuality due to an extreme emphasis on waist and pelvic movements by the women. Since they emphasize eroticism, Sekye dances are described
as *baasifoɔ* or *premanfoɔ asa* (dances of those who do not care about acceptable
social norms in public spaces). The usual gender roles hold that the men play all of
the drums and percussion instruments, but the dance involves both genders. There
are all kinds of situations, both restricted and public, in which Sekye performs.
Restricted performances usually take place in the evening after the Akwasidae
Public Assembly, when the Asantehene and his divisional chiefs are served palm
wine (*nsafufuo*). Referred to as Sadwaase, it is a time to relax, socialize, and catch
up on affairs in the kingdom. There are times when Sekye drumming and dances
are performed privately for the Asantehene, wives of past kings, and females in
the royal household. The performance protocol in such situations require the men
in the ensemble to perform with their heads down without lifting their eyes to
see the girls and women dance. Among the public performances are when they
perform for the Asantehene's *Adɔsowa*, when female dancers are dressed in *kente*
with *dansinkran* hairstyles, and all exposed parts of their bodies are adorned with

precious beads and gold jewelry. Adɔsowa dancers are quite distinct, with exaggerated buttocks that need extra cushions or pillows to express the African aesthetic of a well-endowed woman with curves. There are five dance suites with suggestive titles: Tu Abɔnten (signals the king has stepped out of the palace and is in a procession); Wo to Papim a Na W'ato Kuro (Papim is an indication that you are at the fringes of a town); Ɔhene Re Ba (The king is coming); Bɔme so (play the music for me); and Kramo Densu (name of a major river). The lead drummer and leader of the ensemble were very old, sick, and frail; as a result, we could not record the drum texts.

As in Chapter 3, lived and historical experience along with current experience in Asante are remarkably articulated in the language and poetry of drums. Beginning with Kete and Fɔntɔmfrɔm, the drums and percussion instruments as mediating forms of material culture embody the reign and initial conquest and expansion of the then-Ɔyoko families in Kwaaman under the leadership of Ɔpemsoɔ Ɔsɛe Tutu. The instruments of both ensembles were captured from Tafo as war trophies and when members of the Bɔmaa joined a wave of defections from the royal court of Dɛnkyera to Kwaaman. The result was a new and heavy-sounding fɔnfɔmfrɔm ensemble with two bɔmma drums. Having been kept in a room for several decades, it took the Asante-Gyaaman War of 1818 for the Asantehene Ɔsɛe Asibe Bonsu to reignite the performance of kete. The oral histories of the remaining six ensembles—*Mpintin, Apirede, Mmedie, Kwantenpɔnmuta, Nkukuadwe*, and *Sekye*—similarly embody the chronology of Asante ruler reigns, events, and wars. The analysis of the instrumental texts of these eight drum-based ensembles opens a wealth of historical knowledge of the remote past. We are informed that the thirteen dance suites of kete are associated with historical epochs, and the knowledge of those events informs the selection of pieces for particular situations. For instance, *Adinkra Kofi* is usually performed behind the Asantehene during the annual Remembrance Rites (*Ɛsom Kɛseɛ*), when he is walking in a procession from the outskirts of Brɛman to the mausoleum. *Yɛtu Mpɔ* (we are digging gold) is appropriate for processions and is the preferred piece played behind territorial chiefs (*amanhene*) on their way to greet the Asantehene. During the days of warfare, *fɔntɔmfrɔm Atoprɛtia* was performed on the way to the battlefield, and if they were successful, they returned from the war with *naawea*. In times of peace, the former is performed behind the Asantehene on his way to pay last respects to a deceased royal or territorial chief, or whenever he dramatizes heroic encounters on the battlefield through dance.

In addition to mapping out reigns, events, and wars, each ensemble represents distinct character traits of values in Asante. The music and dances of fɔntɔmfrɔm project Asante militancy (*animsɛm* or *mmɛnsɛm*); mpintin is boisterous, gay, and lighthearted; kete represents matters of grave consequences; and the dense multipart drum texts and never-ending cyclical rhythms are its power and driving force. *Apirede* represents the mysterious and a fear of the unknown, for it is the favorite music of the spirits of the departed; *mmedie* invokes the power of the Creator from the heavens; kwantenpɔnmuta is similar to fɔntɔnfrɔm in the presentation of heroism; the same can be said of the texts of *nkukuadwe* drums; and sekye is lively and sensuous. As stated previously, the value of surrogate texts stems from their ability to express the Asante experience. There is value in bravery, patience, strength, firmness, and persistence, as exemplified by *Abɔfoɔ*, one of the dances of kete and the rationale for dramatizing hunters going after animals in a thick forest at night. The value in being conscious of the impact of human activities on the environment and finding ways of forming harmonious relationships with the environment is encoded in the fɔntɔmfrɔm piece: the path crosses the river, and the river crosses the path. Although lacking absolute dates, the language and poetry of drums are artistic records of reigns, events, and wars that continue to animate rituals and ceremonies in a never-ending continuum from the past to the present, thus ensuring that the Asante past is an inescapable part of the present. A study of the language and poetry of ivory trumpets and drums in no small way contributes to our understanding of Asante history and cultural experience. For the remaining two chapters, we turn our attention to song texts performed separately by members of the kete chorus and the physicians and medical corps, along with verbal poetry performed by chronicle singers or bards and members of the constabulary.

Notes

1 By the mid-twentieth century, a large body of literature was produced especially on the "talking drum," including J.E. Carrington (1949), Ulli Beier (1954), and Henry Balfour (1948), to name just a few.
2 See David Locke (1990: 26–31) for descriptions of Dagbamba *gungon* and *luna* drums. Percival R. Kirby (1968: 36) makes a similar observation that the construction of the Venda *ngoma* (drum) is a long and difficult process, thus affecting its cost, which he estimates it to be "one ox or its equivalent, about five pounds" at that time. Esther A. Dagan (1993) catalogues one of the largest collections of drum varieties, sizes, and shapes from sub-Saharan Africa.
3 Nketia (1974: 41) item number 32, provides another version of this drum text. Photographs of the drums mentioned in this section can be found in Nketia (1974) and Kyerematen (1964).
4 Ben Paulden's (2017) list and pictures include kete groups from Ankaase, Nkwantakese, Tafo, Kokofu, Suma Ahenkro, and Dunkwa.
5 See Nketia (1963: 128–133). For a detailed history of Asantehene's Kete, see Ampene and Nyantakyi III (2016: 240–243). For an analysis of kete rhythms, see William Anku (1988). Ben Paulding (2017) provides an analysis of meter, feel, and phrasing in kete.
6 Nketia (1963) lists *akukuadwo, apentemma, bakoma, kwadum, donno drum,* a gourd rattle (*torowa*), and a gong.
7 Featured performers include The Ghana Dance Ensemble, Choral and Atɛntɛ Music composed by Kwabena Nketia, Agya Koo Nimo's Adadam Seperewa Kuo, Opanin Opoku Mensa Aborofo Sankuo Ensemble, The Original Cultural Centre Agoromma, Manhyia Tete Nnwonkorɔ, and the Royal Drum and Dance Ensemble. The program opened with a dance choreographed by Mawere-Opoku for the Ghana Dance Ensemble, a Sikyi royal court dance, Fontomfrom Akita and Naawea, Akita and Akantam, Sikyi, a Selection from the Adowa Suite, Sanga, Sankuo or Seperewa, Maaney, Manhyia Tete Nnwonkoro led by Nnwonkorɔhemaa, the late Nana Afua Abasa, Choral and Instrumental (Atenteben) Music, Finale: Royal Manhyia Kete Suite.
8 Nketia (1963) lists eight suites of dances, including *Yetu Mpɔ, Mpɛ-Asɛm, Apɛntɛ, Abɔfoɔ, Adaban* (or *Tɔprɛ*), *Dabrɛbuo (Akatape), Adinkra,* and *Adɔsowa Twene (Adampa).*

9 The concept of *topos* or *topoi* in West and Central African drumming and dance traditions is extensively examined by Kofi Agawu (2003: 73–79).
10 Ben Paulden (2017) provides text for the first type of bell pattern, and, although he did not provide his rationale, he refers to it as the Standard kete *dawuro*.
11 Reference my discussion of the great oath in Chapter 2.
12 Ampene and Nyantakyi III (2016: 170–173) contains a history and description of *Tɔprefoɔ*.
13 Nketia (1963: 14–15) includes the dimensions and materials used in constructing all of the drums in the mpintin ensemble.
14 Ampene and Nyantakyi III (2016: 230–231) has a history and group picture of Apirede.
15 In one of the *Abee* introductions by Manhyia Tete Nnwonkorɔ, the late Nana Afia Abasa intones in heightened speech mode: *ye gu Nana ye gu no mmedie o* (we are covering him with *mmedie* drums).
16 See Ampene and Nyantakyi III (2016: 234–239) for a discussion of the Sekye ensemble as part of the royal regalia.

References

Agawu, Kofi. 1995. *African Rhythm: A Northern Ewe Perspective*. Cambridge: Cambridge University Press.

———. 2003. *Representing African Music: Postcolonial Notes, Queries, Positions*. New York and London: Routledge.

Amegago, Modesto. 2015. "The Textual Basis of African Drumming: The Interaction Between Spoken Language and Drumming." In *Discourses in African Musicology: J.H. Kwabena Nketia Festschrift*, edited by Kwasi Ampene, Akosua A. Ampofo, Godwin k. Adjei, and Albert K. Awedoba, 76–95. Ann Arbor, MI: Michigan Publishing.

Ampene, Kwasi, and Nana Kwadwo Nyantakyi III. 2016. *Engaging Modernity: Asante in the Twenty-First Century*. 2nd edition. Ann Arbor, MI: Michigan Publishing.

Anku, William Oscar. 1988. "Procedures in African Drumming: A Study of Akan/Ewe Traditions and African Drumming in Pittsburgh." PhD diss., University of Pittsburgh.

Arom, Simha. 2007. "Language and Music in Fusion: The Drum Language of the Banda Linda (Central African Republic)." *Transcultural Music Review* 11: 1–13.

Balfour, Henry. 1948. "Ritual and Secular Uses of Vibrating Membranes as Voice Disguisers." *Journal of the Royal Anthropological Institute* 78: 45–69.

Beier, Ulli. 1954. "The Talking Drums of the Yoruba." *Africa Music* 1: 29–31.

Carrington, J.E. 1949. *Talking Drums of Africa*. London: Carey Kingsgate Press.

Cudjoe, Emmanuel. 2015. "The Contexts and Meaning in Asante Dance Performance: The Case of Kete." Master's thesis, University of Ghana.

Dagan, Esther A. 1993. *Drums: The Heartbeat of Africa*. Montréal, Canada: Galerie Amrad African Art Publications.

Euba, Akin, 1991. *Yoruba Drumming: The Yoruba Dundun Tradition*. Bayreuth: Bayreuth African Studies.

Keotting, James. 1970. "An Analytical Study of Ashanti Kete Drumming." Master's thesis, University of California, Los Angeles.

Kirby, Percival R. 1968. *The Musical Instruments of the Native Races of South Africa*. Johannesburg: Witwatersrand University Press.

Kyerematen, A.A.Y. 1964. *Panoply of Ghana: Ornamental Art in Ghanaian Tradition and Culture*. New York: Frederick A. Praeger Publisher.

Locke, David. 1981. "Drum Languages in Adzogbo." *Black Perspectives in Music* 9 (1): 25–50.

————. 1990. *Drum Damba: Talking Drum Lessons*. Crown Point, IN: White Cliffs Media Company.

————. 1998. *Drum Gahu: An Introduction to African Rhythm*. Tempe: White Cliffs Media.

Nketia, J.H. Kwabena. 1963. *Drumming in Akan Communities of Ghana*. London: Thomas Nelson and Sons Ltd.

————. 1971. "Surrogate Languages of Africa." In *Current Trends in Linguistics*, edited by Thomas A. Sebeok. The Hague, Netherlands: Mouton & Co., N.V. Publishers.

————. 1974. *Ayan*. Accra: Ghana Publishing Corporation.

Omojola, Bode. 2012. *Yorùba Music in the Twentieth Century: Identity, Agency, and Performance Practice*. Rochester, NY: University of Rochester Press.

Paulden, Ben. 2015. "Kete for the International Percussion Community." In *Discourses in African Musicology: J.H. Kwabena Nketia Festschrift*, edited by Kwasi Ampene, Akosua A. Ampofo, Godwin K. Adjei, and Albert K. Awedoba, 156–185. Ann Arbor, MI: Michigan Publishing.

————. 2017. *Asante Kete Drumming: A Musical Analysis of Meter, Feel, and Phrasing*. Unpublished Master's thesis, Tufts University.

Rattray, Robert Sutherland.1927. *Religion and Art in Ashanti*. Oxford: The Clarendon Press.

5 Rhetoric and history

Kete songs and songs by physicians

Abofra bɔ nwa na ɔmmɔ akyekyedeɛ (A child can crack open the shell of a snail but not the shell of a turtle). Akan Proverb.

In Chapters 3 and 4, I examined texts performed by a variety of ivory trumpets, a flute, and several kinds of drums as stylized accounts of actual events in the past and the present. The focus in Chapters 5 and 6 is on sung texts and poetry that are verbally intoned by the human voice. The genres selected for analysis in Chapter 5 are songs performed by members of the Asantehene kete chorus involving the Asantehemaa, selected ahemaa, and widows of past kings (*ahenyerenom*). Nana Ama Agyeiwaa was the leader of the chorus and Ketehemaa until her untimely death in 2009. Following her passing, Nana Boadi Tutuwaa II replaced her as the leader of the chorus, and it was in that capacity that she led the chorus in my playback analyses of songs during the summer of 2011. The second genre is known as *Nsumangorɔ*, and it describes the songs, dances, and drumming of royal physicians, medical corps, and spiritual advisors. *Nsumangorɔ* is inclusive of both genders, and while female members lead the songs, the group is led by a male chief, Nana Ɔsɛe Bonsu, who is the Asantehene Nnwontofoɔhene (loosely, Chief of singers). By pairing rhetoric with history in my framing title, I would like to draw attention to the incredible skills of the performer-composers of these genres and their ability to use literary devices in narratives and songs to evoke historical experience. The expansive field of rhetoric, with academic departments and an impressive list of journals dedicated to the numerous discourses that animate the field, is too broad for our purposes. Readers are instead referred to Wendy Olmsted (2006) for the intellectual framework, history, and conceptual foundations of rhetoric. For comparative examples in Africa, readers may consult Adebayo Mosobalaje (2017) for Yoruba popular culture in Nigeria, Mcimeli Sisanda Nkoala (2013) for a rhetorical analysis of freedom songs in South Africa, and Kwesi Yankah (2012) for a broader illumination of Akan rhetoric.

Kete Orchestra

As previously discussed, territorial chiefs in Akan areas have only the drum and percussion ensemble, while the Asantehene's Grand Kete Orchestra

involves the drum ensemble and chorus, currently without pipes. Like territorial chiefs, the Asantehene's drum and percussion ensemble performs
consistently without the chorus during court events, including processions.
A combination of the drum ensemble and the chorus is, however, reserved for
special occasions, especially during the late afternoon *Mmaadae* (Adae for
women), which takes place in the inner court and, unlike the Public Assembly
held earlier in the day, restricted to the Asantehemaa and the royal household and widows of deceased kings. Additional performing contexts of the
Asantehene's Grand Kete Orchestra are the all-night performances after the
internment of a member of the royal family. Unlike scholarly engagement
with the drumming and rhythms of kete, no literature exists on the narratives and songs of the kete chorus. In a short description, Nketia describes
three parts to a grand performance, namely the music of the drum ensemble,
pipe interludes and free accompaniment, and a vocal interpretation of the
tunes of pipes. I have never seen the grand performance, and my ethnographic
description in what follows is not only without the pipes but the structure of
the performance is also different from Nketia's description due in part to the
absence of pipes.

Recording Kete songs

It is Sunday, August 2, 2009, and the location is the Asantehemaa's court which
is part of the larger Manhyia Palace. Since kete performances involving the large
chorus of royal wives and the Asantehemaa are restricted to the ruler and a few
courtiers, Nana Kwadwo Nyantakyi III, the Asantehene Sanaahene (Chief of
the Treasury), organized this special performance in order for me to record the
songs. With my video cameraman, soundman, and research assistants, I arrived
at the Asantehemaa's residence around ten in the morning. I met close to thirty
women exquisitely dressed in traditional clothes, from silk head wraps (*abotire*) to the two pieces of printed cloth wrapped around their upper and lower
bodies. The poise and beauty of these women was clear in the early morning
sun, and the atmosphere was somewhat solemn (see Figure 5.1). Across from
the women and sitting under a tent were the Ketehene, Nana Agyei Boahen,
and members of his drum ensemble. There was space between the chorus and
the drum ensemble, thus making it possible for the drum ensemble to face the
chorus. My team and I quickly placed our recording gadgets at strategic positions in order to avoid potential interference with the performance. By 11:15
a.m., Nana Sanaahene gave me a signal that the Asantehemaa was ready to join
us. We quickly turned on our machines, and soon after, all of the women stood
up in deference to the Asantehemaa while the lead singer, the late Nana Ama
Agyeiwaa, began a song:

Example 5.1 Twɛntwɛnko (Indispensable Warrior), Asantehene *kete* chorus.

Twi Text	English Translation
Leader	**Leader**
1. Agoo!	1. Attention please!
2. Twɛntwɛnko e,	2. The indispensable warrior,
3. Yɛretwɛn barima o	3. We are waiting for the warrior
4. Yɛretwɛn barima awisi o	4. We are waiting for the warrior *wisi* o
Chorus	**Chorus**
5. Twɛntwɛnko e,	5. The Indispensable warrior
6. Yɛretwɛn barima o	6. We are waiting for the warrior
7. Yɛretwɛn barima o	7. We are waiting for the warrior
8. Bosompem Kwagyarko e	8. Bosompem Kwagyako e
9. Twɛntwɛnko e,	9. The indispensable warrior
10. Yɛretwɛn barima o	10. We are waiting for the warrior
11. Osinsimu a osi nsuo mu,	11. Osinsimu sits in a river
12. Nanamɔn ayera o	12. But leaves no trail
13. Twɛntwɛnko e,	13. The indispensable warrior
14. Yɛretwɛn barima o	14. We are waiting for you
15. Ɔwerebaani a ɔkoto nsuo so	15. An obstinate fellow who squats in a river
16. Ɔyɛ dadeɛ so adwuma	16. And works on metals
17. Twɛntwɛnko e,	17. The indispensable warrior
18. Yɛretwɛn barima o	18. We are waiting for you
19. Ɔsɛmpani a ɔhwete agyina mu se Kwaw e	19. The one who disperses a council's father Kwaw e
20. Twɛntwɛnko e,	20. The indispensable warrior
21. Yɛretwɛn barima o	21. We are waiting for you
22. Yɛretwɛn barima o	22. We are waiting for a man
23. Yɛretwɛn barima awisi o	23. We are waiting for a man *wisi* o
24. Twɛntwɛnko e,	24. The indispensable warrior
25. Yɛretwɛn barima o	25. We are waiting for you
26. Yɛretwɛn barima o	26. We are waiting for warrior
27. Yɛretwɛn Sɛɛ Ampem e	27. We are waiting for Sɛɛ Ampem
28. Twɛntwɛnko e,	28. The indispensable warrior
29. Yɛretwɛn barima o	29. We are waiting for you

By the middle of the song, the double door opened for the Asantehemaa to step out with Nana Sanaahene holding her right arm, leading her to her seat. Behind Nanahemaa were four maidens (*mmɔdwoafoɔ*) with special haircuts identifying them as coming from the Asantehemaa's court. All of the women in the chorus sat down the moment the Asantehemaa took her seat, but they kept singing the recurring phrase. A brief analysis of the previous opening song is in order. As in earlier examples, the lead phrases are aligned to the left, with the chorus or response phrase indented. The purpose of *Twɛntɛnko* (the Indispensable Warrior) is to inform the Asantehemaa that they, the kete group, are ready for the day's performance and that they are waiting for her to join them with her leadership. The poetic text and the mode of singing follow a set of performance frames, and there is no instrumental accompaniment. The last syllable, *ko* (fight/warrior), in *Twentwenko* establishes the theme of war right from the beginning. They are about to embark on a metaphoric journey or undertaking, and they need a brave person to lead them. Further, the phonology or sound structure of the multisyllabic *twen-twɛn-ko* is a rhetorical device that captures the attention of listeners. The skillful compression of words in a sentence to a single word or formulaic phrase is a mark of rhetorical competence by the performer-composers of kete songs. The regular saying in normal speech is: *yɛ twɛn wo ansa na ye akɔ ko* (we are waiting for you before we embark on war). Additional uses of multisyllabic devices and the compression of words appear at the beginning of Lines 11, 15, and 19 with the phrases *Osinsimu, Ɔwerebaani, Ɔsɛmpani*. Creatively, the singer combines nominals with multisyllabic phrases to create a diverse effect. The nominals are *Bosompem Kwagyarko* (Line 8) and *Sɛɛ Ampem* (Line 27). The first name in the latter, *Sɛɛ*, is a compression of Sɛɛwaa, the third name of Asantehemaa, as in Nana Afia Kobi Sɛɛwaa Ampem II. Further, dialogue between the lead singer and the chorus is established right from the beginning. The leader begins her phrase to announce that they are waiting for the brave one—in this case, Nanahemaa. While the chorus uses repetition (Lines 5 and 6 and all of the responses) to reinforce the statement by the lead singer, the lead singer delves into what Kwesi Yankah calls "metaphorical allusions" to list the traits of the brave warrior they are waiting for (Yankah, 1983: 391). For instance, there is *Bosompem Kwagyarko* (Line 8), who is perhaps a well-known warrior, and other allusions in Lines 11, 15, and 19. Juxtaposition of unlikely pairs is a feature of this song, as Nana Agyeiwaa pairs *nsuo* (water) with metal (*dadeɛ*) from Lines 15–16. Water, as the saying goes, is life, while metal may portray strength or the manufacture of machinery and weapons. With the Asantehemaa formally seated and the opening song over, Nana Agyeiwaa calls for attention in Line 1 and begins a long narrative about the circumstances that led to the discovery of Lake Bosomtwe. As in the opening song, the drum ensemble remains silent.

Example 5.2 Kete Narrative by Nana Ama Agyeiwaa (Ketehemaa), Asantehene *kete* chorus.

Leader
1. Agoo!
2. Ɔkyere ahenemma sɛbe sɛbe o
3. Yɛse dabi hɔ no na woto sɛbe a
4. Wose asɛm biara a yɛnnkyi
5. Asankare a wosi kyɛ mu
6. Aberewa a Nyame ahu
7. Nyampɔn akɔsɔ Akomea Densu
8. Afrɛ Nana a ɔfiri Asankareagya ne Yankamase
9. Afrɛ Nana a ɔfiri Nomenase Kurom ase
10. Ɔsansan tu a ɔfiri he?
11. Akorɔma tu a ɔfiri dua bi so
12. Atetekorɔma a ɔnnim dɔfoɔ akoma te him brɛ brɛ
13. Akorɔma a ɔwe akokɔ na Gyemfua firi Maame Berɛkuwaa ban so
14. Saa mmerɛ a Asante Kɔtɔkɔ twe akofena kɔdi ammɛɛnsɛm
15. Ɔsɛɛ a akobɛn si ne kyinyɛ nkyi ano

16. Okonsi akra
17. Akomea Baafoɔ
18. Ɔsɛkyerɛ Akontire a ɔgye mpanin ne mmɔfra
19. Anim bɛmu a ɔte Bɛnomase
20. Asansa Kɔberɛ e
21. Ɔno na ɔhwe asuo a ɔhwe amena kɛseɛ
22. Obontwi akɔm
23. Akogye dɔm
24. Nana Adomako Ntene
25. Ansa Sasraku a ɔtenaa Asaaman a ne bɔmɔfoɔ sɔree anɔpatuutu sɛ ɔrekɔ ha
26. Ɔkɔ kɔhunuu asu kɛseɛ bi
27. Ɔne ne kraman tutuu mmirika kɔɔ asu kɛseɛ no ho
28. Wɔkɔɛ, wɔhuu ɔtwe, ɔtwe nso de mmirika gidigidi kɔtɔɔ nsuo no mu
29. Wɔn di n'akyi ɛkɔhwɛɛ
30. Ɛna yɛbaa fie no, ɛna Nana Bosompem hene somaa ne bɔfoɔ maa no kɔbisaa asɛɛ
31. Ɔse "me Bosomtwe no no, ɔtwe adondo akoweakra, aberewa dɛɛfoɔ besewee;
32. Adimuadeɛ to Busumuru adeɛ so
33. Maa Nana Sɛi Tutu kɔdaa n'ase daa n'ase eeee
34. Ɔde nipa, ɔde kraman,
35. Ɔde yaawa, ɔde sekan
36. Ɔde nwera ɛde kɔdaa Bosomtwe ase
37. Maa no boaa Ɔsantehene ne ne buu ɔman
38. Kurofi Ampɔn, Agyeman Boadu agyinaman
39. Ɔsei Tutu Nana a wako agye asuo
40. Wote sɛ wo nwom merefrɛ wo?

41. Ɔdanmani ba e
42. Ɔsɛi Tutu a na ogu akuro
43. Nana Kwaku, wako agye Asanteman
44. Ɔdanmani ba, ɔhene nim ko o
45. Wako agye Bosomtwe
     46. Ɔdanmani ba
     47. Ɔhene nim ko o
48. Wako agye Bosomtwe
     49. Ɔdanmani ba
50. Ɔhene nim ko o

51. Wako agye Bosomtwe
52. Ɔdanmani ba
53. Ɔhene nim ko o

54. Ɔdampɔn agye Konama Dwoɔda Kwankwaahene Ɔdanmani ba ei
55. Akorɔma kosɛ awedeɛ
56. Ɔhene nim ko o
57. Wako agye Bosomtwe
58. Ɔdanmani ba
59. Ɔhene nim ko o
60. Ɔdanbarima e wako agye Bosomtwe
61. Ɔdanmani ba
62. Ɔhene nim ko o

63. Ɔsɛi Kwadwo Nana e, Agyeman Appia atudurosoɔ Dwoɔda
64. Osuae twee Bosomuru twee Mponponsuo
65. Osuae kyerɛɛ Kɔtɔkɔ sɛ obiaa ka no a ɔne no bɛdi
66. Ɔsei Tutu Agyeman ɔnnsuro biribiara

(*Continued*)

Example 5.2 (Continued)

67. Ɔdanmani ba ɔhene nim ko o
68. Wako agye Bosomtwe
69. Ɔdanmani ba
70. Ɔhene nim ko o
71. Wako agye Bosomtwe
72. Ɔdanmani ba
73. Ɔhene nim ko o

English translation
Leader
1. Agoo!
2. Captor of chiefs, apologies, apologies
3. It is said that when apologies were used in the olden days
4. Whatever you say is not an abomination.
5. The grandson of Afrɛ who hails from a town of viciousness
6. The old woman who God recognizes
7. Nyampɔn Apɔsɔ Akomea Densu
8. The grandson of Afrɛ who hails from Asankareagya is a citizen of Nyankamase
9. The grandson of Afrɛ who hails from a town of viciousness
10. Where does the hawk fly from?
11. The hawk flies from a certain tree
12. The ancient hawk that does not consider the feelings of a friend, come stealthily
13. Gyamfua the mother of the hawk that eats chicken is from Maame Berɛuwaa's tree
14. And you make Asante Kɔtɔkɔ draw the sword to display bravery
15. Ɔsee, whose war horn is on top of his state umbrella
16. Okonsi akra
17. Baafoɔ
18. Ɔsɛkyerɛ Akontire who redeems the old and the young
19. Anim Bamu who lives at Bɛnomase
20. The dark hawk alas
21. It is he who bails out water from a big channel
22. He bails water from the broadest part of a river
22. Obontwiakwan
23. Akogyeaman. He fights to take over states/nations
24. Nana Adomako Tenten
25. Ansa Sasraku who settled at Asaaman and his hunter got up early morning for hunting
26. And he discovered a big Lake
27. And he ran with his dog to the big Lake

28. When they went, they saw an antelope that ran swiftly and dived into the lake
29. They followed him to see what has happened
30. And when they came home, Nana Bosompem, the chief of Bosomtwe sent his messenger to consult an oracle.
31. He said, "I am Bosomtwe, ɔtwe adondo, akoweakra, aberewa dɛɛfoɔ besewɛɛ.
32. Adimuade to Busummuru adeɛ so
33. Nana Ɔsee Tutu expressed his gratitude
34. He sent a dog
35. He sent a brass bowl and a sword
36. He sent calico to Bosomtwe to express his gratitude
37. And he assisted Asantehene to rule the nation
38. Kurofi Ampɔn, Agyeman Boadu has stabilized the nation.
39. Ɔsee Tutu's grandson who has fought to capture a lake
40. Can you hear your name in your songs?

41. Ɔdommarima e
42. Ɔsɛe Tutu who devastates a town
43. Nana Kwaku, you have fought to redeem the Asante nation.
44. Ɔdammarima, the king is a skillful warrior
45. He has fought to capture Bosomtwe
   Chorus
   46. Ɔdɔmmarima
   47. The king is a skillful warrior
48. He has fought to capture Bosomtwe
   49. Ɔdɔmmarima
   50. The king is a skillful warrior
51. He has fought to capture Bosomtwe
   52. Ɔdɔmmarima
   53. The king is a skillful warrior
54. Ɔdampɔn agye Konama Dwoɔda Kwankwaahene Ɔdanmani ba ei

55. Akorɔma kosɛ awedeɛ
56. The king is a skillful warrior
57. He has fought to capture Bosomtwe
   58. Ɔdɔmmarima
   59. The king is a skillful warrior
60. Ɔdɔmmarima, you have fought and captured Bosomtwe
   61. Ɔdɔmmarima
   62. The king is a skillful warrior

63. Ɔsɛe Kwadwo nana, alas, Agyea Apea carried gunpowder on a Monday
64. He swore the great oath and drew the Bosommuru and Momponsuo swords
65. He swore to Kɔtɔkɔ that he would deal with anybody who dared him
66. Ɔsɛe Tutu Agyeman is not afraid of anything
67. Ɔdɔmmarima, the King is a skillful warrior
68. He has fought and captured Bosomtwe
   69. Ɔdɔmmarima
   70. The king is a skillful warior
71. He has fought and captured Bosomtwe
   72. Ɔdɔmmarima
   73. The king is a skillful warrior

Before I analyze some of the rhetorical strategies in the previous narrative, I would like to situate the narrative in the larger historical context described by Kyerematen (1966: 224–227). Akora Bompe, a hunter from Asaaman, is said to have discovered the only lake in the Asante Region. In one of his hunting expeditions, he shot a duiker (*ɔtwe*) that vanished into the thick growth of bushes. Bampo followed the trail of the duiker and suddenly reached the shores of a lake, and, to his utter astonishment, found that river-water fish (*apatrɛ*) abound in the lake. He fed his dog one of the fish, and when the dog did not die, he also tried one. He reported his discovery to his chief, Nana Akosa Gyima, chief of Asaaman at the time. The chief in turn consulted with an Akan priest who confirmed the existence of the lake and the name, Bosomtwe. The Asaamanhene, Nana Akosa Gyima, then informed his overlord Ɔpemsoɔ Osei Tutu about the discovery of the lake. The king sent items to register his gratitude to the deity of the lake, who is then said to have produced more fish, a source of protein, to sustain and support the kingdom.[1]

As in all narratives and poetry recitals, it is the unique artistic skill of the narrator in particular situations that brings a story to life. Nana Agyeiwaa, as the narrator, stood on her feet while the rest of the chorus sat and listened attentively for their cue to join. In that sense, her facial expressions, the intermittent swinging of her arms, her bearing, the rate of delivery of her text, and using literary devices for emphasis were all crucial to the overall excitement in the story. The seventy-three lines of the previous narrative skillfully combine referential poetry and narrative, in addition to projecting a tripartite division unified by a single theme: the discovery of Lake Bosomtwe. The three broad sections are Lines 1–24, 25–40, and 41–73. As usual, Nana Agyeiwaa begins with a call for attention with the word *Agoo!* (Attention). She follows with a request to her listeners to absolve her from the narrative she is about to perform with the phrase in Line 2, *sɛbe sɛbe o* (apologies, apologies). In case her story infringes on contested historical facts or rekindles deep-seated animosity for current inhabitants around the lake, she offers her apologies. For instance, there are twenty-two villages surrounding Lake Bosomtwe, and there were hostilities among them in the past, which as we shall see in the narrative, sometimes included disagreements concerning the rightful owner of the lake. *Sɛbe sɛbe o* (apologies, apologies) mitigates any potential hard feelings and ensures legal immunity from prosecution.[2] Having calmed down nerves, Nana Agyeiwaa proceeds with a complex mix of literary devices from Lines 5–24 that emphasizes militancy and braveness in the discovery of the lake, including names and places of abode, metaphoric allusions, the use of nominals, referential parallelisms, and other devices. Instances of places of abode are *Asankare* (Line 5), *Asankareagya, Nyankamase* (Line 8), *Nominasekrom* (Line 9), Maame Berekuwaa Abanso (Line 13), and Bɛnomase (Line 19). Metaphoric allusions include *Ɔsansa, Akorɔma, Atetekorɔma* (all three names refer to the hawk), and *Ɔsansa Kɔbere* (the Dark hawk) in Lines 10, 11, 12, 13, and 20. Examples of nominals and referential parallelisms are *Akomea Densu* (Line 7), *Afrɛ Nana* (Lines 8 and 9), *Gyanfuwaa* and *Maame Berekuwaa* (Line 13), *Ɔsɛe* (Line 15), *Ɔsɛkyerɛ Akontire* (Line 18), and *Nana Amoako Ntene* (Line 24). A quick note about *Akorɔma* and *Ɔsansa* (the hawk) and Afrɛ (a deity) is in order. As a bird of prey, the hawk (*akorɔma* or its by-name, *ɔsansa*) is admired by the Akan for "its majesty in streaking down towards its target" on the ground (Yankah, 1983: 383). The action of diving down and swooping its prey from the ground requires exceptionally fast mobility and agility, and that is the reason for the hawk's high regard. Since the hawk is also known for hopping from tree to tree in search of its prey, the Akan use it as a metaphor for restlessness, thus earning it the by-name *ɔsansa*. Depending on the context in which the hawk is invoked, it may refer to an individual without focus in life, but when it is used in relation to bravery or heroism as in the previous narrative, it refers to a powerful ruler who is restless because he or she is engaged in the affairs of state. Conversely,

Afrɛ is a powerful deity that is part of thc Asantehene *Nsumankwaafoɔ* (priests, spiritual advisors, and physicians) group. It is made up of three deities: Afrɛ Sika, Afrɛ Bom, and Afrɛ Pensan (see Ampene and Nyantakyi, 2016: 319).

Having prepared her audience with appellation poetry that grounds Ɔsɛe Tutu as the recipient of the epithets, Nana Agyeiwaa launches into the Second Section relating the circumstances leading to the discovery of Lake Bosomtwe from Lines 25–40. Line 25 is quite distinct, as Nana Agyeiwaa delves into a torrent of words loaded with syllables and phonemes, resulting in a spectacularly long phrase. In Line 28, the phrase *gidigidi* describes the wounded duiker's running and diving into the lake. Nana Bosompem in Line 30 is a reference to Nana Bosompem Boakye Ntow Kuroko, Chief of Bɔaman, in the vicinity of Lake Bosomtwe. Nana Bosompem's last name, Kuroko, features in the *Abrafoɔ Apae* poetry as: *Woyɛɛ saa, yɛɛ saa kum Kuroko ne ne yere Keraka* (You succeeded in killing Kuroko and his wife Keraka). The previous phrase in *apae* heroic poetry recalls the hostilities between the villages surrounding the lake.[3] In order to highlight the ruler's gratitude and presentation of gifts, Nana Agyeiwaa resorted to reduplications in Line 33, as in *kɔdaa n'ase daa n'ase eeee*. In addition to her hand and body gestures, she also prolonged the last particle *e* for emphasis. Towards the end of this section, she refers to the ruler as the one who fought and captured the lake and entreats him, in Line 40, to listen to his praises not only in songs but also in drum poetry, the instrumental verses of ivory trumpets, the durugya flute, and others. The entire phrase in Line 40 is a prompt for the chorus to be ready for the third section that is marked for choral responses.

Nana Agyeiwaa begins the Third Section with a big bang. Although a relatively short phrase consisting of two words and a particle, compared to the beginning of the Second Section, her manner of delivery by raising her voice and appending and sustaining her voice on the particle *e* as long as she could hold her breath places unmistakable weight on the two-word phrase in Line 41. Her choice of *Ɔdɔmmani* as the opening phrase focuses on the character traits of Ɔpemsoɔ Ɔsɛe Tutu as a brave warrior, for the word literally means just that. As I stated previously, Ɔsɛe Tutu is said to have fought and won seventy-seven wars during his reign. Seen in this light, the heroism in the opening phrase is undeniable, for the ruler is said to have destroyed towns (Line 42), to have fought to redeem the Asante Kingdom (Line 43), to be a skillful warrior (Line 44), and finally to have fought to capture Lake Bosomtwe (Line 45). The repetitive chorus phrases throughout the Third Section are composed to reinforce the opening theme in Line 41, established by Nana Agyeiwaa, that the ruler is truly a brave and a skillful warrior. But for the artistry and Nana Agyeiwaa's reliance on referential poetry from Lines 54–56 and 63–66, along with the text substitution of *Ɔdɔmbarima* (Line 60. lit. the warrior is truly a man) in place of *ɔdɔmmanin*, we would have been saddled with thirty-three lines of repetitive singing. The result is a subtle variety of rhetorical devices in the lead parts and a sequential build-up of phrases as in the long, multisyllabic, and phonology-laden Line 54 and the appearance of the hawk in Line 55. Although the discovery of Lake Bosomtwe took place in Ɔpemsoɔ Ɔsɛe Tutu's reign in the seventeenth century, mentioning the Fourth King Ɔsɛe

Kwadwo, who reigned in the in the eighteenth century, in Line 63 and linking his territorial conquests to the first king is quite remarkable. For, Asantehene Ɔsɛe Kwadwo extended Asante territory to as far as Dahomey, and he was known as Ɔsɛe Kwadwo a Ɔko Awia (he fights in broad daylight).[4] Whatever the reasons might be for introducing King Ɔsɛe Kwadwo, Nana Ama immediately returned to Ɔsɛe Tutu, and the chorus rounded up the narrative with the recurring response. It bears stating that whenever members of the kete chorus perform this narrative for a reigning king, it does not matter whether his stool name is Opoku Ware or Ɔsɛe Kwadwo; a reigning king, according to the Asante, is the embodiment of all past kings. In Line 43, the lead singer introduces the soul name (*kradin*), *Kwaku*, of the current ruler, Ɔsɛe Tutu II (he was born on Wednesday) in order to recontextualize and personalize the narrative for the present ruler.[5] *Bosomuru* and *Mponponsuo* are two important swords in the Asante kingdom. Actually *Mponponsuo* (actual name is Mpɔnpɔnson) came first during the reign of Ɔpemsoɔ Ɔsei Tutu, when his priest and counselor Ɔkɔmfoɔ Anɔkye created a miniature sword for his nephew, the newly born Opoku Ware. On the other hand, Ɔpemsoɔ Ɔsɛe Tutu captured the Bosomuru sword from Onoo Adu Gyamfi, a powerful chief who ruled over a wide territory from present-day Kumase to as far as Asante Mampong. The historical precedence of the *Bosmru* sword over the *Mponponsuo* is that Opoku Ware succeeded Ɔpemsoɔ Ɔsɛe Tutu and introduced the *Mponponsuo* sword during his reign. Both swords are carried by the Sword Bearers (Afenasoafoɔ).[6] A newly enstooled king first swears the oath of office with the *Mpɔnpɔnson* sword, but it is only after swearing the Great Oath of Asanteman with the *Bosomuru* sword, as part of the *Pampaso* rituals, that he is recognized as Asantehene. The *Mpɔnpɔnson* is part of the Swords of the Soul (*Akrafena*), while the *Bosumuru* sword is part of the Deity Swords (*Abosomfena*).[7] Truly, there is value in being a skillful and brave leader.

There are instances when songs do not necessarily follow a narrative, making the historical impulse as well as the meaning of the songs difficult to decode by the general audience. In such cases, the ancient song texts are coded with subtexts, thus limiting the meaning to a few knowledgeable courtiers and chiefs. Let us consider the following stanze, Example 5.3, from the Kete chorus with Nana Boadi Tutuwaa as the Lead Singer.

The Asante and the relatively older kingdom of Takyiman had several encounters even before the advent of Asante as a kingdom, and it is no wonder some of the historical incidents between the two kingdoms are recorded in kete songs. Opoku Ware (1720–1750) is credited with capturing the treasury vault (*Sanaa*) from Takyiman, bringing it to Kumase, and creating a stool for it. Before this incident, members of the Treasury (*Afotosanfoɔ*) were entirely responsible for the finances of state. Chief of Treasury Nana Kwadwo Nyantakyi III's version of the oral history is not devoid of mythical undertones. According to him, when the chiefs and people of Takyiman found out that the Sanaa had been taken away, they sent a rescue team to retrieve it. In order to avoid being caught, the Asante soldiers took refuge in an abode of the bush pig, and, strangely, the armadillo (*aprawa or apra*) that inherited the space from the bush pig covered the entrance with a huge

Example 5.3 Wankyi Asa (The bush pig is dead) Lead Singer, Nana Boadi Tutuwaa-Asantehene kete chorus.

Call	English Translation Call
1. Agoo	1. Get ready
2. Ɔwankyi asa, apraa anya bɔn	2. The bush pig is dead and the armadillo has got a burrow
3. Ɔsee Tutu	3. Ɔsee Tutu
4. Ɔwankyi asa, apraa anya bɔn	4. The bush pig is dead and the armadillo has got a burrow
5. Ɔbɔɔ Nyankonsoroma bebiree	5. From the ancient times he created numerous stars
6. Srane ne hene o	6. But the moon is king of all
7. Ɔfiri tete bɔ nipa bebiree,	7. From the ancient times he created several humans
8. Ɔsɛe a na man wɔ no	8. Ɔsee owns the nation/is king of the nation
9. Ɔsɛe biribi reba!	9. Ɔsɛe the terror is coming!
Chorus	**Chorus**
10. Ɔwankyi asa, apraa anyaa bɔn o	10. The bush pig is dead and the armadillo has got a burrow
11. Ɔsɛi Tutu	11. Ɔsee Tutu
12. Ɔwankyi asa, apraa anya bɔn	12. The bush pig is dead and the armadillo has got a burrow
13. Ɔbɔɔ Nyankonsoroma bebiree	13. From the ancient times he created numerous stars
14. Srane ne hene o	14. But the moon is king of all
15. Ɔfiri tete bɔ nipa bebiree,	15. From the ancient times he created several humans
16. Nana na man wɔ no	16. Ɔsee owns the nation
Call	**Call**
17. Yie Ɔwankyi asa, apraa anya bɔn	17. Indeed, the bush pig is dead and the armadillo has got a burrow
18. Ɔsɛe Pemsoɔ	18. Ɔsɛe Pemsoɔ
19. Ɔwankyi asa, apraa anya bɔn	19. The bush pig is dead and the armadillo has got a burrow
20. Ɔbɔɔ Nyankonsoroma bebiree	20. From the ancient days he created numerous stars
21. Srane ne hene oo	21. But the moon is king of all
22. Ɔfiri tete bɔ nipa bebiree,	22. From the ancient times he created several humans
23. Ɔsee a na man wɔ no	23. Ɔsee is the owner of the nation
24. Ɔsee Dankagyeaboɔ!	24. Ɔsee, the gourd that receives bullets
25. **Chorus**	25. **Chorus**
26. Ɔwankyi asa, apraa anya bɔn o	26. The bush pig is dead and the armadillo has got a burrow
27. Ɔsee Tutu	27. Ɔsee Tutu
28. Ɔwankyi asa, apraa anya bɔn	28. The bush pig is dead and the armadillo has got a burrow
29. Ɔbɔɔ Nyankonsoroma bebiree	29. From the ancient times he created numerous stars
30. Srane ne hene o	30. But the moon is king of all

(Continued)

Example 5.3 (Continued)

31. Ɔfiri tete bɔ nipa bebiree,	31. From the ancient days he created several humans
32. Nana na man wɔ no	32. Ɔsεe is the owner of the nation
Call	**Call**
33. Yie ɔwankyeε asa, apraa anya bɔn	33. Indeed, the bush pig is dead and the armadillo has got a burrow
34. Ɔsεe Tutu	34. Ɔsεe Tutu
35. Ɔwankyeε asa, apraa anya bɔn	35. The bush pig is dead and the armadillo has got a burrow
36. Ɔbɔɔ Nyankonsoroma bebiree	36. From the ancient times he created numerous stars
37. Srane ne hene oo	37. But the moon is king of all
38. Ɔfiri tete bɔ nipa bebiree,	38. From the ancient times he created several humans
39. Ɔsεe a na man wɔ no	39. Ɔsεe is the owner of the nation
40. Ɔsεe Dankagyeaboɔ!	40. Ɔsεe, the gourd that receives bullets
Chorus	**Chorus**
41. Ɔwankyi asa, apraa anya bɔn o	41. The bush pig is dead and the armadillo has got a burrow
42. Ɔsεe Tutu	42. Ɔsεe Tutu
43. Ɔwankyi asa, apraa anya bɔn	43. The bush pig is dead and the armadillo has got a burrow
44. Ɔbɔɔ Nyankonsoroma bebiree	44. He created numerous stars
45. Srane ne hene o	45. But the moon is king of all
46. Ɔfiri tete bɔ nipa bebiree,	46. From the ancient times he had many subjects
47. Nana na man wɔ no	47. Ɔsεe is the owner of the nation
Call	**Call**
48. Yie Ɔwankyi asa, apraa anya bɔn	48. Indeed, the bush pig is dead and the armadillo has got a burrow
49. Ɔsεe Tutu	49. Ɔsεe Tutu
50. Ɔwankyi asa, apraa anya bɔn	50. The bush pig is dead and the armadillo has got a burrow
51. Ɔbɔɔ Nyankonsoroma bebiree	51. From the ancient times he created numerous stars
52. Srane ne hene oo	52. But the moon is king of all
53. Ɔfiri tete bɔ nipa bebiree,	53. From the ancient times he created several humans
54. Nana a na man wɔ no	54. Ɔsεe is the owner of the nation
55. Ɔsεe biribi reba!	55. Ɔsεe, the gourd that receives bullets
Chorus	**Chorus**
56. Ɔwankyi asa, apraa anya bɔn o	56. The bush pig is dead and the armadillo has got a burrow
57. Ɔsεe Tutu	57. Ɔsεe Tutu
58. Ɔwankyi asa, apraa anya bɔn	58. The bush pig is dead and the armadillo has got a burrow
59. Ɔbɔɔ Nyankonsoroma bebiree	59. He created numerous stars
60. Srane ne hene o	60. But the moon is king of all
61. Ɔfiri tete bɔ nipa bebiree,	61. From the ancient times he had many subjects
62. 63. Nana na man wɔ no	62. Ɔsεe is the owner of the nation

boulder. The rescue team from Takyiman went past the covered hole and, after a fruitless search, returned home without accomplishing their mission. The Asante soldiers, on the other hand, proceeded to Kumase with the Sanaa. Literally a bank vault, the Sanaa is said to contain state funds in the forms of gold dust, gadgets for weighing gold, and possibly ritual objects. The ruler, chief of the treasury (Sanaahene), and the custodians are the only individuals who know its contents beyond what I have listed previously.[8]

Kyerematen reports another version that claims this particular kete song marked one of the youthful escapades of Ɔsɛe Tutu, who had run away from his stay in Dɛnkyera (1966: 145–146). We are informed by Kyerematen that when Ɔsɛe Tutu returned home to Kwaaman from Dɛnkyera for apparently committing a blunder, his uncle Obiri Yeboa sought asylum for him with the chief of Takyiman, who headed a powerful state at the time. While in Takyiman, the young Ɔsɛe Tutu is said to have gotten into trouble again when he killed the Takyimanhemaa one night and carried away treasures of gold dust and precious beads. A group of strong men were sent to arrest Ɔsɛe Tutu, but when the latter realized that the men were closing in on him, he took cover in the cave of an armadillo, and a spider covered the entrance of the cave with its web. The pursuers gave up when they could not find him, and Ɔsɛe Tutu returned to Kwaaman with his loot. Although the incident is true, its link with the previous kete song is unlikely, since Ɔsɛe Tutu was hardly a king and the Asante Kingdom did not even exist at the time of this incident. I doubt that such a commemorative song would be composed for a little-known royal who was, as it were, always on the run. Additionally, it is a well-known fact that Obiri Yeboa secretly sent Ɔsɛe Tutu to Takyiman without informing his elders about his decision. Although kete drum ensembles existed in Akan areas at the time, the Asantehene's grand kete orchestra became popular, as previously stated, at the time of King Ɔsɛe Asibe Bonsu, thus making the first story involving Opoku Ware Katakyie all the more plausible.

At any rate, the metaphoric references to Ɔwankyi (the bush pig) and *apraa* (the armadillo) in Lines 2 and 4, and the further interpolation of celestial bodies *Nyankonsoroma* (stars) in Line 5 and *Srane* (the moon) in Line 6, are codes for informed listeners. The spoken Twi for the bush pig is *wankyi*, without the initial particle ɔ, while that of the armadillo is *aprawa* as opposed to the sung *apraa* (more on this shortly). Using Akan rhetorical devices, Asante composers established a symbiotic relationship between the two animals. The bush pig is known for digging the ground and creating a fairly large abode. A fully-grown bush pig is about forty inches tall and may weigh about 300 pounds, and for this reason, the space is typically big. Unlike the bush pig, the armadillo is relatively small, about eight inches in length, but when threatened it quickly coils into a ball inside its armored shell; it cannot dig into the ground and create a sleeping space like the bush pig. However, it is only after the death of the bush pig or when it is no longer using the space that the armadillo sneaks in and takes over. In short, the little armadillo was in charge of a cave when Opoku Ware and his soldiers got there. In order to celebrate the success of the king, the singers swiftly access celestial bodies and declare that there may be an uncountable number of stars in the sky, but it is only the moon that is king. The references to the stars and moon reinforce the notion that there are several chiefs in the Kingdom, but there is only one king. However, the prefix *Nyanko* (*nsoroma*) in Line 5 is one of the Twi words for the Supreme Being, the Creator, or God. He is Nyame or Nyankopɔn. Since Akan religious and philosophical thought associates heavenly bodies with God, the stars are referred to as God's stars (*Nyankonsoroma*), the rainbow is referred to as God's arch (*Nyankonton*), and the rain from above is none other than God's rain (*Nyankonsuo*).[9] By linking Ɔsee Tutu's political status on earth to heavenly bodies, the performer-composers are signifying that the king's position in the Asante political hierarchy is ordained by God from above, just as the Gold Stool was given to them by God in Heaven. There is value in believing in the omnipotence of God, the Supreme Being.

As in most of these songs, the archetypal call and response form is the preferred compositional procedure. The choral response seems to be fairly stable, with just Line 11 lending itself to processes of recomposition during performance to reflect current issues. For instance, Ɔsee Tutu emphatically situates the song in the present, since the stool name of the current ruler is Ɔsee Tutu II. There is no question that during the reign of the last ruler, Opoku Ware II, the performer-composers used his stool name for the same purpose. Returning to the particle ɔ, which is attached to *(ɔ)wankyi* in Line 2 and all the call-and-response phrases, it is artistically motivated on the part of the lead singer and by no means an accident. For instance, seven out of nine lines in the call phrase begins with the letter ɔ, thus achieving a level of uniformity in the sound structure. Apart from *(ɔ)wankyi*, the remaining phrases are the correctly spoken words in Twi. Interestingly, the spoken form of the moon in Twi is *ɔsrane*, but the first letter (ɔ) is suppressed, resulting in *Srane*. It may well be that, artistically, it breaks the monotony of beginning every line with ɔ. The last line in all the call phrases is unique. Besides the text, the repeated linguistic tone and a sudden rise of the pitch at the end, LLLL H, provide the cue for the chorus to respond at the end of the high pitch. Second, it is strategically placed to instill fear in potential adversaries. That is, Ɔsee the terror is coming in Lines 9 and 55, and Ɔsee the box that receives bullets in Lines 25 and 41. The last line in all the response sections reaffirms the ruler as the only overlord in the kingdom. The choral response is fixed throughout the performance. Finally, all of the calls project an antecedent quality that is logically concluded by the consequent choral response. That brings us to another Example 5.4 in the same category without a narrative but with drum accompaniment however, our focus is on the song text.

War with an adversary is the typical reason for providing a historical impetus for the Example 5.4. Asante defeat of Dɛnkyera in 1701 did not end hostilities between the two foes, for there were several instances when Dɛnkyera attempted to regain their sovereignty through insurrection, but they never succeeded. As the fifth occupant of the Gold Stool, Asantehene Ɔsee Kwame reigned from 1777–1798. Remarkably, the only war associated with his reign is the war with the Dɛnkyera, when the latter sought to break away from Asante domination. According to Kyerematen, when King Ɔsee Kwame and his soldiers reached the banks

Example 5.4 Ɔhene Bi Aba (A New King Has Arrived) Lead Singer: Nana Boadi Tutuwaa-Asantehene *kete* chorus.

Call		English Translation (A king has arrived)	
		Call	
1.	Agoo!	1.	Agoo!
2.	Yeei	2.	Yeei,
3.	Yee Ɔhene bi aba o	3.	Yee a certain king has arrived
4.	Nana e	4.	Nana e
5.	Naa Sɛe Tutu	5.	Nana Ɔsɛe Tutu
6.	Ɔhene bi aba ɔte nkwanta	6.	A certain king has arrived at the crossroads
7.	Woma no apem a ɔnnye,	7.	He refuses a thousand
8.	Ɔgye mmɔdwe o	8.	But demands human jaws
9.	Nana e	9.	Nana e
Chorus		**Chorus**	
10.	Yeei	10.	Yeei,
11.	Yee ɔhene bi aba o	11.	Yee a certain king has arrived
12.	Nana e	12.	Nana e
13.	Naa Sɛe Tutu	13.	Nana Sɛe Tutu
14.	Ɔhene bi aba a ɔte nkwanta	14.	A certain king has arrived at the crossroads
15.	Woma no apem a ɔnnye	15.	He refuses a thousand
16.	Ɔgye mmɔdwe o	16.	But demands human jaws
Call		**Call**	
17.	Yeei	17.	Yeei
18.	Yee ɔhene bi aba o	18.	Yee a certain king has arrived
19.	Nana e	19.	Nana e
20.	Opoku Ware Katakyie	20.	Opoku Ware Katakyie
21.	Ɔhene bi aba ɔte nkwanta	21.	A certain king has arrived at the crossroads
22.	Woma no apem a ɔnnye	22.	He refuses a thousand
23.	Ɔgye mmɔdwe o	23.	But demands human jaws
24.	Nana e	24.	Nana e
Chorus		**Chorus**	
25.	Yeei	25.	Yeei
26.	Yee ɔhene bi aba o	26.	Yee a certain king has arrived
27.	Nana e	27.	Nana e
28.	Opoku Ware	28.	Opoku Ware
29.	Ɔhene bi aba ɔte nkwanta	29.	A certain king has arrived at the crossroads
30.	Woma no apem a ɔnnye	30.	He refuses a thousand
31.	Ɔgye mmɔdwe	31.	But demands human jaws
Call		**Call**	
32.	Yeei	32.	Yeei,
33.	Yee ɔhene bi aba o	33.	Yee a certain chief has arrived
34.	Nana e	34.	Nana e
35.	Naa Serwaa Ampem	35.	Nana Serwaa Ampem,
36.	Ɔhene bi aba ɔte nkwanta	36.	A certain king has arrived at the crossroads
37.	Woma no apem a ɔnnye	37.	He refuses a thousand
38.	Ɔgye mmɔdwe o	38.	But demands human jaws
39.	Nana e	39.	Nana e
Chorus		**Chorus**	
40.	Yeei	40.	Yeei,
41.	Yee ɔhene bi aba o	41.	Yee a certain king has arrived
42.	Nana e	42.	Nana e

(*Continued*)

Example 5.4 (Continued)

43. Naa Serwaa Ampem	43. Nana Serwaa Ampem,
44. Ɔhene bi aba ɔte nkwanta	44. A certain king has arrived at the crossroads
45. Woma no apem a ɔnnye	45. He refuses a thousand
46. Ɔgye mmɔdwe o	46. But demands human jaws
Call	**Call**
47. Yeei	47. Yeei,
48. Yee ɔhene bi aba o	48. Yee a certain king has arrived
49. Nana e	49. Nana e
50. Ɔsɛe Pemsoɔ,	50. Ɔsɛe Pemsoɔ
51. Ɔhene bi aba ɔte nkwanta	51. A certain king has arrived at the crossroads
52. Woma no apem a ɔnnye	52. He refuses a thousand
53. Ɔgye mmɔdwe o	53. But demands human jaws
54. Nana e	54. Nana e
Chorus	**Chorus**
55. Yeei	55. Yeei,
56. Yee ɔhene bi aba o	56. Yee a certain king has arrived
57. Nana e	57. Nana e
58. Ɔsɛe Pemsoɔ	58. Ɔsɛe Pemsoɔ
59. Ɔhene bi aba ɔte nkwanta	59. A certain king has arrived at the crossroads
60. Woma no apem a ɔnnye	60. He refuses a thousand
61. Ɔgye mmɔdwe o	61. But demands human jaws
Call	**Call**
62. Yee ɔhene bi aba o	62. Yee a certain king has arrived
63. Nana e,	63. Nana e
64. Yee ɔhene bi aba o	64. Yee a certain king has arrived
65. Nana e	65. Nana e
66. Opoku Ware Katakyie	66. Opoku Ware Katakyie
67. Ɔhene bi aba ɔte nkwanta	67. A certain king has arrived at the crossroads
68. Woma no apem a ɔnnye,	68. He refuses a thousand
69. Ɔgye mmɔdwe o	69. But demands human jaws
70. Nana e	70. Nana e
Chorus	**Chorus**
71. Yeei	71. Yeei
72. Ee ɔhene bi aba o	72. Yee a certain king has arrived
73. Nana e	73. Nana e
74. Opoku War	74. Opoku Ware
75. Ɔhene bi aba ɔte nkwanta	75. A certain king has arrived at the crossroads
76. Woma no apem a ɔnnye	76. He refuses a thousand
77. Ɔgye mmɔdwe o	77. But demands human jaws

of River Offin, he ordered his men to fill a certain area of the river with stones and, following that, to build a temporary hut on top of the stones for him to retire for the night. The soldiers carried out the orders, and the resulting hut, impressive as it was, was unlike any engineering or architectural feat at the time. The news about King Ɔsɛe Kwame's hut on River Offin was received with extreme fears in Dɛnkyera, leading to a reconsideration of engaging the Asante in another war. In order to prove their resolve, Dɛnkyera Kyei (the reigning Chief of Denkyira at the time) sent one thousand *predwan*, an equivalent of 8000 British pounds at the time, to the king to render an apology. The ruler accepted the money; however, he insisted that the Dɛnkyera people decapitate the chief and bring his head to him. With their backs to the wall, they carried out the order from the ruler and actually presented the head of Dɛnkyera Kyei to him (Kyerematen, 1966: 331). This singular act on the part of the ruler is recorded in the previous kete song. By demanding the jawbone, the ruler is symbolically seeking to seize his speaking chamber.[10] The last call phrase from Lines 62–70 is exceptional, as the lead singer lowers her voice on all the four lines that are unlike the texts in Lines 2 and 3 and all of the analogous lines. The lowered voice is a signal to the chorus that the song is coming to an end. I recorded the last two examples on Wednesday, January 25, 2017 in the inner court at Manhyia Palace. It was six days after the intense burial rites for the Asantehemaa Nana Afia Kobi Sɛɛwaa Ampem II, and it was Awukudae on the Akan calendar. Unlike Akwasidae, where the focus is on the celebratory facets of life, Awukudae falls on a Wednesday and is marked by reflections on death. There were no processions, and apart from a few Royal Spokespersons and Kumase chiefs, music ensembles and several courtiers were conspicuously absent. Towards the end of the ceremony, Nana Boadi Tutuwaa and members of the kete chorus joined the gathering, and after going through formal greetings, they performed five songs that immediately energized all participants (myself included) since we were just recovering from the funerary rites of the previous week.[11] I have selected the second and third songs, *Bɛtentea* (The Tall Palm Tree) and *Ma Yɛ Mmɔ Wo Din* (Let Your Name Be Proclaimed), for our analysis.

Example 5.5 Bɛ Tenten (Tall palm tree) Lead Singer: Nana Boadi Tutuwaa-Asantehene kete chorus.

Leader	**Leader**
1. Agyen Takyi bɛtenteaa e	1. Agyen Takyi the tall palm tree,
2. Wannsɔ nsapa a ɔbɛsɔ ahuro	2. If he does not tap good wine he will tap froth
3. Ɔsɛe Tumfoɔ Kantan Krodo	3. Ɔsɛe the powerful and almighty
4. Ɔsɛe Berima e	4. Ɔsɛe the brave
5. Wansɔ nsapa ɔbɛsɔ ahuro o	5. If he doesn't tap good wine, he will tap froth
Chorus	**Chorus**
6. Yee buobuo o	6. How fortunate
7. Agyen Takyi bɛtentea e	7. Agyen Takyi the tall palm tree
8. Yee Opoku Ware asinanmu e,	8. Opoku Ware's successor
9. Wannsɔ nsapa a ɔbɛsɔ ahuro o	9. If he doesn't tap good wine, he will tap froth
Leader	**Leader**
10. Agyen Takyi bɛtenteaa e	10. Agyen Takyi the tall palm tree
11. Wannsɔ nsapa a ɔbɛsɔ ahuro	11. If he doesn't tap good wine, he will tap froth
12 Ɔsɛe Tumfoɔ Kantan Krodo	12. Ɔsɛe the powerful and almighty
13. Ɔsɛe Berima e	13. Ɔsɛe the brave
14. Wansɔ nsapa ɔbɛsɔ ahuro o	14. If he doesn't tap good wine, he will tap froth
Chorus	**Chorus**
15. Yee buobuo o	15. How fortunate
16. Agyen Takyi bɛtentea e	16. Agyen Takyi the tall palm tree
17. Yee Opoku Ware asinanmu e,	17. Opoku Ware's successor
18. Wannsɔ nsapa a ɔbɛsɔ ahuro o	18. If she doesn't tap good wine, she will tap froth

In the Akan landscape, a growing palm tree is referred to as *abɛ*, while a fully-grown tall palm tree is *abɛten*, which is artistically presented in the song as *bɛtenteaa*. In Akan matrilineal society, members of the all-female kete chorus are performing a song to advise the ruler to not only emulate his predecessors, in Lines 8 and 17, but also to add to the legacy of his forebears. They turn to positive reinforcement as they caution the ruler, but at the same time they express trust that he will make the right decision by appointing the best candidate from the matriclan to succeed the late Asantehemaa. Using imagery, Nana Tutuwaa aligns the ruler with a tall palm tree that either produces excellent-tasting palm wine (*nsapa*), or, in the worst case scenario, produces only froth (*ahuro*) in Lines 2, 5, 9, 11, 14, and 18. Usually, we drink the good palm wine and throw away the froth, but the froth is equally important because it renders the much-needed service of covering the good wine and preventing it from being exposed to dust, flies, bugs, or simply unwanted ingredients in the drink. Either way, they trust the ruler will rise to the occasion.

Example 5.6 Ma Yɛn Mmɔ Wo Din (Let Your Name Be Proclaimed) Lead Singer: Nana Boadi Tutuwaa, Asantehene *kete* chorus.

Leader	Leader
1. Yee na ma yɛmmɔ wo din o ɔkorɔnto o	1. Let your name be proclaimed
Chorus	**Chorus**
2. Peaw! (spoken)	2. Peaw! (spoken)
3. Yee na Tuo Awedeɛ se	3. Tuo Awedeɛ ways
4. (ɛ)yɛ a ma yɛmmɔ wo din	4. Let your name be proclaimed
5. Peaw! (spoken)	5. Peaw! (spoken)
6. Otuo Wedeɛ na ɔkɔbɔɔ Bannaman se	6. Otuo Awedeɛ who conquered Banda State says
7. (ɛ)Yɛ a ma yɛmmɔ din ɔkorɔnto o	7. Let your name be proclaimed
8. Yee na ma yɛmmɔ wo din o ɔkorɔntɔ	8. Let your name be proclaimed
9. Peaw! (spoken)	9. Peaw! (spoken)
10. Yee na Tuo Awedeɛ se	10. Tuo Awedeɛ says
11. (ɛ)Yɛ a ma yɛmmɔ wo din	11. Let your name be proclaimed
12. Mo ɔpeaw	12. Congratulations
13. Otuo Awedeɛ na ɔkɔbɔɔ Bannaman se	13. Otuo Awedeɛ who conquered Banda State says
14. (ɛ)Yɛ a ma yɛmmɔ din okorɔntɔ o	14. Let your name be proclaimed
15. Yee na nkɔdaa nkɔdaa ɛbɔ wo din	15. Babies and children are proclaiming your name
16. Yɛboa bɔ wo din kwa o aye	16. No doubt, they proclaim your name in vain
17. Ayokofoɔ ɛbɔ wo din	17. The Ayokofoɔ clan are proclaiming your name
18. Yɛboa bɔ wo din kwa o aye	18. No doubt, they proclaim your name in vain
19. Kumaseman ɛbɔ wo din	19. The people of Kumase are proclaiming your name
20. Yɛboa bɔ wo din kwa o aye	20. No doubt, they proclaim your name in vain

21. Ghanaman ɛbɔ wo din
  22. Yɛboa bɔ wo din kwa o aye
  23. Ɛyɛ a ma yɛmmɔ wo din o aye
24. Yee na ma yɛmmɔ wo din o
  ɔkorɔntɔ o
  25. Peaw, peaw (spoken)
26. Yee na Tuo Awedeɛ se
27. (ɛ)Yɛ a ma yɛmmɔ wo din
  28. Ɔda yie o (spoken)
29. Otuo Awedeɛ ɔkɔbɔɔ Bannaman se
30. Ɛyɛ a ma yɛmmɔ din okorɔntɔ o
31. Yee na ma yɛmmɔ wo din o
  ɔkorɔntɔ
32. Yee na Tuo Awedeɛ se
33. (ɛ)Yɛ a ma yɛmmɔ wo din
34. Otuo Awedeɛ ɔkɔbɔɔ Bannaman se
35. (ɛ)Yɛ a ma yɛmmɔ din okorɔntɔ o
36. Yee na nkɔdaa nkɔdaa ɛbɔ wo din
  37. Yɛboa bɔ wo din kwa o aye
38. Ayokofoɔ ɛbɔ wo din
  39. Yɛboa bɔ wo din kwa o aye
40. Ghanaman ɛbɔ wo din
  41. Yɛboa bɔ wo din kwa o aye
42. Kumaseman ɛbɔ wo din

  43. Yɛboa bɔ wo din kwa o aye
  44. Ɛyɛ a ma yɛɔmmɔ wo din o
  aye
45. Peaw, peaw (spoken)

21. Ghanaians are proclaiming your name
  22. No doubt, they proclaim your name in vain
  23. Let your name be proclaimed.
24. Let your name be proclaimed
  25. Peaw, peaw (congratulations, spoken)
26. Tuo Awedeɛ says
27. Let your name be proclaimed
  28. He is living well (spoken)
29. Otuo Awedeɛ who conquered Banda State says
30. Let your name be proclaimed
31. Let your name be proclaimed

32. Tuo Awedeɛ says
33. Let your name be proclaimed
34. Otuo Wedeɛ who conquered Banda State says
35. Let your name be proclaimed
36. Babies and children are proclaiming your name
  37. No doubt, they proclaim your name in vain
38. The Ayokoɔ clan are proclaiming your name
  39. No doubt, they proclaim your name in vain
40. Ghanaians are proclaiming your name
  41. No doubt, they proclaim your name in vain
42. The people of Kumase are proclaiming your name
  43. No doubt, they proclaim your name in vain
44. Let your name be proclaimed

45. Peaw, peaw (spoken)

Ma Yɛ Mmɔ Wo Din (Let your name be proclaimed) anticipates the potential fallout of the ruler's final choice to fill the vacant stool—that not all of his subjects will agree with his choice and any inevitable name-calling should not deter the ruler. For, even when his name is mentioned positively, the unspeakable implication is the potential for a reversal of all positive citations. That is, all of the proclamation from infants, members of the Ɔyoko matriclan, the people of Kumase, or Ghanaians may not be genuine, and it all boils down to those who may be satisfied with or dissent from his choice, but he should be resolute and stand firm. It remains to be said, however, that in a typically militant stance, Nana Tutuwaa and her group referenced the Asante-Banda War around 1770 to reinforce heroic values (Lines 6, 13, 29, and 34. See Figure 5.1). I now turn my attention to *Nsumangorɔ*-songs performed by physicians, medical corps, and spiritual advisors.

Figure 5.1 Nana Boadi Tutuwaa (second from right) leading members of the Kete chorus in a performance at the Awukudae ceremony in Manhyia Palace, January 25, 2017.

Source: Picture by author.

Physicians' songs (Nsumangorɔ)

I conclude Chapter 5 with Nsumangorɔ, a spiritual dance that is staged in a restricted ritual by the same name before major events such as Asanteman Adaekɛseɛ (Grand Adae), but it is also performed in public, albeit differently, during royal funerary rites. As part of the preparations ushering in major festivals, a day is selected for the Asantehene and all the chiefs and priests associated with the Nsumankwaafoɔ to perform Nsumangorɔ. The event is highly restricted, with just a handful of chiefs allowed to participate, including Baafoɔ Nsumankwaahene, Baafoɔ Anantahene, Baafoɔ Dominasehene, Ɔheneba Apagyahene, and Nana Sanaahene, whose role is to provide gold dust and other items for the event. A public performance in recent memory was during the final funerary rites of the late Asantehemaa in December 2017 (Figure 5.2). As part of the Pampaso ceremony described in Chapter 2, Nana Ɔsɛe Bonsu and a large contingent of performers were part of divisions and units who converged at the Pampaso Stool House for close to five hours for the arrival of the Asantehene. It took him two hours to be robed in the Great War Tunic (*Batakarikɛseɛ*) and another two hours for the slow procession from Pampaso to Manhyia Bɔnmu—a natural forest reserve—for the battle with death. The songs selected in what follows were performed while they were waiting at Pampaso and during the procession to the imaginary battlefield. My analysis will consider the contextual link, but in order to obtain a better sound file, I recorded the group in an intimate setting on December 13, 2017 at the Nsumankwaa Palace in Kumase. The group is from Donyina (near Kuamse) and the large contingent of chorus is made up of women and men who form the chorus

Figure 5.2 Nana Osei Bonsu, Asantehene Nnwontofoɔhene, and members of his ensemble performing nsumangorɔ at the Nsumankwaa Palace, Kumase, December 13, 2017.

Source: Picture by author.

but only the men play the drums and percussion. The instrumental accompaniment consists of one *kwadum* (the lead drum) and three large *nnawuro* (gongs)—the same type that is featured in the fɔntɔmfrɔm ensemble. Remarkably, there are no accompanying drums or rattles in the instrumental ensemble. Unlike several of the ensembles that we have examined, the bell and drum patterns are the same. The singing style is markedly different from the unique characteristics of choral singing in Asante and Akan genres like *Adowa, Nnwonkorɔ*, Kete Chorus, and even heroic shouts like *ose*. Homophonic parallelism in thirds is totally absent in the singing, as unison and octave duplication of voices are the preferred modes of singing. Songs are accompanied by sporadic ululation, shouts, and other forms of interjections meant to create excitement in the performance. Performances are intense and involve standing and bodily gestures, and, as a result, they have four or more lead singers. The idea is to ensure a sustained performance that lasts for hours, making the rotation of lead singers ideal for such events. Similarly, dancing and hand gestures are nowhere close to the usual Adowa-based dances that we are familiar with. Apart from the instrumentalist, the entire chorus takes part in dancing by jumping up and down while they alternate hands in an up-and-down motion slightly above the head or in front of the body. The second type of dance involves pushing your partner with your shoulder to see if they can stand on their feet. The Nsumankwaahene is the only chief who is allowed to engage the Asantehehe in this shoulder dance. Although they performed nineteen songs in a single performance unit, I present just four songs for my analysis.

Example 5.7 Kanowaa (He Didn't Mean What He Said), *Nsumangɔrɔ* (Priestly Dances).

Leader	**Leader**
1. Kanowaa yaa e	1. He didn't mean what he said
2. Kanowaa yaa e	2. He didn't mean what he said
3. Ɔkanowaa	3. He didn't mean it
4. Kanowaa yaa e	4. He didn't mean what he said
5. Kanowaa yaa e	5. He didn't mean what he said
6. Ɔkanowaa	6. He didn't mean it
7. Kwanowaa	7. He didn't mean it
8. Wa'kum mpem mpem	8. You have killed thousands
9. San wakyi bekum Asante o	9. Return and kill the Asante.
10. Ɔkwanowaa	10. He didn't mean it
11. Kanowaa	11. He didn't mean it
12. Wa'kum mpempem	12. You have killed thousands
13. Sane wakyi bekum Asante o	13. Return and kill the Asante.
14. Ɔkanowaa	14. He didn't mean it
15. Adwoaba kaanowaa yaa e	15. He didn't mean what he said the child of Adwoa
16. Ye buo buo o	16. Really
17. Sɛ biribi wɔ Asante o	17. That there is something in Asante
18. Aye e	18. Aye e
Chorus	**Chorus**
19. Kaanowaa yaa e	19. He didn't mean what he said
20. Kaanowaa yaa e	20. He didn't mean what he said
21. Ɔkanowaa	21. He didn't mean it
22. Kaanowaa yaa e	22. He didn't mean what he said
23. Kanowaa yaa e	23. He didn't mean what he said
24. Ɔkanowaa	24. He didn't mean it
25. Kaanowaa	25. He didn't mean it
26. Wa'kum mpem mpem	26. You have killed thousands
27. San wakyi bekum Asante o	27. Return and kill the Asante.
28. Ɔkwanowaa	20. He didn't mean it
29. Kanowaa	29. He didn't mean it
30. Wa'kum mpempem	30. You have killed thousands
31. Sane wakyi bekum Asante o	31. Return and kill the Asante.
32. Ɔkanowaa	32. He didn't mean it
33. Adwoaba kaanowaa yaa e	33. He didn't mean what he said the child of Adwoa
34. Ye buo buo o	34. Really
35. Sɛ biribi wɔ Asante o	35. That there is something in Asante
36. Aye e English Translation	36. Aye e

The purpose of Kanowaa is to caution potential adversaries not to underestimate the might and resolve of the Asante Kingdom. As previously stated in Chapter 1, the porcupine may not be an aggressor, but that should not be misconstrued as a sign of weakness. As the Twi saying goes: a child can easily crack open the shell of a snail but not the shell of a turtle (*abofra bɔ nwa na ɔmmɔ akykyekyedeɛ*). There are historical accounts of powerful individuals who thought they would be able to attack and defeat the Asante, only to realize that it was impossible. Having defeated several states, an imaginary adversary decided to bring his forces to Asante (Lines 8–9), but he was defeated (Line 17), so he really did not mean what he said (Lines 1–6). The poetic text and the mode of singing follow a set of performance frames. The formal structure at the global level projects a cyclically induced **AB** form, where **A** is the Lead or call phrase and **B** is the Chorus or response phrase. The choral response is an exact repetition of the call phrase. Based on literary devices at the micro-level, the song is in Three Sections. Section 1 is from Lines 1–6, Section 2 is from Lines 7–14, and Section 3 is from Lines 15–18. Sections 1 and 2 are further divided into two sections. The linear repetition in Lines 1 and 2 is temporarily rounded off with the single phrase Ɔkanowaa (He didn't mean it) in Line 3. The process is repeated from Lines 4–6. Without mentioning names, the two sub-sections are meant to introduce the main idea as stated previously. The two sub-sections in Section 2, Lines 7–10 and 11–14, highlight the reasoning underlying the actions of imagined adversaries. He has killed thousands and thousands, and defeated several states (Line 8), so he is going to turn his attention to the Asante Kingdom. Section 3 finally identifies the individual in Line 15 in the beginning phrase Adwoaba (Adwoa's son) by emphasizing the matrilineal source without mentioning his name. Adwoa's son finally realizes the might of Asante in the penultimate phrase (Line 17), but it is too late to surrender, and the reduplication of the word *buo buo* in Line 16 is followed by *Aye* (Line 18), a cry of dejection that he is going to face the unthinkable. *Kanowaa* is a compression of the Akan phrase Ɔkaa no waa, without the first syllable, which implies saying or making pronouncements without really meaning it. The negation of not meaning what an individual uttered is represented by the ending syllable *waa*. Despite my initial interpretation of Kanowaa, the performer-composers artistically use literary devices to reinforce the message in the song. For instance, in Line 1 Kanowaa is used as a noun form to reference an individual without mentioning their name. On the other hand, Ɔkanowaa in Line 3 reinstates the first syllable, Ɔ, in order to revert to a single-word phrase. Lastly, Adwoaba, in Line 15, is variable and the most unstable phrase in the entire song, since it can be recomposed with another name. Adwoa is the soul name of a female child born on a Monday and can be recomposed with another female child born on, say, Tuesday, Wednesday, Thursday, Friday, Saturday, or Sunday. The next example is a graphic description of the predicament of a stranded toucan (Ɔwam) in a palm tree.

Example 5.8 Ɔ*wam* (The Toucan), Nsumangorɔ (Priestly Dances).

Leader		English Translation	
1.	Ɔwam e maka abɛ mu o	1.	Toucan, I'm stranded in the palm tree
2.	Ɔwam e maka abɛ mu o	2.	Toucan, I'm stranded in the palm tree
3.	Ɔwam nkɔdi abɛ	3.	The Toucan has gone to eat the palm fruit
4.	Na abɛ amere e	4.	That has not ripened
5.	Ɔwam nkɔdi abɛ	5.	Toucan, I'm stranded in the palm tree
6.	Na abɛ amere e	6.	That has not ripened
7.	Aboa ɔwam e maka abɛ mu o	7.	Toucan, the great bird, is stranded in the palm tree
8.	Me wu a gyama nkasa	8.	When I die, gyama sticks should inform the world about my predicatment

(*Continued*)

Example 5.8 (Continued)

Chorus	Chorus
9. Ɔwam e maka abɛ mu o	9. Toucan, I'm stranded in the palm tree
10. Ɔwam e maka abɛ mu o	10. Toucan, I'm stranded in the palm tree
11. Ɔwam nkɔdi abɛ	11. The Toucan has gone to eat the palm fruit
12. Na abɛ amere e	12. That has not ripened
13. Ɔwam nkɔdi abɛ	13. Toucan, I'm stranded in the palm tree
14. Na abɛ amere e	14. That has not ripened
15. Ɔwam e maka abɛ muo	15. Toucan, the great bird, is stranded in the palm tree
16. Me wu a gyama nkasa	16. When I die, gyama sticks should inform the world about my predicatment

Example 5.8 is based on the evocative image of the toucan (*ɔwam*) caught stranded in a palm tree and mobbed for feeding on another person's toils—in this case, palm fruits. For those familiar with the toucan, ripe palm fruits are its main staple, but unfortunately these particular palm fruits were not even ripe (they were still green). But events soon turned ugly when, for some unexplained reasons, the toucan became trapped in the palm branches and was unable to fly away. The owner of the farm found the toucan way up in the branches and immediately gathered dried and fallen branches and sticks (*gyamma*) from the ground and started beating the toucan to death. The moral lesson in the song is greediness in several manifestations of life. The proverb in Twi is: *sika anibrɛ da owuo afa.* Thus, the insatiable pursuit of riches by greed will lead to unforeseen consequences—death. The use of imagery in Asante songs eliminates the feeling of personal bias and allows for an open-minded reception of songs across a wide spectrum of masses, including children. The performance frames in Example 5.8 are similar to Kanowaa, taking the usual **AB** form, where the Leader's phrase is represented by the letter **A** while the choral response is identified as **B**. The choral response is an exact repetition of the lead phrase, creating a cyclical and interactive form. The moral lesson in the song is accomplished by the use of literary devices, including the linear repetition of phrases. Lines 1–2 introduce the toucan's quandary, Lines 3–6 establish the causes of the toucan's predicament, and, finally, Lines 7–8 are a commentary about the fatal consequences of the toucan's actions. The median phrase, *maka* (I'm stranded) in Lines 1–2, 7, and the chorus use the first-person pronoun to personalize the song for the toucan. In a move to predict its demise, the toucan is rescinded to his ultimate fate that his death is not the result of being stranded in the palm branches, but rather to the mob action—the beating he received from dried sticks (*gyamma/egya mma*) under the palm tree (Lines 8 and 16).

As we can imagine, Example 5.9 is a favorite of the Nnsumankwaa group for obvious reasons. For all of his accomplishment in founding Asanteman, Ɔpemsoɔ Ɔsɛe Tutu could not have done it without the spiritual advice of the foremost priest, Ɔkɔmfoɔ Anɔkye. With this song, the performers are assuring the masses that while they have the best medications for physical and spiritual well-being, they do not practice spirituality with greed, for the great priest's word of caution is their guiding star. Bad medicine is not good for society.

Example 5.9 Kɔmfoɔ Anɔkye-Nsumangorɔ (Priestly dances).

Leader	Leader
1. Yɛ wɔ nnuro e	1. We have medicine
2. Bɛrima kae o	2. The brave man said
3. Yɛ wɔ nnuro	3. We have medicine
4. Kɔmfoɔ Anɔkye kae o	4. Kɔmfo Anɔkye said
5. Ɔben nyɛ o	5. Bad medicine is not good
6. Nsuo bɛ tɔ a, ɛde mframa di kan	6. Heavy winds precede thunderstorm
7. Kɔmfo Anɔkye kaa sɛ ɔben nyɛ	7. Kɔmfo Anɔkye warned against bad medicine
Chorus	**Chorus**
8. Yɛ wɔ nnuro e	8. We have medicine
9. Bɛrima kae o	9. The brave man said
10. Yɛ wɔ nnuro	10. We have medine
11. Kɔmfoɔ Anɔkye kae o	11. Kɔmfo Anɔkye said
12. Ɔben nyɛ o	12. Bad medicine is not good
Leader	**Leader**
14. E nsuo bɛ tɔ a, ɔde mframa adi kan	14. Heavy winds precede thunderstorm
15. Kɔmfo Anɔkye kaa sɛ ɔbɛn nyɛ	15. Kɔmfo Anɔkye warned against bad medicine
Chorus	**Chorus**
16. Yɛ wɔ nnuro e	16. We have medicine
17. Bɛrima kae o	17. The brave man said
18. Yɛ wɔ nnuro	18. We have medicine
19. Kɔmfoɔ Anɔkye kae o	19. Kɔmfo Anɔkye said
20. Ɔben nyɛ o	20. Bad medicine is not good

Example 5.10 compares human life with an imaginary journey that we have examined throughout this book including Examples 4.18 and 5.1. Similar to life's journey, the performer-composers caution us that we should make thorough preparations before we embark on the journey of life. And while embarking on the journey, we should be strategic and move slowly to avoid missteps since slow moving is associated with caution-being alert and scouting our environment to avoid pitfalls. Crucially, we should use major pathways or main streets, and avoid by-paths or side streets, where the enemy may be hiding. In the final analysis, genuine intentions will overcome bad schemes of the enemy.

Example 5.10 Yɛ Nam Nyaa (We are traveling/moving slowly)-Nsumangorɔ (Priestly dances).

Leader	Leader
1. Ɔpaa	1. Ɔpaa
2. Ohwi	2. Ohwi
3. Ɔpaa	3. Ɔpaa
4. Ohwi	4. Ohwi
Leader	**Leader**
5. Yɛnam nyaa yɛnam nyaa e	5. We are traveling slowly
6. Yɛnam nyaa yɛnam nyaa e	6. We are traveling slowly
7. (ɛ)Kwan bi a yɛkɔ	7. We are embarking on a journey
8. Yɛnam nyaa sɛ neɛ yɛnkɔ o	8. We are traveling slowly as if we are not moving
9. Yɛnam kwantensoɔ	9. We are traveling on main streets
10. Yɛmfa mfikyire da	10. We shall not take side streets
11. Ɔtamfo nya yɛn a ɔbɛyɛ yɛn	11. Our enemy will hurt us

(Continued)

Example 5.10 (Continued)

Chorus	Chorus
12. Yɛnam nyaa yɛnam nyaa e	12. We are traveling slowly
13. Yɛnam nyaa yɛnam nyaa e	13. We are traveling slowly
14. (ɛ)Kwan bi a yɛkɔ	14. We are embarking on a journey
15. Yɛnam nyaa sɛ neɛ yɛnkɔ o	15. We are traveling slowly as if we are not moving
16. Yɛnam kwantensoɔ	16. We are traveling on main streets
17. Yɛmfa mfikyire da	17. We shall not take side streets
18. Ɔtamfo nya yɛn a ɔbɛyɛ yɛn	18. Our enemy will hurt us
Leader	**Leader**
19. Yɛnam nyaa yɛnam nyaa e	19. We are traveling slowly
20. Yɛnam nyaa yɛnam nyaa e	20. We are traveling slowly
21. (ɛ)Kwan bi a yɛkɔ	21. We are embarking on a journey
22. Yɛnam nyaa sɛ neɛ yɛnkɔ o	22. We are traveling slowly as if we are not moving
23. Yɛnam tinponso	23. We are traveling on main streets
24. Yɛmfa kwankyɛn kwankyɛn	24. We shall not take side streets
25. Ɔtamfo nya yɛn a ɔbɛha yɛn	25. Our enemy will harm us
Chorus	**Chorus**
26. Yɛnam nyaa yɛnam nyaa e	26. We are traveling slowly
27. Yɛnam nyaa yɛnam nyaa e	27. We are traveling slowly
28. (ɛ)Kwan bi a yɛkɔ	28. We are embarking on a journey
29. Yɛnam nyaa sɛ neɛ yɛnkɔ o	29. We are traveling slowly as if we are not moving
30. Yɛnam kwantensoɔ	30. We are traveling on main streets
31. Yɛmfa mfikyire da	31. We shall not take side streets
32. Ɔtamfo nya yɛn a ɔbɛyɛ yɛn	32. Our enemy will harm us

We began this chapter with a kete song talking about imaginary travel, and we end the chapter with the same metaphor by a different group. In all their undertakings, the Nsumankwaa group prides themselves on being cautious and paying critical attention to the environment and their surroundings. Walking in haste may not be ideal, since it is relatively easy to lose your focus and miss traps by potential adversaries. Not only do they walk slowly, but they also avoid side streets and use main streets because bad elements may be hiding in the alleys. Genuine intentions may overcome the diabolical plans of adversaries. There is value in moving cautiously.

The use of rhetorical devices by performer-composers of kete songs to evoke historical and embodied experience is quite remarkable. The very first song (Example 5.1) sets the tone for the theme of war by compressing sentences into single words. Thus, *Twentɛnko* (indispensable warrior); *Osinsinmu* (literally, an individual squatting in a river); *Ɔwerebaani* (an obstinate fellow); and *Ɔsempani* (one who disperses a council) are rhetorical devices meant to invite the Asantehemaa to the performance. They are about to embark on an imaginary war or journey, and they needed the guidance and leadership of the Asantehemaa, for there is value in leadership. In Example 5.2, Nana Agyeiwaa's narrative uses rhetoric to emphasize militancy and braveness in the discovery of Lake Bosomtwe. Ɔsɛe Tutu fought to redeem Asante; he is a skillful warrior, he fought and captured the lake. The strategic recall of names, places of abode-communities that are still part of the landscape around the lake-metaphoric allusions to the hawk or black hawk, and the use of nominals and referential parallelism stir up emotions for collective action. Additional references include the hostilities between Asante and Takyiman in the reign of Opoku Ware, the capture of the treasury vault (Sanaa) in Example 5.3, and the Asante-Banda War (Banasa, c. 1770). In the context of a staged battle with death as part of the final funerary rites of the late Asantehemaa, the *nsumangorɔ* songs *Kanowaa* (He/she didn't mean what they said), *Ɔwam* (the Toucan), *Kɔmfoɔ Anɔkye* (Priest and Spiritual Advisor), and *Yɛ Nam Nyaa* (We are moving slowly) tap into deep-rooted emotions of the heroic past in order to urge the fighting divisions and units on to the encounter with death. These are relatively peaceful times, and the Asante do not embark on wars anymore. Thus, we can interpret walking or traveling in Example 5.10 as metaphors for daily life or daily pursuits for social well-being, as well as calls for the political and economic uplift of all.

Notes

1 Kyerematen (1966: 219–277) provides a detailed account of the discovery of Lake Bosomtwe.
2 For a list of all the villages and their history, see Patrick Elliot Ofosu (2006).
3 Kyerematen (1966: 219) offers a detailed historical account of the issues involved with Nana Bosompem Boakye Ntow Kuroko.
4 Kyerematen (1966: 288–327) includes a detailed account of Asantehene Ɔsɛe Kwadwo's reign.
5 *Kradin*—the soul name, or, literally, the birthday of Ɔpemsoɔ Ɔsɛe Tutu is Friday, hence the name Kofi.
6 Ampene and Nyantakyi III (2016: 122–143) contains a history and detailed description of the swords and sword bearers.
7 For a history and description of both swords, see Ampene and Nyantakyi III (2016: 122–143).
8 For a brief history and description of the *Sanaa* and *Afotosanfoɔ*, see Ampene and Nyantakyi III (2016: 182–187).
9 For Akan religious and philosophical thought, see Kofi Asare Opoku (1982: 61–73).
10 A type of Asante trumpet, *mmɔdwemmɔdwe*, now in the British Museum in London, has a human jawbone attached to the end to draw attention to the importance of the spoken word in Akan.
11 I examine power dynamics and some of the issues involved in such performances in a forthcoming publication, titled *Petitioning the King: Kete Songs, Lineage and Kingship in Asante*.

References

Ampene, Kwasi, and Nana Kwadwo Nyantakyi III. 2016. *Engaging Modernity: Asante in the Twenty-First Century*, 2nd edition. Ann Arbor, MI: Michigan Publishing.
Kyerematen, A.A.Y. 1966. "Ashanti Royal Regalia: Their History and Functions." PhD diss., Oxford University.
Mosobalaje, Adebayo. 2017. "Ebenezer Obey and the Rhetoric of Contradiction." *African Identities* 15 (1): 116–131.
Nkoala, Sisanda Mcimeli. 2013. "Songs That Shaped the Struggle: A Rhetorical Analysis of South African Struggle Songs." *African Yearbook of Rhetoric* 4 (1): 51–61.
Ofosu, Patrick Elliot. 2006. *Lake Bosomtwe: The Pride of Ashanti*. Kumasi, Ghana: Deszyn Origin Publishers.
Olmsted, Wendy. 2006. *Rhetoric: An Historical Introduction*. Malden, MA and Oxford: Blackwell Publishers.
Opoku, Kofi Asare. 1982. "The World View of the Akan." *Tarikh* 7 (2): 26, 61–73.
Yankah, Kwesi. 1983. "To Praise or Not to Praise the King: The Akan 'Apae' in the Context of Referential Poetry." *Research in African Literatures* 14 (3): 381–400.
———. 2012. *The Proverb in the Context of Akan Rhetoric*. New York: Diasporic African Press.

6   Rhetoric and history

Chronicle and referential poetry (*kwadwom* and *apae*)

Obi nto anansεm nkyerε Ntikuma (no one narrates Ananse stories to Ntikuma-the son of Ananse).[1] Akan Proverb.

Moving away from songs to verbally intoned poetry, rhetoric, and history in chronicle and referential poetry is also a continuation of the key issues introduced in Chapter 5. Here, I describe two distinct genres, *kwadwom* and *apae*, as verbal arts in order to distinguish both artistic forms from instrumental and song texts. Despite the noted lack of absolute dates, the contents of chronicle and referential poetry provide candid records of reigns, events, and wars with the extensive use of rhetorical devices and imagery. The textual resources in *kwadwom* are dense and heavily-coded—Akan poetics at the highest level—while that of *apae* is direct and straightforward, although both genres are based on ancient texts and therefore not easily comprehensible to Twi speakers and the Akan. I begin with *kwadwom*.

Kwadwom (chronicle songs)

Kwadwom is a form of verbal poetry that recounts historical events by using rhetorical and literary devices that are also commonplace in *apae*. They are close to what is described in English as bards or minstrels (Nketia, 1987: 201). In Twi, they are known as *Kwadwomfoɔ*. At the Asantehene's court, two men who either walk behind the ruler in processions or stand behind him when he is formally seated perform *kwadwom*. The mode of performance is such that one of the men is identified as the leader (*kwadwom kandifoɔ*), and the second man the responder (*agyesoɔ*), who repeats or echoes the exact phrase that the leader intones. There are different strands in the unsubstantiated sources regarding the beginnings of *kwadwom* in Akan. In an unpublished manuscript on the genre, Nketia (1962) describes a practice where women performed *kwadwom* in the days of three Denkyera Kings: Boadu Akafu (around the mid-seventeenth century), Boa Amponsεm (circa 1637–1694), and King Ntim Gyakari (1694–1701). Although Nketia does not mention the gender of those who performed during Ntim Gyakari's time, the revelation that it was the practice during the time for all three kings of Denkyera to cut off the lower cartilage of their nose in order to render the performance aesthetically pleasing indicates that his consultants were referring to the Akan *nsui* (funeral cries). Interestingly, my consultant at Manhyia Palace, Opanin Kofi Fofie, traced the origins of *kwadwom* to one Akwaa who lived in Dɛnkyera near Bonwire. Dɛnkyera, he told me, has since been abandoned, but it is striking that the name of Akwaa's village is the same as the once-powerful kingdom we have been referring to in this volume. Akwaa, in Opanin Fofie's own words, grew up with a mental disorder that led to bouts of crying, which he combined with utterances while he roamed around the village. The elders in the village started to create poetry out of Akwaa's words and in the process they polished his crying words by using the praise names of the ruler, labeling the resultant poetry Akwaa-nnwom (literary, Akwaa's songs). Surprisingly, no one could recall the motive behind the choice of using the word for songs (*nnwom*, singular, *dwom*), as opposed to *Akwaa su* (cries), to describe Akwaa's utterances, since that would have been the best description for what he was doing. For, the manner of reciting *kwadwom* is described in the Akan Twi language as *be* (a verb) while the noun form, *abeɛ*, illustrates the heightened speech mode of reciting poetry.[2] Kwa-dwom may mislead those who take the word in the literal sense as Akwaa's songs. When I posed the question to Opanin Fofie, he was resolute in declaring, "*yɛ be kwadwom*" (we recite kwadwom, emphasis my own), which makes sense because the Akan will say, "*yɛ to nnwom*" (we sing songs). In his unpublished manuscript referenced previously, Nketia's very first sentence confirms the mode of reciting *kwadwom*: "*[A]nwensɛm a ɛwɔ nwoma yi mu yɛ kwadwom a wɔbe ma Asantehene*" (the collection of poems in this book are *kwadwom* that are recited for the Asantehene. Emphasis mine).

Further, Nketia identifies two types of *kwadwom*: real *kwadwom*, where two men perform behind the ruler, and *sɛn-kwadwom*, which involves a group of six to more than a dozen men. It is plausible that the prefix, *sɛn*, refers to *Ɛsɛn* (court criers) with the first letter elided.[3] It appears that *sɛn-kwadwom* was already in decline over five decades ago, when Nketia recorded *kwadwomfoɔ* in Asante, since he did not provide samples of their repertoire. My work covers the real *kwadwom* type. *Kwadwom* poetry falls under two broad categories, namely, *Nnwontene* (Long Verse) and *Nnwontia* (Short Verses). *Nnwontene* is further divided into three subcategories: *Anyane Anyane* (Awakening), *Amankum* (Destroying Nations), and *Asafo* or Asafodeɛ (the name of a paternal group). As its name implies, the Short Verses usually consist of four to six lines that are performed in unison, as opposed to the relatively long verses where the leader recites a phrase while the responder repeats it verbatim. In a plural performance environment, all performances are truncated the moment they hear the *kwadwomfoɔ* begin the very first phrase of one of the long verses. Participants behave in a similar manner, as all murmuring or whispering ceases and yields to the long verse that usually lasts for about eight to ten minutes. At the end of the poetry, all court musicians play short pieces to congratulate the bards before they begin to take turns again. Short Verses are performed when the Asantehemaa, territorial chiefs (*amanhene*), Kumase Abrempɔn, and Ɔyoko chiefs greet the Asantehene by shaking his hands when he is formally seated. In those instances, the handshake freezes until the end of the verse, and then both ruler and ɔhemaa will lift their right hands up (while they are still holding hands) and make brief remarks to each other before breaking up the handshake. Unlike members of the constabulary (Abrafoɔ), who perform *apae* within the royal space in front of the Asantehene, the position of the bards is immediately behind the formally seated ruler. Consequently, with the exception of the tone of their voices and rapid delivery of texts, dramatic gestures are entirely missing from the *kwadwom* performance (Figures 6.1-kwadwom in context; 6.2-apae in context).

For our purposes, I will present Nnwontene, Amankum, Asafo, and two examples of short verses. Each example will be followed by an in-depth analysis. In the summer of 2009, I recorded Opanin Fofie and members of his group inside Manhyia Palace in Kumase and subsequently met with him over the years to clarify the dense ancient texts. Example 6.1 is usually performed at dawn (between 4 and 5 a.m.) on Akwasidae (Sunday) morning to wake the ruler in order for him to prepare for the day's rituals. Following on the heels of the *kwadwomfoɔ* are the Ɔkyeremma (the Divine drummer), who perform drum poetry (*ayan*) on the pair of atumpan drums. The short trumpeters (*mmɛntiafoɔ*) are next in line, followed by the *ntahera* and *kɔkroanya* trumpet groups, tribunal drums *mpebi ne nkrawiri*, and the pair of *nkukuadwe* drums, in that order. The Asantehene will be ready to begin the day's rituals by the time the last sound-producing instrument is played. As I explained previously, the responder repeats the leader's phrase exactly; but for lack of space, I have left out the repetition in my transcriptions.

Figure 6.1 Yaw Frimpong (right and holding a microphone) and Osei Akwasi (also holding a microphone) performing *kwadwom* in their prescribed position behind the formally seated Asantehene, July 2013, Bogyaweɛ, Manhyia Palace.

Source: Picture by author.

Figure 6.2 Kwabena Poku reciting *apae* in the prescribed royal space directly facing the Asantehene during the Akwasidae public assembly, July 30, 2017.

Source: Picture by author.

Example 6.1 Nnwontene (Long Verse)-Kwadwom by Opanin Kofi Fofie and the bards.

1. Ɔsagyefoɔ nyane dasuo mu o
2. Okuru Asante Naadu nyane nge.
3. Kɔtɔkɔhene nyane
4. Korɔbeahene nyane nge.
5. Merema wo Korɔbea ayirifie anwoma ne Kɔtɔkɔ nge
6. Asante atwa ne tiri Twum o Kyampɔn noforobo nge
7. Asante asiesie bo Sumantete.
8. Korɔbea Asante Naadu nyane nge.
9. Ɔsɛe Kyeretwie me mmɔ wo dinwe awisi o
10. Hwan na obenya sɛ Ɛdweso Owusu Panin ne Akua Bakoma sikaboɔ ba ne wo?
11. Obi nyaa saa bi a anka ɔbɛyɛ bi.
12. Ɛmaanu Atia Dufie ba e demirefi e nyane nge
13. Kyerewaa ne Ntofie Mmogye naa.
14. Odoforo dadeɛ Twum o Kyampɔn noforobo nge
15. Osuo aninkurowi o Sumantete.
16. Agyarko Agyare na adeɛ aseɛ do nge
17. Akusibiekumborɔ Twum o Kyampɔn noforobo nge
18. Agyarko a ofiri Sɛe Frampɔn o damirifua awisi.
19. Ɔsɛe Tutu e me mmɔ wo din nwe awisi o
20. Hwan na obenya se Kantinkyire Boakye Dankwa ne Sɛɛwaa Ampem sikaboɔ ba ne wo?
21. Obi nyaa saa bi a anka ɔbɛyɛ bi
22. Birago Abakan Nana e Frampɔn o damirifua awisi.

(*Continued*)

Example 6.1 (Continued)

23. Meremawo Juaben do Adarkwa Yiadom nge.
24. Yiadɔm nana yede akoboɔ gyegye wo taataa o Twum o Kyampɔn noforobo nge
25. Ɔtɔ sika Asaman Naa Agyigyarko nge
26. Agyarko Yeboah Abaankoro edwom fere wo
27. Ɔheneafrewoɔ e Frampɔn o damirifua o
28. Opoku Ware memɔ wo din nwe awisi
29. Hwan na obenya sɛ Gyaakye Opoku Panin ne Akyaa Yikwan ba ne wo?
30. Obi nyaa saa bi an anka ɔbɛyɛ bi.
31. Aseneɛ Gyambibi ɔhene Twum o Kyampɔn noforobo nge.
32. Ɔhemaa Akyiaa Yikwan ba o Sumantete.
33. Bobbie Ntra Akwasi Pepe nge
34. Ntodimaa Akyeamfoɔ Twum o Kyampɔn noforobo nge.
35. Bobbie Kɛse Brempon ba o Sumantete.
36. Bobbie Naadu Nyane nge
37. Owusu Akyiaw ba e demirefi e nyane nge
38. Gyampirefiafo Osuo a onintiriboɔ Twum o Kyampɔn noforobo nge.
39. Onofo Fori Amankuampem o Sasa Fori Amankuapem nge
40. Osafo Adu Sekyeaman okum Agyeiba Twum o Kyampɔn noforobo nge.
41. Osafoboɔ se oreba Sumantete
42. Osafo Naadu nyane nge
43. Awurade a okura nipa biaku ɔdefata ɔborɔfoɔ senkyera ɔde fata ɔhene bi nge
44. Okuru bɛdi atɔpereba Twum o Kyampon noforobo nge
45. Okuru anitete Brempɔn ba o Sumantete
46. Okuru kaka Naadu nyane nge
47. Wahye yɛn Frampɔn demerefa o
48. Obaa bɛn adifɔ adi maa Akyeamfoɔ tete Agyankɔ da bɔn nge
49. Ofosu Pema Naa Bɔneamo nge
50. Ɔkwakuo nuntɔn Boafo aforoboɔ nge
51. Ɔkyere Nkwatia na ɛkosi Frimpɔn nge
52. Awurade Akyenebo Ofobiriti Adwurodwuro bia Sakraboten nge
53. Awuraa Tipanin a yɛne no goro fuafua no ɔse nnɔsoa kwa o Twum o Kyampon noforobo nge
54. Ɔtɔ sika Asaaman Naa Agyigyarko nge
55. Agyarko Yɛboah Abaankoro ɛdwom frɛ woɔ
56. Ɔsagyefoɔ Frampɔn o demerefa o.
57. Ɔsagyefoɔ manya mfrɛn nge
58. Okuru Asante Naadu nyane nge
    Lead and Response
    59. Okuru bɛdi atɔprɛba demirefi su nna nyane awo
    60. Dɔmaako Sakyi asono aworobɛn

English Translation
1. Ɔsagyefo wake up at midnight
2. Okuru Asante Naadu wake up
3. Kɔtɔkɔhene wake up
4. Korɔbeahene wake up
5. I am greeting you as the overall king of Kɔtɔkɔ
6. Asante has beheaded Twum Kyampɔn noforobo
7. Asante has fortified itself with the charm Sumantete
8. Korɔbea Asante Naadu wake up
9. Ɔsɛe Kyeretwie, I do not mention your name in vain
10. Who would not enjoy being the son of Owusu Panin of Ɛdweso and Akua Bakoma the gold nugget?

11. Had someone gotten this privilege, the one would brag
12. Demirefi; son of Maanu Atia Dufie wake up
13. The grandchild of Kyerewaa and Ntofi mmogye
14. Odoforo deadɛɛ Twum Kyampɔn noforobo
15. Osuo aninkurowi o, Sumantete
16. Agyako Agyare's orioerty elsewhere has been destroyed
17. Akusibiekumborɔ Twum Kyampɔn noforobo
18. Agyare who hails from Sɛe Frampɔn condolence
19. Ɔsɛe Tutu I do not mention your name in vain
20. Who would not enjoy being the son of Kantinkyire Boakye Dankwa and Sɛɛwaa Ampem the gold nugget?
21. If someone else had this privilege he would boast of it
22. Birago Abakan Nana Frampɔn, condolence
23. I am greeting you, Adarkwa Yiadɔm of Dwaben
24. The grandson of Yiadɔm who is welcomed with bullets, we greet you Twum Kyeampɔn
25. Asaman Naa Agyigyarko who trades in gold dust.
26. Agyarko Yeboah Abaan whose name is used in composing songs
27. Frampɔn, who has been summoned by the king, condolence
28. Opoku I do not mention your name in vain
29. Who would not enjoy being the son of Gyaakye Opoku Panin and Akyaa Yiakwan?
30. If someone else had this privilege he would boast of it.
31. Asenɛɛ Gyambibi ɔhene Twum o Kyampɔn
32. Sumantete, the son of Ɔhemaa Akyaa Yiakwan
33. Bobbie Ntra Akwasi Pepe
34. Ntodimaa Akyeamfoɔ Twum Kyampɔn noforobo
35. Sumantete, the son of Bobbie Kɛse Brempɔn
36. Bobbi Naadu wake up
37. Demirefi, the son of Owusu Akyiaw, wake up
38. Gyampirefiafo Osuo a Onintiriboɔ Twum Kyampɔn noforobo
39. Onofo Fori Amankuapem, sasa Fori Amankuapem
40. Ɔsafo Adu Sekyeaman who killed Twum Kyampɔn the son of Agyei
41. Sumantete, Ɔsafoboɔ has announced that he is coming
42. Ɔsafo Naadu, wake up
43. The king who uses one captive to pacify the whitemen and Senkyera to pacify a certain chief
44. Twum Kyeampɔn the son of Okuru bedi atɔperɛ
45. Sumantete, the son of Okuru anitete Brempɔn
46. Okuru kaka Naadu, wake up
47. He has killed Frampɔn, condolence
48. Which woman was found guilty in place of Agyankɔ da bɔn of Akyeamfoɔ of old?
49. Ofosu Pema Naa Bɔneamo
50. Ɔkwakuo nuntɔn Boafo has climbed the rock
51. The death of Ɔkyere Kwatia was attributed to Frimpɔn
52. Awurade Akyenebo Ofobiriti Adwurodwurobia Sakraboten
53. Awura Tipanin with whom we have been trailing closely is carrying an empty load
54. Asama Naa Agyigyarko who trades in gold dust
55. Agyarko Yeboa Abaankoro who is being praised with songs
56. Ɔsagyefoɔ Frampɔn, condolence
57. Ɔsagyefoɔ, I am calling you
58. Okuru Asante Naadu, wake up
   Lead and Response
   59. Demirefi, the son of Okuru bedi atɔprɛ, wail and wake up
   60. Dɔmaako Sakyi, the elephant's tusk trumpet

Compared with other text-based genres in the Akan court, kwadwom is astoundingly dense, with an overwhelming amount of indirection, opaque phrases, metaphoric allusions, and lots of rhetorical devices. Additionally, there is an abundant use of nominals in the form of personal names, by-names, and strong appellations, and it is especially in the nominals that we are able to infer reigns and events associated with historical figures. It bears noting that, despite their emphasis on defeated commanders, kings, and chiefs of enemy states, the Asante did not escape the costs of the battlefield, since they also lost several brave soldiers and leaders. Recalling various wars of conquest and expansion in poetic verses by the *Kwadwomfoɔ* therefore reminds participants in a given event of the grave incidents in the inter-war years and provides the usual solemn background that is filtered through lived experience and social values. Such dense texts require multiple levels of analysis, and it is my goal here to peel off layers upon layers of expressions that hinges on embodied experience and values as the basis for symbolic communication. Example 6.1 is given in five broad sections: Lines 1–8, 9–18,19–26, 27–37, and 38–60. A distinctive feature is the discrete use of formulaic phrases as end patterns to encode the text in symbolic language and provide prompters for the Responder to repeat the Leader's phrase. In most cases, the noted formulaic phrases have no syntactic relationship with the preceding words of the same line, while others may be names or by-names. The first formulaic phrase, *nge*, is non-lexical, and it is used as an end phrase in Lines 2, 4–6, 8, 12, 17, 23, 24, 25, 31, 33, 34, 36–39, 42–46, 48–54, and 57–58. The second end-phrase pattern, *sumantete*, in Lines 7, 15, 32, 35, 41, and 45 refers to the remote source of deities; that is, deities of the Asante are from the beginning of time. The third type of formulaic phrase is a name from the medial position to the end of the phrase: *Twum o Kyampɔn noforobo* in Lines 6, 14, 17, 24, 31, 34, 38, 40, 44, and 53. The fourth type is a term of endearment, Naadu, a compressed form of the name Nana Adu, in Lines 2, 8, 36, 42, 46, and 58. The fifth and last formulaic phrase is the name Frampɔn, in Lines 18, 22, 27, 47, 51, and 56.

Section One, Lines 1–8 is Opanin Fofie's artistic solution to the unnerving task of being first in the line of performers to wake up the Asantehene around four in the morning. Thus, he delves deep into Akan referential poetry with heroic undertones. He begins by avoiding the stool name of the ruler, but instead generates a list of some of the strongest appellations of Asante kings. For instance, Ɔsagyefoɔ (literally, the redeemer; one who goes to war to deliver his people from their enemies) is in Line 1. For his success in delivering his people from the tyranny of Ntim Gyakari and the Dɛnkyera, Ɔpemsoɔ Ɔsɛe Tutu and successive kings were given the title Ɔsagyefoɔ. Okuru (one who carries the entire burden of the kingdom on his shoulders) is in Line 2; Kɔtɔkɔhene (reference to the attributes of the porcupine) and Korɔbeahene (by-name of Asante and metaphor for the king of Asante) are in Lines 3 and 4. In Line 5, Opanin Fofie positions himself as a messenger of the masses, "I am greeting you as the overall king of Kɔtɔkɔ," for it is the people who fought with the kings to overpower adversaries (Line 6). Even the gods of the land are not left out, and Line 7 signifies the readiness of all of the deities from the ancient times—the beginning of time. Opanin Fofie finally

concludes Section One with a considered appeal to the ruler—still without mentioning his name—but using a deep-seated reference to the beginning of Asante
in the remote past in Line 8, that it is time for him to serve his people. In Section
Two, Opanin Fofie invokes some of the attributes of a specific ancestor king, Ɔsɛɛ
Agyemang Prempeh II, again avoiding his stool name and using his strong appellation (*abodin*), Ɔsɛɛ Kyeretwie. Literally, this means "Ɔsɛɛ who captures a live
leopard with his bare hands." Opanin Fofie follows the previous reference by trac-
ing the parentage of King Prempeh II for the benefit of those who were not aware
of the coded reference in Line 9. The name Owusu Panin refers to Prempeh II's
father, who was from Ɛdweso, while Akua Bakoma was his mother. The epithet
sikaboɔ (the gold nugget) added to his mother's name is a reference to the Gold
Stool (Sikadwa Kofi), thus confirming the matrilineal link and establishing that
the ruler is a royal of the most potent stool in the kingdom. Another interpretation
for Lines 9–11 is that the ruler's enviable position as the overlord of the entire
kingdom (king of Kɔtɔkɔ) was highly contested, but he was the ultimate choice.
Line 11 sums up the previous sentiment that it is the wish of others to have been
the beneficiaries of such a great honor. However, his privileged status comes with
a huge burden and responsibilities like waking up at four in the morning.

Prior to that, he apologizes in Line 9 for mentioning the name of the ruler
without his usual honorifics, using the phrase "*me mmɔ wo dinwe awisi*," which
means that it is not my intention to just call your name without your title. The
key word here is *dinwe*, meaning "just your name without your title" and *awisi*,
a greeting response for a Sunday-born (Akwasi or Kwasi) that confers the utmost
respect. Since King Prɛmpɛ II's day-name was Kwame, I am not sure why the
bards appended *awisi* as the formulaic end phrase. At any rate, the deliberate use
of *awisi* in Lines 9, 18, 19, 22, and 28 exempts the bards from potential sanctions
for not using the ruler's honorifics. By the beginning of Section Three, Opanin
Fofie is comfortable enough to introduce the reigning king with his stool name,
Ɔsɛɛ Tutu, in Line 19 but without an honorific like his forebear in Line 9, followed
by the usual procedure of mitigating text that absolves him from punitive measures. Similar to Section Two, he interpolates the king's father, Boakye Dankwa,
who hails from Kantinkyiren and the immediate past ɔhemaa, Sɛɛwaa Ampem
(full name, Nana Afia Kobi Sɛɛwaa Ampem II), in Line 20.[4] But he goes further
this time to include the name of the maternal grandmother of the Ɔsɛɛ Tutu II,
Nana Yaa Birago, whose praise name is Bakani and is referenced here as Brago
Abakan in Line 22.[5] Adarkwa Yiadɔm in Line 23 was a chief of Dwaben, one of
the divisional towns founded by the Ɔyoko and historically considered to be the
last-born of the Ɔyoko family.[6]

Opanin Fofie begins Section Four by calling on Ɔheneafrɛwoɔ, Nana Yaa
Birago's sister whose full name was Nana Akosua Ɔheneafrɛwoɔ, and the maternal grandmother of Opoku Ware II, the predecessor of the present ruler whose
name is invoked as the beginning phrase in Line 27.[7] Opanin Fofie follows with
similar mitigation devices with respect to Opoku Ware II—his father is Opoku
Panin from Gyaakye, and his mother is Akyaa Yikwan. Her full name was Nana
Akua Akyaa Mansa, and the by-name of Akyaa is Oyiakwan (one who paves the

way), but the (o) is deleted in Line 29. From here on, Opanin Fofie embarks on a series of by-names, strong appellations, allusions, and proverbs in Section Five that is meant to empower and fortify the current ruler. I have analyzed some of the poetic devices, and I will analyze the remaining ones from beginning to the end in the next paragraph. But first, I would like to take note of the procedure for concluding the previous poetry (*Nnwontene*). Opanin Fofie's signal for his responders to know that he is about to conclude the recitation is the formulaic phrase *Ɔsagyefoɔ Manya mfrɛn nge* in Line 57. The two bards then take turns, as usual, reciting Line 58, and then a fleeting pause enables them to take a deep breath before rapidly unleashing the torrent of words without break from Lines 59–60. As I mentioned previously, all of the instrumentalists who have been quiet until now spontaneously respond by congratulating the bards and taking turns to sound their instruments. The plural response soon yields to each group and individual taking turns. So, for instance, the short and large ivory trumpets, flute, mpebi ne nkrawiri drums, and nkukuadwe drums take turns while the Abrafoɔ and Kwadwomfoɔ interject verbal verses into the fray. I will now continue to analyze the remaining rhetorical devices in the previous verse.

The beginning phrase Ɛmaanu in Line 12 is Maanu, a name given to a male or female second child, to which the bards added the particle ɛ at the beginning. The reference here is female, Maanu Atia Dufie, and together with Kyerewaa and Ntofie Mmogye, they were all family members of Prɛmpɛ II mother's lineage. The entire phrase in Line 16 is a reminder to the kingdom to be resolute in their values and not to concede to the poisonous schemes of Akusibiekumborɔ in Line 17. The archaic word for poison is *borɔ*, the two syllables at the end of the beginning phrase. As in Line 10, *sikaboɔ* in Line 20 aligns the same Ɔyoko matrilineage with the ruler as evidence of his royal bloodline, and thereby also a true son of the Gold Stool. With that established, he is reminded of his oath of office that stipulates among other things that, besides sickness, he will avail himself whether his subjects call upon him during the day, at night, or in the rain. *Akoboɔ* in Line 24 refers to the shield (*ɛkyɛm*), which is referred to by the archaic phrase *nkataboɔ*. *Abaakorɔ* in Line 26 is the name of a river and a common practice in Akan; sometimes individuals are named after a river. Ɔhemaa Akyaa Yikwan (Line 32) was the 10th Asantehemaa who reigned from 1880–1917. Ntɔdimaa Akyɛmfoɔ in Line 34 is the appellation of the chiefs of Asafo, a suburb of Kumase, whose title is Akyɛmfoɔ and head of the Akwamu Division in Kumase. Lines 33–36 recall the name of Bobbie Ntra Akwasi, a powerful and influential chief whose son was one of the chiefs of Asafo. Lines 37–42 recall wars with equally powerful Akan kingdoms in Akuapem and some of their leaders, to encourage the ruler to be as brave as his illustrious forebears. Line 43 demonstrates the power of the ruler in a didactic reckoning that a thousand could be one, and one could be a thousand. Line 44 points to the ruler, who is capable of ordering the executioner group *Tɔprɛfoɔ* to follow up with capital punishment for a convicted criminal. Up until the end of the nineteenth century, executioners usually performed *Tɔprɛ* on Monday (*Adaedwɔɔda*), following the Sunday Adaɛ for convicted criminals. Line 53 describes an imaginary woman, Awuraa Tipanin, who despite dressing in kente and jewelry from head to toe is described in Akan as *Adɔsoa*, or not up to the task. In other words, no chief can claim that his stool and authority equals that of the Asantehene. As I mentioned previously, Opanin Fofie and his Responders conclude the verse by reciting Lines 59–60 in a rapid succession to the end without a break. In the penultimate phrase, they are signaling the ruler with the code *su nna nyane*—literally, wake up, for the ivory trumpeters are ready to perform as soon as they, the bards, conclude the awakening verse. The reference to the variety of ivory trumpeters who are ready to take turns is described in graphic terms with the phrase *asono aworobɛn*, a contraction of the sentence "*ɔmo bɛ woro asono abɛn agum*." That is, they are ready to unleash sounds of the elephant-tooth trumpets.

Lastly, I would like to bring our attention to two phrases, *demirefi* and *demiri-fua*. The former is a metaphoric allusion to a type of dog in the forest or an animal who hardly sleeps, and it is represented in Lines 12, 37, and 59. The latter, an expression of condolences, shows up in Lines 18, 22, 27, 47, and 56. Each phrase consists of four syllables, and Opanin Fofie skillfully plays with the sound structure of the two words for poetic effect. It is striking that *demirefi* is preceded by a single syllable and a particle, ba e (child; literally son or daughter of), and immediately followed by *nyane* (wake up). On the other hand, the two-syllable name and particle, Frampɔn o, launches *damirifua*. Unlike the first phrase, the second phrase is either followed by *awisi*, a form of greeting, or the particle o. The Kwadwomfoɔ refer to the next example as Amankum (literally, destroying nations or defeating nations), and it is performed during the public assembly on Akwasidae, when the king sits in state to receive divisional and Kumase chiefs who have come to congratulate him for successively leading and concluding the morning's worship. The general public, and visitors from both near and far, are present to engage the ruler in interactional routines and receive blessings from the morning worship (*adae tɔkye*). It is at the end of the long series of greetings that the Kwadwomfoɔ recites one of the long verses, *Asafo* or *Amankum*, to pave the way for the *Akyeame* (Royal Spokespersons and diplomats) and other officials to present guests to the ruler. I recorded the following *Amankun* (Example 6.2) on July 16, 2009 at Manhyia Palace. Opanin Fofie was the leader (*kwadwom kandifoɔ*), while his son, Ɔsɛe Akwasi Fofie, was the responder (*ɛngyesoɔ*).

In terms of poetic verses that list names of defeated commanders and towns, *Amankum* is comparable to Kwabena Kyeremeh's referential poetry (*apae*) in Example 6.8. Unlike the fifteen lines of the apae verse that makes direct reference to various chiefs and towns and may be easily understood, the sixty-two lines of Amankum are challenging and incomprehensible at several levels if we factor in the mode of delivery, archaic texts, indirection, metaphoric allusions, and an overwhelming amount of coded rhetoric. All of this is compounded when three or four lines are recited in a single breath. For instance, Opanin Fofie recited Lines 26–29 in a single breath, paused for a split second, and then concluded with Line 30 also in a single breath. The heroic militancy in Amankum and the historicized poetry of *Kwadwom* are expressed in two broad sections, Lines 1–19 and 20–57, and five lines of closing gestures from 58–62 that can be considered an appendage. The dense texture is similar to Example 6.1, but with added intensity and momentary

Example 6.2 Amankum (Destroying Nations)-by Opanin Kofi Fofie and the bards.

Twi Text

1. Okuru Anim Naadu a
2. Adu Dwaben ɔhene Twum o Kyampɔn noforobo nge
3. O! Dwaben Sεε Naa Agyei Gyaako nge
4. Ɛbereankyε Panin Sereboɔ Siakwan ama wako agye Mampɔn
5. Ofiramani nana o Sumantete awisiε
6. Ɔkɔdeε Akrasi Sεbere tɔɔ ne mu o Twum o Kyampɔn noforobo nge
7. Ofiramani Akrasi yεyere Nana o Sumantete
8. O Dwabena Akrasi nana o Sumantete awisi ε
9. Ase ase ɔkwa?
10. Ɔsεε Tutu tie sε wo dwom frε wo ε
11. Ɔnkasakyire bɔmmɔfoɔ
12. Ɔpatako Kyereko agye ko abɔ ne bo
13. Yεmfa nkɔdi abranee mmɔ no ose
14. Yε Ɔpenemankoma su nna kɔ a ma ɔkwan bεdi awisi
15. Ɔkesεduamoa kεse di ayeyeε ne ademmire atifi
16. O! Sεε Dufianwoma de kyεm ne afena ako ako ayen
17. Ɔhawfoɔ kyε me nnyawa nini bieku na wako ama wo awisi
18. Na asuo annya tire a anka wan sen.
19. Obiri Kwaa na yεrebɔ no nkotie ne nsεm kwa nge
20. Emireku Akyeamo tene Pobi Asomanin
21. Pobi Asomanin nso antumi ammɔ wo kyεm so
22. Kwaakwaa de akyerεma kɔe
23. Kwaakwaa de akyerεma bae
24. Ampata Twum mesom no bi wɔ akonoano
25. Ampata-Twum a osie funu Bempa bi nso antumi ammɔ wo kyεm so
26. Ɛnsɔkɔhene Gyamfi Ameyaw
27. Borɔfoɔhene Gyamfi Ameyaw
28. Yεebiebie, mmofra hunu a yεyare awia
29. Dwabuntwerεbuo nua Ampaforako
30. Adu Gyamfi Bempa bi nso antumi ammɔ wo kyεm so
31. O osi nkɔtoɔ, ɔda nkɔtoɔ, berε nkɔtoakwa Adanse Yankyemaduo
32. Yaw Akyeamotene Boafo Anwoma
33. Anti Kyei Bempa bi nso antumi ammɔ wo kyεm so
34. Asene, asene agye Mampɔn Asene
35. Asene nifa Abaakorɔ ba Dootibo
36. Dootibo nso antumi ammɔ wo kyεm so.
37. Yεnko mma wo nwe? Nko mma wo nwe?
38. Na yεne Adawu Atakyi Dεmkyεmfo Dεnkyεmerεson
39. Dεnkyera Amoako Atta Bempa bi nso antumi ammɔ wo kyεm so
40. Ebitibiti Aduenya Berabata Aduenya
41. Adomahene ne Takyi Amoa ne Kyerεbeduedu
42. Meso m'akatakyie hinampɔn akɔ sa
43. Ɔhene Ameyaw Kwaa Twee nso antumi ammɔ wo kyεm so.
44. Ɔtenkwaa Panin Konadu kunu Amonu
45. Ɔfitiε pam adeε Boafo Adu Anwoma
46. Akyemhene Boafo Owusu
47. Owusu Pebɔɔ nso antumi ammɔ wo kyεm so.
48. Ɛwoso woso ne Ampem
49. Kofi Sini Ampem
50. Adinkra Kwadwo Bempa bi nso antumi ammɔ wo kyεm so.
51. Merebεse ko, na mase nno,

52. Brɛnkoto Akwa Bɔfoɔbi Nkwanta,
53. Akwasi Kasa Bempa bi nso antumi ammɔ wo kyɛm so.
54. Ɔkyere ahene kwa?
55. Pɔtɔeɛ Kwaku bi nso antumi ammɔ wo kyɛm so.
56. Ɔsɛe a okum Bɔdwesɛanwo Adu Gyamfi e.
57. Okum Ampatatwum a ɔsie funu a ɔte Foase.
58. O! Kyerefo damirifua, damirifua, damirifua nge
59. Bobbie Aboagye Sɛe Frampɔn o damirifua awisi.
60. Ɔsagyefoɔ manya mfrɛn nge
61. Okuru Asante Naadu nyane nge
    Lead and Response
62. Okuru bɛdi atɔperɛba demirefi su nna nyane ao Dɔmaako Sakyi asono aworobɛn.

English Translations
1. It is Okuru Anim Nana Adu
2. Adu, the chief of Dwaben, Twum Kyampɔn noforobo nge
3. Oh! Ɔsɛe Nana Agyei Gyaako of Dwaben nge
4. Ɛberankye Panin Sereboɔ Siakwan has rescued Mampɔn from battle
5. Sumantete, the grandson of Ofiramani, Awisi
6. Ɔkɔdeɛ Akrasi Sɛbɛre embraced Twum Kyampɔn noforobo nge
7. Sumantete the beloved wife of Ofiramani Akrasi
8. Sumantete, the grandson of Dwamena Akrasi Awisi
9. They call you in-law in vain?
10. Ɔsɛe Tutu, listen, they are calling you with your songs
11. Don't murmur behind the hunter
12. The mediator who gets involved in a war
13. He who is being hailed for his gallantry
14. Is Ɔpenemankoma who wails and clears the path awisi
15. The canopy of Ɔkesɛduamoa forms on top of reeds
16. Oh! Ɔssɛ Dufianwoma has fought with shield and sword to rescue us from battle
17. Afflicter, offer me one very brave man to fight for you
18. For without a watershed the stream could not flow
19. It is Obiri Kwaa whose feat in war is being narrated to him nge
20. Emireku Akyeamo trails Pobi Asomanin
21. And Pobi Asomani could not stand your might
22. Kwaakwaa brought the drummers away
23. Kwaakwaa brought the drummers back
24. I serve Ampata Twum at the battlefield
25. Ampata Twum who buries the dead also couldn't stand your might
26. Gyamfi Ameyaw the chief of Nsɔkɔ
27. Gyamfi Ameyaw the chief of Borɔfo
28. The exposure of the war machinery scares children to become sick in broad daylight
29. Ampaforako, the brother of Dwabuntwerɛbuo
30. Adu Gyamfi Bempa also could not stand your might
31. Ubiquitous Adanse Yankyemaduo, whether one moves or stays at the place, one still meets you
32. Yaw Akyeamotene Boafo Anwoma
33. Anti Kyei Bempa also could not stand your might
34. The Asenes have captured the Asene clan of Mampɔn
35. Dootibo, the son of Abaakorɔ, the Right Wing chief of Asene
36. Dootibo also could not stand your might
37. Should we fight for you to enjoy the booty? Should we fight for you to enjoy the booty?

(*Continued*)

Example 6.2 (Continued)

38. And we are referring to Adawu Atakyi Dɛmkyɛmfo Dɛnkyɛmerɛson
39. Dɛnkyera Amoako Atta Bempa also could not stand your might
40. Ebitibiti Aduenya Berabata Aduenya
41. Adomahene and Takyi Amoa and Kyerɛbeduodu
42. I move my great worriors to war
43. Ɔhene Ameyaw Kwae Twee also could not stand your might
44. Amonu the husband of Ɔtenkwaa Panin Konadu
45. Boafo Adu Anwoma whose presence disperses the crowd
46. Boafo Owusu the chief of Akyem
47. Owusu Pɛboɔ also could not stand your might
48. Ampem who stirs the crowd
49. Kofi Sini Ampem
50. Adinkra Kwadwo Bempa also could not stand your might
51. I am going to count one and count two (so prepared)
52. Brɛnkoto Akwa, the junction of a certain hunter
53. Akwasi Kasa Bempa also could not stand your might
54. Does he capture chiefs in vain?
55. Pɔtɔɛɛ Kwaku also could not stand your might
56. We are calling you, Ɔsɛe who killed Adu Gyamfi of Bɔdwesɛanwo
57. He killed Ampatatwum of Foase who buries the dead
58. Oh! Kyerefo, condonlence, condolence, condolence nge
59. Condolence, Bobie Aboagye Sɛe Frampon awisi
60. I have captured the large drums
61. Okuru Asante Naadu wake up nge
    Lead and Response
62. Okuru who keeps vigils over the ivory trumpets with Dɔmaako Sakyi

refractions, especially in Section 2, along with the strategic placement of formulaic phrases as coding devices. Opanin Fofie constructs a series of referential poetry in Section 1 with surprisingly minimal use of some of the formerly identified formulaic phrases in the previous example. For instance, there are only four appearances of the phrase *nge* in Lines 2, 3, 6, and 19, while *Twum o Kyampɔn noforobo* emerges only twice in Lines 2 and 6.

The phrase in Line 1 invokes the name of Asantehene Kwaku Dua, with the usual contraction of Nana to Naa. Like all of the rulers who carry the burden of the kingdom on their shoulders, a visitor cannot easily navigate the royal space, with all of the customs and the ever-watchful eyes of courtiers, before appearing in his presence. The fast-paced delivery shifts to a once-powerful chief of Dwaben, Adu in Line 2, and Akrasi, a royal name in the same locality. References to Dwaben should be understood in the larger context of locations and interactions of Ɔyoko matriclans in the kingdom. In that sense, Lines 1–8 use praise names and appellations for Asantehene Kwaku Dua and the affirmation that he is protected by all the deities, Sumantete, in the land. As a compound word, Suman-tete means deity from the beginning of time. Line 9 warns against making frivolous claims and of their potential consequences (you may recall Example 5.7). Despite distractions at ceremonies, Opanin Fofie entreats the ruler (in Line 10) to pay attention to symbolic communications and coded phrases embedded in his poetic verse, the poetry of drums, the cane flute, ivory trumpets, apae referential poetry, and songs. The general public is also asked to desist from murmuring or whispering in the background during the recitation of *Amankum*. These expectations are framed in the graphic imagery of a hunter stalking an animal in the forest in Line 11, *Ɔnkasakyire bɔmɔfoɔ*, implying one does not make noise behind a hunter in such ominous situations. Court Criers (*Nsɛneɛfoɔ*) are noted for making these kinds of comments when there seems to be unnecessary chatter during public assemblies. Typically, when the Asantehene is giving a formal speech or passing judgement during court proceedings, the Court Criers intone the formula: *ɔnkasakyire, ɔkasakyire* (literally, no murmurings). The bravery of the ruler comes up, again, in the metaphoric allusion to the eagle (*ɔkɔdeɛ*) in Line 12 and the loaded sound structure of the phrases /ɔpata-ko kyere-ko agye-ko/. The eagle is known in Akanland to mediate fights between two birds, but it turns around to slap (and even kill) the unyielding bird with its wings. That is, as a peaceful person, the ruler settles fights among feuding towns or individuals, absorbs those fights, and takes over fights if one of the feuding parties takes an uncompromising stance. The placement of *ko* at the end of the phrases and the repeated sound of the letter *k* are well noted. For his gallantry, muscled men and women (*abrane* in Line 13) are chanting heroic songs (*ose*) behind him to urge him on. Further testimony to his bravery is revealed by the notion of staying awake in the night (*su nna* in Line 14) to ensure safe passage in the bush path, thus ensuring peace in the kingdom, for which he is said to be *Ɔpenemankoma*. That the ruler is high on the totem pole among his peers is conspicuous in the metaphoric allusion to the cane, ayeyeɛ (*ɛyeɛ* in regular spoken language). For the Akan, *ɛyeɛ* is a relatively large type of cane, followed by *demire* that is in turn followed by *mfea* in terms of size and utility. That sheds light on the hierarchy within the cane family. The ruler is now referred to as *Dufianwoma*, the only one who fights with a shield and sword (in Line 16). As the source of strength (Lines 17 and 18), the people are ever-ready to fight like the metaphoric river that may flow long distance, and although it may be spatially far from its source, its continued existence is dependent on its source. As the last phrase in Section 1, Line 19 prepares the audience for Section 2 by recalling Obiri Kwaa, who was well-known as a pathological liar, and as such, conveys that those who spread false rumors about the ruler will not succeed. The formulaic phrase *nge* brings temporary closure to Section 1. In Section 2, Opanin Fofie generates a list of some of the powerful kings and chiefs whose spears or bullets could not metaphorically penetrate the shield (*kyɛm* or *ɛkyɛm*), with the first letter ɛ elided. Put in simple terms, they could not defeat the Asantehene.

As in the first section, I will begin Section 2 by identifying a new formulaic phrase, *Bɛmpa bi*, that is markedly different from the previous ones and located in Lines 25, 30, 33, 39, 50, and 53. It may well be that the noted phrase is strategically placed as a decoy to divert attention from the intended target as the historical referent. A brief discussion of the said referent is in order. The chief of Onoo, Nana Adu Gyamfi Bɛmpa, and his paternal brother, chief of Bɔdwesɛanwo Nana Adu Agyamfi, were described as men of valor. Due to the similarity of their names, they are referred to in Asante lore, poetry, and song texts by the names of their towns. That is, Onoo Adu Gyamfi and Bɔdwesɛanwo Adu Gyamfi, respectfully. Two critical regalia objects that are central to Asante success in the inter-war years were captured from these two brothers. Ɔpemsoɔ Ɔsɛe Tutu captured Onoo Adu Gyamfi's Bosom-uru sword and later succeeded in capturing the silver treasure casket, *Dwetɛ Kuduo*, from Bɔdwesɛanwo Adu Gyamfi after he had defeated them. The previously-named regalia objects are also essential to the enstoolment rites involving Asante kings. The king-designate had to swear the oath of office to Asanteman, with the Bosomuru sword as part of the Pampaso ceremony. Without the silver casket (*Dwetɛ Kuduo*), a newly installed Asante king could not lay claim to the office, and it is the last regalia object presented to him after his enstoolment.[8] When it comes to the silver cas-ket (Dwetɛ Kuduo), Baafoɔ Ɔsɛe Asibe (Dɛɛboɔsohene) informs us that one of the bloodiest and fiercest battles that Opoku Ware fought, close to Kumase, was against the chief of Bɔdwesɛanwo, Nana Adu Gyamfi (see for instance, Kyerematen, 1966: 272). With the previous historical events, we can appreciate the poetic devices that Opanin Fofie deployed, including indirection, oblique phrases, and metaphoric allu-sions, in order to render the direction of his intended target ambiguous. For instance, Ampata Twum in Line 25 has nothing in common with Bɛmpa bi. Structurally, Lines 26 to 30 are grouped together, but the name of the chief of Nsɔkɔ, Gyamfi Ameyaw, is totally different from that of Adu Gyamfi Bɛmba, chief of Onoo. Simi-lar conditions are at play in Lines 33, 39, 50, and 53 until he gives us a straight target in Line 56 by referring outright to Bɔdwesɛanwo Adu Gyamfi. Opanin Fofie invariably engages in similar techniques of indirection before introducing the name of an adversary who could not defeat the Asante. For instance, the intended target in Lines 20–21 is the Akyem Abuakwa chief Pobi Asomanin; however, he begins Line 20 with the name Emireku Akyeamo Tene. In the war against the combined forces of Akyem Abuakwa, Akuapem, Assin, and Fante, the Asantehene Ɔsɛe Kwadwo (Ɔko Awia, 1764–1777) defeated them after sustaining large casualties. There was no question that King Pobi Asomanin led one of the most formidable forces, but the Asante forces eventually defeated him in what has come to be known as the War Against Thousands (Dɔmpem Sa).[9]

It took three lines of oblique phrases and metaphoric allusions to the crow (*kwaakwaa dabi*) and the divine drummer (Ɔkyerɛma) in Lines 22–24, before we were finally presented with Ampata Twum as the next target in Line 25. His-torically, Lines 22–23 remind us of the selfless devotion of Ɛdwesomhene Dako Pim, one of the seven chiefs who voluntarily gave themselves up for sacrifices before the war of liberation with the powerful Dɛnkyera kingdom. We are told that Edwesohene's body was chopped into pieces and scattered in the forest for scav-engers (vultures).[10] Unlike the previous chiefs, the chief of Nsɔkɔ Nana Gyamfi Ameyaw was introduced in Line 26 with the addition of the letter (Ɛ)nsɔkɔ, but this is not until we are made to navigate a plethora of nuanced rhetorical expres-sions from Lines 27–30, immediately followed by the formulaic phrase *Bempa bi*—all in a fast-paced and breathtaking delivery. But that is not all, since Line 28 is a huge diversion, when Opanin Fofie submits that children or those not mature enough are traumatized when they are exposed to hidden secrets (*asumasɛm*), even in broad daylight.

Similar processes are at work when three formidable chiefs from Adanse—Nana Yankyemaduo, Nana Yaw Akyeamotene, and Nana Ante Kyei—are presented in Lines 31–33. In particular, I would like to draw reader's attention to the phonology of Line 31: *osi nkɔtoɔ, ɔda nkɔtoɔ*, and *berɛ nkotoɔakwa*. The Asene chief, Nana Abakorɔ, and his son, Tibo, both rebelled against the Asante, and Lines 34–36 recall those incidents. Dɛnkyera Amoako Atta is the goal of all of the indirections in Lines 37–39, but not until the intended pun on *Dɛmkyɛmfo Dɛnkyemerɛson* in Line 38 is linked to the beginning phrase, Dɛnkyera, in Line 39, did the intended target becomes clear. One of the great kings of Takyiman, Nana Ameyaw, is the objective of Lines 40–43.[11] The king of Akyem, Nana Boafo Owusu, comes up in Lines 44–47, while the powerful king of Gyaaman, Adinkra Kwadwo, is the subject of coded nuances from Lines 48–50. The uncompromising attitude of the Gyaase chief in Manso Nkwanta, Akwasi Kasa, is the target of Lines 51–53. After causing undue problems in the vicinity, he was captured and decapitated. The two phrases in Line 51, *Merebɛse ko, na ma'se no*, denotes two unheeded stipulations from the Asantehene to Akwasi Kasa, characterized by the single-syllable words *ko* and *no*, meaning one and two respectively. Pɔtɔeɛ Kwaku is the next victim in Lines 54–55, followed by one of two phrases without indirection (Line 56) that I have already discussed in connection with Bɔdwesɛanwo Adu Gyamfi. The second direct phrase is Line 57, which is linked to the same king in the previous line, Ɔsɛe Tutu, without repeating his name. Ampatatwum was a chief of Asante Akyem Foase. Technically, Line 57 marks the end of Opanin Fofie's list of defeated kings and chiefs. In the larger scheme of things, Lines 58–62 are laudatory phrases that append praises to Section 2 and highlight the ruler for such extraordinary achievements. He begins Line 58 with a sudden outburst, exclaiming, "O!" to signify a sense of bewilderment at the impressive list of powerful and fearful kings and chiefs who have been defeated. In that context, *damirifua* in Line 58 means congratulations as opposed to condolences, the usual English translation. It is Opanin Fofie's mode of conferring gratitude to the Asantehene by repeating *damirifua* three times (recall the spiritual potency of the number three in Akan), to stress the import and value of expressing gratitude to the king for devoting his reign to the daunting tasks of territorial conquests and expansion in the name of nation building. For that, the king is given the praise name Kyerefo—literally, one who captures kings and chiefs or simply defeats kings and chiefs. The word in spoken Twi is Ɔkyerefoɔ, with the beginning and ending letter *ɔ* muted in the poeticized version. Line 59 offers further praise names, and for the first time we encounter one of the formulaic phrases, *Frampɔn*, that we identified in Example 6.1. Line 60 is the usual phrase that alerts the Responder, Osei Akwasi Fofie, court musicians, courtiers, and the general public that they are about to end the seemingly long verse. The additional formulaic phrase *nge* comes up as the end pattern in Lines 60 and 61, followed by a split-second pause, and then, finally, the rapid deployment of the text in Line 62 in a single breath to bring the verse to an end. The next example is titled Asafo, another dense and ancient verse by the bards that focuses on attributes of valor, courage, and fearlessness as idealized values.

Example 6.3 Asafo (Valor, Courage, and Fearlessness), *Kwadwom*. Opanin Kofi Fofie and
the Bards.

Twi Text
1.   Ɛdwom deɛ e nyane e,
2.   Ntikora Nana nyane,
3.   Ntikora Nana Kusi nyane nge.
4.   Mere ma wo Dwapɔn Bɔdɔmmɔwuo ne nani amoa gyinan Freduedu nge.
5.   Yaa ɔkaakyire bɔɔ wo hwerɛmoasu nge.
6.   Yaa ɔbɔ wo suo bɔ wo peabɛde.
7.   Adu Ansere,
8.   Bɔdɔm nua a ɔbɔɔ Kankyerekyere maa Onyame si aseɛ sokurodo,
9.   Dwantire nim hyeaduro a ɔfra w'ani e.
10. Adu Agyei bɔ wo hwerɛmoo asu nge
11. Adu Agyei bɔ wo peabɛde
12. Asafo Akwa manya mfrɛn Ampoma Ankoma akɔ ko m'adawuro e
13. Adu Boyi Safo Awisi, Safo Ɔpeabɛde adwo e
14. Ɔbɔ wo tim kyɛm bɔ wo hwerɛmo asu nge
15. Ɔbɔ wo tim kyɛm bɔ wo peabɛde
16. Mmabaduam Apea Kusi krapim nge
17. Ɔbema Nsia, Ɔbaabasia a w'awo dɔm nana Gyinanfredua Akyeaw Opoku
     Agyemang
18. Agya Panin Afari Naa Gyinafredua Akyeaw Opoku Asu nge
19. Agya Panin Afari Naa Gyinafredua Akyeaw Opoku Agyemang
20. Amakom Akosa krapim nge.
21. Ampɔn Nyinamoa nekyɛno tete Gyinanfi Akua Kusi nge
22. Opoku a okum sɛfoo, kum kwayɛfoo.
23. O! Safo Poku damirifua, damirifua, damirifua nge
24. Ɔsafo Poku e Frampɔn o dɛmirifa adwo.
25. Worakɛse Worakɛse,
26. Worakɛse Adwumakaase Abirem Agyen Pepra,
27. Yɛmfa hene mma hwan?
28. Yɛmfa hene ma Gyaanaadu Asare,
29. Ɔhene kwa? Ɔhene ne hwan?
30. Ɔhene kɔ ɔbosom asu, ɔhene kɔ ɔbosom asu,
31. Tera bosom asu, tera Bosomtwe, Kwarteng bosom asu,
32. Akokɔ fufuo a obata Bosomtwe,
33. Emire mire mire nson,
34. Ɔhene kwa? Ɔhene ne hwan?
35. Ɔhene ne Adwumakaase Abirem Pepra nge
36. Asiedu Papakɛseɛ a ɔde ne nyedua guu nsuo kotɔɛ baa akoronkɔtɔ nge.
37. Ofosu Dwamoa Boaboafo ɔko no anini nge
38. Ofosu Pem, Yaw Buroniba o ɔkɔ Asante amere
39. Asante amere Frampɔn dɛmirifa adwo
40. Wo Naa Dwaben Bema Daa ɔsoa ne nkuku, ne ne nkaka, ne ne nkɛntɛn kɔɔ awadeɛ
41. Ampɔfo Kwaamoa ɔbaa dwomfoo.
42. O! Dwaben Akɛntɛn,
43. Ɔsɛe Tutu na yɛn wura ne no.
44. Ɔpemsoɔ e, tie sɛ wo dwom referɛ wo ɛ.
45. Ɔnkasakyire bɔmmɔfoo
46. Ɔpatakoo Kyerɛkoo agyekoo abɔ ne bo.
47. Yenfa nkodi abranee bɔ no ose.
48. Tu atam a otu adɔfoo tam
49. Yaa Ɔpenemankoma su nna kɔ a ma ɔkwan bedi adwo
50. Ɔkesɛduamoa kesɛ di ayeeɛ ne ademire atifi
51. O! Sɛe Dufianwoma de kyɛm ne afena ako ako adwo.
52. Ɔhawfoo kyɛ me nyao nini bieku na w'ako ama wo adwo
53. Na asuo annya tire a anka wansene.

54. Ohiri Kwaa na yɛrebɔ no nkotie ne nsɛnko nge
55. Emireku Akyeamotene Pobiasomanin,
56. Pobiasomanin nso anntumi ammɔ wokyɛm so.
57. Kwaakwaa de akyerɛma kɔe
58. Kwaakwaa de akyerɛma bae
59. Ampata Twum mesom no bi wɔ akonoano
60. Ampata Twum a osie funi Bɛmpa bi nso antumi nso ammɔ wo kyɛm so
61. Yɛnko mma wo nwe? Nko mma wo nwe?
62. Na yɛne Adawu Atakyi Dɛnkyɛmfo Dɛnkyɛmmerɛnson,
63. Yɛn nso apeaa, yɛnso atwenee na yɛ'yan,
64. Amamramadu atwenee tokuro,
65. Ampɔn Kɔtɔkɔ Kyebi Baa Kwanti Bɛmpa bi nso anntumi ammɔ wokyɛm so.
66. Agya Panin, Panini
67. Agya Panin Afari Abamoo aforo Kantanka,
68. Yɛɛ hyɛ asɛɛ na anka ɔnni biribi,
69. Ewie akyire yi, sikabɛn mmienu na ebu n'abuguo gyina Fredua Akyaw Opoku Agyeman.
70. Agya Panin Afari Naa Gyina Fredua Akyeaw Opoku Asu nge.
71. Agya Panin Afari Naa Gyina Fredua Akyeaw Opoku Agyemang.
72. Opoku a okum sɛfoɔ kum kwayɛfoɔ.
73. O! Safo Poku damirifua, damirifua, damirifua nge.
74. Ɔsafo Poku Frampɔn o demerefa adwo.
75. Entera Agyekum Kyere Dɔmaako Sakyi ɔdi Amoako ntene nge.
76. Obi yare nsamansuo Anima gyae nsateafoɔ ntene nge

Lead and Response
77. W'ahye ɛdɔm to afanu a koto amen ɔdehye brane a ɔko animia ɛne wo adwo.

English Translations
1. The head of songs wake up,
2. Ntikuma Nana wake up,
3. Ntikuma Nana Kusi wake up
4. I'm greeting you, the grandson of Dwapɔn Bɔdɔmmɔwuo Amoa Gyinan Freduedu
5. Yaa Ɔkaakyire who cleansed you with hwerɛmo thorns?
6. Yaa who cleansed you, tied your spears together?
7. Adu Ansere
8. The kinsman of Bɔdɔm who created things from the very beginning before God'screation,
9. The wise man knows the concoction that can cause blindness
10. Adu Agyei who cleansed you with hwerɛmo thorns?
11. Adu Agyei tied your spears together
12. Asafo Akwa has alerted Ampoma Ankoma to go to war with my dawuro (gong?)
13. I am greeting you, Adu Boe Safo Awisi, Safo Ɔpeabɛdɛ, good evening
14. He creates a shield for your head and cleanse you with hwerɛmo thorns
15. He creates a shield for your head and ties your spears together
16. Apea Kusi Kerapɛn of Mmabaduam
17. Ɔbema Nsia the grand daughter of Gyinani Fredua Akyeaw Opoku Agyeman a prolific woman who has countless progeny.
18. Agya Panin Afrɛ Nana Gyinafredua Akyeaw Opoku Asu
19. Agya Panin Afrɛ Nana Gyinafredua Akyeaw Opoku Agyeman
20. Akosa Krapem of Amako
21. Amponyinamoa (the Earth deity) and Kyɛno Tete Gyinanfi Akua Kusi
22. Opoku who killed the savanna dweller and the forest dweller
23. Oh! Safo Poku Frampɔn condolences, condolences, condolences
24. Osafo Poku e, Frampɔn o, I bid you condolence
25. Worakɛse, Worakɛse,
26. Worakɛse Adwumakaase Abrɛmu Agyen Pepra,
27. Who should be enstooled king?

(*Continued*)

Example 6.3 (Continued)

28. Gyaanadu Asare Should be ensetooled king.
29. Is someone called a king for nothing? Who is king?
30. The king goes to the river deity, the king goes to the river deity.
31. He goes beyond the river deity. Goes beyond the Lake Bosomtwe Kwarteng's river deity.
32. The white fowl that lives near Bosomtwe.
33. The seven emire trees.
34. Is someone called a king for nothing? Who is king?
35. Adwumakaase Abremu Pepra is the King.
36. Asiedu Papakɛse who fought across the river and lost his life, we salute you.
37. Ofosu Dwamoa Boaboafo who fights against brave worriers nge
38. Ofosu Pem, the son of Yaw Buroni who fought against Asante amere
39. Asante Amere Frampon, condolence, condolence
40. It is your grandmother, Juaben Bema Daa who carried her odds and ends to her matrimonial home.
41. Ampofo Kwaamoa, the expert singer.
42. Oh! Dwamena Akenten,
43. It is Ɔsɛe Tutu who is our Lord.
44. Ɔpemsoɔ listen to your praises
45. Don't murmur behind the hunter
46. The mediator who gets involved in a war and conquers the warriors
47. Let us use him to exhibit our valiancy
48. One who snatches the loin cloth of his enemies
49. The dirge singer, Yaa Ɔpenemankoma whose wailing creates peace along the path
50. Ɔkɛseduamoa Kɛse that feeds from the top of rattan species
51. Oh! Sɛe Dufianwoma has fought with the shield and the sword and has become powerless
52. Tormentor, lend me one of your strong limbs. For you have become powerless after the fight since a river cannot flow without a source
53. It is Obiri Kwaa who is receiving praises in war songs and tales nge
54. Emireku Akyeamotene Pobiasomanin
55. Emireku Akyeamotene Pobiasomanin also could not withstand your valor
56. Should we fight for you? Should we fight for you?
57. We are talking about Atakyi Dɛnkyɛmfo, Dɛnkyɛmmerɛnson.
58. We are not carrying trumpets, we are not carrying drums so we don't perform drum poetry.
59. The drums of Amenamadu.
60. Ampɔn Kɔtɔkɔ, Kyebi Baa Kwanti Bempa could not withstand your valor
61. Agya Panin, Panin,
62. Agya Panin Afari Abamoo Aforo Kantanka.
63. He had no paraphernalia at the beginning.
64. But in the end he possessed two gold trumpet bracelets that he wore on his arms to establish the dynasty of Fredua Akyeaw Opoku Agyeman nge.
65. Agya Panin Afari Nana Gyina Fredua Akyeaw Opoku Agyeman
66. Agya Panin Afari Nana Gyina Fredua Akyeaw Opoku Agyeman
67. Opoku who kills warriors from both the Savana and the Forest zones
68. Oh! Safo Poku, condolence, condolence, condolence nge
69. Safo Poku Frampɔn, condolence, adwo
70. Entera Agyekum Kyere Dɔmaako Sakyi who is mounting surveillance on Amoako
71. Somebody is being fortified with ghost water so Anima desist from mounting surveillance on nsateafoɔ
72. Ayi Buruku, the deity who killed his priest Twum Kyeampɔn noforobo
    Leader and Responder
73. You are the one who annihilates the multitude. The great royal who kills with both sides of his sword.

Similar to *Nnwontene* (Example 6.1) and *Amankum* (Example 6.2), Asafo is typically performed to prepare participants at Akwasidae Public Assemblies, major ceremonies, or formal situations for a speech by the ruler. *Asafo* is also interchangeable with *Nnwontene* as the preferred verse performed by the bards at dawn on Akwasidae to wake up the Asantehene in order to prepare for the morning worship, as I described in the Prologue and Example 6.1. Since all three examples are fairly long verses, it is tempting to designate the verses as Nnwontene (literally, Long Verses); however, Opanin Fofie and Opanin Kwame Bɔɔ, two elderly bards and leaders of Kwadwomfoɔ, are precise with their taxonomy by referring to the verses by their respective titles—that is, *Nnwontene, Amankum,* and *Asafo.* On the other hand, all of the short verses have designated titles, but they are collectively grouped under the single umbrella term, *Nnwontia.* The archaic textual content of *Asafo,* in addition to all of the rhetorical devices discussed in connection with *kwadwom,* is woven into the core of symbolic metatexts, which presents enormous challenges to the listener while also rendering this verse incomprehensible to the uninformed. In order to understand the historical experience and values that are expressed in the previous verse, I will begin my analysis with a historical interpretation.

The title Asafo initially leads listeners to associate this verse with either a suburb in Kumase with that name, or simply as a reference to combatants—that is implied in the compound word ɛsa-foɔ (fighters) and, in general, Akan Asafo warrior organizations. However, Asafo is a contraction of *Asafodeɛ,* the subdivision of Asantehene Opoku Ware's paternal deity (*ntorɔ*). Since his grand uncle is Ɔpemsoɔ Ɔsɛe Tutu, they share the same paternal deity, the *Bosomuru Ntorɔ,* but the latter belongs to the *Adufudeɛ* subdivision. It bears pointing out that, in his unpublished script, Kwadwom, Nketia refers to this verse as Asafodeɛ (Nketia, 1962: 25–30). It may well be that over the years *deɛ* has been dropped from the original title, leaving the phrase, Asafo, as the title that Opanin Fofie and Opanin Bɔɔ assign to this verse. The title of Example 6.3, *Asafo,* then, is a historical narrative that encompasses the valor, courage, and fearlessness of Opoku Ware Katakyie, who succeeded Ɔsɛe Tutu in 1720.[12] Apart from the overwhelming use of nominals (praise and strong names) and processes of individuation, the rhetorical devices include the use of imagery, metaphoric allusions, and all of the devices that I previously referenced. Interestingly, Opoku Ware's name is not mentioned in full in this verse, but the historical reference is apparent, as we shall soon discover.

Before going through linguistic analysis in *Asafo,* it bears pointing out that the discrete method of formulaic phrases that encode a system of metatexts serves as an identifying marker of end phrases and rhetorical ideas, along with the sense of importance they convey. Similar to Example 6.1, the first formulaic phrase, *nge,* appears as an end phrase in Lines 3, 5, 10, 14, 16, 20, 23, 35, 36, 37, 54, 70, 73, 75, and 76. As an end phrase in Line 3, it concludes the initial thought in the verse—that is, waking up the ruler with the parallel repetition of the end phrase *nyane* (wake up). Line 5 is a graphic description of adversaries unknowingly stepping on thorns and prickles (*hwerɛmo* in archaic Twi, and *nkasee* in modern

Twi) and sustaining wounds. The non-lexical end phrase lends weight to the ominous predicament of those unfortunate individuals. Line 10 identifies Adu Agyei
as the true likeness of thorns and prickles that adversaries should avoid, hence
the formulaic end phrase for emphasis. Line 14 is a caution for individuals to be
watchful for friends who pretend they are shielding them from their enemies,
only to turn around to stab them in the back with thorns and prickles. That calls
for another emphasis with the formulaic phrase. Appia Kusi and Amakom Akosa
are well-known for their bravery and the noted end phrase lends weight to that
claim in Lines 16 and 20. The end phrase in Line 23 is meant to reinforce the
honorifics of Opoku Ware Katakyie for his remarkable achievements as the second Asantehene. The formulaic end phrase in Line 37 reinforces Ofosu Dwamoa
Boaboafo's valor in combat, while the end phrase in Line 54 marks the beginning
of Section 4.

Another formulaic end phrase, *adwo*, has linguistic meaning and provides a
contrasting feature to the non-lexical phrase *nge*. The former phrase tactically
appears eight times in Lines 13, 24, 39, 49, 51, 52, 74, and 77. *Adwo* is a compression of the Akan day-name Ɛdwɔɔda or Dwɔɔda (Monday). Akan cosmology
assigns calmness (or coolness), peacefulness, and tranquility to those born on a
Monday. A typical response to greetings for those born on Monday is *yaa adwo*,
and there are special events that are reserved for Mondays. For instance, after
the internment of a deceased family member on Saturday, Mondays are usually
set aside by family members to tabulate the monetary cost or gain of the funeral
and to resolve family feuds. So Mondays are for the resolution of conflicts and
to bring about peace and normalcy.[13] In light of the preceding, all of the eight
occurrences of *adwo* as a formulaic end phrase follows a line or two of agitated
combat, and the bards are artistically either congratulating a soldier or soldiers
(*Asafo*) or pleading for calmness and a return to peace and normalcy. In Line 12,
the bards are assured that Ampoma Ankoma fought and recovered their inheritance, represented by *m'adawuro* (my metal gongs). Now that the war is over, he
can lay down his sword and cool off (end phrase in Line 13). The end phrase in
Line 24 is in response to Lines 22–23, that Opoku Ware conquered as far as the
savannah grasslands and the forest areas, and *adwo* is appended to Line 24 as an
imagined response to his subjects congratulating him. The formulaic end phrase
in Line 39 follows a similar procedure, since it is the logical goal of Lines 37–39,
where Ofosu Dwamoa is said to fight like a man in all the difficult battles he
encountered. He is recognized and honored for bringing peace and tranquility to
the area. The end phrase in Lines 49, 51, and 52 are configured as responses to
greetings, while the end phrase in Line 74 is in response to Lines 72–74. With the
inherent characteristic of Monday (*Ɛdwɔɔda*), it is not entirely out of place that
Asafo, a verse that focuses on the Asante lived experience during numerous com-
bats, is concluded with our noted formulaic end-phrase, *adwo*. The bottom line
is, as in the tactical placement of the end phrase *awisi* in Nnwontene (Example
6.1), *adwo* is a mitigating phrase that absolves the bards from punitive measures,
in case the historical verse of *Asafo* reminds some influential individuals of grave
and/or contested historical experiences.

Lived experience and values are mediated in Asafo through five sections that flow sequentially and fluidly: Lines 1–24, 25–35, 36–53, 54–65, and 66–77. Section 1 is made up of twenty-four lines of opening material. As a verse that is performed at dawn to wake up the ruler, the opening phrases in *Asafo* (Lines 1–6) share similar compositional processes with the opening phrases in Nnwontene, Lines 1–8 (Example 6.1). Opanin Fofie's artistic solution to being the first performer to wake the ruler at dawn is to probe deep into Akan referential poetry, without negating heroism as the overarching theme in Asafo. After the opening phrase, *Edwom dee* (literary head of songs), Opanin Fofie and his responder artistically spin out a list of strong appellations, including the parallel repetition of the beginning phrase *Ntikora Nana* in Line 2 and *Ntikora Nana Kusi* in Line 3. The previous is followed by three lines of parallel repetition of end phrases, *nyane* (wake up) from Lines 1–3. The bards then extend greetings after imploring the ruler to wake up in Line 4 with a poetic presentation of precious beads, *Bɔdɔmmɔwuo*. The rest of the lines in Section 1 deliver a run-down of heroic encounters with a plethora of nominals, while avoiding direct references to the stool names of past kings, or that of the current ruler, for seventeen lines. The first reference to Opoku Ware, eventually comes up in the parallel repetition of Lines 18 and 19, but in the amalgam of nominals, only the first name Opoku is given. The bards round off Section 1 with three iterations of Opoku by placing it as the beginning phrase in Line 22, preceding the first name with one of his praise names, Safo, in Line 23 and Ɔsafo in Line 24. Although Asafo is dedicated to the valor and fearlessness of Opoku Ware, it is not until Lines 17, 18, and 19 that the bards begin to mention Opoku as the penultimate end phrase by the mechanics of parallel repetition. Issues of parentage are part of the nomenclature, and here the middle name of Opoku Ware's mother, Kusi, is invoked as early as Line 3 but cloaked in terms of endearment, Ntikora Nana. In Lines 16 and 21, there is additional mention of Kusi, whose full name was Nyaako Kusi Amoa, the first Asantehemaa who reigned from 1695–1722. Another interpretation of Kusi is that Ntikora Nana (Line 2) and Ntikora Nana Kusi (Line 3) refer to the son of Nana Nkɛteaa Abamo, the second Asantehmaa who succeeded Nana Nyaako Kusi Amoa and reigned from 1722–1740. Depending on the historical weight underlying the performance context, either interpretation is acceptable, and it may well be that it is precisely the ambiguity implied in the choice of words that is the hallmark of *kwadwom*. Opoku Ware's father was one of three successive chiefs of Amakom: Akosa Yiadɔm, Adu Boyi, and Adua Mɛnsa. Scattered references to the three chiefs, beginning with the elder Amakom Akosa, is the second phrase in Line 20, Adu Boyi in Line 13, and most of the references in Section 1. We may also presume that Adu is the shortened form of Adua Mɛnsa, the youngest of the three brothers and the addressives in Lines 7, 10, 11, and 13.

Bɔdɔmmɔwuo (Line 4) are precious beads that were given to Opoku Ware, together with large quantities of gold dust and coarse blankets (*nsaa*) by the Konghemaa during The Barehyia War, when the former pursued fugitives from Takyiman to Kong.[14] It is said that the Konghemaa was captivated by the looks of the Opoku Ware and assisted him in capturing over 300 of the fugitives. She further asked to add Opoku to her name, and she became known as Abrewa Poku. Another form of encryption in the imagery that points to Opoku Ware as the addressive is the end phrase *peabɛde* in Lines 6 and 11, *Ɔpeabɛde* in Line 13, and a return to *peabɛde* in Line 15. Oral history has it that soon after the birth of Opoku Ware, Kɔmfo Anɔkye placed a miniature sword in his quivering right hand and named the sword *mpɔnpɔnsɔn* (literally, sword of responsibility), predicting that the newly born baby would carry the burden of the state on his shoulders in the future. When Opoku Ware accompanied Ɔsɛe Tutu to the Akyem Kotoku War, he led a battalion and used the sword to keep his men under control. His battalion came to be known as Pea-dɔm (the arrow infantry), and he used this same sword to swear the oath of office when Ɔsɛe Tutu died on the battlefield. An additional story that links Opoku Ware with spears is when Kɔmfo Anɔkye is said to have predicted the successor of Ɔsɛe Tutu by planting two spears at Pampaso, where Opoku Ware lived, and at Asaman, where Ɔsɛe Tutu's nephew Boa Kwatia also lived. While the spear at Pampaso attracted a number of birds, the spear at Asaman did not even attract a single bird. Anɔkye's interpretation was that the spear at Pampaso suggested Opoku's ability to rally the whole nation behind him, and he subsequently named the location *Pease* (under the arrow), while the other was called *Kwadani*—literally, the spear has upturned. From all indications, the previous varied evidence, the noted end phrase, and *peabɛde* are representational references to Opoku Ware by the bards, but they are artistically concealed in rhetorical devices.

Additional metatexts that are part of the coded rhetoric in this verse are Lines 22–24. The entire phrase in Line 22, "*Opoku a okum sɛfoɔ, kum kwayɛfoɔ*, is *Opoku a okum ɛsremfoɔ, kum kwayɛmfoɔ*," in spoken Twi. Thus, *sɛfoɔ* is a contraction of *ɛsremfoɔ* (Savanah dwellers), while *kwayɛfoɔ* is the same for *kwayɛmfoɔ* (forest dwellers). Referentially, it is well-known that in the days of conquests and territorial expansion, Opoku Ware conquered far and near, and by the end of his reign, he expanded Asante to the Dagomba and Gonja kingdoms in the North and Northeastern Savannah area. Sefwi, Wassa, and Gyaaman in the Northwest and several states in the Forest area including but not limited to Takyiman, Akyem Kotoku, Akyem Abuakwa, the Afram Plains, and Bɔdwesɛanwo were defeated one way or the other. With such daring accomplishments, Line 23 opens with a single syllable and an exclamation sign, O!, to express bewilderment, followed by a compression of the subdivision of his paternal deity, *Asafo*, preceding his name, Poku, with the first syllable *O* suppressed, which is followed by repeating *damirifua* three times. Instead of its literal meaning, condolences, *damirifua* in this context confers congratulatory greetings to Opoku Ware for expanding and consolidating the gains of the kingdom. Line 24 concludes the three phrases with praise and greetings, *adwo*, to literally cool off hectic historical events in order to usher in temporary relief.

Section 2 begins with a big bang, as Opanin Fofie raises his voice two notches higher than that with which he ended Section 1. A peculiar trait of this verse is located in this section, as Opanin Fofie intones eleven phrases all alone before the responder echoes the same lines. Further, the single theme of finding a suitable leader runs through the entire section; it is the dilemma that has befallen the people of Worakɛse (near Adwumakase) who are in search of a leader or chief. It seems that the popular choice is Agyen Pepra, who, it turns out, is not immediately available since he has traveled to a far-off land, perhaps to trade. Gyaanadu Asare is the likely choice in the absence of Agyen Pepra, but either the character or leadership of the former is highly questionable. The imagined and confused state of affairs leads to several rhetorical questions from Lines 27–29. In an attempt to locate Agyen Pepra, the bards unleash a fast-paced delivery and torrent of words from Lines 30–31. It seems that the favorite candidate had crossed a big river, ɔbosom *asu*, past Lake Bosomtwe in his travels, and, as a result, is out of reach. In order to ensure Agyen Pepra returns to assume his rightful place, a section of the people suggested performing a ritual offering of a white fowl and seven *emire* trees to the deity of Lake Bosomtwe. Another rhetorical question follows the previous suggestion, for while there may be potential candidates, none surpasses the character and leadership skills of Agyen Pepra. The people are resolute in their choice, as indicated by their persistence in Line 35, the last phrase in Section 2. The logical resolution of the gridlock in Section 2 is marked by the strategic placement of the noted formulaic phrase at the end of Line 35. Here, it functions in the dual role of marking the end of the section, as well as giving prominence to the final selection of Adwumakaase Abremu Pepra as the leader.

Section 3 projects referential poetry by Opanin Fofie's choice of nominals, praise names, and epithets to establish value in sacrifice and selflessness. The opening phrase in Line 36 presents Asiedu Papakɛseɛ, who fought to defend his people but paid the ultimate price in the end. Ofosu Dwamoa Boaboafo fights like a man in difficult battles, and for that they honor him (Line 37); Ofosu Pem and Yaw Boniba receive similar recognition (Lines 37 and 38). Naa Bema, whose by-name is Daa, was possibly the ɔhemaa of Dwaben, and her praise is found in Ampɔfo Kwaamoa's songs (Lines 40–41). In the context of a ceremony, using his artistic license, Opanin Fofie draws the ruler's attention to all of the heroic activities of his subjects in Line 44. The bards then move on to request attention from the general public in Line 45, that they should not murmur or engage in distractions. I have previously analyzed the remaining texts, from Lines 46–53, at the end of Section 3. Section 4 continues the theme of valor with the imagery of members in the community rushing out to listen to the message from the battlefront that Obiri Kwaa has brought to them. The successes and challenges in the battlefield comprise the message from Lines 55 to the end of the section. That none of the perceived adversaries survived the might of the Asante army is represented with the metaphoric allusion to the ruler's shield (*ɛkyɛm*). The subtext in Line 65 is that Kyebi Baa Kwanti succeeded the ruler of Akyem Abuakwa Ofori Panin, who was defeated and killed in the *Ahantan Sa* (the War of Pride). As revealed by Kyerematen, the former unsuccessfully revenged the defeat of his predecessor, but he met a similar fate in the last major war that Opoku Ware led against Akyem Abuakwa (*ibid*, 277–280). The median phrase, *Abamoo*, in Line 67 triggers events surrounding the Asante campaign against the Afram Plains. Overwhelmed by the combined forces from Dwaben, Nsuta, Kumawu, Kwaaman,

Agogo, and Kwawu, the King of the Afram Plains, Antaadafinam, committed sui-
cide by drawing in the Afram River with large quantities of his regalia. All of
the rulers of the previously-named towns, who were also captains of the same,
shared Antaadafinam's regalia, and a particular copper statue of a mother with
three children with an umbrella covering them called *Abamoo* went to the chief
of Kumawu. The artistic beauty and value of the Abamoo statutes were held in
high esteem to the extent that expectant mothers made every effort to set eyes on
them with the understanding that their newborn children would be as beautiful or
handsome as the Abamoo statutes. Since the statutes are carried on the head, the
entire phrase projects the elevated imagery of *Abamoo* and artistically plays with
the double meaning of *Kantanka*. First, Kantanka is the by-name of Ɔsafo (literally, a brave warrior), which is also the praise name for Opoku Ware (Ɔsafo Poku)
to delineate heroic militancy. The second has to do with the graphic description of
an elevated *Abamoo* radiating beauty in all directions—*kan-tan* in Twi).

Finally, Section Five continues to express courage and fearlessness with a similar projection of by-names, strong appellations, allusions, and proverbs. The hum-
ble beginnings of Opoku Ware and his later fortunes resulting from his conquests
are foregrounded in Lines 68–69. The formulaic end phrase in Line 70 is the
penultimate phrase in the six prior lines, 66–69, which foreground the achievements of Agya Panin and the first time that the bards rattled the nominals (praise
names) of Agya Panin. Lines 70–71 are saturated with strong names and praise
names of Opoku but crucially expound on the initial iterations of praise names in
Lines 66–67. Lines 70–71 seamlessly merge into the last metatexts from Lines
72–74, which are an exact repetition of Lines 22–24. This further reinforces my
initial submission that Asafo is a historical verse expressing the Asante experience
in the early years of the kingdom, and how the brave and militant Opoku Ware
Katakyie expanded and consolidated the kingdom following the passing of the
founder, Ɔpemsoɔ Ɔsɛe Tutu. Since the overarching theme in Asafo is to highlight
valor in combat, the end phrase in Line 73 is to stamp a code of approval for the
recognition of Opoku Ware Katakyie, who conquered territories in the savannah
and forest Zones (Line 72). Line 70 is immediately followed by a parallel repetition in Line 71. The formulaic end phrase in Lines 75 and 76 is the usual stress
on the unique characters of the nominal—unique in the former line and brave in
the latter. Towards the end of the verse, the bards express a profound appreciation of the kingdom to Opoku Ware for his extraordinary achievements during
his thirty-year reign. In that sense, the last phrase (Line 77) aptly summarizes the
main theme of Asafo and concludes with the extremely appreciative formulaic
end phrase, *adwo*. All pointers are located in the goal of Asafo—brave and courageous combatants. Truly, there is value in courage.

In addition to the rhetorical devices noted with *Nnwontene* and *Amankum*, *Asafo*
indexes a set of features worth discussing. It is the longest verse, and although
not entirely unique, it leans heavily on textual borrowings and thus establishes
intertextual linkages with *Nnwontene* and *Amankum*. At the same time, however,
it retains its distinctive character as *Asafo*. For instance, the theme of wake up,
nyane, which appears in Lines 1–4 of Example 6.1 is expressed in Lines 1–3 in

Asafo; this is followed by greetings in Line 5 of the former and Line 4 of the latter. One of the formulaic end phrases in Nnwontene is *awisi*, typically a response to greetings for those born on Sunday, but it is uniquely *adwo* in Asafo. The intertextual relationship with Amankun (Example 6.2) is more elaborate than Nnwontene, since it involves several lines. For instance, Lines 10–13 in *Amankum* is the same as Lines 44–47 in *Asafo*. The only difference between the two is the beginning phrase—Ɔsɛɛ Tutu in *Amankum* and Ɔpemsoɔ in *Asafo*—but Ɔpemsoɔ is the praise name of Ɔsɛɛ Tutu. Lines 14–21 in Amankum are quoted in Asafo from Lines 49–55, while Lines 22–25 in the former are the same as Lines 52–60 in the latter. Lines 37–38 in Amankun are cited in Lines 61–62 in Asafo, while Dɔmaako Sakyi in the rapidly delivered last line in Amankun is quoted in Line 75 in Asafo. Some of the distinct phrases in Asafo include Line 48, *Tu atam a otu adɔfoɔ tam* (One who snatches the loin cloth of his enemies). While the text is unique, it is also the manner of delivery that draws attention to the entire phrase. Line 63 deserves a brief comment. *Yɛn nso apea, yɛn so atwenee na yɛ'yan* is a forceful statement by the bards that establishes their identity as one of two verbal art forms in the court (Abrafoɔ Apae is the other) that do not depend on instrumental surrogacy but rather use the human voice to perform. Although the entire phrase in Line 65 is modeled on *Amankun*, the textual content is fresh and original. The procedure for ending the fairly long verse in *Asafo* diverges significantly from that of *Nnwontene* and *Amankun*. As I pointed out previously, the signal in the previous verses is located in Line 57 in Nnwontene (Example 6.1) and Line 60 in Amankun (Example 6.2), followed by another line to prepare for the final gesture. Since Lines 72–74 are exact repetitions of Lines 22–24, it may well be that the phrases in the three lines are prompters that they are about to end the verse. Although the penultimate phrase in Asafo does not confer the same closing gesture as those in the previous two verses, the bards follow similar ending procedures, with a momentary pause and then unleashing a torrent of texts in Line 77 at a fast pace to end the verse. As usual, all of the instrumentalists are then activated with a plural response to congratulate the bards. I will now present two examples of *Nnwontia* (Short Songs) to conclude our analysis and discussion of *Kwadwom*.

Unlike the three previous examples where the bards take turns, with the second bard echoing the same phrase as the first, the two bards perform the following example at the same time. Example 6.4 is performed after the ruler distributes offertory drinks (*Adae Nsa*) to chiefs, courtiers, and guests participating in the Akwasidae

Example 6.4 Nom Nsa Gu Ase (Have Your Drink), *Kwadwom*. Opanin Kofi Fofie and the Bards.

Twi Text	English Translation
1. Ɔsagyefoɔ nom nsa gu ase nge	1. Ɔsagyefoɔ have your drink nge
2. Okuru Asante Naadu berɛdwo nge	2. Respectfully, Okuru Asante Naadu nge
3. Okuru bedi atɔperɛ ba dammirifua	3. Condolence, the son of Okuru Bedi Atɔperɛ
4. Nom nsa gu ase awo	4. Enjoy all your drinks, my Lord.
5. Ɛdwom ne akyerɛma wura.	5. The Master of songs and drummers

Public Assembly. As its name suggests, and compared with the previous three examples, Example 4.6 is relatively terse, with the five lines possessing intertextual affinity with *Nnwontene* and *Amankum*, respectively. In that case, Lines 1–2 are variations of the same in *Nnwontene*. Line 3 is a modified version of Line 44 in *Nnwontene*, while Lines 3–5 are a variation of Lines 59–60 in Example 4.3. Like the concluding phrases in *Nnwontene*, Lines 3–5 are rapidly intoned, from beginning to the end, in a single breath. We are by now familiar with literary devices and the function of the end-formulaic phrase *nge*. The only new phrase is in Line 5: *ɛdwom ne akyerɛma wura*, meaning the king is the ultimate patron or master of songs and drummers. The usual plural response by all sound-producing instruments immediately follows the end phrase in Line 5 to express their gratitude to the ruler for the offertory drinks. Example 6.5 is our last example of Short Verse performed by the bards.

Example 6.5 Ɛntera Agyekum (A name)-Kwadwom. Opanin Fofie and the bards.

Twi Text	English Translation
1. Ɛntera Agyekum Kyere Dɔmaako Sakyi o a ɔdi Amoako ntene nge	1. Ɛnterɛ Agyekum Kyere Dɔmaako Sakyi who trails Amoako nge
2. Obi yare nsamansuo Anima gyae Amoako Agyaako nge	2. Anima, leave Amoako the victim alone nge
3. Ayi Buruku a ɔkum n'akomfoɔ Twum o Kyampɔn noforobo nge	3. Ayi Buruku deity that kills its priest, Twum Kyampɔn noforobo
4. Sɛ woahye w'akyiri ban a,	4. Since you have a child,
5. Ma yɛmfa nyɛ ban nnya wo na yɛtu a yɛgye wo abayɛn	5. Permit us to leave our children with you for upbringing.

Towards the end of a Public Assembly, such as the referenced Akwasidae in the Prologue, the Ɔkyerɛma (the Creator's Drummer) will begin a series of drum poetry (*Ayan*) on the pair of atumpan drums, imploring His Majesty to rise. Concurrently, the bearer of the *Mpɔnpɔnsɔn* sword goes around to inform the chiefs, courtiers, guests, and all gathered that the ruler is about to rise. The *Abrafoɔ* (members of the Constabulary) take turns reciting one or two verses, while through instrumental surrogacy, the ivory trumpeters also sound short verses known as *Honam Sin* to prepare for the end of the ceremony and the recession from the Courtyard. The moment the bearer of *Mpɔnpɔnsɔn* sword returns to his position, the bards usually perform Ɛnterɛ Agyekum (A name) as a signal to the chiefs, courtiers, guests, and the general public that the Asantehene is about to rise. Right at the end of the concluding phrase, all present stand in deference before the ruler rises for the recession. The bards skillfully lift Lines 1–2 from Lines 75–76 in *Asafo* (Example 6.3), while Line 1 is the exact phrase of Line 75, and the text in Line 2, Amoako Agyaako, is recomposed as the end phrase. The multisyllabic *nsamansuo* in Line 2 is a reference to the herbal medicinal preparation used in the past for bathing a terminally sick person for spiritual cleansing. Ayi Buruku was a deity said to have killed its priests for unexplained offences. As in all *kwadwom* verses we have analyzed, the concluding phrases in Lines 4–5 are delivered at a relatively fast tempo in a single swoop of breath, followed by the archetypal plural response. Since this is the end of the assembly, the collective response leads to a recession performance involving all ensembles.

Apae (referential poetry)

I shall now turn my attention to *Apae* by discussing and analyzing four archetypal verses performed by the Abrafoɔ (members of the constabulary). Described as referential poetry by Kwesi Yankah, as opposed to praise poetry, *apae* fundamentally historicizes military conquests in heroic poetry to remind the reigning king and people of the sacrifices and accomplishments of their fore-bears (Yankah, 1983). Similar to *kwadwom*, historical experience is woven into the fabric of *apae* poetry, thus leading to symbolic codes that are difficult to untangle by the uninformed. It bears noting that a variety of sound-producing instruments are deployed, either as solos or in varied combinations with other instruments such as ivory trumpets, flutes, and drums to provide supplemental channels for expressing referential poetry. However, *apae* shares the spotlight with *kwadwom* as the only two verbal art forms at the court of the Asantehene that use the human voice as a performance medium. *Amoma* is another type of referential poetry comparable to *apae*; however, it is no longer performed in Akan courts. The only known collection of Amoma verses is Nketia (1978). In addition to epithets and praise for individuals, there are appellations that embody well-known characteristics of the Akan stool as the seat of authority. Referential poetry, according to Yankah, is not limited to the royal space, but it is a daily occurrence in formal and informal situations where individuals are show-ered with strong appellations (*abodin*), praise names (*mmrane*), and dirge names (*nsubaa*). Informal situations may arise when friends socialize, and, as a form of teasing, they engage in some kind of praise to recognize success, while parents may resort to praise names when playing with their infants. Formalized situa-tions, however, are institutionalized as part of the political apparatus. Unlike informal practices, *apae* and *kwadwom* fall under the spectrum of institutional referential poetry that are performed by professionals in the court of Akan kings and chiefs (Yankah, 1983: 381–400).

The vast majority of *apae* verses were composed in the days of territorial con-quests and wars of expansion, and that explains the predominant themes of war, heroic pronouncements, and militancy. Akosua Anyidoho further elaborates that, in those days, the war theatre "was considered the supreme test of manhood, and those who excelled were considered exemplary individuals" (Anyidoho, 1991, 1993). In addition to Nketia, Yankah, and Anyidoho, I would like to add that *apae* is also part of an elaborate system of verbal and non-verbal symbolic com-munication designed as a form of security clearance performed to spiritually and physically protect the ruler during court ceremonies, funerary rites, and festivals. As I noted previously, court musicians, including the bards and members of the constabulary, do not speak in formal situations; even during court cases, where they might have been witnesses to a crime, they are not able to make comments. The only medium at their disposal is the use of rhetorical devices in poetry and musical constructs to caution the ruler about the potential misrepresentation of facts. Using the rhetorical and musical devices at their disposal, they are able to prevail on the Asantehene to occasionally postpone a hearing to enable him to confer behind closed doors with, say, the courtiers. At other times, members of the constabulary unusually take turns to recite *apae* in order to caution the rulers about potential adversaries in the immediate area. As I stated elsewhere, the expression in the Akan proverb is *kɔkɔsakyi kasa kyerɛ boninkyerefoɔ a ɔte, nanso ɔte no abɛbuom* (lit. when the vulture speaks to the hyena, the latter understands, but it is understood in proverbial language).[15] In the present when there is relative peace, *apae* aligns the heroic past with challenges in the present as a source of inspiration for the ruler and society at large. Apart from the use of ancient Twi texts and the associated drama during performance, *apae* texts are reasonably clear and straightforward, while *kwadwom*, on the other hand, is full of antiquated texts deliberately delivered with extreme codes and symbolism.

The office of a constabulary that enforces laws was well established in Akan courts before the founding of Asante, but under the latter the constabulary was enlarged to accommodate three distinct groups, namely, Tɔprɛfoɔ, Animosum (or Anadwosekan), and Abrafoɔ. We may recall that when Ɔsɛe Tutu was returning from Akwamu to the then-Kwaaman to succeed his diseased uncle, the King of Akwamu appointed a leading member of his constabulary, Anum Asamoa, and his group to guard him all the way to his destination. Upon reaching their destination, Ɔsɛe Tutu settled Anum Asamoa and his men at Adum in what is now part of downtown Kumase. The current name of the suburb, Adum, is a corruption of Anum, and as time went on, they became known as Adumfoɔ. Referencing Kyeremten's account, there was a split somewhere along the line, and while one group retained the name Adumfoɔ, the other became known as Abrafoɔ. Literally, *abra* means to restrain, so *abrafoɔ* is understood as those who restrain people from going against the laws of the land. So the actual duties of the *abrafoɔ* are to ensure that individuals and groups become law-abiding citizens. The *Adumfoɔ*, on the other hand, are responsible for punishing or carrying out the executions of those who break the laws of the land. Essentially, the *abrafoɔ* cry out and appeal for peace, while *Adumfoɔ* punish those who ignore the appeal. It is the *abrafoɔ* who recite history in the form of referential poetry, and as a result, I agree with Yankah that the usual English label executioners is a misnomer (Yankah, 1983: 381–384).[16]

There are four distinct groups of Abrafoɔ with their respective chiefs: the Nkram Abrafoɔ, Anoo Abrafoɔ, Bɔamang Abrafoɔ, and Tweneduroase Abrafoɔ. Nkram Abrafoɔhene is the overall chief (Abrafoɔhene). All of the four groups of Abrafoɔ are always present to recite apae when the Asantehene sits in state during the periodic Akwasidae Public Assemblies or the Convocation of Chiefs at the Grand Adae (Adaekɛseɛ) that takes place every five years. Royal funerary rites and those for divisional chiefs and Kumase Abrempɔn are additional occasions for the Abrafoɔ to recite referential poetry. The *Atrane* (symbolic firing of a gun) is another event in which the *abrafoɔ* participate, particularly when the Asantehene wears the Great Tunic War dress (*Batakarikɛseɛ*). For the symbolic firing of the gun, the king shoots the gun three times, and each one is preceded by *apae* referential poetry. Apart from ceremonies, *Abrafoɔ* are on duty during purification rites in the Chapel of Stools (*Nkonwafieso*), when the black stools of past kings are brought out for cleansing. In those situations, they stand ready outside the entrance to the stool room and recite the verses for a particular ancestor-king as soon as his black stool is brought out. The stools are usually carried on the nape of the Stool Carrier's neck, and the Stool Carrier will stop and only proceed at the end of the verse. When it is part of processions, the *Abrafoɔ* walk on both sides of the Gold Stool and intermittently recite *apae* referential poetry. Additional duties include keeping order during ceremonies and court cases.

When reciting *apae*, the *Abrafoɔ* lift the sword, with the right hand holding the grip between the two pommels, making a fist with the left hand, placing the fisted left hand on the gilt, and directly facing the king as he formally sits in state and recites the poetry while looking directly at his face. Performance is a crucial element that combines taking steps towards the Asantehene with the manner of raising and tilting the head to the right, the tone of the voice, the reciter's person-ality, and his gait and demeanor—all of which contribute to the overall drama.[17] At the beginning, all four chiefs take turns, starting with the overall chief Nkram Abrafoɔhene and followed by Anoo Abrafoɔhene, Bɔamang Abrafoɔhene, and finally Tweneduroase Abrafoɔhene. Then comes the non-office-holding Abrafoɔ, who are identified as the "children" of the chiefs. While the children are reciting the verses, the corresponding chief whose "child" is reciting will immediately stand up, alert and ready to step in to continue with the poetry in case they forget a line. When that happens, the individual steps back immediately to regain his composure before rejoining the *Abrafoɔ*. The dress code for the *Abrafoɔ* consists of a leopard-skin hat (*etwiekyɛ*), and some of the hats have two ears and red eyes carved into the forehead, while others have talismans (*suman*) on the forehead. All four chiefs wear a variety of necklaces and keep a bunch of small knifes (*sɛpɔ*) in leather sheaths (*bɔha*), which are tucked into the cloth close to the chest. The four knifes used by the Nkram Abrafoɔhene, Baafoɔ Asumang Kofi Ababio, are known as *kumamani* (lit. killer of townsmen), *kumahɔhoɔ* (killer of visitors), *kumadehyeɛ* (killer of royals), and *sɛpɔ* (knife). Similarly, the swords (*mfena*) are identified with names: Nkram Abrofoɔhene has Kontonkronwi (death is like the hair around the human neck, we all have it and we shall all die someday). The *Gye Me Di* (Trust Me) knife belongs to Anoo Abrafoɔhene, Baafoɔ Kofi Antwi Baah. We now turn our attention to rhetoric and history in apae.

The unfolding drama and apparent confusion that are inevitable consequences of wars such as those involving Asante and Dɛnkyera are vividly captured in the following *apae* (Example 6.6) performed by Kwabena Kyeremeh, a member of the constabulary at Manhyia Palace in Kumase. Apart from ceremonies and ritu-als, I recorded the Abrafoɔ and their chiefs in the summers of 2009 and 2011.

Oral history narrated by the Abrafoɔ informs us that Ɔpemsoɔ Osei Tutu sent a group of his spies (*Kwanserafoɔ*) to Assen Atandanso, and another group on top of a hill near Manso Nkwanta, where they could easily monitor the valley below for troop movement on the part of the Dɛnkyera. According to oral tradition, the

Example 6.6 Agya Nyane, Agya Nyane (Wake Up Father, Wake Up Father), Apae by Kwabena Kyeremeh.

Twi Text	English Translation
1. Ɔno no!	1. That's him!
2. Agya nyane, agya nyane	2. Wake up father, Wake up father
3. Ɔse Agya wonte sɛ anwam na esu yi?	3. Father, don't you hear the cries of hornbills?
4. Buei! Wo abɔfra yi wo yɛ abɔfra pa	4. You are a child indeed
5. Mesee wo sɛ anwam na ɛresu?	5. Did I tell you that this was the cries of hornbills?
6. Ɔse Ɔsɛe Tutu Ntahera retwa Amantam nsu a	6. When Ɔsɛe Tutu's Ntahera are crossing the Amantam river
7. Wose anwam na ɛresu yi	7. You refer to them as cries of the hornbill?
8. Ɔse Agya e! Agya e!	8. He calls father! Father!
9. Sɛ woretwa asuo a,	9. When you are crossing the river,
10. Sɔ wo tuo mu o	10. Hold your gun firmly
11. Na Ɔsɛe Tutu no ara ka ho bi na ɔreba	11. For Ɔsɛe Tutu himself is leading the charge
12. Ɔno a, adummɔ, adammɔ, adankaweaboɔ	12. That's him, knocking of doors and building, the gourd that disperses bullets
13. Ɔpanin a ɔte Da	13. The elderly man who lives at (O)Da
14. Afari a ɔko mpenten	14. Afari who fights briskly
15. Ɔsɛe Tutu no no,	15. That's Ɔsɛe Tutu.
16. Yetua wo mpenten so a	16. When you are besieged suddenly
17. Wote mu anɔpa tutuutu	17. You escape at dawn
18. Nyankopasakyie a wo ti ho apa	18. The vulture that has a baldhead
19. Wo ka fra fra!	19. Wo ka fra fra!

name of the town, Manso Nkwanta, is in reference to *ɔman aso*, the ear of the
nation. That is, those living in that village at the time were acting as the ears of
the kingdom, and it was their duty to report any troop movement or suspicious
maneuvers on the part of the Dɛnkyira to Kumase. *Ɔman aso* later became Manso,
while Nkwanta refers to a major intersection, a crossroads in the area. On their
way to the two locations, they were accompanied by the Ntahera ivory trumpeters, and a child thought the sound they were hearing in the night were the cries of
hornbills in the forest, but the father corrected the child's delusion from Lines 4 to
7 asking, "when Ɔsɛe Tutu's Ntahera are crossing the Amantam river, do you refer
to their sound as the cries of hornbills?" The child then cautions his/her father to
hold on tight to his gun when crossing the river.

Kyeremeh begins with a compelling moniker, *ɔno no*, in Line 1 that immediately draws attention to him and especially the Asantehene, who is the focus
of his performance.[18] There is a broad overarching sequence that begins with a
dialogue between father and child from Lines 2–11, followed by processes of
individuation that settle on Ɔsɛe Tutu as the object of reference and whose heroic
qualities are deserving of attention. In that sense, this is one of the few heroic
recitations in the *apae* repertoire, with the first section artistically configured as a

form of dialogue. The dialogue is between a father and his child, though we are not sure of the gender of the child. Rhetorical devices include the duplication of phrases as in Line 2, *Agya nyane, Agya nyane*; the cautionary Line 8, *Agyae e! Agyae!*; Lines 3 and 5, *sɛ anwam na esu yi?*; and Line 7, *anwam na ɛresu*, which are striking in terms of their implicit rhetorical devices. Although the repetitions in Lines 3 and 5 are framed in the form of a question, the inherent meanings are slightly different. In Line 3, the child prods the parent, "can't you hear the cries of hornbills?" The father retorts: "did I ever tell you that these are the cries of hornbills?" Line 7 jettisons *sɛ* at the beginning of the phrase and ends up with: *Wose awam na ɛresu yi* (did you refer to them as "the cries of hornbills?"). The formulaic phrase, *mpenten*, in Lines 14 and 16 is the same but conveys strikingly different meanings by means of referential parallelism. It refers to an individual who "fights briskly" in Line 14, while Line 16 refers to an individual who has been ambushed by an imaginary army. Thus, Ɔsɛe Tutu (Line 15) is like Afari who fights briskly when he is surrounded by an army (Line 14), but Ɔsɛe Tutu finds a way to escape when he is ambushed (Line 16). There is also a phonological configuration that targets the sound structure in the vowel *ɔ* as an end-pattern in a repeated sequence in Line 12, as in *adumm(ɔ)*, *adamm(ɔ)*, and *adankaweabo(ɔ)*. The repetition of *mm* in the medial position in Line 12, in addition to ending the line with the compressed and multisyllabic *a dan-ka-we-a-boɔ*—that is, the box that receives bullets—is quite striking. *Nyankopasakyie* (the bald-headed vulture) is yet another formulaic phrase with multiple syllables that reinforces the bravery and heroism of the Asantehene. As a scavenger, the vulture lacks recognition in Akan folklore, since they associate it with laziness. The vulture, for instance, can-not cultivate its own farm or engage in a rewarding vocation, and, as a result, it is left to forage on discarded food in the dumpster. Conversely, one of the Akan proverbs that acknowledges the bald-headed vulture signifies strength and the ability to absorb hardships by proclaiming: *asem a ɛto kɔkɔsakyi maa ne tiri ho pae yɛ, sɛ ɛkaa aboa kwakwaadabi a, anka wawu ama yɛ 'sie no*. Literally, this means that the crow would have been long dead and buried if it had to deal with the challenges that caused the vulture to lose the hair on its head. In short, most chiefs would not have the strength to survive what the king had to contend with on a daily basis. Placing the multisyllabic *Nyan-ko-pa-sa-kyie* at the beginning of the penultimate phrase (Line 18) is a method of recasting the usual pitch contrast in reciting apae for dramatic effect. Instead of beginning with a high-pitched voice and tapering off with a low-pitch, the opening phrase in Line 18 injected energy into the poetry until the very last line, when Kyeremeh rapidly delivered the con-cluding phrase in lower tones. The hornbill, river, and vulture are symbolic allu-sions that Kyeremeh incorporates into the poetry to expand the semantic field of epithets for the king. At the end of the referential poetry, the ivory trumpet groups, *durugya* (cane flute), and *kwadwomfoɔ* (minstrels) usually take turns perform-ing praise poetry from their repertoire. The pair of *Mpebi ne Nkrawiri* drums is always on hand to punctuate the cadences in the verses, or sometimes to play in such a way as to overlap with the voice. For instance, in Example 6.6 the Mpebi ne Nkrawiri drums begin playing to emphasize the cadences from Lines 12 to 19,

Example 6.7 Mpebi ne Nkrawiri drums punctuate Apae.

---

12. Ɔno a XX adummɔ XX adammɔ XX adankaweaboɔ XX
13. Ɔpanin a ɔte Da XX
14. Afari a ɔko mpenten XX
15. Ɔsɛe Tutu no no XX
16. Yetua wo mpenten so a XX
17. Wote mu anɔpa tutuutu XX
18. Nyankopasakyie a wo ti ho apa XX
19. Wo ka fra fra! XXXXXXX

Example 6.8 Apae by Kwabena Kyeremeh.

Twi Text
1. Ɔno no,
2. Ɔsɛi Tutu,
3. Woyɛɛ saa yɛɛ saa kum Wasa tomfoɔ
4. Ama ne dadeɛ aka pata
5. Woakum Bɔaman Kwadwo Awua
6. Woakum Amansee Barima ɛna
7. Woakum Agyei Ntiri Mansah
8. Woakum Kuroku ne Keraka ne ne wɔfaase Yaw Pipim
9. Woakum Buroni tekɔɔ
10. Woakum Agyei Sumanfo
11. Woakum Nsɔkɔhene Agyeinim ama na yera wɔ atɛ ase
12. Woakum Werɛkyɛwerɛkyɛ ama kwan nkyɛn adwo
13. Woakum Ɔdomanko Buroni Mankata
14. Ɔkankan Buroni se ɔpa wo kyɛw
15. Ɛmmfa nea wo de yɛɛ Mfante no, mfa mmɛyɛ no.

English Translation
1. That's him
2. Ɔsɛe Tutu
3. You intentionally killed blacksmith from Wasa
4. And he left his tools on the barn
5. You have killed Bɔaman Kwadwo Awua
6. You have killed the strongman of Amansee
7. You have killed Agyei Ntiri Mansa
8. You have killed Kuroku ne Keraka and his nephew Yaw Pipim
9. You have killed the tall whiteman
10. You have killed Agyei Sumanfo
11. You have killed the chief of Nsɔkɔ, Agyeinim, and we can't find him around atɛ game
12. You have killed Werɛkyɛwerɛkyɛ and there is peace along the path.
13. You have killed Charles MacCarthy
14. The Dutch is pleading with you
15. Don't treat them the same way as you did the Fante

---

as shown in Example 6.7. The XX are the punctuation sounds of the Mpebi ne Nkrawiri drums.

If we doubt the intended goals of apae poetry, Example 6.8 squarely projects heroic militancy, to use Yankah's (1983) memorable interpretation, onto the Asantehene. Although he did not participate personally in the various wars that led to the defeat of the previously listed names, he is considered to be an embodiment of all past kings. In his recitation, Kyeremeh generates a list—either the name of a chief, a commander of the opposing army, or a combination of a name of a chief and his state—to historicize Asante victories in various wars. In Line 3, Wasa refers to a state northwest of Kumase, while *tomfoɔ* is an ironsmith implying the extraordinary skills of a chief from Wasa who could manufacture iron implements. Despite his perceived skills, he was killed and his tools remained useless on top of his hut (Line 4). From Kyerematen (1966: 219–221), we learn that Bɔaman is a town near Lake Bosomtwe, and Kwadwo Awua is perhaps the name of a chief in Line 5. Amanseɛ in Line 6 is a reference to towns south of Kumase that are separated into Amanseɛ Central and West Districts, with Bekwai as the capital of the former and Manso Nkwanta the capital of the latter. In Line 7, Agyei Ntiri Mansah is the name of a chief in the same locality, but the full name of Kuroku in Line 8 is Bosompem Boakye Ntow Kuroku, an influential chief of Bɔaman, and his wife Keraka. Kuroku had lodged a complaint with Ɔpemsoɔ Ɔseɛ Tutu that one of his subjects, Adu Yeboa Korantwe, had been made head of the Vanguard of the army without his knowledge. Perhaps such a remonstration by Kuroku would not have led to an attack by his superior, but the reports by the chief of Asaaman, Akosa Gyima, that Kuroku was claiming ownership of the lake and had been harassing and preventing those who were not his subjects from fishing in the lake led to the attack and subsequent defeat of the latter. Facing imminent defeat, Kuroku fled to the south in the company of some of his men and established Akyem Bosome. Buroni in Line 9 is the Akan word for the white man/woman, or any human with light skin, while *tekɔɔ* is the compression of *tenten* (a tall person) and *kɔɔ* (a light-skinned person). In Line 10, Agyei is the name of a fearful priest (*Nsumankwaafoɔ*) that has been reduced to *Sumanfo*. *Nsɔkɔhene* refers to the chief of Nsɔkɔ, whose name was Agyeinim. Nsɔkɔ is the Akan name for the seventeenth-century trading town northwest of Kumase, which Mande traders from Mali and other areas in the Sahel Region called Bi'u or Begho. Nsɔkɔ was strategically situated on the trade route from Kumase to Bondugu and further west to Kong in present day Côte d'Ivoire, and then northward to Wagadugu in Mali west of Jenne, and then finally to Timbuktu.[19]

The multisyllabic *Werɛkyɛwerɛkyɛ* and its unique sound structure in Line 12 is not the name of a person, but rather describes the rustling of dry leaves on the undergrowth and footpaths in the forest. The rustling sound is the result of robbers who hide in the forest and ambush unsuspecting travelers and traders who travel long distances to market centers to trade their wares. It may also stand for enemy soldiers who use the cover of the thick undergrowth to ambush unsuspecting opponents. In the larger scheme of things, *werɛkyerɛwerɛkyerɛ* is a metaphoric allusion to the referent Ɔpemsoɔ Ɔseɛ Tutu and his accomplishments, not only on the battlefield but also in eliminating armed robbers along trade routes. Further, the previous allusion recognizes Ɔpemsoɔ for forming a lasting union of states, in addition to formulating wide-ranging constitutional laws that ushered in relative peace, prosperity, and security. Ɔdomanko Buroni Mankata in Line 13 is a reference to the British Governor Sir Charles MacCarthy, who was killed by Asante soldiers. Upon hearing of the death of Ɔsɛe Asibe Bonsu in November 1823, writes Wilks, Governor MacCarthy who had been engaged in all kinds of schemes to create dissent among outlying states in the Asante Kingdom, decided to attack Asante in January 1824. In what ushered in almost a century of Anglo-Asante wars, on January 21, 1824 Asante soldiers killed Governor Mac-Carthy and eight of his officers (Wilks, 1975).[20] Ɔkankan Buroni in Line 14 refers to the Dutch at Anomabo during the reign of Ɔsɛe Asibe Bonsu. Lines 14 and 15 capture, in poetic verse, the same event as Chapter 2, involving the Asante and Fante in the early nineteenth century. Three Assene Chiefs—Amo, Apotoe, and Tibo—rebelled against the kingdom and had sought refuge on the coast with Fante chiefs in Abora, Cape Coast, and Anomabo. Against the combined forces of the Fante, the Asante faced a formidable foe, but they eventually triumphed, and the Dutch governor who was stationed at Anomabo sent messengers to Ɔsɛe Asibe to plead for peace on behalf of the Fante. A unique literary device in Example 6.8 deserves our attention. *Woakum* as a beginning phrase from Lines 5–13 may well be a contraction of Line 3, which in the process conveys prominence to Wasa tomfoɔ as evident in the two lines, 3 and 4, that constitute the phrase. Second, the prefix Wo in Line 3, and from Lines 5–13, creates a unified thread that connects the variety of strands, names, and places in this verse. Third, the sequences of *w* in the beginning phrase, and *k* in the middle of the same phrase, generates a reliable sound pattern for listeners. Kyeremeh provides us with yet more poetry in the next example.

Example 6.9 joins Example 6.6 in setting up a dialogue between an adult and his child for dramatic effect. With the day-names of females in Akan, we can say with certainty that the dialogue is between a man and, probably, the women in a household. Akosua is the day-name for a Sunday-born, Adwoa is a Monday-born, Abena is a Tuesday-born, Akua is a Wednesday-born, Ama is a Saturday-born, and, finally, Yaa is the day-name of a Thursday-born. The three broad sections of this verse are Lines 1–5, 6–14, and 15–19. The First Section dwells on referential parallel lines, and although a nominal individuating the ruler is entirely absent, the presence of imagery leaves no doubt about the referent in this poetry. That our imagined referent is as powerful as a small-but-dangerous river is marked with the duplication of two syllables as in Line 2, *keteketekete* and *krakyɛ ne krakyɛ*. His overgrown beard is compared to the buffalo bull's horns in Line 3. The crocodile provides another formidable trait in Line 4, when Kyeremeh combines the sound structure of the compressed *Ɔ-dɛn-kyɛm-dua-tram*, the long tail of a crocodile that in regular spoken language is *dɛnkyɛm a ne dua atra no*. Line 5 finally throws in a code for the informed that Kyeremeh is signifying none other than the heroic attributes of Ɔpemsoɔ Ɔsɛe Tutu, and for that, we need to draw in the historical setting for the multisyllabic opening phrase Okurusono in Line 5. This is the oral history of a wounded elephant shot by a hunter, Atia Boro, which had fallen into a pit. With the help of his men, Ɔsɛe Tutu lifted the humongous elephant from the pit, and that led Anum Asamoa and his *abrafoɔ* to compose this particular line: If you have to lift an elephant, you lift one that lies in a pit (see Kyerematen, 1966: 133). I will highlight a few phrases and the dialogue

Example 6.9 Asuo Keteketekete (A Small Stream), Apae by Kwabena Kyeremeh.

Twi Text

1. Ɔno no!
2. Asuo keteketekete ne krakyɛ ne krakyɛ
3. Na bɔdwesɛ poma no sɛ ɛkɔɔnini abɛn
4. Ɔdɛnkyɛmduatram
5. Okurusono a, okukuru deɛ ɛda amena mu
6. Ɔse Akosua eei, Adwoa eei, Abena eei, Akua eei, Ama eei, Yaa eei,
7. Ɔse fa me ntomaban brɛ me oo
8. Ɔse na adɛn o?
9. Seɛ nnaano Ɔsɛi Tutu asɛm a ɛbaaɛ na ebi aba biom no
10. Ɔse wo abɔfra wei manse wo?
11. Manse wo ne Ɔsɛi Tutu agorɔ yi?
12. Ɔsɛi Tutu de ne nsa, anaasɛ abaa, anaasɛ ɔde tuo na ɔbɔɔ wo sei?
13. Ɔse wo abɔfra wei si wo tiri aseɛ
14. Si wo tiri ase ma mogya ngu wo
15. Ɔsɛi Tutu, woyɛɛ saa yɛɛ saa guu mogya tradaa
16. Akokɔnini a wo yam yɛ
17. Ɔsɛi Tutu, wo na woma a apinikum si nipa mu
18. Apini kum no o!
19. Hmmmmm!

English Translation

1. That's him!
2. A small stream with a steep raven
3. His beard is as fixed as a buffalo bull's horn
4. The crocodile's tail is fairly long
5. If you have to lift an elephant, you lift one that lies in a pit
6. Akosua e, Adwoa e, Abena e, Akua e, Ama e, Yaa e
7. Bring me my piece of cloth
8. She says what is the matter?
9. It is Ɔsee Tutu's problem that occurred that other day that has reoccurred
10. He says, you this child didn't I warn you?
11. Didn't I warn you not to play with Ɔsee Tutu?
12. Did Ɔsee Tutu use his hand, or a club, or a gun to hurt you this way?
13. He says, you this child lower your head
14. Lower your head for the blood to drain
15. Ɔsee Tutu, you intentionally caused blood to flow profusely
16. A generous cock
17. Ɔsee Tutu, you caused people to die out of groaning
18. He died out of groaning
19. Hmmmmm!

in the Second Section for our attention. *Ntomaban* in Line 7 is a loincloth (known as *danta* or *amoase*) that was in popular usage in the seventeenth century and preceded short or long pants. The phrase *abofra* (child) in Line 10 is alluding to the fact that only adults with childish thoughts will not take grave matters associated with Ɔsee Tutu seriously, and that explains the use of the phrase play in Line 11. Although European merchants introduced guns in Akan areas by the end of the seventeenth century, there were not that many guns in circulation and weapons of war were predominantly sticks, tree branches, stones, the bare fist, swords, and any projectile. A possible answer to the question raised in Line 12 may be that a stick struck the victim's head, leading to blood draining from the nose. The man went to the aid of the victim by instructing him to "lower your head for the blood to drain" from your nose to avoid internal bleeding.

The Third and final Section, in Lines 15–19, magnifies the fast-paced events of Lines 6–14. Kyeremeh begins the final section by identifying an attribute of the referent with nominal and epithets that, although causing pain and anguish to his enemies, the king is referred to as a generous cock. For it is not lost on his audience that, while it is the hen that takes care of its chicks, the cock is sometimes observed grabbing termites and feeding them to the chicks. In other words, the ruler might kill his enemies in the battlefield, but surviving members of a victim cannot cry out openly, as that will result in further destruction and anguish. In the absence of an external display of grief, the people resort to crying within, as expressed in the last phrase, Hmmmmm, in Line 19. Baafɔɔ Kwadwo Kuma, Bɔaman Abrafoɔhene, performed the last apae.

Example 6.10 Ɔpampam Bi (One who chases people)-Apae by Baafɔɔ Kwadwo Kuma.

Twi Text
1.   Ɔno no
2.   Ɔno no
3.   Ɔpampam bi e
4.   Ɔpampam bi e
5.   Ɔsɛi Tutu
6.   Wo pampam Kwaku Atta kɔkuu no too Yompa
7.   Yompa Ɔkyere se ɔma wo mo ne ko
8.   Ne deɛ nyɛ dɛ nti na Onyankopɔn buaa no atɛn
9.   Okukurutoɛ Gyinaampanduodu gyina afuo so a
10. Yɛnte ntodie
11. Ɔsɛi Tutu Bediako,
12. Wogyina ako no a yɛnyi wo mene
13. Ɔka fra fra!

English Translation
1.   That's him
2.   That's him
3.   One who chases people
4.   One who chases people
5.   Ɔsɛi Tutu,
6.   You chased Kwaku Atta and killed him at Yompa
7.   Yompa Ɔkyere congratulates you for fighting hard
8.   His cause was not right hence God found him guilty
9.   When thunderstorm moves across the farm
10. We cannot harvest the farm produce
11. Ɔsɛe Tutu the warrior
12. At the war front no one can kill you
13. Ɔka fra fra

The emphasis on *ɔpampam bi* and the prolongation of the particle *e* at the end of the phrase by Baafoɔ Kwadwo Kuma opens a window into the circumstances that led Kwaku Atta and his men to take to their heels and take refuge with Ɔkyere, the chief of Yompa. But not long after arriving, Kwaku Atta, together with his people and his deity, perished under strange circumstances, and that led Nana Ɔkyere, the Yompa chief, and his people to conclude that Kwaku Atta was a bad character after all, to the extent that he and his followers were struck dead by the Supreme Being. In that sense, the ruler is compared with the thunderstorm and lightning and the fearful sound described as *Okukurutoɛ Gyinaampanduodu*. The combination of phonology and multisyllabic devices describe the normal response of Akan farmers to the sudden onset of thunderstorms while they worked on the farm. The advice is for farmers to quickly abandon work and run home, instead of trying to harvest a few pieces of produce like tomatoes, garden eggs (a type of eggplant), peppers, and others. A warning to adversaries is to hide, just as Kwaku Atta did, without challenging the Asantehene to a fight.

Summary

In the foregoing analyses of chronicle songs (*kwadwom*) and referential poetry (*apae*), we have encountered the overwhelming use of coded rhetoric to outline historical events related to reigns, events, and wars. All of our historical references in Chapter 2, and several others, are recorded in these two verbal art forms with different modes of presentation. While *apae* is direct and makes no effort at covering up names, locations, and incidents, *kwadwom* uses a special mode of delivery including archaic texts, indirection, metaphoric allusions, imagery, opaque references, and coded language artistically concealed in rhetorical strategies. A unique feature of *Asafo* (Example 6.3) is intertextual borrowings from *Nnwontene* (Example 6.1) and *Amankum* (Example 6.2). Despite the *kwadwom* emphasis on defeated adversaries, the Asante did not escape the agony of the numerous wars, as they also lost several brave soldiers and leaders. Recalling those incidents by the bards is therefore a constant reminder of grave incidents in the inter-war years. In his *Apae*, Kwabena Kyeremeh delves into the imagery of the hornbill, a river, and the vulture to create symbolic allusions in order to expand the semantic field of epithets for the ruler. Another rhetorical device is the parallel repetition of *Wo* (you) in Example 6.8, which creates a unified thread connecting a variety of strands, names, and places into a single work of poetry. Kwadwom is not limited to the name-calling and recognition of past kings but also the masses. For instance, the ruler is reminded of sacrifices of some territorial chiefs, including the Ɛdwesohene Diko Pim, who gave themselves up to be sacrificed to ensure the triumph of the Kwaaman coalition over Dɛnkyera. Knowledge of history, as previously noted, is power, and the public recall of honorable sacrifice encourages the younger generation to emulate the bravery and valor of their forebears. There is value in sacrifice and selflessness.

After my ethnographic account of the Akwasidae Public Assembly in the Prologue, I observed that court music and verbal arts are integral to the socio-political and religious life in Asante. Additionally, I noted how every event is a performance of aspects of Asante history, experience, and social values and followed this with a series of questions: 1) How do we access the text-laden performances involving *fontomfrom*, *mpintin*, and *kete* drum ensembles? 2) What were the ivory trumpeters—both short and long—expressing in the instrumental texts? and 3) How do we unpack ancient song texts, the verbal poetry of the bards, and the referential poetry of the constabulary? The search for answers guided the analyses, focus, and scope of my discussions, and I have no doubt that my discussions will generate additional questions. The intersection between lived and current experience is expressed through a complex system of instrumental and song texts, as well as verbal poetry for the orderly functioning of the political order and the state in Asante.

Notes

1 Ntikuma is the son of Ananse, the main character and originator of all stories in Akan; hence the stories are named after him, *Anansesɛm* (Ananse Stories). There is no doubt that Ntikuma possesses firsthand knowledge of Ananse Stories, and, as such, outside the Ananse household no one is expected to narrate Ananse stories to Ntikuma.

2 See Ampene (2005: 52–63) for a detailed description of *abeɛ* in nnwonkorɔ.

3 At Manhyia Palace, court criers (*ɛsɛn*) are part of the *Nsɛneɛ* group with additional responsibilities. For a description of the court criers, see Ampene and Nyantakyi III (2016: 190–193).

4 The late Asantehemaa, Afia Kobi Sɛɛwaa Ampem II, reigned from 1977–2016 (thirty-nine years). She was 111 years old when she passed away on November 7, 2016 and was interned in the Royal Mauseleoum at Brɛman on Thursday, January 19, 2017, after four days of national mourning with people from all over the world paying their last respects. The newly enstooled Asantehemaa, Nana Ama Konadu II, is the daughter of the late ɔhemaa and the elder sister of the reigning king, Otumfoɔ Ɔsee Tutu II.

5 In his biography of the late Afia Kobi Sɛɛwaa Ampem II, Ɔheneba Akwasi Abayie (2019: 58–63) traced the matriline of members of the Kumase Ɔyoko family. Nana Yaa Birago was the daughter of Nana Akua Afriyie (Akua Dehyeɛ), whose mother was Nana Afia Kobi I (Asantehemaa from 1857–1880).

6 In addition to the Asante king's stool in Kumase, additional Ayoko matriclan stools include Kokofu, Nsuta, Bekwai, Worawora, Dwaben, Kuntenase, and Dikoman.

7 Nana Akosua Ɔheneafrɛwoɔ gave birth to Nana Ama Sɛɛwaa Nyarko, the 12th Asantehemaa, and Nana Akua Akyaa Mansa, who also gave birth to Otumfoɔ Opoku Ware II, the 15th Asante king.

8 Reference Kyerematen (1966: 193–194) and Irene K. Odotei and George P. Hagan (2003: 19–22). For a history of the Bosomuru sword and Dwetɛ Kuduo, see Ampene and Nyantakyi III (2016: 124, 255–257).

9 See Kyerematen (1966: 298–299) for an account of this war.

10 For a considered discussion of the three-year preparation for the Dɛnkyera War and Kɔmfo Anɔkye's requests and advice about the nature of sacrifices that will ensure victory, see Kyerematen (1966: 196–213).

11 Takiymanhene Ameyaw hosted fugitives in his kingdom and gave them a place to settle in what is now known as Nkoranza, and the ensuing hostilities and his eventual defeat by King Opoku Ware can be found in Kyerematen (1966: 264–268).

12 My discussion of Opoku Ware's paternal affiliation owes a lot to the eloquent biographical information and description of the activities of his reign by Kyerematen (1966: 250–282).

13 It is considerations such as these that underlie the decision to begin the four-day events around the royal burial and funerary rites of the Asantehemaa, Nana Afia Kobi Sɛɛwaa Ampem II, on Monday, January 16, 2017. They began the royal funerary rites on a calm day and gradually built up to a day of pain, Yawɔɔda (Thursday), for the burial.

14 See Kyerematen (1966: 269–272) for the pursuits of fugitives from the Takyiman War to Kong by Opoku Ware.

15 See Ampene and Nyantakyi III (2016: 39–40) for a description of the 2014 Adaekɛsɛɛ and how the ivory trumpeters use surrogate speech to caution the king before he takes his seat.

16 Kyerematen (1966) is a brief historical account of Ɔsɛe Tutu and Anum Asamoa's journey from Akwamu to Kwaaman. For a brief history of Abrafoɔ, Tɛprɛfoɔ, and Animosum, see Ampene and Nyantakyi III (2016: 166–175), which includes the oral history and pictures of all three groups.

17 Yankah (1983: 386) describes another form of performance, perhaps in Akwamu and/or Dɛnkyera, where the reciter covers half of his mouth with his left hand, while he points a sword held in his right hand at the chief. He also references other areas in Africa, precisely in Bahima where the reciter of royal poetry faces the audience with a spear in his right hand in a horizontal pose above his shoulder.

18 My analysis in this section owes a great deal to earlier publications by two literary scholars, Kwesi Yankah (1983) and Akosua Anyidoho (1991). Yankah's article is based on his field research in the 1970s in three Akan states—Denkyira, Akwamu, and Asante—as well as a compilation of *apae* verses by J.H. Kwabena Nketia. Akosua Anyidoho's is a stylistic analysis of poems written in the style of *apae* by the renowned national spokesperson, Okyeame Boafo Akuffo, titled *Kotokohene Dammirifua Due* (1975).

19 Nsɔkɔ features prominently in historiography, and references to a few are in order: Kwame Ampene (2013); James Anquandah (1982); Kwasi Konadu (2014); and Ivor Wilks (1975).

20 Kyerematen (1966: 62) contains a brief entry on this line in *apae* poetry, with additional material on pages 348–349.

References

Abayie, Oheneba Akwasi. 2019. *Otumfuo Osei Tutu II, Asantehene 20th Anniversary Brochure*. Accra, Ghana: Buck Press Limited.

Akuffo, Boafo Okyeame. 1975. *Kotokohene Dammirifua Due*. Accra: Ghana Publishing Corporation.

Ampene, Kwame. 2013. "The Story of Nsoko." Originally published in *The Spectator*. Online: http://www.s158663955.websitehome.co.uk/ghanaculture/mod_print.php?archiveid=2186 (Accessed: 3 April 2020).

Ampene, Kwasi. 2005. *Female Song Tradition and the Akan of Ghana: The Creative Process in Nnwonkorɔ*. Aldershot, England: Ashgate Publishing Ltd.

Ampene, Kwasi, and Nana Kwadwo Nyantakyi III. 2016. *Engaging Modernity: Asante in the Twenty-First Century*, 2nd edition. Ann Arbor, MI: Michigan Publishing.

Anquandah, James. 1982. "The Archaeological Evidence for the Emergence of Akan Civilization." *Tarikh* 7(2): 9–21, 26.

Anyidoho, Akosua Love. 1991. "Linguistic Parallels in Traditional Akan Appellation Poetry." *Research in African Literatures* 22 (1): 67–81.

———. 1993. "Gender and Language Use: The Case of Two Akan Verbal Art Forms." PhD diss., University of Texas, Austin.

Konadu, Kwasi. ed., 2014. *The Akan People: A Documentary History*. Princeton: Markus Wiener Publishers.

Kyerematen, A.A.Y. 1966. "Ashanti Royal Regalia: Their History and Functions." PhD diss., Oxford University.

Nketia, J.H. Kwabena. 1962. *Kwadwom*. Unpublished manuscript. Institute of African Studies, University of Ghana.

———. 1978. *Amoma*. Accra and Tema: Ghana Publishing Corporation.

———. 1987. "Asante Court Music." In *The Golden Stool: Studies of the Asante Center and the Periphery*, edited by Enid Schildkrout, vol. 65. New York: American Museum of Natural History.

Odotei, Irene K., and George P. Hagan. 2003. *The King Returns: Enstoolment of Asantehene Otumfuo Osei Tutu II and the Ayikesee (Great Funeral) of Otumfuo Opoku Ware II*. Accra, Ghana: Institute of African Studies, University of Ghana. Education and Cultural Heritage Series.

Wilks, Ivor. 1975. *Asante in the Nineteenth Century: The Structure and Evolution of a Political Order*. Cambridge: Cambridge University Press.

Yankah, Kwesi. 1983. "To Praise or Not to Praise the King: The Akan 'Apae' in the Context of Referential Poetry." *Research in African Literatures* 14 (3): 381–800.

Epilogue
Concluding Akwasidae public assembly

Asɛmpa Yɛ Tia (A Good Case Must Be Argued in Brief). Akan Royal Spokes-persons Staff (*Akyeamepoma*) without a finial.

Continuing from where I left off in the Prologue, a series of events follow the dis-tribution of offertory drinks. The Royal Spokespersons lead the chiefs and ahemaa, and all present, in a collective expression of gratitude, with the bards performing the type of Short Songs translated into English as Ɔsagyefoɔ Have Your Drink to register their appreciation (see Example 6.4). A combined force of ivory trumpet-ers perform *Akokɔ* (the Hen) for the same purpose, while the Creator's Drummer rattles a short phrase (*mo ɔkorontɔ*) expressing profound gratitude, and continue with playing the *topos* for one of the fɔntɔmfrɔm dance suites, *Atopretia*. Momen-tarily, the *Mpɔnpɔnsɔnhene*, Nana Ɔsɛe Boadu, who usually sits to the immediate right of the ruler, goes around to the assembled chiefs to inform them that the ruler is about to rise. The bards recite another Short Verse, *Ɛntera Agyekum* (Example 6.5), as soon as Nana Boadu takes his seat, and, as if on cue, the Asantehene rises up from his chair. In a split second, all of the chiefs, courtiers, and guests also stand up in deference to the Asantehene. The recession from the courtyard is remi-niscent of the procession, as all of the ensembles continue the plural performance with intensity and renewed vigor. The Asantehene makes the usual rounds for another form of interactional routines—to express gratitude and exchange a few words with the chiefs and guests. He also acknowledges the performers, including the Popular Bands. Just as he did on his way in, he pauses to listen to the *mme-die* drums before exiting the courtyard, with the gourd drum ensemble (*mpintin*) still performing behind him. One by one, the participants begin to file out of the courtyard, and eventually the fɔntɔmfrɔm drummers stop performing while one of the Popular Bands keeps playing for a while. Led by Akyɛmpemhene Ɔheneba Adusei Poku, the *Kyidɔm* (the Rear Guard) converge in the exact space where the Asantehene was seated and wait until the latter goes to the inner chambers of *Asankroase* before dispersing. The end of the day's Akwasidae event marks the beginning of another cycle. While we are not sure of the scope of the next event, we are certain that there will be another Akwasidae in forty-two days, for the Akan world is organized around circular mappings—the infinite and never-ending universe that continuously renews itself. Like the manifold repetition and variation in the instrumental texts and songs, every forty-two days come with their own challenges that are unique on several levels.

Basing my ethnography on an event such as the Akwasidae Public Assembly encapsulates lived experience, values, aesthetics, ideology, philosophy, and much more, as it allows us to see not only what is done but *how* it is done. Events, in the short- and long-term, assemble and reinforce embodied experience and crystallize disparate creative sensibilities and social relations into a single space. Knowledge of history is power, and the periodic Akwasidae Public Assembly at Manhyia Palace provides space for the performance of aspects of Asante history, lived and current experience, and social values. It is worth mentioning that all of the diverse court musicians and poets learn their repertoire separately in the villages and towns where they live, without reference to the larger whole. Astoundingly, during events they do not perform alone, but they are still able to coordinate with other court musicians, poets, and courtiers to form a larger interconnected whole. Although they work on their own in the village, they have a conception of how the parts will fit together. For instance, they are keenly aware of their place in processions; where they will sit after processions; when to sound an ivory trumpet, short trumpet, or *durugya* flute; when the bards perform Long or Short Verses; and when members of the Constabulary take turns to recite Referential poetry. These are artistic sensibilities or a form of ritual memory, which instinctively come out during events and are highly valued by participants. Issues of materiality—wearing appropriate costumes, props, and the sharing of ritual drinks—are integrated into events. Ultimately, events provide the space to capture not only the unfolding history but also the continuity of Asante history and musical culture in its present manifestations. Herein lies the musical evidence for embodied experience and values encoded in the complex system of metatexts and meta-communicative devices in the diverse presentation of court music and verbal art forms. These provide compelling evidence that musical and allied arts are inextricably knit into the fabric of Asante history and socio-political organization. In one of his authoritative history books on the Asante, Ivor Wilks states, among other things, "the Asante past is memorialized in spoken rather than written word" (Wilks, 1993: 331). In addition to the spoken word, I would also add artistic forms, from sound-producing instruments as mediating material objects, to instrumental and songs texts and verbal poetry. The performance arts for the Asante are complex sites for recording and storing lived experience, while events such as the recurring forty-two day Adae, annual festivals, funerary rites, and court ceremonies provide multifaceted media for recalling and transmitting lived experience from generation to generation. Mossi musicians, we are informed, "transmit the history of their empire, dating back to the fourteenth century, by the use of gourd, hourglass and cylindrical drums" (Agawu, 2016: 127).

My focus on the intersections between music, lived experience, and values is in line with research paradigms that continue to enliven a large body of texts in ethnomusicology and allied disciplines in the humanities. Throughout this monograph, I have created space for the views of my interlocutors—court musicians and verbal artists, chiefs and cultural experts—to be part of the larger discourse.

My approach resonates with heuristic ethnography in the works of McCall (2000), Apter (1992), Jackson (1982, 1989), Stoller (1989, 1997), Stoller and Olkes (1987), Turner *et al.* (1992), and Feld (2012). By recognizing the knowledge base of culture bearers and custodians of court ensembles, I am keenly aware of the inherent problems with oral traditions, but, at the same time, and like McCall, it is not lost on me that all knowledge is a socially situated construct and not an objective model of social reality. Embodied experience recorded in artistic expressions, including court music and verbal arts, should be subject to rigorous verification and analysis in the same way that written sources should not be taken for granted. In this volume, the history of Asante court music and verbal arts are examined, first and foremost, by linking Asante with the Akan past to establish continuity with the remote past. Following that, I examine Asante court music and verbal arts through reigns, events, and wars occurring within each reign. Wars of conquest and expansion inspired creativity in the arts, as heroic encounters generated a large corpus of songs and instrumental texts, and poetry became a record of lived experience. However, as is generally the case with oral narratives, while events provide us with chronological episodes, they lack absolute dates. Since dates in Akan are not cumulative, the best method of recording incidents and reigns are the myriad artistic expressions; but for our purposes, I have focused on music and verbal arts as well as mediating material culture. Further, I have discussed the seeming lack of innovation in Asante court music in the context of the current lived experience of my interlocutors and presented my own views on the subject. The noticeable lack of creative impulse, the creation of new instruments, ensembles, songs and instrumental texts, and poetry to commemorate events is due in part to the end of Asante militarism, along with conquests and expansion in 1896 and then in 1901. These were the events and imagery that provided inspiration for innovations, but there are new creative outlets. With a new political framework and Asante as part of Ghana, sources of creativity are less visible than in the pre-colonial era. Currently, court musicians and poets recompose existing texts in order to recontextualize the verses and make them relevant to contemporary Asante. The exception is the creation of new short ivory trumpets (*mmɛntia*) and a philosophical statement by succeeding kings. However, due to the integration of court music and verbal arts with the social and political order, oral traditions are guided by contextual usages, thus making recall comparatively possible. Incredibly, the vast resources of Asante court music and verbal arts are activated for landmark events such as the restoration of the Asante Confederacy in 1935, after the truncation of the socio-political order for nearly four decades following the defeat by the British in 1896 and 1901 and the subsequent exile of Asantehene Agyemang Prɛmpɛ. Another landmark event was the burial and final funerary rites for the late Asantehemaa in January and December 2017. It was the first time in 209 years that a reigning Asantehene performed funerary rites for an Asantehemaa who was also his birth mother. The combination of oral traditions, political authority, and national unity with the visual, musical, and performance arts during the collective mourning of the late Asantehemaa was unprecedented in over a generation. Without reference to written documents, the contextual relevance of oral traditions in Asante took center stage, as the final funerary rites were staged as battles with an imaginary enemy, death. A mock battle was created and, led for two days by the Asantehene wearing his Great War Tunic (*Batakarikɛseɛ*), Divisional chiefs in Kumase (also wearing battle dresses) marched to a forest behind the palace to perform the ritual firing of guns. Territorial chiefs wearing battle dresses were carried in the palanquin while their retinue followed on the second day. This seemingly perfect coordination of multifaceted activities was as though they had been thoroughly rehearsed over weeks, but it was the product of embodied experience and the contextual manifestation of purely oral traditions.

Having established the historical framework, I based my discussions from Chapters 3 to 6 on a combination of historical narratives and analyses of texts. Chapters 3 and 4 were based on instrumental texts, with the framing titles indicating the language and poetry of ivory trumpets and *durugya* flute, and the language and poetry of drums. The instrumental texts were filtered through a sophisticated system of surrogate speech to elucidate embodied experience and social values. Chapters 5 and 6 are based on the human voice—songs and verbally intoned poetry—and focused on the use of rhetorical strategies and illuminated embodied experience and social values. Through an analysis of text, we encountered the brilliant use of rhetorical devices by performer-composers of kete songs to evoke historical and lived experience. In the context of a staged battle with death as part of the final funerary celebration of the late Asantehemaa, priestly songs (*nsumangorɔ*) and performances tapped into deep-rooted emotions of the heroic past to urge the fighting divisions and units on to an imaginary battle with death (*baamoa wuo*). In the chronicle songs and referential poetry performed by bards (*kwadomfoɔ*) and members of the constabulary (*abrafoɔ*), we came across the special delivery of archaic texts, indirection, metaphoric allusions, imagery, opaque references, and coded language artistically concealed in rhetorical devices. Despite an emphasis on defeated adversaries in *kwadwom* and *apae*, the Asante did not escape the vagaries of numerous wars, as they also lost several brave soldiers and leaders. Recalling those incidents by the bards and *abrafoɔ*, therefore, are constant reminders of grave incidents in the inter-war years.

In addition to music and experience, I expanded my theoretical framework to include the concept of musical value, for the value of the surrogate texts in this monograph stems from their value in expressing Asante historical experience. The events that led to the creation of the *kwantenpɔnmuta* drum and the drum text exemplified value in persistence. Additional instances include value in sacrifice, courage, and gratitude (Example 1.1); value in recognizing authority by not making false claims (Example 3.1); value in the motivation to succeed at all costs and value in bravery and patience and value in expressing gratitude (Example 3.3); value in a compassionate and generous leader (Example 3.7); value in diplomacy and strategic planning (Example 3.14); and value in the spiritually perfect number seven and its internal divisions of three and four (see Chapter 3). Example 4.17 is a case study of value in patience, while Example 4.18 highlights value in the harmonious relationship with the environment. Examples 5.1 and 5.2

bring to sharp focus values in courageous, skillful, and unwavering leadership. There is value in believing in the omnipotence of God and in moving cautiously (Example 5.10), and several instances throughout Chapter 6 enrich the analysis in this volume. A study of Asante court music and verbal arts is inherently a case study of the evocative subtitle, the porcupine and the Gold Stool. The founders adapted the biological attributes of the crested porcupine (*kɔtɔkɔ*) as the sacred totem of Asanteman to register a non-aggressive stance in all matters, thus preferring diplomacy over war. Metaphoric allusions to the porcupine (*kɔtɔkɔ*) are one of several stock expressions in compositions for instrumental and song texts and verbal arts in this volume. The heavenly origins of the Gold Stool (*Sikadwa Kofi*) ascribe a divine origin—a special gift from God (*Onyankopɔn*), the Creator of all things and the Sovereign Lord of all. Also referred to as *Abɛnwa*, this singular object embodies the soul, the identity, the strength, and the power of the Asante kingdom, and it has undoubtedly been the single-most unifying force in Asante. The relevance of the Gold Stool to my overall discussion of court music and experience is the sound-producing and musical instruments attached to it, as well as those that are part of the regalia, which provides evidence for the integral role of expressive arts and mediating material culture in Asante. Ultimately, there is general interest among scholars and the general public in the musical heritage of pre-colonial kingdoms in Africa, and I am optimistic that the present volume will add to the growing list of scholarly publications in this area. Several of these kingdoms still exist, albeit under new political structures, in Africa. Until we are able to access the vast resources and wealth of the artistic bedrock in these kingdoms, we will be missing a huge portion, if not all, of the historical and lived experience and values encoded in court music and verbal arts in Africa. Indeed, a good case must be argued in brief!

References

Agawu, Kofi. 2016. *The African Imagination in Music.* New York: Oxford University Press.

Apter, Andrew. 1992. *Black Critics & Kings: The Hermeneutics of Power in Yoruba Society.* Chicago: University of Chicago Press.

Feld, Steven. 2012. *Sound and Sentiment: Birds, Weeping, Poetics, and Song in Kaluli Expression.* 3rd edition. Durham, NC: Duke University Press.

Jackson, Michael D. 1982. *Allegories of the Wilderness: Ethnics and Ambiguity in Kuranko Narratives.* Bloomington, IN: Indiana University Press.

———. 1989. *Paths Toward a Clearing: Radical Empiricism and Ethnographic Inquiry.* Bloomington, IN: Indiana University Press.

McCall, John C. 2000. *Dancing Histories: Heuristic Ethnography with the Ohafia Igbo.* Ann Arbor, MI: University of Michigan Press.

Stoller, Paul. 1989. *Fusion of the Worlds: An Ethnography of Possession Among the Songhay of Niger.* Chicago: University of Chicago Press.

———. 1997. *Sensuous Scholarship.* Philadelphia: University of Pennsylvania Press.

Stoller, Paul, and Cheryl Olkes. 1987. *In Corcery's Shadow: A Memoir of Apprenticeship Among the Songhay of Niger.* Chicago: University of Chicago Press.

Turner, Edith with William Blodgett, Singleton Kahona, and Fideli Benwa. 1992. *Experiencing Ritual: A New Interpretation of African Healing*. Philadelphia: University of Pennsylvania Press.

Wilks, Ivor. 1993. *Forests of Gold: Essays on the Akan and the Kingdom of Asante*. Athens, OH: Ohio University Press.

Appendix A

The genealogical structure of the royal Ɔyoko dynasty of the Gold Stool of Asante from the seventeenth century to the twenty-first century

	Name	Position	Period	Century
1.	Ɔpemsoɔ Ɔsee Tutu	1st Asantehene	1680–1717 (37 years)	17th/18th
2.	Nyaako Kusi Amoa	1st Asantehemaa	1695–1722 (27 years)	17th/18th
3.	Opoku Ware (Katakyie)	2nd Asantehene	1720–1750 (30 years)	18th
4.	Nkatia Ntim Abamo	2nd Asantehemaa	1722–1740 (18 years)	18th
5.	Akua Afriyie	3rd Asantehemaa	1740–768 (28 years)	18th
6.	Kusi Obuodum	3rd Asantehene	1750–1764 (14 years)	18th
7.	Ɔsee Kwadwo (Ɔko-Awia)	4th Asantehene	1764–1777 (13 years)	18th
8.	Konadu Yiadɔm	4th Asantehemaa	1768–1809 (41 years)	18th/19th
9.	Ɔsee Kwame	5th Asantehene	1777–1798 (21 years)	18th
10.	Opoku Fofie	6th Asantehene	1798–1799 (1 year)	18th
11.	Ɔsee Asibe Bonsu (Bonsu Panin)	7th Asantehene	1800–1823(23 years)	19th
12.	Akosua Adɔma	5th Asantehemaa	1809–1819 (10 years)	19th
13.	Ama Sɛɛwaa	6th Asantehemaa	1819–1828 (9 years)	19th
14.	Ɔsee Yaw Akoto	8th Asantehene	1824–1834 (10 years)	19th
15.	Yaa Dufie	7th Asantehemaa	1828–1836 (8 years)	19th
16.	Kwaku Dua (Fredua Agyeman Pamboɔ)	9th Asantehene	1834–1867 (33 years)	19th
17.	Afia Sapɔn	8th Asantehemaa	1836–1857 (21 years)	19th
18.	Afia Kobi	9th Asantehemaa	1857–1883 (26 years)	19th
19.	Kofi Karikari	10th Asantehene	1867–1874 (7 years)	19th
20.	Mɛnsa Bonsu	11th Asantehene	1874–1883 (9 years)	19th
21.	Yaa Akyaa	10th Asantehemaa	1883–1917 (34 years)	19th/20th
22.	Kwaku Dua II	12th Asantehene	1884–1884 (40 years)	19th
23.	Agyeman Prɛmpɛ I	13th Asantehene	1888–1931 (43 years)	19th/20th
24.	Konadu Yiadɔm II	11th Asantehemaa	1917–1945 (28 years)	20th
25.	Sir. Ɔsee Agyeman Prɛmpɛ II	14th Asantehene	1931–1970 (39 years)	20th
26.	Ama Sɛɛwaa Nyaako	12th Asantehemaa	1945–1977 (32 years)	20th
27.	Opoku Ware II	15th Asantehene	1970–1999(29 years)	20th
28.	Afia Kobi Sɛɛwaa Ampem II	13th Asantehemaa	1977–2016 (39 years)	20th/21st
29.	Ɔsee Tutu II	16th Asantehene	1999-Present	20th/21st
30.	Konadu Yiadɔm III	14th Asantehemaa	2017-Present	21st

Originally published in the 20th Anniversary Royal Souvenir Brochure by Ɔheneba Akwasi Abayie, Otumfoɔ Akɔmfɛrehene. Used with permission by Ɔheneba Akwasi Abayie.

Appendix B

The genealogy of Asante kings and ahemaa (queens)

As noted in the preceding chapters, reigns and events occurring within each reign provided a wealth of resources for the artistic impulse as court musicians and poets composed songs and poetry to embody historical experience and social values. My aim for including an organogram in the appendix is to trace the line of descent beginning with Nana Gyamfua Manu Kotosi (Nana Manu) from roughly the mid-seventeenth century. Nana Manu was the daughter of Nana Gyapa and Grandaughter of Brempɔmaa Piesie. These women preceded the Kwaaman Purchase and the founding of the Kwaaman Coalition. A. A. Y. Kyerematen's discussion takes us as far back as five generations before Ɔseɛ Tutu's time. Due to space constraints, I begin with Nana Manu and as we shall see in the flow chart and my notes in what follows, it was Nana Manu's son, Ɔseɛ Tutu, who became the founding king of Asante while her granddaughter, Nana Nyaako Kusi Amoa, became the first Asantehemaa. On September 7, 2019, I met with Ɔheneba Akwasi Abayie in Maryland to discuss his updated version of the genealogy in the 20th Anniversary Brochure for the current Asantehene, Ɔseɛ Tutu II. Ɔheneba is the son of Otumfoɔ Sir Ɔseɛ Agyeman Prɛmpɛ II-the 13th Asantehene (1935–1977), hence his name Ɔheneba (meaning, the son of a king). Ɔheneba is also the current Otumfoɔ Akɔmfɛrehene and he was among the delegation of Asante chiefs who accompanied the Asantehene to the United Nations for his keynote speech on September 13, 2019. Owing to his closeness to the Stool and his current office, his knowledge of the Ɔyoko royal family is quite extensive. In my meeting with him, therefore, we reviewed his updated version of the "Genealogy of Asante Kings and Queenmothers." Ɔheneba's organogram is elaborate and highly informative and, as he rightfully acknowledges, it draws on a similar chart by J.O. Agyemang-Duah, which in turn has been revised by Thomas K. Aning. It bears mentioning that all the previously-named charts owe a great deal to Ivor Wilks' reconstruction of the genealogy of Ɔyoko royals (Wilks, 1975: 327–373). My organogram is inspired by updates initiated by Ɔheneba and our extensive discussion during his visit to Maryland. I used shapes to distinguish between the first female ancestress, female royals, kings, and ahemaa.

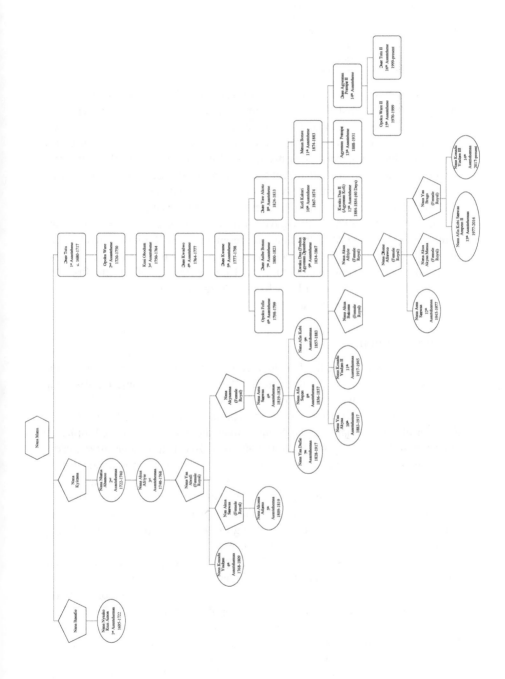

Key

Hexagon	Female Ancestress
Pentagon	Female Royal
Rectangle	Asante Kings
Oval	Asante Queens

The organogram shows the female line of descent to the left and the male line to the right. The Akan matrilineal succession ensures that the male line is dependent on the female royals and ahemaa. On the organogram, the relationships between the Asantehene and Asantehemaa are not readily apparent so, where necessary, I have provided explanations in my notes. With the exception of a few areas, I avoid detailed explanation of contested spots in the genealogy. Readers are referred to the comprehensive discussion by Kyerematen and Wilks referenced previously. Although there may be several female royals and children of ahemaa, I include one or two who either gave birth to a king or ahemaa or both. I have avoided the use of the label, the first—represented by the Roman numeral I—as a reference to rulers with the first stool name as in, Afia Kobi I or Prεmpε I—since it should be implied that Afia Kobi, Ͻsεe Tutu, or Prεmpε refer to the first. Afia Kobi II, Prεmpε II, Ͻsεe Tutu II, or Konada Yiadɔm III are those who used stool names of previous kings and ahemaa.

The organogram

I begin with Nana Manu, the female ancestor who gave births to Nana Bɔnafie, Nana Kyirɔma, and Ͻsεe Tutu. Around 1680, Ͻsεe Tutu became the first king, Ͻpemsoɔ, of the Kwaaman coalition that later became known as the Asante Empire. Approximately 1695, Ͻsεe Tutu appointed Nana Nyaako Kusi Amoa, the daughter of Nana Bɔnafie, as the Asantehemaa, the first in the Asante Empire. As indicated in the organogram, Nana Bɔnafie was Ͻsεe Tutu's older sister, making Kusi Amoa his niece. When Ͻsεe Tutu died in 1717, Kusi Amoa nominated her own son, Opoku Ware, to the Gold Stool in 1720. Contrary to common belief, Opoku Ware was not the nephew of Ͻsεe Tutu but his grandson (or Tutu was Opoku Ware's great uncle). It is worth noting that it took three years for Kusi Amoa to find a successor after the passing of Ͻsεe Tutu and the unusual delay certainly points to a possible succession dispute.

When his mother passed away in 1722, Opoku Ware appointed his aunt, Nana Nkεtia Abamoo, the daughter of Nana Kyirɔma, as the 2nd Asantehemaa. Nkεtia Abamoo passed away in 1740 and this presented Opoku Ware a second opportunity to appoint another Asantehemaa. He appointed Nana Akua Afriyie (1740–1768), the daughter of Nkεtia Abamoo and his cousin, as the 3rd Asantehemaa. When Opoku Ware passed on in 1750, Akua Afriyie nominated her brother, Kusi Obuodum, to the Gold Stool. Kusi Obuodum (1750–1764) is the cousin of Opoku Ware and according to oral history, abdicated the stool after losing his eyes sight. Nana Yaa Abrafi and Ͻsεe Kwadwo were the children of Akua Afriyie so she nominated her son, Ɔsɛɛ Kwadwo to succeed his uncle, Kusi Obuodum, in 1764. He became known as Ɔsɛɛ Kwadwo a Ɔko Awia (literal meaning: he who embark on war in broad daylight). He reigned from 1764 to 1777.

According to Ɔheneba Akwasi Abayie, Yaa Abrafi (the daughter of Nana Akua Afriyie) had three children: Nana Konadu Yiadɔm, Nana Akua Sɛɛwaa, and Nana Akyaamaa. Ɔsɛɛ Kwadwo appointed his niece, Nana Konadu Yiadɔm, as the 4th Asantehemaa, when Akua Afriyie passed on in 1768. On her part, Konadu Yiadɔm nominated Ɔsɛɛ Kwame as the 5th Asantehene to succeed Ɔsɛɛ Kwadwo in 1777. Ɔsɛɛ Kwadwo was Nana Akyaamaa's son. In 1798, Ɔsɛɛ Kwadwo was destooled and Konadu Yiadɔm nominated her son, Opoku Fofie, as the 6th Asantehene. Opoku Fofie passed on in 1799, allowing Konadu Yiadɔm the third opportunity to make a nomination. She selected her son, Ɔsɛɛ Tutu Kwame, as the 7th Asantehene. His stool name was Ɔsɛɛ Asibe but he is also known as Ɔsɛɛ Asibe Bonsu Ɔbɔɔ Hyɛn. When Konadu Yiadɔm passed in 1809, Ɔsɛɛ Asibe Bonsu became the second Asantehene (after Opoku Ware) to perform the burial and funerary rites for his biological mother. Ɔsɛɛ Bonsu then went on to nominate his cousin, Nana Akosua Adɔma, as the 5th Asantehemaa. Akosua Adɔma was the daughter of Nana Akua Sɛɛwaa, sister of Konadu Yiadɔm, the 4th Asantehemaa, and Nana Akyaama, and as we may recall, all three sisters were the daughters of Nana Yaa Abrafi.

With the passing of Akosua Adɔma in 1819, Ɔsɛɛ Bonsu appointed his cousin, Nana Ama Sɛɛwaa, Akyaamaa's daughter, as the 6th Asantehemaa. Ɔsɛɛ Bonsu passed away in 1823 and Ama Sɛɛwaa nominated her brother, Ɔsɛɛ Yaw Akoto, as the 8th Asantehene in 1824. Ɔsɛɛ Yaw Akoto and Ama Sɛɛwaa are the children of Nana Akyaamaa. In 1828, Ɔsɛɛ Yaw Akoto appointed Nana Yaa Dufie as the 7th Asantehemaa to fill the vacant stool when Ama Sɛɛwaa passed away. Yaa Dufie was the daughter of the 4th Asantehemaa, Konadu Yiadɔm, and, as a result, the former is the cousin of Ɔsɛɛ Yaw Akoto. When the Gold Stool became vacant in 1833 following the passing of Yaw Akoto, Yaa Dufie nominated Kwaku Dua in 1834 as the 9th Asantehene. Also known as Fredua Agyeman Ɔpamboɔ, Kwaku Dua was the son of Ama Sɛɛwaa, the 6th Asantehemaa and the nephew of Ɔsɛɛ Kwame, Opoku Fofie, Ɔsɛɛ Bonsu, and Yaw Akoto—the 5th, the 6th, the 7th, and the 8th Asante kings, respectively. It was Kwaku Dua who appointed his sister, Nana Afia Sarpɔn, as the 8th Asantehemaa in 1836. She was destooled in 1857. Kwaku Dua then appointed Afia Sarpɔn's daughter, Nana Afia Kobi, as the 9th Asantehemaa in 1857 to fill the vacant stool. Afia Kobi, the niece of Kwaku Dua, had five children: Kwaku Anim, Kofi Kakari, Mɛnsa Bonsu, Yaa Akyaa, and Akua Afriyie. Upon the passing of Kwaku Dua in 1867, Afia Kobi nominated her son, Kofi Kakari, to fill the vacant stool as the 10th Asantehene but he abdicated in 1874. Afia Kobi then nominated Mɛnsa Bonsu as the 11th Asantehene but he was also destooled in 1883. I have described this era of succession disputes as a period of instability and civil strife, among others, in Chapter 2. The crushing defeat of Asante in 1874 by the British forces during the reign of Kofi Kakari (Sagrenti Sa) was the main reason he was forced out of power. Agitations and several factions emerged and for the third time, Afia Kobi nominated her younger son, Kwaku

Dua II, to succeed Mɛnsa Bonsu as the 12th Asantehene in 1883. Also known as Agyeman Kofi, Kwaku Dua II reigned for only 40 days and is suspected to have died under a mysterious circumstance.

After a series of succession disputes and civil war, Nana Yaa Akyaa managed to push her Mother, Afia Kobi, aside and become the 10th Asantehemaa in 1883. In that sense, Yaa Akyaa was not appointed by a male king. At any rate, after a bitter three-year civil war, Yaa Akyaa succeeded in nominating her own son, Agyeman Prɛmpɛ, as the 13th Asantehene in 1888. Agyeman Prɛmpɛ was also known as Kwaku Dua III or Kwaku Dua Saamu. Yaa Akyaa died in exile in Seychelles in 1917 and while in exile, Agyeman Prɛmpɛ appointed her sister, Nana Konadu Yiadɔm II (Konadu Adusa), as the 11th Asantehemaa in 1917. Nana Akua Aba-koma and Konadu Yiadɔm II are the daughters of Yaa Akyaa—the 10th Asante-hemaa. Konadu Yiadɔm II nominated Akua Abakoma's son, Ɔsɛe Agyeman Prɛmpɛ II (Kwame Kyeretwie), to succeed his uncle-Agyeman Prɛmpɛ—as the 14th Asantehene in 1931. Akua Abakoma's mother is the 10th Asantehemaa, Yaa Akyaa. When Konadu Yiadɔm II passed on three years later, Prɛmpɛ II appointed his cousin, Nana Ama Sɛɛwaa Nyaako as the 12th Asantehemaa in 1945. Sɛɛwaa Nyaako is the granddaughter of Nana Akua Afriyie and the daughter of Nana Akosua Ɔhene Afrɛwoɔ and the sister of Nana Akua Akyaa (Akua Akyaa Mansa). The Gold Stool became vacant in 1970 with the passing of Prɛmpɛ II and Sɛɛwaa Nyaako nominated Opoku Ware II as the new occupant of the Gold Stool. Opoku Ware is the son of Akua Akyaa Mansa who is the sister of the 12th Asantehemaa, Nana Ama Sɛɛwaa Nyaako. In 1977, Opoku Ware had to choose the 14th Asante-hemaa and he appointed his aunt, Nana Afia Kobi Sɛɛwaa Ampem II—daughter of Nana Yaa Brago to succeed Sɛɛwaa Nyaako. Afia Kobi Sɛɛwaa Ampem II was the daughter of Nana Yaa Brago, who was the daughter of Nana Akua Afriyie. In 1999, Afia Kobi Sɛɛwaa Ampem II nominated her son, Ɔsɛe Tutu II (Osɛe Tutu Ababio), to succeed Opoku Ware II as the 16th Asantehene. Since Afia Kobi was the aunt of Opoku Ware, he was the first cousin of Ɔsɛe Tutu II and that makes them brothers in Akan. When Afia Kobi Sɛɛwaa Ampem II passed on in 2016, Ɔsɛe Tutu II appointed her older sister, Nana Konadu Yiadɔm III, to succeed their mother as the 15th Asantehemaa.

Index